Forecasting, Warning and Responding to Transnational Risks

Also by Christoph O. Meyer

ECONOMIC GOVERNMENT OF THE EU: A Balance Sheet of New Modes of Policy Coordination (*Co-edited with Ingo Linsenmann and Wolfgang Wessels*)

THE QUEST FOR A EUROPEAN STRATEGIC CULTURE: Changing Norms on Security and Defence in the European Union

TOWARDS A EUROPEAN PUBLIC SPHERE? THE EUROPEAN COMMISSION, THE MEDIA AND POLITICAL ACCOUNTABILITY (*in German*)

Forecasting, Warning and Responding to Transnational Risks

Edited by

Chiara de Franco
Research Associate, King's College London

and

Christoph O. Meyer
Senior Lecturer in European Studies, King's College London

palgrave
macmillan

Softcover reprint of the hardcover 1st edition 2011 978-0-230-29784-5

First published 2011 by
PALGRAVE MACMILLAN

Palgrave Macmillan in the UK is an imprint of Macmillan Publishers Limited, registered in England, company number 785998, of Houndmills, Basingstoke, Hampshire RG21 6XS.

Palgrave Macmillan in the US is a division of St Martin's Press LLC, 175 Fifth Avenue, New York, NY 10010.

Palgrave Macmillan is the global academic imprint of the above companies and has companies and representatives throughout the world.

Palgrave® and Macmillan® are registered trademarks in the United States, the United Kingdom, Europe and other countries.

ISBN 978-1-349-33422-3 ISBN 978-0-230-31691-1 (eBook)
DOI 10.1057/9780230316911

This book is printed on paper suitable for recycling and made from fully managed and sustained forest sources. Logging, pulping and manufacturing processes are expected to conform to the environmental regulations of the country of origin.

A catalogue record for this book is available from the British Library.

Library of Congress Cataloging-in-Publication Data

Forecasting, warning, and responding to transnational risks / edited by Chiara de Franco, Christoph O. Meyer.
p. cm.
Includes bibliographical references and index.
1. Risk – Forecasting. 2. Risk assessment. 3. Emergency management. I. De Franco, Chiara, 1977– II. Meyer, Christoph O., 1973–

HM1101.F67 2011
363.34′2—dc22 2011011754

10 9 8 7 6 5 4 3 2 1
20 19 18 17 16 15 14 13 12 11

Contents

List of Illustrations vii

Acknowledgements viii

Notes on Contributors ix

1 Introduction: The Challenges of Prevention 1
Chiara de Franco and Christoph O. Meyer

Part I Forecasting Harm

2 The Coastline of the Future: Some Limits on Forecasting and Prediction 19
Sir David Omand

3 Epistemology of Forecasting in International Relations: Knowing the Difference between 'Intelligence Failure' and 'Warning Failure' 33
Jan Goldman

4 FORESEC: Lessons Learnt from a Pan-European Security Foresight Project 47
Ville Brummer, Clementine Burnley, Henrik Carlsen, Ana-Maria Duta, Bastian Giegerich and Raphaële Magoni

5 Modelling Transnational Environmental Risks: Scenarios for Decision Support 65
Fabian Wagner

6 Risk, Uncertainty and the Assessment of Organised Crime 85
Tom Vander Beken

Part II Communicating and Learning from Warnings

7 Mediatised Warnings: Late, Wrong, Yet Indispensable? Lessons from Climate Change and Civil War 99
Chiara de Franco and Christoph O. Meyer

8 Do They Listen? Communicating Warnings: An Intelligence Practitioner's Perspective 117
William Shapcott

9 Responding to Early Flood Warnings in the European Union 127
David Demeritt and Sebastien Nobert

10 Dark Secrets: Face-Work, Organisational Culture and Disaster Prevention 148
Marc S. Gerstein and Edgar H. Schein

Part III Responding to Warnings

11 Transnational Risk Management: A Business Perspective 169
Corene Crossin and James Smither

12 From the 'Neurotic' to the 'Rationalising' State: Risk and the Limits of Governance 187
Henry Rothstein, Olivier Borraz and Michael Huber

13 Silos and Silences: The Role of Fragmentation in the Recent Financial Crisis 208
Gillian Tett

14 Forecasting, Warning and Preventive Policy: The Case of Finance 217
Thomas F. Huertas

15 Prospective Sense-Making: A Realistic Approach to 'Foresight for Prevention' in an Age of Complex Threats 227
Warren H. Fishbein

16 Conclusion: New Perspectives for Theorising and Addressing Transnational Risks 241
Christoph O. Meyer and Chiara de Franco

Bibliography 258

Index 281

Illustrations

Tables

6.1 Predictors of low-risk and high-risk businesses, from Albanese (1987: 109) 91
10.1 Reasons why insiders do not warn about risks 150
10.2 Specific suggestions for committed organisations 158
16.1 Variables influencing warning-response performance 243

Figures

1.1 The warning-response-loop: four challenges for prevention 7
2.1 Different levels and purposes of warning 31
6.1 Relationship of risk, harm, threat and vulnerability 89
6.2 Threat assessment scheme, based on Brown (1998) 89
9.1 Deterministic v. ensemble forecasting methods 128
9.2 An example of an ensemble 'spaghetti' hydrograph for a hindcasted flood event 141
11.1 Phases of risk assessment 172
11.2 Impact-likelihood-matrix 177

Acknowledgements

For Homer warnings were the stuff of tragedy. They were either not heeded, as in the case of Cassandra's warnings about the Trojan horse, or the very action designed to avoid the harm in fact caused it, as in the case of Oedipus. If the contributors to this book had shared this fatalistic outlook, this book would have never seen the light of day. Fortunately, they mustered all their optimistic realism and gave generously of their time to contribute papers and thoughts to a workshop at King's in September 2009. This gift is all the more precious from those whose day job is outside of academia in the area of intelligence, risk and business consultancy, journalism or financial-market regulation, not to mention those who endured the six-hour jet lag from the United States in order to participate. We hope this book is also evidence that genuine curiosity does help to overcome disciplinary and professional divides and produce new thoughts, rather than collecting incommunicable pieces of wisdoms.

The workshop itself would not have been possible without the funding provided by a grant from the European Research Council (No. 202022), following its first ever call for proposals. The Foresight project focuses primarily on early warning in the area of violent intrastate conflict, but deliberately tried to branch out and learn from other areas of risk communication. We would also like to thank the members of the Foresight advisory group, who participated in the workshop either as paper givers or as participants in the discussion. These include Brooke Rogers, Michael Goodman, Sir David Omand and William Shapcott. The editors would also to thank John Brante and Florian Otto for helping to organise and run the workshop as well as for their comments on individual contributions, particularly on the editors' three chapters. Jayne Peake, the publicity officer at the Department of War Studies, did a great job in helping to organise an event which was not public at all, perhaps hoping that something good would eventually come out of it.

The editors and publishers finally wish to thank Dr Tim Bynum and Professor Jay S. Albanese for permission to reproduce Table 6.1 from Jay Albanese (1987) 'Predicting the Incidence of Organized Crime: A Preliminary Model' in Tim Bynum (Ed.) *Organized Crime in America: Concepts and Controversies*. New York: Criminal Justice Press.

Contributors

Olivier Borraz is a research professor at the Centre National de la Recherche Scientifique (CNRS), based at the Center for the Sociology of Organizations at Sciences Po, Paris. His main research interest is the governance of risk, with a focus on environmental and health issues. In 2008 he published *Les Politiques du risque*, in which he analyses the role of social movements, controversies, expertise, decision-making and non-state actors in the governance of risk. He is currently co-director of the risk governance concentration of the Master of Public Affairs degree at Sciences Po.

Ville Brummer is head of R&D for the Crisis Management Initiative, Helsinki. Earlier, he worked as a lecturer, researcher and project manager in the Systems Analysis Laboratory at Helsinki University of Technology (TKK), where he was responsible for several large-scale foresight studies and strategic decision-support activities. Brummer has published widely on foresight and decision-support methodologies in various journals, including *Technological Forecasting and Social Change*, *Technology Analysis and Strategic Management* and *International Journal of Technology Management*.

Clementine Burnley is a senior project manager for Adelphi Research in Berlin. Her work focuses on early warning and management of crises, and environmental security is one of her areas of expertise. Her current projects include the European Commission-funded research projects G-MOSAIC and SECURENV. Previously, she spent six years at the European Commission's Joint Research Centre in Ispra, Italy. She is the author of several peer-reviewed papers, as well as numerous reports, and has provided editing and writing services to various companies. She has lectured at the University of Manchester and at the University of Bedfordshire.

Henrik Carlsen is Deputy Research Director of the Division of Defence Analysis, Swedish Defence Research Agency (FOI), Stockholm, and project manager of projects on the ethics of future robotics and on socio-economic scenarios for climate change adaptation. Prior to joining the FOI, Carlsen worked as a consultant in the information security business. His main research focus is foresight and strategic planning – translating the broad uncertainty of future developments into specific guidance for decision-making. Areas of application include climate change mitigation and adaptation, emerging and disruptive technologies, defence material acquisition and European security research.

Corene Crossin leads the Asia Pacific political-risk consulting practice of Control Risks, London, managing complex-risk projects for clients across the region. She writes and speaks regularly on identifying and managing risks in emerging markets. Before joining Control Risks, Crossin worked in the non-profit sector and specialised in examining the risks faced by financial institutions involved in investments in politically unstable areas. She has also conducted extensive research into extractive-sector activities in developing countries and has been involved in high-level work with the UN Security Council, IMF and International Finance Corporation as well as OECD governments.

Chiara de Franco is a research associate in the War Studies Department, King's College London. She was previously a research assistant at the European University Institute, a lecturer in war representations at the University of Florence, and a lecturer in European affairs at Florida State University. At King's she is working in the framework of the FORESIGHT project, concentrating on the Balkan conflicts, on the early-warning systems of France, the OSCE and the UN, and on political communication and text analysis. Her first monograph, on the impact of international TV networks on foreign policy-making, is forthcoming.

David Demeritt is Professor of Geography at King's College London, specialising in social theory and the environment. His research focuses on the articulation of environmental knowledge, particularly scientific and technical knowledge, with power and the policy process. He currently serves as a convenor of the Hazards and Risk Group and as Director of Graduate Studies. Demeritt is book review editor for *Environment and Planning A*, a member of the editorial boards of *Geoforum* and *Cultural Geographies*, and a member of NERC's Peer Review College.

Ana-Maria Duta is a conflict specialist at the Institute for the Protection and Security of the Citizen, European Commission Joint Research Centre, Brussels. She is involved in research into political conflicts, conflict risk modelling and related topics.

Warren H. Fishbein is coordinator of the Global Futures Forum (GFF) in the US State Department's Bureau of Intelligence and Research, Washington, DC. Previously, he served as deputy director of the CIA's Global Futures Partnership, where he helped develop GFF and led projects involving the application of foresight methodologies and academic outreach. He is the author of *Wage Restraint by Consensus: Britain's Search for an Incomes Policy Agreement, 1964–79* (1984) and of the Sherman Kent Center occasional paper 'Making Sense of Transnational Threats' (2004, with Gregory Treverton).

Marc S. Gerstein heads Marc Gerstein Associates, New York, a management consulting firm, and is president of the Organization Design Forum. He has taught and held research positions at Columbia Business School, MIT Sloan School of Management, Cambridge University, and McGill University. He is a former executive vice president and head of strategy for Instinet, Reuters' electronic share trading firm. He is the author of three books, including *Flirting with Disaster: Why Accidents Are Rarely Accidental* (2008, with Michael and Daniel Ellsberg), and his work on strategy and organisational dynamics has been published by *Sloan Management Review, Journal of Business Strategy, People and Strategy* and Stanford University.

Bastian Giegerich is a senior researcher at the Bundeswehr Institute of Social Sciences (SOWI), Strausberg, Germany. He was previously Research Fellow for European Security at the International Institute for Strategic Studies (IISS), London. He has carried out a research project on future European security trends supported by the European Commission. He was a Fulbright Scholar at the University of Maryland, a research associate at the National Defense University in Washington, DC, and a project manager at the Aspen Institute, Berlin. Giegerich has published widely on European security issues in various scientific journals and newspapers.

Jan Goldman is a member of the faculty of the National Defense Intelligence College, Washington, DC, and the author or editor of several textbooks and reference works on intelligence analysis and strategic warning. He has assisted in the development of several all-source intelligence warning centres and is the only person to have been awarded the title Current Intelligence and Indications and Warning Expert by the Defense Intelligence Agency.

Michael Huber is Professor of Higher Education Studies in the Faculty of Sociology and the director of the Institute of Science and Technology Studies at the University of Bielefeld, Germany. His main research interests relate to risk and regulation, organisation theory and higher education studies. Recent publications in these areas are 'Colonised by Risk: The Emergence of Academic Risks in British Higher Education' (in B. M. Hutter, ed., *Anticipating Risks and Organizing Risk Regulation in 21st Century*, 2010) and 'Fundamental Ignorance in the Regulation of Reactor Safety and Flooding' (in N. Stehr and B. Weiler, eds, *Knowledge and the Law: Can Knowledge Be Made Just?*, 2008).

Thomas F. Huertas is vice chairman of the Committee of European Banking Supervisors and director of the Banking Sector, Financial Services Authority (FSA), UK. He is also a member of the Basel Committee on Banking Supervision. Huertas is responsible for strengthening the FSA's risk identification and mitigation capabilities in the banking sector (especially with respect to problem banks). He has extensive practical experience in banking and finance from his previous career with Citigroup. He is the author of *Crisis: Cause, Containment and Cure* (2010) and co-author *Citibank, 1812–1970* (1985, with Harold van B. Cleveland). He is a guest professor at the Goethe University, Frankfurt.

Raphaële Magoni conducts research into migration flows, the permeability of the EU external border and related security issues at the European Commission Joint Research Centre in Brussels. With a background in public international law and conflict analysis, Magoni has been active in the field of migration and human rights. After working as a refugee coordinator with Amnesty International in Brussels, she became a researcher for the Migration Policy Group, contributing to a number of projects relating to policy development in the field of migration at the European level.

Christoph O. Meyer is a senior lecturer in the War Studies Department of King's College London and director of the FORESIGHT research group on early warning and conflict prevention, funded by the European Research Council. He specialises in political communication, European integration and governance, and constructivist approaches to foreign and security policy. He is the author of *The Quest for a European Strategic Culture* (2006) and has authored articles on forecasting, early warning and persuasion, European responses to and perceptions of terrorism, and European security and defence policy.

Sebastien Nobert is a post-doctoral research associate in the Risk and Hazards Group in the Department of Geography, King's College London. His work concerns the contested understandings of uncertainty and modelling involved in flood forecasting. His publications include 'Challenges in Communicating and Using Ensembles in Operational Flood Forecasting' (*Meteorological Applications*, 2010, with D. Demeritt, H. L. Cloke and F. Pappenberger) and 'Using Ensemble Predictions for Operational Flood Forecasting: Lessons from Sweden' (*Journal of Flood Risk Management*, 2010, with D. Demeritt and H. L. Cloke).

Sir David Omand GCB is a visiting professor in the War Studies Department, King's College London. He was the first UK Security and Intelligence Coordinator, as Permanent Secretary in the Cabinet Office responsible to the prime minister for the professional health of the intelligence community, national counter-terrorism strategy and 'homeland security'. He was the UK government's chief crisis manager for civil contingencies. He served for seven years on the Joint Intelligence Committee. He was Permanent Secretary of the Home Office, director of GCHQ (the UK signals-intelligence and cyber-security agency) and Deputy Under Secretary of State for Policy in the Ministry of Defence.

Henry Rothstein is Senior Lecturer in Risk Management and deputy director of the Centre for Risk Management, King's College London. His main research interests relate to the institutional factors shaping the emergence, operation, failure and reform of risk governance regimes across policy domains. His publications include *The Government of Risk* (2001, with

Christopher Hood and Robert Baldwin) and articles in a wide range of academic journals, including *Science, Technology and Human Values, Economy and Society* and *Public Administration*.

Edgar H. Schein is the Sloan Fellows Professor of Management Emeritus at the MIT Sloan School of Management, Cambridge, MA. He previously worked at the Walter Reed Institute of Research and later at MIT, where he taught until 2005. His extensive list of publications includes *Organizational Psychology* (3rd edition, 1980), the organisational culture texts *Organizational Culture and Leadership* (4th edition, 2010) and *The Corporate Culture Survival Guide* (2nd edition, 2009), *DEC Is Dead, Long Live DEC* (2003) and *Helping* (2009, on the theory and practice of giving and receiving help). He was the 2009 recipient of the Distinguished Scholar-Practitioner Award of the Academy of Management.

William Shapcott is Director General for Personnel and Administration at the General Secretariat of the EU Council of Ministers, Brussels. He was director of the EU Situation Centre from 2001 to 2010, and for the previous two years was counsellor to Javier Solana, Secretary General of the European Council and High Representative for the Common Foreign and Security Policy. Before working for the European Union, Shapcott was a member of HM's Diplomatic Service. He was previously Counsellor for Politico-Military Affairs at the British Embassy in Washington, DC. He joined the Foreign Office in 1988 after eight years in the Royal Tank Regiment.

James Smither is Director of Consulting Projects at Control Risks, London. In his role heading the company's political-risk consultancy business, he has led a variety of consulting assignments across sectors including energy, pharmaceuticals, mining and defence. He has authored works on political risks for the Institute of Risk Management's 'Managing Business Risk' compendium, is a regular keynote speaker at major business conferences and is frequently interviewed by international news media such as CNN, the *Financial Times* and the *Wall Street Journal*. He has previously worked for an international foreign policy think tank.

Gillian Tett is managing editor of the US edition of the *Financial Times*. In March 2009, she was named Journalist of the Year at the British Press Awards. In June 2009, her book *Fool's Gold* won Financial Book of the Year at the inaugural Spear's Book Awards. In 2007, she was awarded the Wincott prize for financial journalism. She joined the *FT* in 1993 and was posted in 1997 to Tokyo, where she became the bureau chief and returned to become deputy head of the Lex column. She is the author of *Saving the Sun: How Wall Street Mavericks Shook Up Japan's Financial System and Made Billions* (2004).

Tom Vander Beken, a lawyer and criminologist, is a professor at Ghent University and director of the Institute for International Research on

Criminal Policy (IRCP). His main focus of research is on criminal justice-related issues and on risk and other future-oriented methodologies to assess organised crime. Vander Beken has published extensively and has been involved in many national and international research projects on crime and justice.

Fabian Wagner is a senior research scholar at the International Institute for Applied Systems Analysis, Laxenburg, Austria. His research into integrated assessment and systems modelling intersects a variety of academic disciplines, including climate science, biophysical processes, engineering, economics, sociology, governance and decision theory. He has gained intimate knowledge of the Intergovernmental Panel on Climate Change, first as a staff researcher at the IPCC Technical Support Unit in Hayama, Japan, and then as lead author. He has also consulted several times for the UN Framework Convention on Climate Change secretariat and has developed various quality control tools for national greenhouse gas inventories.

1

Introduction: The Challenges of Prevention

Chiara de Franco and Christoph O. Meyer

Diplomat 1: I'm confused. I thought you were talking about global warming, not an ice age.

Dr Hall: Yes, it is a paradox, but global warming can trigger a cooling trend [...]

Diplomat 2: Excuse me. When do you think this could happen, professor? When?

Dr Hall: I don't know. Maybe in a hundred years, maybe in a thousand. But what I do know is that if we do not act soon, it is our children and our grandchildren who will have to pay the price.

Diplomat 3: And who's going to pay the price of the Kyoto Accord? It will cost the world's economy hundreds of billions of dollars.

Dr Hall: With all due respect, Mr. Vice President, the cost of doing nothing could be even higher. Our climate is fragile.

The Day After Tomorrow, Scene III

In the opening sequence of Roland Emmerich's blockbuster *The Day After Tomorrow* (2004), a palaeoclimatologist played by actor Dennis Quaid reports on his findings on climate change at a United Nations conference in New Delhi. The diplomats and politicians present, including the Vice President of the United States, remain unconvinced by his vague if forceful warning. We draw attention to this film not for its cinematic qualities or its popularisation of climate science. Rather, it illustrates western, and in particular US, concern over potentially catastrophic perils in the future, which is also reflected in subsequent academic writing about new global threats and vulnerabilities: the meltdown of the financial system, terrorism with nuclear and biological weapons, the unintentional dangers of new technologies and sudden changes in the earth's environmental system (Posner, 2004; Homer-Dixon, 2006; Delpech, 2007; Fukuyama, 2007; Perrow, 2007; Bostrom and Cirkuvic, 2008). The film also encapsulates popular mythology about warning and prevention, which portrays decision-makers as cynical and narrow-minded, while expert 'warners' are extraordinarily foresighted and altruistic individuals who put their reputation on the line to speak (scientific) truth to power and prevent the worst. Implicit in this Cassandra-mythology is the expectation that warning is bound to fail.

Contrast this popular scepticism with the growing enthusiasm among governments, international organisations and non-governmental organisations for early warning and preventive policy across many different issue areas such as genocide, pandemics and tsunamis. While *prevention* is focused on removing the causes of potential harm altogether, *mitigation* aims at minimising the harmful consequences of an unpreventable event. In both cases uncertainty remains about whether the anticipated harm will ever manifest – not only because of the difficulties in forecasting accurately the behaviour of complex environmental systems, new technologies or extremist political groups, but also because knowledge itself is to varying degrees contested not only within societies, but also within expert communities. As a consequence, a number of states such as the UK, Singapore and, to some degree, the United States have established systematic and structured foresight capabilities (Habegger, 2008, 2010); also, non-governmental organisations and businesses are investing more resources into in-house 'long-range risk assessment', 'horizon-scanning', 'forward planning' or contract consultancies for the purpose of identifying future risks and opportunities (Armstrong, 2001; Humanitarian Futures Programme, 2010).

Amidst popular scepticism and official enthusiasm, we increasingly learn that effective prevention or mitigation depends on difficult cognitive, normative and political judgements, involving a range of actors in different organisational and national settings and varying across types of risk and interest constellations. In the case of the financial crisis of 2008–2009, politicians, bankers and regulators were accused of not recognising the emerging asset bubble. The accused, however, retorted that the particular dynamics and transnational scope of the crisis made it an essentially unpredictable surprise, a Black Swan event considered highly implausible through the prisms of beliefs dominant at the time and predictable with the benefit of hindsight (Taleb, 2007; also Chapters 13 and 14). Similarly, just a few months before terrorists turned airliners into missiles in September 2001, the director of the Defense Threat Reduction Agency in the US Department of Defense was confident that '[we] have, in fact, solved a terrorist problem in the last twenty-five years... The problem was aircraft hijacking and bombing' (cited in Posner, 2004: 174). Subsequent enquiries into the intelligence failures prior to the 9/11 attacks illustrated the problems of spotting weak signals and effectively sharing information among government agencies.

In contrast to these cases of risks being underestimated, some alleged cases of overreaction to warnings, such as swine flu (2008–2009) and the volcanic ash flight ban over northern Europe (2010), show that the potential to over-warn, misunderstand and overreact is just the flipside of the frequently lamented warning-response gap (George and Holl, 1997). Above all, these latter cases testify to the difficult judgements involved in identification, communication and management of transnational risks. Indeed, the rapidly escalating warning alerts from the World Health Organization (WHO) in relation to the swine flu virus (H1N1) triggered expensive national pandemic plans, public anxiety and costly shutdowns of countries' tourism industries, but were judged in retrospect to be insufficiently sensitive to evidence concerning the severity of the strain, which turned out to be milder than seasonal flu in its effects and considerably milder than the bird flu variant everyone had expected and prepared for (Chan, 2010). The complete ban on air-travel over northern Europe in response to the ash cloud emanating from an Icelandic volcano was instead the result of a lack of pre-existing agreement about safe ash levels and the rigid application of aviation protocols (Sammonds et al., 2010). It caused massive disruption to travel and trade within Europe, imposing substantial financial costs and hugely increasing the risks of accidents as people drove rental cars for long hours across Europe.

Hence, some key issues demand answers. Which of the risks are sufficiently knowable to justify preventive action and how much uncertainty is acceptable to whom? How can risk communicators break through high attention thresholds and scepticism of users, and how can users separate the credible and important warnings from the self-interested and less important? Are organisations and decision-makers equipped to encourage, recognise and adequately respond to inconvenient warnings that highlight failure and challenge key projects? Are decision-makers sufficiently incentivised to take precautionary measures, given the problems of claiming credit for them in public, or can public anxiety about certain risks also induce overreaction to avoid blame? How is it possible to make informed judgements about when and how to mobilise preventive or mitigating action, especially when there is uncertainty about the magnitude of the risk, as well as the risks created by preventive action itself? Is it possible for decision-makers to agree on collective strategies for tackling transnational risks when they are rooted in, and accountable primarily to, national communities and if future harm and gain are unequally distributed across national boundaries?

This book will not be able to answer all of these difficult questions, but the thrust of the various contributions is to challenge both technocratic and popularised accounts of the warning-response problem from the dual perspective of researchers and practitioners working in different areas of risk. The technocratic account holds that risks are best assessed by experts who 'educate' policy-makers in a timely fashion about what is the most effective and efficient response to such risks, on the basis of cost-benefit calculations. The popularised account notoriously suffers from hindsight biases, in so far as decision-makers are blamed for missing warnings when things go wrong but are accused of self-interested fear mongering when certain preventive policies are being advanced. In fact, reading the contributions in this book together, we can see that recognising risks, warning about them, prioritising between them and taking preventive action against them hang together in complex ways and involve balancing judgements. Both warning and acting on warning are far more difficult than much of the contemporary commentary suggests, especially when risks acquire transnational character. Acknowledging these difficulties, the contributors suggest ways in which such challenges can be handled, if not fully managed away, by individuals, public and private organisations, the news media, and scientists.

1.1 The state of the art

Research into transnational risks as such is not new. Since the path-breaking study by the German sociologist Ulrich Beck on the emergence of a risk society on the background of societal concerns over nuclear power, acid rain and polluted rivers (Beck, 1986), risk research has truly taken off in sociology, psychology, geography as well as in environmental and health studies (Beck, 1999; Renn, 2008). The literature has identified a wide range of factors that influence how experts, organisations, the news media and the general public perceive and communicate risks (Pidgeon et al., 2003; Breakwell, 2007). However, most of the literature dealing with warning and prevention failures focuses on commercial organisations and much of the writing has so far been focused on the risks connected to the disastrous failure of technologies and production systems, most of it in the US context (Perrow, 1999; Bazerman and Watkins, 2008; Gerstein and Ellsberg, 2008). Similarly, studies of regulatory approaches to risk are typically focused on environmental and health risks arising from new products and the negative externalities of human production and consumption, but few comparative efforts have been made in other policy areas such as crime eradication and finance regulation risk. Likewise, in the arena of international governance, much of the writing focuses on environmental risks, in particular climate change, but only recently have scholars used concepts from risk research to think about future risks of terrorism, civil war or inter-state war (de Goede, 2008; Dunn Cavelty and Mauer, 2009). One key aspiration of this book is to explore how different expert communities deal with varying degrees of uncertainty, which methods they use to explore such potentially unknowable risks, and what kind of boundary problems emerge at the intersection of expert analysis, warning and decision-making. Can we identify key obstacles and ways of overcoming them across different types of risks, institutional structures and interest constellations? Are there lessons to be learned for both scholars and practitioners, or is each area too idiosyncratic for such cross-fertilisation?

One of the shortcomings of most risk research has been the lack of conceptualisation of the linkages between risk forecasting, communication, learning and preventive action. There has been a tendency to regard these activities as either wholly distinct or to study 'risk management' in such a holistic way that the specific challenges of knowing, communicating, perceiving, deciding and acting in different governance settings and situations are squeezed into a single technocratic paradigm. While each of the authors represented in this book may place a stronger emphasis on either forecasting, communication of risks or responses to them, virtually all of them emphasise how these issues are interconnected in professional practice, and how problems in one domain affect other domains. For instance, David Demeritt and Sebastian Nobert show in Chapter 9 that national decision-makers are not necessarily interested in more accurate and earlier 'ensemble forecasts' of floods from the EU, but in later and more certain national forecasts that allow them to shift the responsibility for decisions to evacuate to national experts. A key characteristic of the relationship between producers and consumers of forecasts is thus not only the debate over who has superior knowledge, but also about who can be blamed under what conditions. In the case of national security, Jan Goldman (Chapter 3) highlights the importance of distinguishing between intelligence (forecasting) and warning failures. But users of warnings can also cause analytical flaws when, for instance, politicians repeatedly ask intelligence services to investigate hypotheses that suit their political agendas, or when intelligence services are asked to make their products more precise and confident than would be 'professionally responsible' in order to justify particular policies in public (see Chapters 2 and 16). Similarly, users may not consider warnings in terms of their substance, but whether warning producers can be considered politically suspicious given their attributed self-interest, such as certain minority ethnic groups or humanitarian non-governmental organisations (NGOs) warning of impending or actual genocide (e.g. Chapter 8).

Finally, there is a tendency in the literature to neatly separate contributions from academics and practitioners in terms of theory and application. While not all writing by practitioners can help to advance our understanding of the dynamics at work, we feel the contribution of practitioners is undervalued. Academic research comes with its own specific biases toward certain theories, methods and worldviews, and research happens also in non-academic settings. Reflective practitioners with years of experience at the highest levels of their profession, as presented in this book, are not only shapers of social, economic, and political conditions, but also astute analysts of current practice who do not need a scholarly spokesperson. This is why we have brought together practitioners and scholars to reflect on a common set of questions but based on their different areas of expertise. Practitioners contributing to this book are drawn from the UK Financial Services Authority (Thomas Huertas), *The Financial Times* (Gillian Tett), the consultancy Control Risks (Corene Crossin and James Smither), the EU Situation Centre (William Shapcott), British Joint Intelligence Committee (former member David Omand), the US State Department's Bureau of Intelligence and Research (Warren H. Fishbein), and the International Institute for Applied Systems Analysis (Fabian Wagner). Each of the three thematic sections of the book – Forecasting, Communication, Responding – will thus contain a healthy mix of both scholarly and practice-based thinking.

1.2 Analytical framework and contributions

The structure of this book follows from the distinction we make between forecasting, communicating, learning, and mobilising some kind of action (for the three-fold approach, see Bazerman and Watkins, 2008: 153–157). These are the four main challenges that need to be addressed in order to place relevant knowledge about risks at the service of effective and proportionate action at both national and international level. Together they form a warning-response loop as illustrated in Figure 1.1. While the labels above imply a sequential logic of one stage following neatly after another, the reality is considerably more complex. In finance for instance, risk analysis, warning and response are continuously linked. Risk perceptions are reflected in prices, which in turn affect risk indicators as market participants react to these changes almost instantaneously (Chapter 14). The feedback loops between the stages are also visible when experts are influenced by users' expectations, either through power asymmetries and fear of being blamed for false positives or negatives, or simply because the specificity and certainty of forecasting depends on users' risk appetite as risks and opportunities often go together, as Crossin and Smither point out (Chapter 11). Despite these inter-linkages and the concurrent character of risk recognition, communication, learning and mobilisation, the four activities do entail distinct challenges and usually involve different kinds of specialised actors related in different ways to each other. For the dynamics within the warning-response loop it matters whether risk forecasters, communicators and managers are all in the same hierarchically structured organisation, whether they are contractually or legally linked, as in the case of rating agency or public watchdogs, or whether warnings originate from NGOs or individual experts via the news media. Both producers and consumers of warnings can thus operate according to different professional rules, within different relations of power and on the basis of divergent worldviews. In the following, we will discuss the questions raised by each of these challenges, as well as the challenges themselves, in more depth. On the way, we will clarify key terms like 'forecasting', 'warning', 'risk', 'threat', and 'prevention'.

1.2.1 Forecasting risks

What do we mean when we talk about forecasting and risk? Risk is commonly defined as *a composite measure of the probability and (negative) consequences of a given phenomenon,* whereas a threat is linked to *the intentions and capabilities*

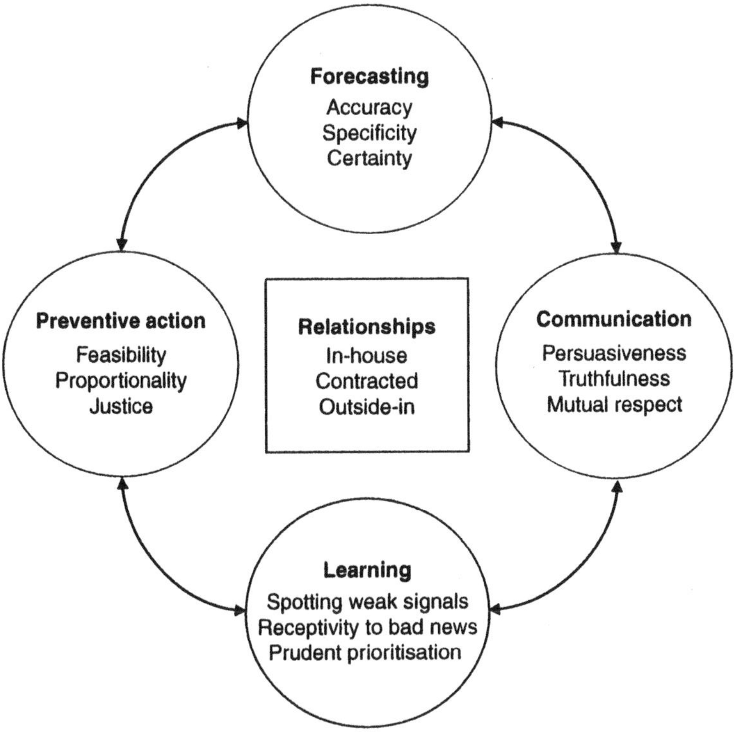

Figure 1.1 The warning-response-loop: four challenges for prevention

of a particular source to inflict harm (Chapters 6 and 11). Harm is the negative consequence when a risk materialises from a given user's perspective, as the same event may also have positive effects for the same or other users. The foundation of any policy aimed at prevention or mitigation is knowledge claims about future events and their harmfulness. Forecasts can be based on the natural and social sciences or a mixture of both, which will affect social credibility. But forecasts can also involve knowledge generated by warning systems (Chapter 9), journalists, academic experts, field officers working for NGOs and even individual citizens. The contributions in this book cover a range of different actors involved in forecasting such as risk consultancies (Chapter 11), regulators (Chapter 12), multi-nationally funded scientific institutions (Chapter 5) and consortia of research institutes (Chapter 4) and even individual whistleblowers within organisations (Chapter 10), each of which uses different forms of expertise in different ways.

Forecasting is understood broadly as all activities relating to making sense of the future, and here in particular, identifying risks that may affect negatively a given individual, social group, organisation or state. Typical performance goals for risk forecasting exercises are their accuracy, their specificity and their level of certainty. In this book we are primarily concerned with non-routine future risks involving significant uncertainty about the probability, timing and nature of their manifestation. This uncertainty could stem from the low frequency of their occurrence, fundamental uncertainty about their causes, or a lack of information about future conditions to project existing knowledge of causes. While most anticipatory analysis in organisations is non-systematic and intuitive, one notes a shift towards using a range of techniques for assessing risks and dealing with uncertainty, such as extrapolation, model-based forecasting, expert-surveys, market-based risk assessment, deliberative and counter-factual scenario-building, as well as simulations of various kinds. For some of types of risk, the goal of a forecasting technique is to produce single point 'predictions', whereas others will generate probabilistic assessments depending on different contingencies and policy choices. David Demeritt and Sebastien Nobert, for instance, investigate the origin and evolution of the European flood alert system and examine the reasons why national users rely on the more sensitive and earlier 'ensemble' forecasting methods less than might be expected (Chapter 9). A third approach questions the utility of probabilistic forecasting for many types of risk and across longer-time horizons, and focuses rather on challenging conventional wisdom and unquestioned assumptions through developing scenarios, role-play and simulations. Fabian Wagner writes about his experience with the non-probabilistic GAINS model in Chapter 5. A group of authors involved in the FORESEC project (Chapter 4) reflect on the experience of exploring security risks facing the EU over a time period of 15 years (until 2025) on the basis of cross-national participatory scenario-building. Similarly, Tom Vander Beken (Chapter 6) critiques the rise of (mainly) quantitative risk assessments in the area of combating organised crime, and highlights the potential of alternative forecasting techniques to get a better grip on future criminal activities.

The problem of high uncertainty regarding contemporary forecasting as compared to the bipolar, less rapid and less interconnected world before the end of the Cold War, has been at the centre of a number of recent contributions in both risk research and intelligence studies (Cavelty and Mauer, 2009). Warren Fishbein argues in this book (Chapter 15) that complexity, obscurity and novelty have increased in the post-Cold War globalised world to a degree that a new analytical approach is required. While most forecasting is concerned with pre-identified risks and the monitoring of indicators related to them, the 9/11 attacks and the financial crisis have taken most decision-makers as well as publics by complete surprise. For observers such as Nicholas Taleb (2007) these are 'Black Swan' Events, which are rare but have a high impact. This does not mean that such events have not been imagined or forecasted, but they negate the prevalent expectations. We can indeed identify some warnings retrospectively about 9/11-style attacks and jihadist extremism (Clarke, 2004; Czwarno, 2006) and about the risk building up in the subprime mortgage sectors and the overleveraging of institutions in small and big countries (Chapter 14). Gillian Tett shows in Chapter 13 how 'technical silos' within banks account for why the risks generated by new financial products went largely undetected, but argues that such silo mentality is baked into the twenty-first century with its reliance on increasingly fine-grained specialisation and division of labour.

This raises the question of how to handle uncertainty and avoid intelligence failures (Betts, 2007; Jervis, 2010). One approach is to highlight problems of connecting the dots to address 'intelligence failures' of the nature preceding the 9/11 attacks (Chapter 3). David Omand (Chapter 2) is interested in how intelligence analysts can provide accurate early warning of future threats to decision-makers given the increasing complexity of contemporary security threats. He also reflects on how this challenge is magnified by political demands for implausibly precise and certain advice. Jan Goldman (Chapter 3) expands on this theme by investigating different kinds of epistemological problems relating to forecasting on the one hand and the problem of measuring the performance of intelligence agencies on the other.

1.2.2 Communicating risks

Risk communication is concerned with the way information, interpretations and opinions about risks and their management are transmitted, discussed, amplified and transformed as they become part of a communication process involving individuals, groups and institutions (for an overview see Renn, 2008: 201–271). The nature and effects of risk communication can be analysed in terms of characteristics of the source, message, channel, transmitters, contextual factors as well as the receivers. Research on risk perceptions and the psychology of risk, in particular on cognitive and motivational biases, demonstrates considerable differences in how risks are being communicated and perceived, depending on whether they are man-made or natural, evoke weak or strong emotional responses, technical or politicised, certain or uncertain, and whether they are culturally distant or close (Pidgeon et al., 2003; Breakwell, 2007). For instance, de Franco and Meyer (Chapter 9) find substantial differences in the way the news media convey warnings about climate change as compared to intra-state conflict. Effectiveness of risk communication can be defined from various normative perspectives depending on expectations related to the role of expertise and experts in public policy and business, as well as on different assessments about the nature of different types of risks. As different expectations are also reflected in different relationships between the sender and receiver of messages, this book presents, on the one hand, some contributions that highlight risk communication in terms of a two-way-dialogue, such as in the cases of responses to air pollution (Chapter 5), and advice to business (Chapter 11). On the other hand, other contributors focus on warnings as intentional communicative acts aimed at persuading recipients to pay attention to impending harms and mobilise some action, for instance through intelligence about imminent attacks (Chapters 2 and 3), ensemble forecasting of floods (Chapter 9), or whistle-blowing about dangerous organisational malpractice (Chapter 10).

Whereas warning is by its very nature a bottom-up process involving an initiative by experts, or organisations with access to such experts, de-facto much of the warning practice is hardwired into organisational and governmental practices, blending into regularised risk communication involving a range of in-house or externally contracted experts. Warnings in this more mundane form are being actively solicited by different types of users, either because they are required to do so by regulation before introducing new products to the market, or because governments and business want to be aware of potential risks before they take action, whether to launch a particular computer-system, build a plant in a potentially unstable country, or launch military action against a foreign government or rebel group.

Key generic challenges from the communicator's perspective are how to establish credibility with recipients, how to frame messages in a way that ensures they will be noticed and processed with sufficient motivation, and under what circumstances risk communication is persuasive. Corene Crossin and James Smither (Chapter 11) from the consultancy *Control Risks* elaborate on how they seek to preserve their long-term organisational credibility when clients see advice as inconvenient for planned projects. Contributors also stress the challenges of intercultural and cross-national risk communication. William Shapcott, for instance, reflects on communicating intelligence in the EU, where consumers have different worldviews, values and preferences, not to mention different levels of English language proficiency (Chapter 6).

From a normative perspective, risk communication involves the challenge of reconciling truthfulness with the minimum simplification and repackaging required to ensure attention and understanding on the part of recipients with little pre-existing knowledge and limited time to process new information. As Fabian Wagner of the International Institute for Applied Systems Analysis argues (Chapter 5), some forecasts can only be fully understood through knowledge of advanced mathematics, but models can not only be used as instruments of discovery but also as languages for a dialogue between experts and various stakeholders. If warning communicators want to make themselves understood among non-experts, they need to accept the trade-off in accuracy that comes with higher intelligibility among warning recipients (Betts, 1978). But this process of adjustment can easily lead to oversimplification and exaggeration to maximise effect as, for instance, in the claim contained in British intelligence of September 2002 about Iraq's

Weapons of Mass Destruction (WMD) programme, which asserted that Iraq had WMD and was 'able to launch in 45 minutes'. Another case was the decision of the British Advertising Standards Authority (ASA) to ban two advertisements commissioned by the British Department for Energy and Climate Change in 2009 that were judged to go beyond established science in their predictions of future flooding and drought (ASA, 2010). The advertisement also raised problems with regard to the respect for recipients' autonomy as it evoked fearful images of drowning people in a bed-time story setting. Or consider the case of scientists sitting on advisory committees complaining to the news media that their advice on drug classification was 'ignored', because it did not lead to a particular policy decision by the government.

Another type of normative problem in risk communication arises when risk communicators have a hidden agenda which is likely to seep into message, content, and framing. In the case of swine flu, some of the health experts involved in assessing the harm have been found retrospectively to have financial links to pharmaceutical companies that stand to profit from large-scale vaccination programmes. Rather than acting as self-negating prophecies, warnings may be self-fulfilling and create the conditions that accelerate the harm instead of stopping it, a phenomenon aptly described by Karl Popper as the 'Oedipus-Effect' (Popper, 1957: 11). In few areas is the linkage between warning and action as apparent as in the financial markets, where prices can be highly responsive to warnings as Huertas explains in Chapter 14. A warning about a lack of liquidity, for instance, may directly contribute to panic in the market, rather than enabling preventive action, as happened with the Rating Agency's downgrading of Greece's credit rating in May 2010. Moreover, warnings can be exploited by market participants who can spread rumours that will turn the market to their own advantage.

1.2.3 Learning from warnings

In the context of this book, learning can be conceived as a cognitive process which aims to put the best available knowledge at the service of decision-making. The legitimate expectation is that those with delegated authority to take preventive action should take reasonable steps to be receptive to warnings in order to be able to act on them if they agree with the risk communicator about the urgency, probability and gravity of a given risk. In some cases, learning can take the form of a convergence of users' with analysts' judgements about the probability and harmfulness of a given phenomenon (Brante, 2009: 6), whereas in other cases, users may have legitimate grounds for dismissing a warning as biased, unimportant or non-urgent. But how can users recognise, understand and prioritise those risk messages that are accurate, urgent and important as to their implications? Each of these three steps involved in the cognitive processing of risks is fraught with problems and is generally more difficult than is commonly assumed in post-mortems. We will look briefly at three of the main challenges.

The *first* challenge for organisations and decision-makers is to spot weak (warning) signals at a time when they have become increasingly inundated by the rising flow of information from both internal and external sources. Warning messages are easily drowned out by a low signal-to-noise ratio determined by the volume and nature of messages competing for the attention of a given decision-maker in a given situation (Wohlstetter, 1962). This is one of the key lessons from many disasters that have afflicted private and public organisations (Boin et al., 2005; Bazerman and Watkins, 2008). Failure to recognise warnings can be attributed in part to forecasting problems in not being able to reach sufficiently certain and unambiguous judgements, or to communicating risks in a way that resonates with a given recipient, but receptivity also has a 'pull-dimension'. If organisations and leaders are solely focused on information related to opportunity-seeking, or do not actively resist simplification nor pay attention to detail and operations (Weick and Sutcliffe, 2007), they are much more likely to miss those weak signals. Warren Fishbein (Chapter 15) argues that governments and intelligence services can learn from nuclear power plants and aircraft carriers on how to become 'mindful' of potential errors.

The *second* challenge relates to the fact that risk communication may conflict with motivational biases of recipients, in so far as warning messages might be inconvenient or downright embarrassing if they were accepted as credible. While decision-makers are entitled to disbelieve knowledge claims, they should not do so without any rational basis. A senior diplomat such as the former EU High Representative Javier Solana may well have a unique insight leading him to dismiss the conclusions of intelligence briefings about the intentions of a given foreign government, because of his long experience of its leaders. However, the same cannot be said about the former South African President Thabo Mbeki when he dismissed overwhelming medical evidence about the causes of and potential remedies for AIDS. Often inconvenient warning messages are not just disbelieved, but they are actively discouraged and suppressed. Shooting the proverbial messenger will discourage experts from coming forward with inconvenient truths in the future. Openness to inconvenient news and adversarial arguments is therefore an essential precondition for organisational learning from warnings, but has often not been practised. Marc Gerstein and Edgar Schein (Chapter 10) look at the importance of empowering individuals within organisations to blow the whistle on grave risks, highlighting the various ways organisations tend to retaliate against those who reveal their 'dark secrets'.

The *third* challenge is that, even if a given recipient does muster sufficient initial attention to process a warning and accepts its underlying knowledge claim, it is still not self-evident that she/he shares the warner's beliefs about why this particular warning deserves to be prioritised. The warner may not understand the recipients' preferences or the situational context, or may not know what instruments are available to respond. In fact, what is a harmful event for some may represent for others an opportunity to be exploited (rather than a problem to be prevented at all costs). For some political actors the financial crisis may represent a unique opportunity to mobilise political action that would under normal circumstances be impossible, whereas for others it is a threat to their livelihood. Similarly, in foreign affairs, seasoned diplomats may welcome a 'security crisis' arising from a 'state of concern' around missile testing because it supplies an opportunity to exploit fears of neighbours and build a new coalition to advance medium and long-term objectives. Other less benign reasons for not prioritising certain risk messages relate to the phenomenon that decision-makers discount the future far more than is prudent, both for themselves but particularly for their constituents, whether they are voters, consumers or shareholders. Many decision-makers are trained and incentivised to focus on the agenda of the day and their immediate tactical advantage, rather than consider issues that are likely to manifest as problems tomorrow or beyond the next election. Consider for instance, the way warnings about the impending insolvency of Greece were handled by European leaders, especially the German government, in late 2009 and early 2010. They delayed for months sending a clear signal to financial markets that the EU would act to help Greece in order to avoid a negative electoral fall-out in important regional elections. The end result was that European finance ministers had to agree on a €750 billion bail-out package to meet all Greece's debt payments for the next three years and prevent both that country's bankruptcy as well as a domino effect on other Eurozone members such as Spain, Portugal, Ireland, and Italy (Barber, 2010).

1.2.4 Mobilising preventive action

Preventive action is aimed at tackling the causes of a problematic phenomenon so that the probability of it happening, and its likely impact, are reduced to zero. It may also be defined more broadly as an action aimed not at tackling the problem itself, but rather more selectively at reducing some of its most harmful consequences. This second broader definition could also be called mitigation, resilience, or preparedness, with all labels referring to a particular view of what policy is possible. In current discussions about climate change, for example, both prevention (reducing CO_2 in the atmosphere) and mitigation measures (building higher dams) are being discussed.

Given the diversity of risks and their potential interplay, preventive action can take the form of direct action aimed at preventing a particular harm from occurring such as regulation, or the creation of regulatory bodies, unilaterally or internationally coordinated changes in domestic and international policies, or the creation of tailor-made early warning systems. Another type of response relates to cognitive and instrumental readiness, which will not necessarily prevent the phenomenon from occurring, but may substantially limit harmful effects (Chapter 15). Some responses, such as developing and practising evacuation plans for large cities or creating a stand-by civilian engineering unit, can have mitigating effects across a range of possible risks. Finally, an important precursor to preventive action in response to initial warning might be to do more research widely defined to increase confidence in risk forecasting and a better understanding of the costs, impact, and downsides of different policy responses.

The dynamics of preventive policy can be expected to differ across the policy spectrum, depending on the instruments available for a response. If a low-cost and low-risk instrument is at hand for early preventive action against a particular risk, the chances of it being used are higher in comparison with those areas where the costs and risks of preventive action are very high. Moreover, the emergence of novel risks may require the creation of new instruments, forms of international collaboration, coordination and resource pooling, while in other areas of more conventional risks existing instruments just need to be used earlier and better. However, it is well-known that global governance and regulation is lagging behind the transnational spread of economic and social activity and is struggling to manage risks within the current institutional framework that originates in its basic features, from the post-World War II period. As one could observe during the recent financial crisis, there is both over- and under-lapping of competencies to deal with different types of risks, which create confusion over who is expected to act. Asymmetric consequences of different types of risks can lead to potentially very different assessments of how harmful a given risk is. This can be reinforced by culturally conditioned differences in worldviews, values and norms, which may lead to different assessments of the costs and benefits of a phenomenon as well as costs associated with preventive policy (Douglas and Wildavsky, 1982). Other complicating factors arise from transnational debates over who has caused a given new risk (if it is man-made) and who should therefore bear the costs of adjustment.

These perceptions matter because preventive action is far from being a self-evident choice, particularly in those areas where action is costly and may create new kinds of risks (Sunstein, 2005). Preventive action may turn out to be grossly disproportionate to the probability and scope of a certain harm occurring when compared with alternative uses of the same resources for a range of public goods. This mismatch is most apparent when mortality rates can be calculated for a course of action and compared with statistical value of life, or the lives saved if the same resources were channelled into alternative policy measures. In the area of national security, there are often questions about whether the use of particular instruments, in particular military force, creates more problems than it solves. In fact, in the area of counter-terrorism, often the overreaction of the state is a major risk-accelerator rather than an instrument of prevention. Moral dilemmas also arise when warnings suggest sacrificing the few for the many. David Omand

(Chapter 2) reminds us that Winston Churchill refused to utilise intelligence to redirect enemy fire to less densely populated and strategically important areas of London.

Three chapters in this book address problems of preventive policy directly. Thomas Huertas examines the potential for making the global financial system meltdown-proof, placing particular emphasis on measures necessary for allowing banks to fail without endangering the whole system (Chapter 14). Warren Fishbein makes the case for enhancing the resilience and mental preparedness of government given that it would be unrealistic to expect early warning always to be available and preventive action to work (Chapter 15). Finally, Chiara de Franco and Christoph Meyer draw on the insights from the previous chapters to theorise which variables tend to help or hinder the identification, communication, and response to different types of transnational threats. In a second step, they attempt to draw on these analytical insights to formulate four arguments about how warning-response dynamics can be improved by dealing better with uncertainty, enhancing international collaboration, better scrutiny of international risk management and, finally, combining prevention and resilience.

Part I
Forecasting Harm

2

The Coastline of the Future: Some Limits on Forecasting and Prediction

Sir David Omand

2.1 Introduction

Governments hate surprises. They hate it when they have to perform U-turns and ditch cherished policies in the face of unexpected events. They hate it even more when headlines shriek 'government caught napping'. An inability by government to spot trouble approaching and to act to prevent or mitigate it is liable to be regarded by the public as a major weakness and a sign of lack of competence. There are some types of human activity that cannot by their nature be known in advance – the workings of stock-markets, or the incidence of 'acts of God' such as extreme weather events and earthquakes. Even in circumstances (such as international affairs) that are closely tracked by governments and their diplomatic, military and intelligence establishments, there are practical limits as to how much forewarning should be expected of untoward developments. This chapter therefore sets out briefly to examine what should be a realistic aspiration to forecasting and prediction by governments of developments that they could most benefit from knowing about in advance whether in international affairs, technology or social attitudes.

2.2 Problems of epistemology

How does anyone begin to predict the future? Looking backwards, we have our knowledge of where we have been to help guide us. Looking forwards, the possibilities are infinite – and the more precisely we try to enumerate those possibilities the more complicated they become. We can imagine the task of the horizon-scanner as that of a sailor peering ahead through the mist trying to map from offshore the distant coastline of the future without ever being able to reach it. There is a simple analogy here with the old question, how long is the British coastline? The answer depends on the size of your measuring ruler. The finer the scale of the measuring instrument the larger the answer becomes, as every bend and inlet has to be measured (see Chapter 5). The best model of a coastline is that of a fractal. So it is with the complex boundaries of the web of events that make up the transition from the past into the future. The finer the detail that the analysts try to bring to bear in their mapping of the future, the more interrelationships are discovered that have to be taken into account, and the less precise the answer. The fractal nature of reality means that it is not possible for the analyst to establish how the possible sets of cross-currents or side winds will influence us and thus in which future we will arrive. It is impossible to plot a precise course from here to the future. The old military expression, big hands, small map, comes to mind. The only way to is to approximate, to try to identify from the distance of the present the larger features and archipelagos that stick out from the coastline and about which mariners seeking to navigate safely towards the future should certainly be warned.

A reasonable stab at forecasting can be made by assuming that tomorrow will be like today, only more so, as obvious trends are assumed to continue on into the future. That inductive approach gives good results most of the time, but when the unexpected intervenes it can lead governments dramatically astray. Low probability events occur, and occur more frequently (in the security domain as elsewhere) than those conditioned to think in terms of the law of large numbers, in which extremes tend to cancel out, would expect. There are obvious inherent dangers, for historians, intelligence analysts and horizon-scanners alike, of relying on inductive reasoning without having a satisfactory explanation of the underlying situation. Scientific method is the best methodology for supporting predictive analysis, based on the development and testing of alternative hypotheses regarded as the provisional explanations of observed reality that best accord with the available evidence.

Forecasting, on the other hand, can proceed from a broad identification of factors, whether economic, environmental, technological, social or international, that may shape possible futures. A distinctive feature of many recent reports on national security (e.g. IPPR, 2009) is that they attempt to provide forecasts by identifying major drivers of threat (hostile ideologies, proliferation of weapons of mass destruction, global issues such as climate change and demography), and then seek to identify the 'threat actors' (terrorists, rogue states), and finally the 'threat domains' in which such actors can influence our path to the future (in cyber-space, in regions of instability and conflict around the world, in our cities as modern urban living becomes ever more vulnerable to the effect of large-scale disruptions). The Labour Government in the UK published a National Security Strategy (Cabinet Office, 2008 and 2009) that is a case in point, designed at the outset from the point of view of the future protection of the citizen, and based on principles of good risk management covering the full range of major disruptive events (not just malicious threats such as terrorism, proliferation and international crime, but also the impact of serious natural hazards such as pandemics or extreme flooding). The intention of such analysis is less to guide prediction of what will happen than to provide a rational basis for the identification of national and international capabilities that may be needed to cope with the range of futures thus identified.

New demands are thus placed on government both to acquire strategic notice of plausible emergent risks as well as, wherever possible, to provide actionable forewarning – prediction – of when and how those risks are likely to erupt, in the interests of trying to manage events so as to maintain the normality of everyday life.

That approach begins to suggest a new definition of national security as *a state of trust on the part of the citizen that the major risks to everyday life, whether from man-made threats or impersonal hazards, are being adequately managed to the extent that there is confidence that normal life can continue or if disrupted will be quickly restored.* In the circumstances of the early twenty-first century, government's ability to exercise reasonable management of responses to key threats and hazards will rest substantially on its ability to anticipate trouble, and thus stay one step ahead. An important part of maintaining this public confidence in government is honesty about the limits of forecasting and prediction, as well as the limitations to state power to prevent risks from arising or to mitigate their impact even when they are have been forecast (see Chapter 13).

2.3 Improving the use of forewarning

A definition of intelligence also flows from this approach. We can see 'the purpose of intelligence as improving decision-making by government through reducing ignorance and, further, the purpose of secret intelligence as achieving this end in respect of information that others are seeking to prevent us knowing' (Omand, 2010). It is important in considering the value of intelligence in improving government decision-making on security issues (and thus, for example, how much to invest in collecting and assessing it) to recognise that information may be used to reduce uncertainty (or ignorance, as I prefer to call it) on the part of the decision-maker in three distinct stages. It is the combination of these stages that usually leads to an ability to make at least a rough predictive assessment of future conditions. In that way we improve the odds of acting more in alignment with our goals than we would have achieved had we simply tossed a coin to decide between courses of action, or acted on hunch or wrong information, or allowed events rather than prior decision to decide the outcome.

The *first* step in using information in this way is what could be termed *building situational awareness.* Specific intelligence can help to build up awareness of a hidden domain of interest to the policy maker. Individual intelligence reports can be seen as building blocks, but it would be misleading to think of the purpose of such intelligence effort as just to heap up presumed facts in data bases and lists. Individual reports contribute to overall situational awareness and may turn out be the missing pieces in the jigsaw that transform awareness of the overall picture that the puzzle represents (see Chapter 8). In terms of terrorism, for example, it is important to try to find out:

1. The identities, and aliases, of those suspected of supporting or engaging in terrorism and their past personal history and criminal record;
2. Biometric details identifying the root identity of terrorist suspects;
3. The location of terrorist suspects;
4. Their patterns of behaviour and association;
5. Their modus operandi for attacks;
6. Their counter-surveillance understanding and the measures they take;
7. The movements of suspected terrorists;
8. The logistics, training and financing of their networks.

Such detailed information gathering is the part of the intelligence iceberg below the surface. To give an example from a completely different area, a considerable intelligence effort would be needed to track Chinese strategic missile developments, both submarine launched and road mobile, and their development of future weapons systems such as an anti-satellite capability.

The *second* step of using information in supporting decision-making can best be described as *explanatory*, examining hypotheses from which explanatory theories of past and present behaviour can be built, how a situation has arisen, the dynamics between the parties and what the motivations of the actors involved are likely to be. Thus, in terms of terrorism, an understanding is needed of the belief systems of terrorist groups, what really motivates them, how and why does individual radicalisation take place and so on. To revert to the Chinese example from the military domain, intelligence can be used to examine possible rationales for the Chinese missile and ASAT programmes: for example, are these best explained as a defensive move driven by Chinese fears of a future US first-strike capability with precision guided conventional weapons against old first-generation Chinese silo-based missiles? Or do they reflect an aggressive doctrine of military superiority? Intelligence is unlikely to provide unambiguous answers, but can contribute greatly to a rational examination of possible explanations (see Chapter 15).

The *third* use of intelligence is potentially the most valuable, but also the most fraught, and that is for *prediction*. It is a small, but significant, step to use an explanatory theory of present behaviour to predict likely future attitudes and behaviour and to generate forewarning (see Chapter 5). To take the terrorism example, can we predict the next move of a terrorist group? It could be a single intelligence report from inside a terrorist group that enables prediction of a terrorist attack on a crowded place to trigger anticipatory security action, thus saving scores of lives. It could be a predictive assessment based, not on specific intelligence reporting but on judgments made about a developing situation in an unstable country overseas, that extends the explanatory into the predictive. How will the future threat mutate, and so on? To continue the Chinese military example: if we have good awareness of the situation now reached by weapons systems developments, and if we have sound explanations of present behaviour what, for example, could our intelligence model tell us by way of prediction about how the People's Liberation Army would respond to future US arms control initiatives? Such predictive assessments need not of course be point estimates. It can still be extremely helpful to governments to have ranges of prediction, or 'not before' dates, for example in relation to a proliferator's ability to develop a nuclear weapon.

The history of intelligence prediction by national intelligence communities of emerging threats is nevertheless patchy, especially in predicting revolutions and the collapse of empires. The main problem appears to be the inductive fallacy, of imagining that tomorrow will be like today since today was like yesterday, with perhaps some adjustments for the effect of known trends. This approach fails when paradigm shifts occur – Black Swans – and thus the predictive models fail to make sense of reality, usually because the assumptions about human behaviour underlying the models no longer apply. Like phase changes in physics, new relationships come into play. It is the shift from one model to another that is hard to predict. The parable of Cradock's egg comes to mind: Sir Percy Cradock, as chairman of the Joint Intelligence Committee (JIC), used to imagine the task of predicting such movements as like holding a raw egg in one's hand, squeezing, and trying to predict which microscopic cracks will suddenly become fissures and the integrity of the structure collapse inward. Intelligence is rather better at predicting more mundane things, within a relatively stable frame of reference, such as the arrival of new military capabilities in the armed services of a potential adversary.

If nevertheless reliable pre-emptive secret intelligence is available, then it can be of great value to government in the security, military or diplomatic domains. In counter-terrorism it can allow the security authorities to protect the public with the rapier rather than the bludgeon of state power: it protects the public directly by disrupting and preventing criminal acts before they occur; it lowers the level of violence, gaining time for long-term measures to address the roots; it provides the leads for criminal investigations that will lead to prosecutions, thus reassuring the public, reducing the threat and upholding the rule of law; and, crucially it helps the authorities operate in ways that reassure the communities in which the terrorists seek support, not alienating them through blunt measures such as house-to-house searches, stop-and-search or roadblocks and controls or, at its most extreme, mass internment.

Governments will therefore continue to strive to gain predictive knowledge to reduce uncertainty in their decision-making. Since, however, the defining characteristic of secret intelligence is that others are actively trying to stop it being acquired, we should note that it follows that exceptional means will be needed to collect and manage it. That in turn raises significant ethical issues in a democracy as to the limits to be placed on the type of method that would be justified to provide this predictive power. Forecasting and warning of threats that others seek to hide from us comes at a price. Careful statutory regulation and judicial and political oversight within the framework of human rights is necessary to ensure that the public remains content with what is being done in their name.

2.4 Applying risk calculus

Conceptually, the starting point for using predictive estimates for policy purposes is the risk equation: risk, or expected loss of public value = likelihood × vulnerability × impact × duration (and similarly for expected gain in public value from the combination of likelihood, opportunity, payback and payback period). A good example is the way that since 2003 the UK has been following a long-term counter-terrorism strategy, CONTEST (Home Office, 2009), built around a modern national security objective: to reduce the risk from international terrorism so that people can get on with everyday life, freely and with confidence. The strategy was designed explicitly to be an exercise in risk management, with the Pursue (short to medium term) and Prevent (medium to longer term) campaigns designed to reduce the likelihood of future terrorism directed against the UK and its interests overseas. The Protect campaign is aimed at reducing the vulnerability of society, especially its critical national infrastructure. The Prepare campaign is aimed at reducing the scale and duration of disruption when attacks do get under the security radar.

The guiding principle for government has to be to find sets of policies that manage the expected risks down to the lowest reasonably achievable level (the ALARP principle), explaining to the public that a zero-risk position is not generally attainable. Nor is it desirable as an aim given the likely costs that might be incurred, ethically as well as financially. Examples of such potential costs abound in the area of counter-terrorism where tensions are bound to exist in balancing within the framework of human rights such needs as security and privacy, the right to life and the right to a fair trial. Specific policies followed by the United States as part of the Bush Administration 'war on terror' resulted in significant cost to the international reputation and 'soft power' of the United States as well as giving rise to individual injustices.

A principle of subsidiarity also has to be applied by government so that problems are dealt with at the lowest level at which a reasonable level of risk can be achieved in practice. At the same time, government needs to take care that it is not falling into the trap of 'securitising' all its ills as national security issues. If every problem is treated as a security threat then security measures will become the only response. In government planning, relevant major risks have to be individually assessed in terms of their likelihood, the vulnerability of society to them, and the impact they would have if they did occur (see Chapter 11). The all-risks approach has also to take account of the internationally interdependent nature of most of the issues, given that they cannot in future be neatly divided up for action into domestic and overseas compartments.

Risk management of security issues by government on behalf of the public cannot, however, simply be a technical exercise in utilitarian welfare economics, 'the greatest good for the greatest number'. With limited resources to spend, whose security is to be safeguarded first? Are the metrics of the insurance industry and government cost-benefit analysis applicable, such as number of Qualys, the quality-adjusted life-years, to be saved through differential investment in protective measures? (see, e.g. DEFRA, 2009). And what if added protection of some crowded places from terrorism is predicted to lead to the displacement of threat on to other groups? The interests of minorities too must be safeguarded. Winston Churchill famously initially turned down the request from his World War II intelligence advisers to use double-agents to deceive the Germans into adjusting their V-1 attack on London so that more of the rockets fell on the less densely populated suburbs of South London rather than the centre of the city, on the grounds that he was not prepared to take the moral responsibility for redirecting the enemy's fire, for which they alone must take responsibility, from one part onto another of the British population despite the predicted overall savings in casualties.

Should we concentrate today on tackling what are seen as the top risks in the 'national risk register' (in terms of likelihood, vulnerability and impact) and working down the list until the security budget runs out? The Cold War games theorists would call it a 'minimax' strategy, of minimising the maximum damage that might be done to the life of the nation; for example, ensuring the protection of the essentials of life through safeguarding the critical national infrastructure (power, communications, water, etc.) from the consequences of major attack. Or should we follow a modern version of a 'maximin' strategy, maximising the minimum level of security that all members of the public ought to enjoy in their everyday lives as they go to work, frequent public spaces or use air travel? The answer so far of course has had to be to have a set of policies that incorporates a judicious admixture of both approaches. We can be confident that the measures taken so far in the UK have added to overall public welfare, such has been the combination of elevated level of threat and vulnerability of much of the infrastructure, but there will come a time when it will be harder to choose what to protect and by how much and how to balance the opportunity costs impact on other public policies that might have benefited from these resources.

Particular difficulties arise in judging the level of investment justified against low probability events, those described by so-called 'fat-tailed' distributions, when it is known that they would carry very serious societal consequences, such as a radiological device or 'dirty bomb' in the hands of terrorists. Very rare events do nevertheless happen as, to general surprise, the international financial sector discovered in the banking and credit crisis of 2008. The UK Government spent a significant amount of public money after 9/11 in stockpiling smallpox vaccine against the very low probability that the disease could become a terrorist weapon, knowing that huge loss of life would be likely should that occur. In that case, therefore, it was judged worth the significant opportunity cost in terms of other public benefits foregone' in order to take the risk off the table. In circumstances where risks from threat events are correlated, the calculations become even more difficult. There may also be externalities. The risk to society in terms of the effect of loss of national and international confidence of having a run of terrorist attacks may be very much greater than the sum of the risks to the individuals directly caught up in the attacks. Weaknesses in security in one country (say in public health, commercial aviation, or affecting the safety of nuclear power plants) will have an impact on the risk carried by citizens of other nations. International functional organisations such as the International Civil Aviation Organisation (ICAO), the International Maritime Organisation (IMO), the International Atomic Energy Agency (IAEA), and the World Health Organisation (WHO) are used to taking a systemic, global approach to the risks inherent in their areas of activity. Regional bodies such as the EU have come rather later to the realisation of the need to cooperate on the transnational nature of many modern risks and to share national risk assessments through bodies such as the EU SITCEN (see Chapter 8).

2.5 Providing government with forewarning

What the policy maker traditionally wants first of all from the intelligence analyst, meteorologist, seismologist, political scientist or futurologist in managing risks is the estimate of likelihood, the first factor in the risk equation. A key question therefore is what it will take to generate useful and useable intelligence-based warning for government.

The intelligence community over the next few years will have to surmount a number of upheavals if it is to continue to be able to provide adequate forewarning of future threats. Rapid developments in the relevant technologies fuel an explosion in the volume, complexity and ubiquity of communications in the Internet age, and enable the possibility to access multiple data stores of different kinds of personal information about individuals that can be useful for criminal investigation, counter-terrorism and other purposes. There is now an overwhelming amount of potentially relevant open source information that could be accessed creating real challenges for intelligence analysts, but also creating opportunities for new linkages with the wider strategic futures and horizon-scanning communities in government. There is also much greater public awareness of the part that intelligence is playing in security activity and concerns over the proper limits on the methods that government and its agencies should exercise on their access to and use of intelligence, whether acquired by traditional intelligence sources, from overseas liaisons, or from the new opportunities opened up by the technologies of electronic surveillance and data analysis (see Chapter 15).

The modern operational intelligence cycle can best be seen (Omand, 2009) as a network of activities involving close interaction between producers of raw intelligence and analysts on the one hand, as they work together to access the information they need, and analysts and their customers on the other, as they work together to elucidate the meaning of the intelligence thus derived. Such networks can be seen, for example, when looking at tactical and operational level support for domestic counter-terrorism and at the arrangements for supporting military activity overseas. At the same time, when it comes to the writing of national strategic assessments, such as produced by the JIC, the respective roles of the policy and analytic communities need to be carefully preserved, with appropriate psychological distance between them, as both the US and UK inquiries into intelligence assessments on pre-war Iraqi weapons of mass destruction have reminded us.

There is also a link here that must be made to horizon-scanning in providing cuing for intelligence collection and assessment. Horizon-scanning as an activity does not usually rely on secret intelligence, and has an open, sharing and peer review culture rather than the restrictive and regulated approach associated inevitably with information acquired through secret sources and methods. Such analysis can very usefully complement intelligence assessment in providing situational awareness and strategic notice of possible impending developments.

Effective horizon-scanning does, however, also need strong high-level political support, since its greatest value lies in being able to present from time to time unexpected or uncomfortable pictures. There is no necessity, and there may be a disadvantage, in government trying to corral all horizon-scanning within a single organisation. This is a field of activity in which multiple competing visions may offer more enlightenment. But the need to provide high-level support, professional culture, to feed intelligence assessments, and to have assurance that the results are not biased by political preferences, would suggest that the activity across government should be overseen and protected by the national intelligence leadership.

The essential dilemma of generating and using intelligence analysis is that unconscious biases and motivations, on the part of policymakers, analysts, and management alike, may well affect the quality of judgements reached – but being unconscious, such influences are that much harder to bring to the surface and thus to neutralise. The UK has developed instruments for producing authoritative all-source assessment through the JIC, set up in 1936 and charged with the responsibility 'to monitor and give early warning of the development of direct and indirect foreign threats to British interests, whether political, military or economic, and to keep under review threats to security at home and overseas'. The JIC sits in a unique position within Whitehall because it crosses the intelligence producer/consumer divide. For the most part, such assessments will draw on secret intelligence – but the judgments of the JIC about the future in such cases will inevitably have the nature of mysteries and complexities, rather than the more straightforward assessment of secrets uncovered. Horizon-scanners too have to manage carefully their relationship with policy makers, since there is a crucial difference between the world of the analyst and of the policy maker. For the former, judgements are only as good as the fit of the explanation and there is no shame in revision in the light of new evidence (indeed, the reverse, the shame is in failing to update one's theories); for the latter, policy-making is about shaping the world in the image of the desired policy outcome, and contrary evidence is just another obstacle to be overcome by the application of greater resources and will. Having to admit publicly that one's opinion on a matter has changed is very hard for a politician; it has to be second nature for an analyst.

One factor not to be forgotten is that in the realm of military affairs there is usually an adversary who is actively seeking to deceive and thus to achieve surprise. Good generalship often consists of achieving tactical surprise – the when and where – even (or especially) in circumstances when it is not possible to conceal their strategic intent. The 1944 Allied landings in Normandy, the 1968 Soviet invasion of Czechoslovakia, the 1973 Egyptian and Syrian attack on Israel, the 1982 Argentine invasion of the Falkland Islands, the 1998 Iraqi invasion of Kuwait, and other examples too numerous to list, testify to the ability of the offence to deceive watching intelligence services even when there is strategic notice available to them of the possibility of attack. The record of savants in predicting the development of useable new technologies is poor (the telephone: 'every town should have one'; the electromagnetic wave: 'it's of no use whatsoever', the computer: 'the world market for computers would add up to five'; and similar sayings). In the same way, predicting the moment at which a dictatorial regime will be toppled by uprisings, or democratic governments ousted by voting swings, remains as much art as science.

2.6 Assessing performance in prediction

Assessment of performance in providing predictive intelligence warning is problematic where it has led, as it usually does, to some form of policy response or pre-emptive action. The true comparison that ought to be made is between the situation before the warning and what would have happened without the warning if events had been allowed to run their course, an exercise in counter-factual thinking. Where warning was not given, it may still be difficult to judge whether the absence of warning constituted a culpable failure, or resulted from one of the inevitable gaps in knowledge that are part of the reality of intelligence work (see Chapter 3).

There have been two powerful criticisms of the track record of the US and UK intelligence communities over the last few years in elucidating the meaning of the information potentially available: *on the one hand,* criticism of lack of imagination leading to failure of the US community to join up the dots over 9/11, and most recently the failure to link the fragments of intelligence that might have prevented the attempt to bring down an airliner over Detroit on Christmas Day 2009, with comparable criticisms of UK services over the failure to link one of the 7/7 bombers to earlier intelligence; and *on the other hand,* of over-imaginative interpretation of sparse and fallible intelligence in the case of pre-war US and UK intelligence assessments of Iraqi weapons of mass destruction (WMD).

The intelligence analysts thus balance precariously on the horns of the dilemma of Type I or Type II errors: of joining dots up into plausible but erroneous combinations, or of failing to recognise, or to accept as genuine, new patterns of threat. Occam's razor[1] continues to be a good guide, and analysts would do well to heed the dangers of Crabtree's bludgeon (Jones, 1989): 'No set of mutually consistent observations can exist for which some human intellect cannot conceive a coherent explanation, however complicated'. Here we also need to recognise that there can be cases where the quality of the intelligence warning depends as much on the analysts' ability to understand the intentions of their own government and the potential interactions with those of the adversary. In that respect, forecasting natural hazards that are not reflexive is likely to be considerably simpler in methodological terms than threats with an opponent that reacts and adapts.

Intelligence has been described as often contradictory and sometimes plain wrong (Clausewitz, 1873: Vol. I, Book I, Chapter VI). It is frequently incomplete. Intelligence gaps are to be expected, given the nature of the activity, and should not necessarily to be regarded as 'intelligence failures' in the sense of being blameworthy. Taking a leaf from the study of disasters (Perrow, 2002) we can categorise the task of providing estimates of the likelihood of unwelcome surprises as covering three forms. There are *unique events,* those surprises that are infrequent acts of God that cannot be affected by policy measures, and whose broad probability it may be possible to estimate statistically in terms of time since the last occurrence, but where individual point predictions are inherently hard to forecast. Then there are those *discrete events,* whose frequency can be rationally influenced by policy measures and can be estimated. The likelihood of such events may be expressible in an alert state given a system of indicators and warnings or alerting methodology. Further security measures to reduce the likelihood can then be taken if it is judged cost effective to try to reduce the overall risk. Finally, there are *normal events,* which are the inevitable consequence of living with highly complex interactive systems, that Perrow (2002) in his analysis of the Three Mile Island nuclear disaster labels 'normal accidents'. In the field of warfare, there is Clausewitz's fog and friction, and there will be surprises. Similarly, in complex (that is in virtually all) security and intelligence work there will be unexpected developments. For example, as resilience planners know, nasty surprises can come from the unexpected interaction of elements of the critical national infrastructure when there is a disruptive event. Policy makers, including those responsible for authorising military, security and intelligence operations, must not confuse these categories. The inevitable post-mortems after a major disruptive event usually lead to demands that 'this must never be allowed to happen again'. The result is often a set of stable-door-closing measures that, if the problem is a 'normal accident', may well just add more complexity and thus paradoxically increase the risk of future accidents. Similarly, getting rid of the people in charge at the time may simply waste the learning opportunity and introduce fresh inexperience. It is inevitable in risk management that sometimes the downside happens.

2.7 The value of strategic notice

At the outset of this chapter I referred to the distinction between forecasts and predictions. Getting point predictions right or wrong is not all that matters. It is also important that government has a sense of the broad range of relevant issues and events that will shape the coming years, to give a sense of the global agenda, to which decision-makers ought to be paying more attention. This phenomenon is what I describe as having 'strategic notice' (Omand, 2010). With strategic notice, intelligence agencies are more likely to be attentive to material that may bear on the problem and government will be more attuned to signs that would otherwise be passed over as noise in the system.

It is possible to imagine a hierarchy of analysis as shown in Figure 2.1. Strategic notice normally sits above the traditional world of secret intelligence. It is usually derived from open source analysis, often originating outside government and then picked up by government horizon-scanners and strategy staffs.

Without strategic notice the risk increases that relevant intelligence that could have been accessed will be passed over, or that if it is collected and disseminated, the policy customers will fail to see any reasons to be

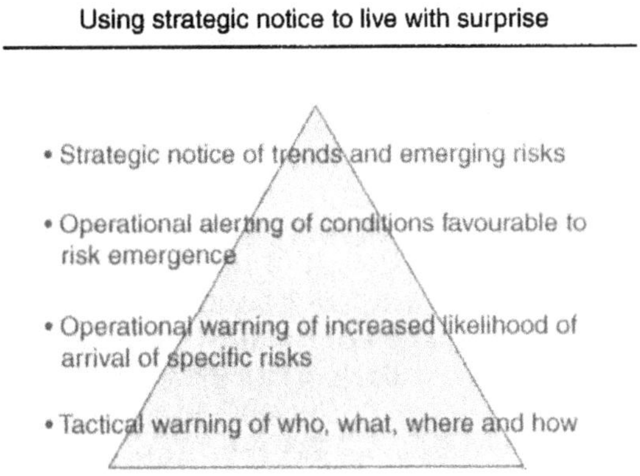

Figure 2.1 Different levels and purposes of warning

interested in it. The risk of warning failure thus increases through a chain of consequences:

- inability of the analysts to be able to access sufficient information that bears on the issue. The risk increases that there will not be sufficient dots to connect into the right pattern.
- biases and errors by the intelligence analysts in interpreting correctly the reliability or the meaning of the intelligence that was obtained, including knowing to how process it in a sufficiently timely fashion. Past over- or under-estimates may, for example, lead to over-correction the next time the problem is encountered.
- difficulties in communication between the analytic and user communities, leading the former (consciously or unconsciously) to be overly influenced by the expectations of the latter, and leading the latter to fail to appreciate the proper significance attributed to the assessment by the former. Analysts may, for example, fear the consequences of failure to warn of an event such as a coup much more than the risk of crying wolf (and there are many plausible ways to explain away a prediction that did not materialise, whereas absence of warning will be seen as a straight intelligence failure).
- policy failure on the part of the decision-makers even on receipt of warning, again an inevitable occurrence from time to time, but made more likely if they have not earlier spotted the significance of strategic notice of the issue early on and prepared themselves mentally for the possibility of receiving bad news.

The reason things appear to go wrong when crisis looms is usually a combination of these factors, often due to poor levels of mutual understanding and trust in the relationships involved between leaders and advisers, and at times between analysts and their intelligence management. Personality clashes can interfere with the correct processes of assessment, and the emotional pressures of a crisis can distort receptivity to warning messages.

We can be sure that the coming generation will judge the quality of government today by how far strategic issues were grasped and the groundwork laid to prepare for the risk landscape of the future. No government can afford to invest against every possible contingency that can be envisaged, nor is it wise to have a population constantly in fear of the highly unlikely event. So governments need some basis on which they can assess the full range of risks, seen as a product of likelihood, vulnerability and impact should the event transpire. How can security, the first duty of good government, be maintained at a bearable and sustainable cost? How do we avoid becoming obsessed with security risks, and how do we avoid the benefits of security turning to the taste of ashes in our mouth if the methods used to deliver security, and the essential intelligence that underpins it, were to turn out to have undermined and even violated the very values we seek to defend? These are questions that will in the future increasingly separate what we will recognise as the signs of good government from those of bad government. They deserve serious attention from academics and practitioners alike, working together to explain and model the processes involved.

Note

1. *Entia non sunt multiplicanda praeter necessitatem*, or entities must not be multiplied beyond necessity. So, other things being equal, the simplest explanation should be preferred.

3

Epistemology of Forecasting in International Relations: Knowing the Difference between 'Intelligence Failure' and 'Warning Failure'[1]

Jan Goldman

3.1 Introduction

Too often 'intelligence failure' and 'warning failure' are used interchangeably. These terms are considered equal parts of a forecasting equation, if they are considered separate entities at all. Mostly, they are perceived as two interchangeable terms, with the assumption that one necessarily leads to the other. This may be because analysts (those who are involved in producing intelligence products) and policymakers (those who are involved in consuming intelligence products) do not, or care not to, understand the different values and variables placed on 'warning' and 'intelligence'.

When reporting about Greens, Senator Bob Brown's request for a parliamentary inquiry into suspected intelligence failures ahead of the Bali massacre in October 2002, an Australian newspaper reported that this inquiry was prompted by a declaration by the Australian Prime Minister, John Howard, that there had been no intelligence that specifically warned of a bomb attack at that time. The same article, however, also reported that, in response to threats identified by the CIA (Central Intelligence Agency), the United States had changed its travel notice twice before 20 September 2002 and had specifically warned US and western citizens to avoid all those places in Indonesia where ex-pats are accustomed to gather (Allard and Wilkinson, 2002).

Clearly, Prime Minister Howard's observation that no intelligence specifically warned of the bomb attack, limits effective warning to hindsight. Consequently, he seems wrongly to believe more oversight may be required to make intelligence warning effective. It is ironic that policymakers as consumers can also be the arbitrators of reviewing warning failures.

Going beyond the intelligence cycle of collecting, processing and distributing information, a theory of knowledge is needed to clarify, explain, and hopefully improve the warning process. The underlying assumption of this chapter is that only by establishing a theory of how knowledge is acquired can we progress to explaining the difference between *intelligence failure* and *warning failure*. Throughout this chapter, the reader is introduced to a vocabulary and theory of ideas that can further develop the delineation of 'warning' as more than a by-product of 'intelligence', rather than assuming incorrectly they are identical terms. It is only after these two terms are clearly understood that we can improve forecasting and intelligence in international relations. In this chapter, intelligence is *defined as the knowledge provided by distilling information and its application at the strategic level for implementing policy.*

3.2 Epistemology and a theory of intelligence

A commonly accepted definition of 'epistemology' is that it is *a branch of philosophy that focuses on the nature and scope of knowledge, addressing the questions of what knowledge is, how knowledge is transferred between people, how we know what we know, and why we know what we know.* Over 2500 years ago, Plato wondered what a person would need in addition his beliefs that would create the conditions of knowledge. In its simplest form, according to Plato, considered the father of epistemology, reality can be divided into two main divisions, which are 'the Sensible World' and 'the World of Forms' (Plato, 2007: 509d–511e). 'The Sensible World' spans from the metaphysical world of 'images' to the epistemological world of imagination and perception, resulting in opinion. 'The World of Forms' spans the metaphysical world from 'mathematical forms' to the epistemological world of understanding and reason, resulting in knowledge. Consequently, epistemology arises from the combination of the Sensible World and the World of Forms, resulting in imagination, perception, understanding and reason (Sophia Project, 2008). How we view information is as important as what the information reveals independently of interpretation. Lock K. Johnson believes that any theory of intelligence must consider the basic human nature, but, 'in a paradox, though, well-heeled nations with behemoth intelligence services are also likely to suffer acute information failures.' (Johnson, 2009: 35).

This is because policy makers and military commanders believe that intelligence is a matter of reporting information and then acting upon it. It is an operational skill, rather than a theory based on a field of knowledge. This may be why intelligence work is typically associated with the term 'tradecraft'. 'Tradecraft' lies between training (typical of an apprentice, and exhibited by vocations), and the current and technical foundation of knowledge needed by professional education (typical of most professions). Deconstructing intelligence, so that some type of theory can exist, would allow the 'tradecraft of the intelligence profession' (for lack of a better term) to move forward in developing itself. In no job is the individual completely responsible and dependent on information from beginning to end, whether it is collecting, processing or disseminating it. Historian David Kahn developed a theory of intelligence based on sources of information. The author believes intelligence theory is divided into two realms of sources of information. These concepts include 'physical intelligence' and 'verbal intelligence', and should not be confused with 'current intelligence' and 'estimative intelligence', which relate to the purpose of intelligence rather than a theory of origin. According to Kahn, physical intelligence:

> consists of information drawn from things, not words. It is seeing marching troops, fortifications, supply dumps, campfire smoke; hearing tank motor noise, smell cooking, feeling ground vibrations. I call it physical intelligence. For centuries it came only from the observations of the common soldier, patrols, the cavalry. But the balloon, the Zeppelin, the airplane provides more physical intelligence more quickly than the deepest-driving horseman. (Kahn, 2009: 5)

Intelligence was obtained through direct observation. Supplemented by technology (e.g., from basic searchlights to infrared radar), we have progressed in our ability to see far beyond our own vision. Nevertheless, we are still limited in our physical ability to observe. Information obtained directly from any of the human and technical sources utilised in the intelligence community support is extremely important and useful. However, it does not replace the more advanced form of intelligence; verbal intelligence. This form of intelligence can furnish an understanding of both a material and a psychological component. Using preparation for war as an example, Kahn states:

> On the other hand, verbal intelligence deals with intentions, and just as the enemy needs time to realize those plans, so a commander who knows about them gains time, to prepare against them. He can shift his forces from an unthreatened flank to an endangered one, for example. In other words, verbal intelligence magnifies strength – or, in the current jargon, is a force multiplier. (Kahn, 2009: 6)

It is this second concept of an historical theory of intelligence that Kahn believes is more significant. According to Kahn:

> The tapping of telegraph wires and the interception of radio messages furnished far more verbal intelligence than the occasional waylaying of a courier ever did. The growth is significant because verbal intelligence can furnish more valuable information than physical. Understanding this must begin with an acknowledgment, that war has both a material and psychological component. The material elements consist of such

> tangibles as troops, guns, and supplies, the psychological comprises such as matters as a commander's will, his tactical ability, and the morale of his troops. The material factors dominate: the most brilliant, most determined commander of a regiment cannot withstand an army. And this factor is served by verbal intelligence, while the less important psychological component is served by physical intelligence. (Ibid.)

Verbal intelligence gets to the heart of understanding the threat. The threat, in simple terms, can be relegated to major factors, including capabilities and intentions. Capabilities are defined in intelligence as *what your enemy possesses*. Typically, this would include the collective military, economic, political, scientific and technical means, methods and capacity of the threat. For countries, this translates to weapon systems, manpower strength and alliances that can be utilised. All of these can easily be determined by physical intelligence collection such as the movement of troops or the announcement of support from one nation to another. However, verbal intelligence is *getting inside the mind of your adversary*, assessing their intentions and willingness to be a threat. This can be determined by analysing the information beyond what can be simply seen and collected. Intentions are translated into an adversary's purpose, plan, commitment or design for action, as possibly exhibited by a leader, decision-maker, nation or a nation's foreign policy (Goldman, 2006: 84). Ultimately, it becomes *a belief* by the intelligence analyst as to what an adversary will do in a future scenario.

In understanding the difference between 'true knowledge' (analysis) and 'what a person believes to be true knowledge' (assessment), it is important to return to Greek philosophy. Plato discusses a search for a condition known as *true belief*. He goes on to state that in order to obtain knowledge, individuals must at the very least believe a true proposition. 'Belief' might be too weak. Indeed, when we go out of our way to indicate that we merely believe a proposition, we are often trying to warn the person to whom we are talking that we lack knowledge. ('Do you know if the bus runs on Saturday?' I'm asked. 'Well,' I respond, 'I *believe* that it does.'). In any event, in at least some contexts, we seem to require something more like a *subjective certainty* in order to have knowledge, which is a belief-like state (an absolutely firm conviction with no trace of doubt) (Fumerton, 2006: 12).

Without doubt, policymakers want absolute certainty from intelligence. Ambiguity is not to be tolerated. Indecision or not taking action is in fact a decision not to act. Policy makers do not want to be on the receiving end of questions as to why the government failed to take action. Consequently, for the intelligence community, it is much easier to send out a warning notice when a coup is in progress, rather than before its outbreak. But is that successful warning? It may be successful at the tactical level, which can affect the outcome of some battles, but is it successful at the strategic level?

The use of intelligence depends less on what is known and produced, and more on the value placed on it by senior government officials. As has been pointed out by Richard Betts, 'observers who see notorious intelligence failures as egregious often infer that disasters can be avoided by perfecting norms and procedure for analysis and argumentation. This belief is illusionary' (Betts, 2009: 87). According to Betts, 'optimal decision in defense policy therefore depends on the use of strategic intelligence: the acquisition, analysis and *appreciation* of relevant data' (Ibid.). The paradox of this knowledge (known as the 'paradox of warning') is that the more successful the warning is in its ability to counter an attack based on timeliness, the less likely it may be that the forecasted sequence of events will occur. In other words, overt preparations to counter a surprise attack could lead the attacker to believe they have lost the element of surprise. This may result in the intelligence of the enemy's initially intended surprise attack appearing to be wrong, based on the change in an enemy's course of action. An example of this occurred in the business world:

> Executives were seeking to sue computer software manufactures after the expected Y2K computer meltdown scheduled for January 1, 2000. The executives were not suing the computer software companies because the newly installed software did not work, but that they had no way of knowing if the Y2K threat was a real attack on their computers. According to the software companies, that the software worked was the reason the computers continued to function without interruption. It could be argued, that because of the success of the software, there was no threat. The moral of this story is that good warning sometimes provide countermeasures that may ultimately prove fruitless because the element of surprise is no longer available to the attacker...thus good warning can make liars out of excellent analysts. (Goldman, 2006: 106)

In seeking to find a definition of 'intelligence', the casual student will find many, all very popular. This term seems to refer to a body of information and the conclusions drawn and furnished in response to the perceived or known requirements of customers. In other words, 'intelligence' can be an added description of the information and its importance to the decision-making process (e.g., this information is extremely important intelligence in understanding the threat.) Typically, this term is used and focused on the end result of a process that includes planning, gathering and analysing information of potential value. The outcome of this process derives from the collection, collation, evaluation, analysis, integration and interpretation of all this information. Intelligence requirements are typically translated and assigned to the intelligence community by decision-makers, regardless of their level.

The consumer may have little understanding of tactical, operational, or strategic indicators. This is unfortunate, because it is they who are at times determining collection requirements that are then translated into the intelligence process. The consumer can be a war fighter at the tactical level, the theatre commander at the operational level or the National Command Authority at the strategic level. While Betts believes that hierarchy, centralisation and specialisation are precisely the characteristics that are the essence of any government, the problem lies in 'the dominance of operational authority over intelligence specialists and the trade-off between objectivity and influence' (Betts, 2009: 91–92).

Regardless of where the intelligence requirements come from, it is usually in response to such basic questions as: what is known about the potential threat's intentions and capabilities, how reliable and valid is the intelligence, how does this intelligence fit with what we already know about the potential threat's intentions and capabilities? In other words, this becomes the epistemology of intelligence, or alternatively, how do we know if we know anything about our adversary? How and when are we aware of knowing the true capabilities and intentions of a threat?

3.3 Intelligence failure vs. warning failure

It may be easy to blame the intelligence community when an unexpected event or action occurs that may pose a threat or the risk of a threat to a nation. Any misunderstanding of a situation that leads a government or its military forces to take actions that are inappropriate, counterproductive or ill-timed in relation to its own interests is through a failure to understand an adversary's capabilities or intentions, is usually labelled an 'intelligence failure' (Schulsky and Schmitt, 2002). There are numerous examples of so-called 'intelligence failures' in the US intelligence community, ranging from its failure to forecast the Japanese attack on Pearl Harbor in 1941, to the 9/11 terrorist attacks in 2001. These so-called 'intelligence failures' are also labelled 'warning failures', directly implying a failure to respond, or an inadequate response, to real and psychological attacks. It is the responsibility of the intelligence community to provide analysis and framework for a proper policy response. An intelligence assessment is the beginning of a synchronous relationship between the intelligence and policy communities. An intelligence failure encompasses all or parts of the intelligence process and system. According to Russ Travers, in 'The Coming Intelligence Failure':

> Despite our best intentions, the system is sufficiently dysfunctional that intelligence failure is guaranteed. Though the form is less important than the fact, the variations are endless. Failure may be of the traditional variety: we fail to predict the fall of a friendly government; we do not provide

> sufficient warning of a surprise attack against one of our allies or interests; we are completely surprised by a state-sponsored terrorist attack; or we fail to detect an unexpected country acquiring a weapon of mass destruction. Or it may take a more nontraditional form: we overstate numerous threats leading to tens of billions of dollars of unnecessary expenditures; database errors lead to a politically unacceptable number of casualties in a peace-enforcement operation; or an operation does not go well because the IC is not able to provide the incredibly specific data necessary to support a new generation of weapons. In the end, we may not suffer a Pearl Harbor, but simply succumb to a series of mistakes. (Travers, 1997)

According to Cynthia Grabo, an intelligence analyst for almost 40 years, 'while these surprises have often been cited as *intelligence failures* – and admittedly there were some serious inadequacies in collection and assessment – gross misperceptions and errors in judgment by policymakers and military command were the real causes of failure. There is no better example of the principle that warning is useless unless it results in action to forestall disaster.' (Grabo, 1987).

Warning failure is failure to anticipate some action, event or decision by a foreign leader that results in detrimental consequences to another nation's national security. Although intelligence failure is often related to the failure to forecast events before they happen, not all warning failures are solely the responsibility of the intelligence community. Intelligence is used to influence decisions that may result in a specific action. For example, if a policy maker receives intelligence that a specific act will probably occur, and the policymaker implements no preventive action, is that a warning failure?

In developing an epistemology of intelligence, a template develops that allows one to understand the difference between intelligence failure and warning failure. Intelligence failure falls in the 'world of forms'. Intelligence emerges from facts, information that can be analysed, and applied understanding and reason. Knowledge is realised from this tangible form of reality. On the other hand, warning failure is perceived from the 'Sensible World', which transcends the metaphysical world of imagination, perception and opinion.

Typically, on my first day of teaching intelligence analysis and warning, I ask my students if anyone has written intelligence analysis reports. Most of the 20 students' hands are raised, since most of the students in my class are mid-career intelligence analysts. However, when I follow up with the question 'how many folks have written intelligence assessment reports?', there tend to be some confused facial expressions. For some students, analysis and assessment is the same term. It is not. For any intelligence analyst, it is vital that they understand the difference between these two terms, since if they are unsure of what they mean, how is the consumer expected to know the difference?

Richards Heuer seeks a middle ground between analysis and assessment. He labels that middle ground *interpretative analysis*. According to Heuer, in *Psychology of Intelligence Analysis*:

> Customers demand for interpretative analysis is greatest within two or three days after an event occurs. The system requires the intelligence analyst to come with an almost instant diagnosis before sufficient hard information, and the broader background information that may be needed to gain perspective, become available to make possible a well-grounded judgment. This diagnosis can only be based upon the analyst's preconceptions concerning how and why events normally transpire in a given society. (Heuer, 1999: 16)

This raises the question that if 'analysis is what you know', and 'assessment is what you believe', what is 'interpretative analysis' for intelligence? 'Analysis' is a systematic approach to problem solving, which involves the processes of separating intelligence information into distinct, related parts or elements and examining those elements to determine essential parameters or related properties (Goldman, 2006: 6). The term 'assessment' is the process of combining all intelligence data into a unified, specific judgment – the result of analysis formed within the context of the intelligence environment. It was the 9/11 Commission that pointed out that the analysis of the terrorist threat was so weak that terrorism was not even on the horizon as an issue. Consequently, the threat was never assessed properly. According to the 9/11 Commission Report:

> If a president wanted to rally the American people to a warlike effort, he would need to publicize an assessment of the growing al Qaeda danger. Our government could spark a full public discussion of who Osama Bin Laden was, what kind of organization he led, what Bin Laden or al Qaeda intended, or what past attacks they had sponsored or encouraged, and what capabilities they were bring together for future assaults. We believe American and international public opinion might have been different – and so might have the range of options for a president – had they been informed of these details. (9/11 Commission, 2004: 341)

It is possible that events *might* have turned out differently or maybe not. Without a doubt this was an *intelligence failure*. But what type of intelligence failure was it? Through the strategic or tactical lens, it becomes clearer what type of intelligence failure it is. According to the 9/11 Commission, the attacks were a *strategic* intelligence failure. If you have a *strategic intelligence failure*, then a *warning failure* will follow. Strategic intelligence provides the context for warning to occur. Intelligence can translate into a warning document, but rarely does a warning document translate into intelligence. *Warning is the product of a process, intelligence is the process producing a product.*

> For example, a disaster *response* plan (associated with warning intelligence) is not the same as a disaster-*preparation* plan (associated with general intelligence). A disaster-*preparation* plan could restructure the conditions that will provide an adequate response as envisioned beforehand. Naomi Zack, in her book *Ethics for Disaster* (2009), delineates the difference by stating three principles between these phrases. According to Zack, 'planning is part of preparation, and it needs to occur before a disaster is present or imminent, if not done beforehand. Disaster planning as a part of preparation needs to be unbiased, and so long as there is assumed time, there is no reason to compromise on what ought to be done because preparation occurs in normal times'. (Zack, 2009: 18)

According to Zack, 'disaster-preparation planning has to be general, but not so general as to be morally or factually vacuous and that disaster planning ... must also be practical or possible to execute' (Ibid.). We are obligated to plan optimistically, in the sense that we ought not to make plans that we know will violate existing moral principles or do not believe will achieve desired goals, that is optimistic planning is based on the assumption that it is possible to plan well (Ibid.). Consequently, planning for contingencies, Zack states:

> without knowing precisely what those contingencies will be, entails that disaster preparation is not the same thing as disaster rehearsal. No matter how many mock disasters are staged according to proper plans, the real disaster will never mirror any one of them. Disaster-preparation planning is more like training for a marathon than training for a high jump competition or a sprinting event. Marathon runners do not practice by running the full course of twenty-six miles; rather, they get into shape by running shorter distances and building up their endurance with cross-training. If they have prepared successfully, then they are in optimal condition to run the marathon over its predetermined course and length, assuming a range of weather conditions, predicated or not. This is normal marathon preparation. (Ibid.)

It is exactly this separation between disaster *preparedness* and disaster *response* that has a similarity to 'general intelligence' and 'warning intelligence' respectively. While preparing for a disaster requires a clear understanding of the context of the threat, responding to a disaster must be much more specific; clearly 'general intelligence' provides the context while 'warning intelligence' must focus on the specific capabilities and intentions of a threat. These terms tend to be confused and used inappropriately at the strategic, operational and tactical levels. When used incorrectly, for example using tactical intelligence for strategic warning purposes, the result is a misuse of, or a lack of understanding of, how intelligence should be utilised. Although this is typically referred to as *actionable intelligence* it should be described as *inadequate intelligence.*

Inadequate intelligence can be defined as *information on an action, event or decision that has already occurred and which requires further action at either the tactical or strategic level.* Typically associated with the present tense and at the tactical level, this information is quickly analysed and assessed at face value. Numerous examples exist where information is gathered on a routine basis from all available sources concerning events of immediate interest. Typically this type of intelligence focuses on descriptive 'snapshots' of generally static conditions, it is highly perishable since it covers events disseminated without delay, and it requires little or no evaluation, interpretation, analysis or integration. Rather, it requires action – if not immediate action – by the consumer of the intelligence.

The fall of the Shah in Iran in 1978 is a classic case of using inadequate intelligence. The first major demonstrations against the Shah began in January 1978. Between August and December 1978, strikes and demonstrations paralysed the country. The CIA and State Department daily reports, which were the primary vehicles for political intelligence, consistently failed to draw Washington's attention to Iran during the early spring and summer of 1978, following the worst rioting in a decade. The early identification of factors, to include the Shah's vulnerability and mounting dissidence, could have prevented the crisis that evolved between the two countries. Arthur Hulnick, a veteran of more than 35 years in the profession of intelligence, including 28 years in the CIA, wrote, 'In 1979, after the fall of the Shah of Iran, and the rise of the theocracy, the CIA warned President Carter and the State Department that if the United States were to provide asylum to the terminally ill Reza Pahlavi, radical elements in Iran might well invade the U.S. Embassy in Tehran. The warning went unheeded' (Hulnick, 2004).

As a consequence, this type of inaccurate intelligence directed decision-makers away from the 'surprise attack' on the US Embassy and the hostage taking of personnel in the building. It was 444 days, before they were released. Some observers have noted that the rise of the Islamic Revolution should be taken in the context of such factors as the leadership role of the Shi`i ulama, the question of political authority in Shi`ism, and the role of the Karbala paradigm in the popular religion. This is nothing new. Thirty-eight years earlier, the Japanese attack on the US naval base in Pearl Harbor, Hawaii was considered a surprise attack. However poor analysis and a strong reliance on current information for preventive intelligence, demonstrate how poorly intelligence was used. It has been argued that, because there was no formal US intelligence community, it relied heavily on inadequate intelligence to focus the threat, resulting in missed opportunities to prevent harm. Some of the indications that were missed include: Human Intelligence (HUMINT) reports from Peru's minister in Tokyo, intercepts of Japanese Foreign Ministry traffic, notification by Japan's Foreign Minister to the US Ambassador that negotiations had to be settled by 29 November or 'things are going to automatically happen', and the Japanese navy abnormally changing its ships' call signs during the week prior to the attack (hence Japan's aircraft carriers and submarines could not be found by US naval intelligence). These were all good indications of the possibility of a surprise attack by the Japanese. Unfortunately, most of the intelligence at the time was focusing on the possibility of sabotage or terrorist acts to US assets. Consequently, reliance on current intelligence such as collecting information on Japanese descendants of US citizens, resulted in missed opportunities to warn at the strategic level. In both the fall of the Shah and the Japanese attack on Pearl Harbor, intelligence for strategic warning was replaced by current intelligence focusing on tactical threats. The warning failure at the strategic level to consider any attack, except sabotage, paved the way for a full-fledged naval assault (Wohlstetter, 1962).

Recently, the 'buzz words' in the national security and intelligence communities are complexity theory, chaos, and uncertainty. Without a doubt the global arena has become complex with information, and the global war of ideas has gone beyond the communist vs. capitalist international arena (see Chapter 4). Former CIA director James Woolsey, for example, has compared the post-Cold War era with having won a 45-year-long struggle against a dragon – the Soviet Union – the United States now finding itself in a jungle with a lot of poisonous snakes that are harder to keep track of than the dragon (Leung, 2005).

Over the last 20 years, our ability to receive and process information has grown exponentially in direct proportion to the dwindling size of the computer chip and its capability to process more and more information. This techno-scientific mindset has created a linguistic impoverishment. According to Adam Elkus, in his article on defence policy and epistemological failure, 'techno-scientific thinking lacks the basic vocabulary to describe and understand conflict because it fundamentally denies and actively minimises politics, often viewed by techno-scientific thinkers as messy or irrational' (Elkus, 2009: 4). This mode of thinking in the business world is referred to as 'info-enthusiasm'. It is the ability to allow the most current information to redirect one's long term knowledge (Brown and Duguid, 2002; Chapter 15).

According to Elkus, one form of 'ad hockery' is the elevation of operational methodologies to strategies, as the now ubiquitous phrase 'counterterrorism strategy' indicates. He states, 'In the face of conceptual chaos, these narrow frameworks are being marshalled to give direction to a largely formless US foreign policy' (Elkus, 2009: 5).

Analysis to support strategic intelligence tends to be in-depth research focused on capabilities and intentions that consider possible scenarios; while tactical intelligence support tends to be rapid response, or current intelligence to support crisis management, plan execution focuses on the current situation and on indications and warnings. The result has been a new term, that had rarely been used, but today seems to be quite commonly uttered: 'actionable intelligence'.

Although there is no agreed definition for 'actionable intelligence', it has come to be a shorthand term for *responding to intelligence, at the tactical level in the absence of policy*. The result has been extremely confusing for both intelligence analysts and policymakers. For example, in the summer of 2001, prior to the terrorist attacks of September 11, National Security Adviser Condoleezza Rice said there were not enough specifics or *actionable intelligence* to justify any meetings between senior intelligence officials and members of the National Security Council. Additionally, President Bush said the intelligence memo he read shortly before the attacks contained no *actionable intelligence* that would have helped him to try to prevent the 9/11 attacks. However, according to National Terrorism Chief Richard Clark, because very often intelligence exists about a major terrorist attack, but not about where or when it will take place, that is all the more a reason to make all necessary efforts to find that *actionable intelligence* (CNN.com, 2004). Clearly, tactical information is the indication and warning knowledge to redirect strategic initiatives and policy.

However, what is the opposite of actionable intelligence? Would it be in-actionable intelligence? When does intelligence become useful? Or is the value and usefulness only something we add ourselves to that information?

Sometimes knowledge is not actionable from the outset, but may still be needed to be acted upon, contrary to the fundamental meaning of actionable intelligence, because of variables unknown to the intelligence analyst. *Murky intelligence* can be defined as *intelligence that is of questionable reliability or validity, information that cannot be placed in the content of typical routine analysis to determine its worth*. Former US Deputy Defense Secretary Paul Wolfowitz has said that the use of murky intelligence is justified in the war on terror if it prevents future attacks. Following a congressional report, which concluded that the September 11 attacks could have been prevented if security services had shared and acted upon information, several television networks interviewed him and every time he insisted that the lesson of 9/11 is that, if you are not prepared to act on the basis of murky intelligence, then you have to act after the fact (BBC News, 2003). Consequently, intelligence may not be based on the knowledge received from the information, but rather on how that knowledge is produced using different analytic methods.

The epistemology of forecasting in international relations, and knowing the difference between intelligence failure and warning failure, can possibly be focused on how knowledge is managed. Edward Waltz, in *Knowledge Management*, develops a functional taxonomy based on the type of analysis and the temporal distinction of knowledge and foreknowledge – warning, prediction, and forecast (see Chapter 5) – which distinguishes the two primary categories of analysis (Waltz, 2003: 11). These two types are descriptive analyses and inferential analyses. According to Waltz, *descriptive analyses* provide little or no evaluation or interpretation of collected data, leaving the consumer to carry out subsequent interpretations of the material. Typical descriptive analytic tasks include organising, compiling, structuring, indexing and cross-checking. Any of the intelligence collection platforms (e.g., Signals Intelligence (SIGINT), Imagery Intelligence (IMINT), and HUMINT) can produce descriptive analysis. Unfortunately, when the information collected under descriptive analysis, requiring little or no evaluation or interpretation, transcends intelligence material, it may incorrectly be put into the context of *warning* intelligence. The result is that the consumer may be forced to do something, or what has been commonly referred to as 'actionable intelligence'. The term 'actionable intelligence' removes the ambiguity that is so prevalent in intelligence. In reality, this almost notional intelligence is a rarity in the intelligence community. The US had intercepted Japanese message traffic prior to the attack on Pearl Harbor, but not one of the messages was deemed intelligence because there was no reporting of the stated day, time, or avenues of approach of the attack. In other words, policy makers were looking unrealistically for intelligence to clearly state the time and location of the impending attack. In part, this is because consumers of intelligence want a theoretical system that provides a clear understanding for intelligence services, to tell them that there will either be an attack or not, so that appropriate counter-mobilisation actions can be taken, or not taken.

While a warning system that policymakers can rely upon so that uncertainty is removed from the decision-making process is attractive, unfortunately it is not a realistic objective. The theoretical problem with this system is that, while there will inevitably be indication of the other sides' intentions to attack, especially in hindsight, these can easily be lost in the noise of contrary or ambiguous indications. Mostly, successful surprise attacks occur 'not out of the blue, but out of a murky grey which did not fit well into the Yes/No warning model' (Brody, 1983: 45).

An inferential analysis requires the analysis of collected relevant data sets (evidence) to infer and synthesise explanations that describe the meaning of the underlying data. Using inferential analysis to view the past, present and future, is explaining past events, describing structure attributes, describing behaviour and predicting future events.

According to Waltz, all analysis can be divided by two types of knowledge, which is either explicit knowledge or tacit knowledge. *Explicit knowledge*, which has been captured and codified in abstract human symbols, is considered the 'better form of knowledge'. It is the basis for logical reason and most importantly of all, it enables knowledge to be communicated electronically and reasoning processes to be automated. Data can be stored, retrieved and analysed (Waltz, 2003: 63).

Tacit knowledge is the intangible, internal, experiential and intuitive knowledge that is undocumented and maintained in the human mind. It is a personal knowledge contained in human experience. This kind of knowledge forms the bridge between perception and the higher forms of (conscious) reasons that we can describe more easily. According to Waltz, 'This is the personal knowledge that is learned by experience, honed as a skill, and often applied subconsciously' (Waltz 2003: 64). *Tacit* knowledge adds value to the process, and allows an analyst to assess any preventive action by an adversary. These two forms of knowledge , as well as two modes of human thought, have been described as 'know-what' (*explicit* knowledge) and as 'know-how' (*tacit*), distinguishing the ability of *tacit* knowledge to put *explicit* knowledge into practice.

3.4 Conclusion

Without doubt, 'intelligence failure' and 'warning failure' are considered equal parts of a forecasting equation when there is a failure to understand these concepts as separate entities. The epistemology of intelligence seems to provide a breakdown of the components of knowledge of intelligence into distinct categories. Using such theories can assist in better intelligence collection, as well as utilising this knowledge in forecasting in international affairs. Throughout this chapter, the reader has been introduced into both the vocabulary and theory of ideas that have the ability to further develop and delineate 'warning' from the general concept of information as 'intelligence'. In the end, it is only after 'intelligence failure' and 'warning failure' are clearly understood and defined that we can improve forecasting and intelligence in international relations.

Note

1. The views and opinions expressed in this chapter are those of the author and do not reflect the official policy or position of the US Government, Department of Defense or any agency in the US Intelligence Community.

4

FORESEC: Lessons Learnt from a Pan-European Security Foresight Project

Ville Brummer, Clementine Burnley, Henrik Carlsen, Ana-Maria Duta, Bastian Giegerich and Raphaële Magoni

4.1 FORESEC and the emerging EU security research agenda

This chapter discusses the methodology and results of a European Commission (EC) funded pan-European security foresight project (FORESEC) conducted in 2008–2009 to help understand how specific international risks might manifest in the lives of European citizens across a set of Member States (MS) of the European Union (EU).[1] Through a participatory foresight process, the project facilitated the emergence of a shared vision and coherent and holistic approach to current and future threats and challenges for European security. In doing so, a further aim of the project was to assess whether a shared European concept of security could be identified. The project provides policy support and advice for researchers and decision-makers, with a view to offering recommendations on European foresight and research priorities. After explaining the methodology employed in the project, the chapter will briefly review some of the outcomes, before critically analysing identified limitations and benefits of using participatory foresight in the field of international security. The chapter finally offers an assessment of the contribution that can realistically be expected from security foresight projects employed to generate policy and research support in international contexts, and makes recommendations about how foresight can be anchored systematically into EU-level security policy and research activities. Using the experience of the FORESEC project, this chapter speaks directly to one of the central ambitions of this book, namely to explore different methods and approaches in dealing with uncertainty and to assess their merits and perils.

Security research within the EU framework has developed significantly over the last decade, and there have been cumulative efforts to define a research agenda and the creation of distinct instruments to drive development forward. While foresight activities as such were not new to the EU, security foresight remained rare outside the national level and the private sector. As implemented by the EC under Framework Programme 7 (FP7), security research has the dual objective of enhancing the security of European citizens and improving the competitiveness of the European security industry.

This very particular institutional context has a significant impact on the overall understanding of security and the prioritisation of security research investments. It has, for example, become apparent that it is easier to involve representatives of the private sector rather than public users in the preparatory work phases designed to define long-term research priorities. Also, that security research has focused so far on internal and civil security because the Commission does not have competence in second pillar issues. However, it is possible to detect a subtle opening towards external security and military security matters in the latest work programmes of the FP7 security theme.

An important step for the development of security research within the EU framework was taken when in 2003 the EC set up a Group of Personalities (GoP) with the primary mission to develop a vision for a secure Europe and to spearhead the process of advancing European industrial potential, with the aim of protecting the European citizen. It was against this backdrop that EU-level civil security research started as a separate programme in 2004, when the EC launched its three year Preparatory Action for Security Research (PASR) with a budget of €45 million.

With PASR underway, the next step, in 2005, was for the EC to establish the European Security Research Advisory Board (ESRAB). ESRAB's purpose was to provide advice to the Commission on the implementation of a European Security Research Programme and desirable priorities for this programme. ESRAB had a major impact on the security theme work programmes of FP7, but maintained a firm focus on internal security. While ESRAB brought together demand articulators and research and technology suppliers from within Europe, and offered a framework against which many national, regional and even private research programmes could be calibrated, it nonetheless focused only on the medium term.

To address this deficit, the European Security and Research Innovation Forum (ESRIF) was established in 2007. It was tasked to develop a mid- and long-term strategy for civil security research and innovation and thus address some of the limitations of ESRAB. The main objective of ESRIF was the development of a Joint Security Research and Innovation Agenda that would link research with policy making and implementation. The hope was that this would lead to more coherent research programming, in turn producing better innovation.

When FORESEC was designed, the most commonly used foresight methodology was based on analyses from subject matter experts bringing together individuals with experience in national government, international institutions and private think tanks or research institutes. Experts conduct analyses of the existing work on European security, including global trends and actors that have an impact on European security. They also conduct work on the current functioning of the European security initiatives. Further background research is conducted by looking at historic situations to anticipate future trends. Once draft papers have been established their results are then most often discussed at seminars or study groups and workshops. These panels help to generate authoritative feedback before the results are published. Participatory elements remained underdeveloped in this standard method. Likewise, many foresight exercises were still conducted at the national or even sub-national level. Furthermore, only a small minority of studies in the public domain dealt with European security challenges and their impact on technology needs. Most were concerned either with security regarding a certain sector or security of a certain country.

Regarding the overall framework of this book, this chapter makes a contribution to our understanding of the first challenge identified in Chapter 1: forecasting risks. Both security research and foresight from a security perspective are still very recent additions to the landscape of EU-level research priorities. At the same time foresight is gaining importance because it is necessary to better understand what a common European security and threat assessment should include, and to continually revisit the analysis in the face of an ever-changing security environment. Doing so is a necessary step to develop shared and common policy responses as well as research priorities. In time these may contribute to the development of a European security culture. Against this background, the consortium involved in the FORESEC project tried to design and implement a pan-European, holistic and participatory foresight process.

4.2 Project methodology

Any political actor is naturally embedded in a context. Given that an actor can rarely shape this context, it must learn to structure contextual uncertainties. Furthermore, once an actor has learnt more about the context, this knowledge must be transferred into actual policy options in order to navigate the complex landscape of choices available. This is certainly the case for the EU with its ambitions in the security field that include ensuring the security of its citizens and being recognised as an important contributor to global security (European Union, 2008).

There is general consensus among scholars as well as policy makers that the security field has witnessed a substantial increase in uncertainty since the end of the cold war (see Chapters 2 and 15). The primary cause for the increased uncertainty is complexity. To date, no universal definition exists of what complexity (or a complex system) is. However, roughly speaking, a complex system is a system with many components whose behaviours are both highly variable and strongly dependent on the behaviour of other components (see Various Authors, 1999). This is indeed a very vague formulation of a complex system and it is tempting to conclude that almost all systems are complex systems. This however is not the case: there are completely ordered systems and there are completely disordered systems, with complex systems filling the gap in between (Huberman and Hogg, 1986).

Within the security field complexity enters in many different ways. An interesting aspect of complexity, particularly relevant in that field, is the interaction of different timescales. If the dynamics of different subsystems are governed by substantially different timescales, this can lead to complex behaviour (Scheffer et al., 2009). For example, during the cold war, policy processes (subsystem 1) could relatively easily keep pace with change in security context (subsystem 2). Today however, many contextual changes happen over much shorter timescales. This resulting time lag between contextual changes and policy responses constitutes a major challenge for the security community. Another relevant aspect inducing uncertainty is the existence of so-called 'tipping points'. The term has become a popular replacement for the more precise term 'critical transitions'. In recent years it has become increasingly clear that complex systems permit critical transitions in which the system changes abruptly between states (Scheffer et al 2009). In the last two decades the end of the Cold War and the 9/11 attacks represent primary examples of critical transitions in international security.

In recent years we have seen increased complexity both with regard to the context – including threats to be addressed – and the policy landscape in which appropriate measures should be developed. Stable and relatively predictable threats have been replaced by a plethora of vague, ill-defined and seemingly unpredictable threats. Today's threats can be divided into 'natural' and 'man-made' threats. In the first group we find examples like the 2010 earthquake in Haiti and the Tsunami in South-east Asia during Christmas 2004. The appropriate toolbox here is usually some statistical analysis based on historical events. Man-made threats can be further divided into 'intentional' and 'unintentional' threats. A key problem area in the class of unintentional threats is the issue of socio-technical systems. For these threats some kind of probabilistic risk assessment is the orthodox methodological approach (Bondi, 1985), while approaches for today's intentional threats are much less developed. From a European perspective an equally important development with regard to increased complexity is the evolution of a European architecture for security. The main point is that the complexity of the current situation calls for novel methodological approaches to support European policy processes of relevance for security.

Acknowledging these complexities has consequences for one's perspective on the future. It has been suggested that different perspectives can be based on the principal questions an actor may want to pose about the future: What will happen? What can happen? How can a specific target be reached?

(Börjeson et al., 2007). This set of questions also reflects earlier attempts (Amara, 1981) to classify scenario typologies within future studies according to whether the goal is exploring probable, possible and/or preferable futures respectively. The discussion of complexity and uncertainty above entails that the second and third questions are the only viable ones for security foresight, that is security foresight should in general explore the possible and/or preferable futures in order to provide policy support.

Security foresight follows in the tradition of two future-oriented policy support processes and scientific disciplines. On one hand, security foresight can be seen as a variant of traditional, science and technology (S&T) related foresight activities whose aim is supporting the identification, analysis and selection of research themes and technologies, and to enhance innovation (Irvine and Martin, 1984; HLEGEU, 2004; TFAMWG, 2004). On the other hand, it has also strong foundations in security and defence planning (NATO, 2003), and risk-analysis (Aven, 2003), that seek to support decision-makers in the development and implementation of actions and policies that ensure the security of citizens and sovereignty of nations.

Originally, both approaches were developed to produce information and support decision-making on resource allocation (Irvine and Martin, 1984; Salo and Cuhls, 2003). Within innovation policy, the focus of foresight activities has traditionally been to support the allocation of resources to thematic S&T activities in view of competitiveness of industries as well as the overall well-being of society (Martin and Irvine, 1989). In security policy, future-oriented activities have traditionally aimed at assisting decision-makers to target resources to actions that protect most vulnerable and relevant assets and thus maximise the overall security of nations and citizens. From the 1990s onward, however, both fields have adopted characteristics of systemic thinking, and increasingly the focus of future-oriented activities is not only on single technologies, single threats or risks, but also on their interdependencies and context (Smits and Kuhlman, 2004; Hekkert et al., 2007). This shift has influenced the perception of what policy makers, industry, practitioners and academia expect from foresight processes.

While foresight activities within innovation policy have increasingly been performed at the international level, the same cannot be said about security foresight. As a consequence of the dominant role of the state in the security field, security foresights have so far been carried out almost exclusively at the national level, and these activities are often linked to the development of national security strategies.

As has been argued elsewhere in this book, the changing security context and the increasing complexity require us to adjust our methods (see Chapters 2 and 15). In order to move beyond the fragmented picture of security-related foresight activities and shift the focus from the national point of departure, the FORESEC project set out to be truly pan-European and thus respond to the problem identified by other contributors. We defined two basic criteria in designing the foresight process. First, in order to cope with the challenges outlined above the approach should facilitate a notion of 'shaping rather than controlling' the future security environment. Second, the approach must be participative in order to incorporate views from as many perspectives and members states as possible, as well as a means to anchor the process and the results as broadly as possible.

In terms of methodological constituents, the foresight process consisted of desk research, interviews, a pan-European Delphi survey, interactive workshops and scenario building. The first phase of the process provided an overview of national and European security-related activities. To this end 12 country reports were compiled covering security-related strategies, institutions, research activities, industry, and public opinion issues in Austria, Bulgaria, Estonia, Finland, France, Germany, Italy, Poland, Slovenia, Spain, Sweden and the UK. These MS were selected to cover a broad spectrum of different political cultures, geographical locations, national strategies and societal challenges that are relevant to security. A second aim of the first phase was to engage a network of people and organisations from different sectors working on security issues across Europe.

As a bridge between the first and second phases of the project, a two day workshop was organised. This workshop brought together some 80 security experts to identify key trends and drivers of European security. The main prepared input for the workshop was a draft synthesis report summarising the findings of the 12 country studies. The workshop aimed at developing a 'broad picture' of drivers, threats and challenges that would subsequently serve as a basis for the online Delphi survey of the second phase and the scenario-building process of the third phase.

In order to facilitate broad participation among the network of security experts, the second phase of the foresight process was centred on an online Delphi survey. A Delphi survey is a survey in two (occasionally more than two) rounds, in which the results of the first round are given as input for the second round. The main idea is that respondents in the second round can react on the basis of their knowledge of all answers from the first round.

The objective of the FORESEC Delphi survey was to identify future trends of relevance to European security. In contrast to many Delphi surveys, especially earlier surveys within technological forecasting, the FORESEC Delphi aimed for neither prediction nor consensus. Instead it tried to identify diversity among respondents (see scenario building below). In the survey, experts were asked to evaluate change factors and impacts in terms of their probability of affecting European security, and their importance for European security up to the year 2025. Areas covered included societal, political, environmental, economic and technological aspects of the future of importance for European security. Subsequently, the Delphi survey was complemented by desk research into the identified change factors.

The FORESEC online Delphi engaged more than 300 security experts from almost all MS.

In the third phase, the results from the Delphi survey and the analysis conducted served as a basis for scenario building. This phase of the process was designed (i) to help understand how specific threats might manifest themselves in the lives of European citizens, and (ii) to identify national- and European-level policy options that could prevent, counter or mitigate the threats. Six parallel workshops were organised in Austria, Bulgaria, Finland, Italy, Sweden and the UK. In order to get comparable results across the countries a workshop methodology utilised in all six MS was developed. Twelve 'risks areas', representing common categories of risks discussed in the EU, were identified in order to assess them against the current situation in each of the six countries. The assessment was performed in several steps. First, each national workshop mapped the twelve risk areas onto a likelihood/impact matrix. Then, the top risk areas in relation to the security agenda of the country in which the workshop was being held were identified. Finally, workshop participants identified possible policy options and actions in order to meet and mitigate the impact of the identified risks by utilising three context scenarios. These scenarios were developed utilising the scenario planning school (Kahn and Wiener, 1967; van der Heijden, 2005; Chapter 15). This methodology involves the development of a set of qualitatively different external scenarios, in the sense of describing factors and developments beyond the influence of the planning entity itself.

4.3 Selected project findings

The various consultations and participatory processes combined with the background research carried out throughout the FORESEC project produced a series of findings which are summarised in this section.[2] As far as public opinion is concerned, traditional security topics are rarely identified as top priorities. Today, security seems to be more about societal and individual well-being in a general sense. Citizens increasingly use individual economic security as a yardstick for their overall sense of security, as shown by the frequent references made to different aspects of economic security in the FORESEC country reports. Concern about future problems that may be caused by increased income disparity and the growing stratification of society is also reflected in the results of the national workshops. This suggests that the concept of 'human security' is becoming more important among citizens in Europe, and takes precedence over the traditional notion of 'national security'. The ensuing impression is that the citizen is now at the centre of the security realm in the EU, gradually replacing the state as the referent object of security.

Generally speaking, opinion polls indicate that societies in EU MS feel relatively safe. Although Europeans see many things as potentially threatening, they do not actually feel threatened or affected by them in their daily lives. However, single events tend to act as catalysts to public threat perceptions: for example, an act of terrorism perpetrated in one country will often have repercussions on the perceptions of security of citizens in other countries.

The FORESEC project has observed that the assessment of threats and trends made by security experts in different EU MS is to a large extent similar. However, the Delphi results have revealed some interesting differences between NATO and non-NATO members. Participants from NATO MS were more concerned about external threats and issues related to internal power distribution, while those from non-members stress the potential consequences that ecological and societal changes may have on security. The Delphi also showed a higher level of confidence in the ability of modern technologies to generate security among participants from NATO MS (FORESEC, 2009: 13). It is interesting to note that the NATO vs. Non-NATO cluster was the only cluster that produced statistically relevant results. Clusters based on geography, member state size, or length of EU membership failed to do so.

The FORESEC results also indicate there is no common concept of security across Europe: in a society as diverse and complex as the EU, it is hardly possible to find a definition that everyone will agree upon (see Chapter 8). Governments' perceptions of security across the EU have been shaped by various historical and geographic factors, and proximity to potential sources of territorial threat or to sources of migration affect a country's security conception. As a result, approaches to security are still fragmented across MS. The consequence of this is that EU MS do not have a comparable set of security strategies or priorities in place to adequately address current security challenges.

In spite of these differences, there is an overlap of threat assessments among MS as far as major government documents are concerned (Giegerich and Pantucci, 2008: 12). It seems commonly accepted that security is an evolving concept, as demonstrated by the radical change of picture in the security environment since the end of the cold war. Our once bipolar world has become a multipolar one with a multitude of actors exerting influence, including non-state entities. Governments' strategies highlight the diffuse and complex nature of the current security threat. At the top of the 'new security agenda', one now finds issues such as transnational organised crime, irregular migration or international terrorism, while 'traditional' state-based threats are generally considered to have lost much of their relevance. Most governments also stress the blurring of internal and external security driven by interlinked, asymmetric and de-territorialised challenges. This is also emphasised in the European Security Strategy (ESS) 'A Secure Europe in a Better World' adopted by the European Council in 2003, which suggests that internal and external dimensions of security can no longer be usefully separated from each other (European Union, 2003).

With regard to institutions dealing with security issues, this new environment requires improved interagency processes and government coordination. The institutional division of labour found in most MS no longer adequately addresses the needs of modern security policy. Therefore, institutional restructuring is currently taking place in several MS in order to bring together diverse instruments across civilian and military spheres into a coherent security response. Governments are trying to create a more joined-up policy involving a wide range of ministries, often assuming new roles, together with actors from the private sector and civil society. This is partly a consequence of the rapid growth of the private security industry across Europe, which has taken over areas where the state was traditionally the main provider of security. As a result, there is increasing debate about who should be responsible for the provision of security: the state, the private sector, or society as a whole?

Security research in EU MS is to a great extent conducted from the perspective of national defence. Many EU MS are also members of NATO and security research in these countries is often conducted and coordinated from a 'hard security' perspective (Rintakoski, 2009). National security research and foresight activities are not coordinated with European-level research programmes, resulting in gaps and overlaps between activities (FORESEC, 2009: 18). However, an interesting fact to note is that security research encompassing the broader meaning of the term and the more traditional 'hard' military research are moving closer together. As this broadened concept of security as a field of research is growing in importance, its size is increasing dramatically and there is considerable potential for new and innovative research efforts (Giegerich and Pantucci, 2008: 12).

4.3.1 Future trends: selected Delphi findings

As FORESEC has shown, the notion of security is one that evolves over time, as do risks and their perception; therefore, the elements which are relevant to the European security agenda need to be constantly redefined (Rintakoski, 2009). A number of changes in global politics and economy will take place in the future. Some were singled out by experts during the Delphi and the scenario workshops as having a high likelihood of affecting European security in the next 15 years, and a high impact if they do occur.

The Delphi participants believed that by 2025, Europe will witness the development of new major power centres around the globe, even though the role of several nations and multilateral organisations remains uncertain. It is generally agreed that the rise of China and India, and how they integrate in the international system, will be a central issue in coming years. According to the participating experts, the EU will not be a major player in the emerging world order, which may even lack a centre of gravity; Europe's ability to shape the international environment will be reduced in the long-term. The EU may, however, take the role of mediator when political crises occur in countries located in its vicinity or in other regions of the world.

While the Delphi survey suggests that the EU neighbourhood will be an area of considerable political stability in the future, there is danger that states in the vicinity might serve as staging grounds for terrorist attacks in the EU. The Middle East in particular is regarded as a breeding ground for Islamist terrorism, which will continue to spread into the EU. Additionally, experts believe that Iran will eventually develop the nuclear bomb, thus becoming a menace to its neighbours and to Europe. This is one of the major threats identified to future European security and it goes hand in hand with the fear that this might ignite a regional arms race as other countries in the region enhance their effort to develop weapons in order to deter Iran (Aguirre-Bastos, 2009).

As far as demography is concerned, Delphi participants expect population growth in developing countries to trigger more migration to the EU. These population movements may be exacerbated by climate change and its possible security implications in terms of natural disasters and conflicts over scarcer resources. Increased levels of illegal immigration may boost the activities of organised crime networks that thrive on people smuggling and the exploitation of vulnerable population groups. They may also lead to a rise in societal tensions, especially as the EU is considered ill-prepared for the integration of immigrants. Additionally, there is growing concern among experts about the increasing pressure that ageing populations will place upon the welfare state and national budgets of EU MS.

Participants in the Delphi considered economic and social stability to be essential requisites for security. Social and economic tensions and marginalisation were repeatedly mentioned as potential risks which could result in radicalisation, unrest and political instability. In this respect, the EU as a political institution and its MS were identified as the most important actors to guarantee security. In particular, national and EU institutions are seen as crucial for managing future financial crises.

One of the most prevalent security issues for Delphi participants was future access to energy resources, as many producer countries are seen as politically unstable. It is widely believed that nuclear energy will become more prominent in the discussion of remedies for the gas and oil bottleneck. Similarly, the risk of critical infrastructure breakdown is one that is often stressed by experts in the various MS. The domino effect that this kind of threat can have is taken very seriously, as it can disturb both the social and economic systems of a country. Participants in the Delphi expressed much pessimism about the increasing vulnerability of infrastructure, from cyber-infrastructure, pipelines and transport links, to energy infrastructure in general. Growing technological capacities, complexity and linkages of critical infrastructure systems will also make the EU more vulnerable to cyber-attacks. In most countries, participants believe that the next five years will see a substantial increase in IT crime and fraud and that this will have a medium to high impact on their countries' security.

4.4 Critical evaluation

Lying between innovation management and security planning, decision support and vision building, security research foresight has to address a mix of different objectives and expectations that are brought to the table by funding organisations and participants. Whether the overall objective of foresight should be to contribute to innovation or to the security of citizens and nations depends on which organisational or professional perspective is dominant. In addition, it is unclear whether security foresight is more suitable for producing information relevant to decision-making on the EU level, or to innovation and security at a structural level by assisting with the identification of mutual interests and joint actions within partly isolated national security systems. In FORESEC, for example, discussions in the kick-off workshop included both (innovation and security) views of what FORESEC should try to achieve. Even in the development of the Delphi survey it was not clear whether some statements, for example concerning climate change, should be formulated as threats causing serious risks to EU citizens, or as triggers for technological innovation driven by European industries. Moreover, on the question of what role foresight should play in EU security research policies, participants presented very different views. On the one hand, some experts presented strong arguments that foresight should concentrate on vision building among national security policy and innovation systems. On the other hand, some participants favoured the role of foresight in advising the EC on how to allocate resources to different research themes. Overall, these different objectives and expectations lead to a situation where foresight managers (i.e. those responsible for design, implementation and dissemination of foresight activities) need to define balanced foresight objectives along the following dimensions (see also Rip, 2003; Rask, 2008; Könnölä et al, 2009; Salo et al., 2009):

1. *Threats and opportunities*: Activities may explicitly focus on increasing the security of different objects such as nations, citizens, the economy or infrastructure. However, foresight activities can also concentrate on enhancing innovation and increasing the competitiveness of industry. Even though these objectives can be seen as convergent at some level, they also stand in conflict. For example, it is not clear whether applications in nano-, bio- and ICT-technologies will mainly cause or solve more threats and risks. Moreover, whether security foresight and research should focus on preventive measures such as development aid and diplomacy, or actions that improve the level of preparedness such as

surveillance and weapon technologies, depends on how much emphasis is put on the security of citizens versus the competitiveness of industry.

2. *Country-level vision building and client recommendations*: Several authors have raised the need to balance foresight objectives between consensual vision building and the development of actionable recommendations (Havas, 2003; Rip, 2003; Rask, 2008). Too much emphasis on finding common denominators between different organisations and MS may lead to analysis and recommendations that are too abstract or obvious to benefit decision-making. However, if research settings are too specific, it becomes difficult to engage experts with diverse cultural, organisational and professional backgrounds and to generate productive dialogue (Keenan, 2003; Rip, 2003; Salmenkaita and Salo, 2002). Within international security foresight, this tension may be even more dominant. Security-related activities are cross-sectoral by nature, and thus it may be difficult to find common actions which are understandable and agreeable to representatives from different backgrounds. Moreover, in multinational foresight processes (e.g. Georghiou, 2001), diverse cultural backgrounds and organisational landscapes may make it difficult to synthesise information from various sources without increasing the level of abstraction in the discussions (Brummer et al., 2008; Könnölä et al., 2009).
3. *Development of novel information and analysis of interdependencies*: Security research related foresight activities can explicitly concentrate on identifying new building blocks for security analysis by developing novel information on threats, risks and technologies that have not been properly examined in earlier studies. However, foresight activities may also focus on facilitating new perspectives and analysing interdependencies between known building blocks such as evolving threats, risks and technologies. These may have been already identified in certain academic communities or governmental bodies, but may need further examination in terms of their linkages to other threats. Foresight can treat novel information and its interdependencies at the same time (e.g. HLEGEU, 2002; Salo and Cuhls, 2003), but, initially, the development of novel information requires a homogenous group of experts whereas the identification of interdependencies requires participants with different organisational and professional backgrounds.

4.4.1 Balanced objectives in FORESEC?

In view of the taxonomy defined above, the FORESEC project was not well-balanced. For example, FORESEC aimed at both facilitating *country*-level vision building *and* providing decision support *for the EC*. It focused on *both* novel threats *and* their interdependencies. It also approached European security from the perspective of *both* diverse threats *and* S&T-related opportunities. Altogether, the objectives of FORESEC reached a level of complexity that made it difficult to achieve the outcomes defined at the beginning of the project.

However, the methodological toolbox developed for the project was well-balanced in term of the dimensions described above. For example, country reports, the kick-off workshop and Delphi were suitable approaches for analysing the European security context and there was no reason to expect that project phases conducted through scenario workshops and further desktop work, would not be feasible approaches for complementing the context analysis by identifying policy and S&T-related actions. The methodology included also parts dedicated to shared vision building (workshops and Delphi) as well as activities designed to support EC decision-making (Delphi, scenario workshops, desktop work). Special emphasis was put on balancing novel information (Delphi and international scenario workshops) and interdependencies (national scenario workshops). Considering the participatory element of the FORESEC approach, the consortium succeeded in engaging a diverse and balanced group of different European security actors.[3] It thus provided a fruitful base for networking and vision building as well as more detailed analysis on certain threats and opportunities.

While FORESEC produced many valuable outputs, especially in the area of risk perceptions, it proved difficult to identify genuinely new threats, opportunities or linkages, at least on a level of abstraction that would provide unique added-value for EC decision-making. Of course, wide participation in both country and EU-level activities is valuable in itself, and FORESEC facilitated several seeds for collaboration which are likely to generate long-term benefits. However, it is not clear whether it will succeed in producing sustainable collaboration beyond FP7. The key area for improvement of future activities similar to FORESEC is a closer alignment of the methodological toolbox and the group of stakeholders involved in participatory work.

The selected methodologies were of a complexity that made them very challenging to apply with the diverse and wide group of participants that were engaged in the project. On one hand, the participant base was well suited for a vision building process, while on the other, methodological choices mainly concentrated on producing rather complex information to benefit EC decision-making and hence not on vision building. Even though the methodological choices as such were suitable for analysing the complex landscape of European security and supporting EC decision-making, the diverse composition of participants made it difficult to apply the methodologies consistently and coherently over time. For example, the variety of participants' backgrounds made it problematic to find a level of abstraction that would make statements in the Delphi survey understandable to all the respondents, and at the same time design them in way that went beyond obvious and already well-established information on European security.

Likewise, in the scenario workshops, diverse backgrounds made it challenging to find a common language, which in turn made it difficult to deal with the complex workshop setting.

In theory, the diverse participant range would provide a fruitful base for analysing interdependencies between evolving threats, developments and actions. However, many methodological choices were more suitable for producing information on new threats and opportunities, not on their interlinkages. The Delphi concentrated on scoping the European security landscape at large. While it developed vast amounts of information on certain threats, the fact that the participants evaluated pre-defined statements limited the potential to discover and analyse linkages. Activities that concentrated on interdependencies, such as development of macro-scenarios and some reports, were mainly done through desktop work, and input from the participant base was not fully exploited.

Systematic, future-oriented and participatory processes are crucial in the development of shared strategies and the integration of isolated security and innovation systems at the EU level (European Union, 2008). FORESEC was the first foresight project concentrating on civil security in which ambition, scope and engagement justify the labels holistic and pan-European. As such, it broke new ground and the critical reflections presented here should provide fruitful 'lessons identified' helping with the design and implementation of similar security research foresight activities, which are certainly in the pipeline for FP7 and beyond (ESRIF, 2009).

In the design of foresight activities, there is a need to distinguish between the facilitation of vision building and networking on one side, and processes trying to assist decision-making on the other. Important methodological choices need to be driven by a clear understanding of where the balance is struck and which emphasis is appropriate to meet overall objectives. This would enable a coordinated approach to methods and the involvement of stakeholders.

The more vision building-orientated the foresight process is, the more diverse the group of participants must be. The more diverse the composition of stakeholders, the simpler the process has to be. Thus, when the focus is on decision-making, and the participant group is rather homogenous, methodological choices can be more complex, and processes can have divergent objectives. On the other hand, when the focus is on vision building, and a diverse group of stakeholders is invited to participate, there is need for simple methodological choices and strong trade-offs between different objectives.

Even though shared vision building, networking, and the need for contributing to EU innovation and security get more attention in the political debate, there are no suitable methodologies that help managers of foresight activities to adjust the process in that direction. Most of the foresight methodologies are, in essence, developed for assisting decision-making (e.g. TFAMWG, 2004) and thus there is a need for methodological development that takes into account the challenges of engaging experts from different professional and cultural backgrounds in the development of shared visions.

4.5 Role of foresight in policy support

Foresight studies have been carried out regularly since the 1980s on the regional, country and sometimes EU level, mainly in S&T and industry contexts (Georghiou and Keenan, 2005; Rasmussen and Anderssen, 2009). However, there are wide differences between countries in terms of resources allocated and influence on the decision process. In the UK, government departments and many government agencies have futures groups and the scope of activities has widened as their work has been recognised and valued. A similar process is occurring in Singapore (Sutherland and Woodroof, 2009). There are examples of regional coordination/networking, such as within the Nordic Foresight Forum and APEC. In other regions, like Central and Eastern Europe and the newly independent states (CEE/NIS), there has been a slower uptake and differing degrees of scepticism from both industry and policy actors (Keenan, 2006).

In order to align with the Lisbon strategy objectives of improving competitiveness, EU innovation policy is supposed to be based on 'implicit or explicit visions of the future' (JRC-IPTS, 2001). The EC's strategy to achieve this objective has been one of support and coordination by the now defunct Foresight Unit K2, in the old EC Directorate General RTD, mainly through funded studies, platforms and networks, and through the work of the EC Joint Research Centre – Institute for Prospective Technological Studies. Foresight has been used in some countries for security and defence planning (NATO, 2003; Sutherland and Woodroof, 2009). Since 2002 there have been a substantial number of national level foresights with a national- or global-level geostrategic focus (Wikman-Svahn, 2009; NATO, 2005). While a number of recent S & T foresights have taken place in fields directly or indirectly coupled to security issues, at EU level relatively few studies have addressed EU security in future or EU security research (Barré, 2001; JRC-IPTS, 2001; Wikman-Svahn, 2009).

FP7, in its Research and Security theme, tries to support EU external policies including peacekeeping, humanitarian and crisis management tasks through S&T, but does so in an indirect manner by underpinning the development of security technologies and applications. The programme on foresight in socio-economic sciences and humanities should also support national, regional and community policy makers in identifying long-term challenges. The Social Sciences and Humanities (SS&H) dimension should be considered a 'key technology' (Gaskell, 2005). The most recent strategic orientation for further security research has been given through the work of ESRIF.

Beyond improving individual technologies, focus on security-integrated concepts is needed for current security missions and civil crisis management (Sieber, 2005). In line with the EU's expanded security concept, ESRIF has expanded the focus of civil security research to a wider range of threats, examined societal questions and emphasised systemic risk assessment and foresight methods, which it has itself used.

ESRIF has highlighted the global dimension of security, the importance of research and innovation to support EU civil security mission areas, and the potential usefulness of foresight for guiding the policy-making process (ESRIF, 2009). The nature of current threats (which are diffuse and interconnected), lack of knowledge about the possible evolution of these threats and their potential social impact, make the use of tools such as those employed in foresight processes attractive.

The EU's new, more comprehensive security approach and its implementation in Common Foreign and Security Policy (CFSP) demands enhanced coordination between MS in security policy. FORESEC found little shared vision either in defining security or in defining threats, and highly specific threat prioritisations for some countries. The analysis of current security concepts in selected EU MS revealed fragmentation in understandings of security, in approaches to security and in use of foresight processes. ESRIF had also underlined the diverse security needs and expectations, and policies in EU MS, and stressed the need for multilevel policy coordination between EU, national and regional levels, while respecting the principle of subsidiarity from EU level to MS level (ESRIF, 2009). In these circumstances it may not be easy to arrive at the consensual, common positions between MS necessary for external actions under CFSP.

4.6 Conclusions

There is now a substantial body of EC and nationally supported resource expertise in foresight. Foresight is widely diffused and used by experts for technological and market forecasting, and its use is being extended to a more widely defined idea of security. Foresights are approaching maturity in S&T and research in some countries, and high-level policy makers at both national and EU level are aware of foresight processes and tools for priority setting, but it is unclear what impact they have on the decision processes (Barré, 2001; Ghiorghiou and Keenan, 2005; Sutherland and Woodroof, 2009). While foresight for security research straddles both innovation policy and decision support, apart from defence scenario-building foresight processes are less used in the security domain (NATO 2005; Wikman-Svahn, 2009).

Adoption of foresight processes has taken place at different rates in different countries and foresights range between one-shot activities that are limited in scope, or on-going, systematic processes (Keenan, 2006). While foresight practices and studies have been evaluated in a number of individual countries, impact measurement is still relatively immature, but this could clarify the relevance and role of foresights in the strategic decision-making process, taking into account other influences on decision-makers (Georghiou and Keenan, 2005).

The implications of FORESEC findings point to continued challenges for shared objective setting in external policy, which, as ESRIF points out, is a recent and evolving competence of the EU (ESRIF, 2009). In general however, foresights could still be useful. The systematic consultation process offers sites for vision building among nominal competitors, offers space for disagreement as well as agreement between constituencies, and allows for the coordination of positions with regard to societal goals (Rip, 1990). The FORESEC experience underlines the difficulty of generating insights that are useable (in the sense providing accurate information), speak to the needs of the end-users and can be queried by critics (see Chapter 16). Much also depends on managing expectations. Foresight exercises are not necessarily predictive and remain exploratory by design.

The ESRIF final report makes several recommendations with regard to foresight. Capabilities must be strengthened through enhanced transnational cooperation; new policies should be initiated in order to deliver the most appropriate solutions; integrated approaches to security should embrace interoperability, standardisation, certification, validation, communication with the public and exchange of best practice; the focus should be put on the global dimension; and the security research that is based on the European Security Research and Innovation Agenda (ESRIA) must include a transparent mechanism involving all stakeholders.

The EC reacted to ESRIF's findings and recommendations on the next steps to be taken at the European level. The first phase is the social aspect of security, which should become the main focus, reinforcing the legal, ethical and societal dimensions. The second phase consists in improving the competitiveness of the European security industry by overcoming market fragmentation and strengthening the industrial base. The third phase aims at investing in the future, with the help of the R&D activities that need to be reappraised, strengthened and amplified. As threats to European security are not easy to predict, the security R&D should focus on strengthening Europe's resilience to threats and on its ability to recover from crises efficiently. The fourth step involves implementing the ESRIA.

Notes

1. FORESEC was funded under the European Commissions' Framework Programme 7 Security Theme. The project was led by the Crisis Management Initiative (Helsinki). The other consortium partners were the Austrian Institute for Technology (Vienna), the Centre for Liberal Studies (Sofia), the International

Institute for Strategic Studies (London), the Joint Research Centres (Ispra) and the Swedish Defence Research Agency (Stockholm). This chapter draws on a variety of reports that the FORESEC consortium published. They can be downloaded at www.foresec.eu.

2. Findings are presented in much greater detail alongside some of the raw data that went into the analysis in the FORESEC reports. All of them are available for download at www.foresec.eu.
3. For example, in the Delphi study, 346 registered users from over 20 European countries participated. The composition of participants was well-balanced in view of different organisational backgrounds; approximately 35 per cent of the participants were from government, 35 per cent from academia, 15 per cent represented NGOs and civil society organisations and 15 per cent came from the private sector. In different workshops the participant base was well-balanced in view of both organisational and geographical background as well.

5

Modelling Transnational Environmental Risks: Scenarios for Decision Support

Fabian Wagner

> How is it possible to expect that mankind will take advice, when they will not so much as take warning?
>
> Jonathan Swift

5.1 Introduction

Predicting the future has a long history. In European culture it can be traced back to prehistoric versions of astronomy, codified in Stonehenge and the Nebra Sky Disk. The notions of a well-ordered cosmos, of cyclical time, are intimately linked with the belief in a future that can be divined (Gould, 1987; Eliade, 1991).

In the ancient world knowledge of the future was often associated with the mythical lower world of the dead, as we read in the Odyssey (Book XI), the Aeneid (Book VI), in Dante and in Milton. The Etruscans believed they could read the future in the sliced-up livers of sacrificed animals, and the professions of augurs and astrologers followed in this tradition. Jesus spoke largely in the future tense (Steiner, 1998) and the relation between myths, religion and prophecies is a close one. Even in worldly matters, or maybe particularly so, the belief in order and stability was paramount. As late as the end of the nineteenth century in central Europe life was seen as fundamentally predictable and stable (Zweig, 1964), before the advent of modernity and World War I changed this attitude profoundly.

There is another long, literary tradition of dealing with the future. Utopian and dystopian writers, such as Plato, Andreae, More, Hobbes, Zamyatin, Huxley, Orwell and others did not predict. They *projected* hopes and fears onto future societies, they described what we would call today *scenarios* or 'possible worlds' – laboratories located somewhere in time and space.

To know the future has always been considered useful. To know enough to be prepared for the dangers and opportunities lurking beyond the horizon of our immediate field of vision can be vital for survival. Our ability to imagine and anticipate a variety of dangers and to plan ahead – even if we do not *know* the future – may even explain why our species has spread so successfully on this planet. For us, dealing with risks has always been an everyday challenge.

A *risk* is an expected damage. That is, negative things may happen with certain probabilities, and the risk is just the average of the damages weighted with the probabilities that they occur. Thus, risk involves negative consequences and lack of knowledge of the future. The starting point for this paper is the following pair of questions: (i) Can science predict environmental risks? (ii) How can these risks be reduced, once identified? (see Chapter 11)

I shall argue that asking question (i) stems in many ways from a misunderstanding of what *science* is and what a *prediction* is. I will therefore first clarify some of the terminology, and reformulate question (i) as: *How do we identify risks*? Obviously, we always use some kind of model for this – models work like our organs, or as McLuhan has it, the 'medium' of the future (McLuhan, 2001) – and one purpose of this chapter is to show how models inform us about environmental risks. I will illustrate this briefly with examples from air-quality science and atmospheric pollution.

There is a simple universal answer to the second question, at least in the field of environmental risks: reduce the likely causes of these risks and you reduce the risks themselves: reduce the release of toxic chemicals into rivers and air and you reduce the risk of poisoning humans, animals and plant life; reduce the number of smokers and you reduce the risk of lung cancer; reduce the emissions of greenhouse gases and you reduce the risks of climate change.

However, reducing environmental risks, like other risks, always comes at a cost, either as a straightforward monetary cost to someone, or in the form of an opportunity cost, or as a cost in the form of loss of power or influence. It therefore comes as no surprise that stakeholders often disagree on whether or not to change the status quo for the sake of reducing environmental risks. This can be observed both in international climate-change negotiations, but also in regional and local scenarios.

More fundamentally, it has been argued that different people assess environmental risks differently, depending on their knowledge, culture and other background factors (Douglas and Wildavsky, 1983). There is probably some truth to this, but it must not be overlooked that it also lends itself as an excuse for an arbitrary ex post facto value-relativism. Even the same people may not apply the same principles for different risks. It is somewhat ironic that the Bush administration argued for pre-emptive military strikes as a means of weapons of mass destruction (WMD) control, but opposed most vehemently a precautionary approach to environmental risks, even though the evidence for the latter was incomparably better. Thus, one may add ideology as one of the key determining factors in risk assessment.

With multiple and potentially conflicting interests at stake, with multiple actors, different backgrounds and objectives, there may not be a simple answer to the second question above, acceptable to all stakeholders. There are, however, situations where scientific assessment can help not only to identify risks, but also guide the process of reaching a consensus among stakeholders on how to reduce the risk.

One of the key messages of this chapter is that decision-makers need a clearer picture of the role the sciences can play in risk assessment. On the one hand, they need to appreciate that science is the best we have when it comes to environmental risk assessment, and even though our understanding of complex systems is limited and fragmented, the things we do know give rise to substantiated concerns, for example about climate change. Yet scientists must not fall into the trap of overselling their results (believing they might not otherwise be heard); referring to model results as 'predictions' is a case in point, as we shall see in the next section. Scientists, on the other hand, cannot expect that their results are directly translated into policy: the sciences alone cannot settle questions that involve fairness and equity (and most policy decisions do), and policy makers may not feel comfortable with models that are beyond their grasp.

In the following sections I will argue that precise terminology can help to communicate the exact role the sciences, and in particular scientific models, can play in assessing environmental risks. There are different types of scientific models, each designed for a different purpose, and here we will focus on those designed for risk identification on the one hand, and for facilitating policy processes that lead to risk reduction on the other.

Over the past few years I have been involved in integrated assessment (IA) modelling in the field of air pollution and greenhouse-gas mitigation, and I will describe some of the challenges and successes of GAINS, an IA model developed at, and operated out of, the International Institute for Applied Systems Analysis (IIASA). Drawing on the GAINS model, I will also illustrate the parallels between scientific models and languages, how models can be used to share knowledge and assumptions about complex systems in an international policy context, and what are favourable conditions for building up trust in scientific models.

5.2 Forecasting risks

Let us begin by clarifying some terminology. The terms *prediction, forecast, projection, scenario* all refer to ways of viewing aspects of the future from the vantage point of the present. Unfortunately they are often used interchangeably, even though they are not synonymous. While *prediction* (Latin *praedicere,* to foretell, to say before, or to prophesy) clearly relates to the notion of certainty, infallibility or even necessity or inevitability (as in Greek tragedy – see Sophocles' *Oedipus*), the other terms convey the notion of possibility.

Can we know, can we predict the future? For most people the answer is yes, some things can be predicted; for example the laws of physics tell us that the sun is going to rise tomorrow. But the notion of *prediction* really is rather problematic for various reasons: (i) natural laws are empirical laws that merely describe what has been observed in the past. While mathematical truths can be considered timeless, natural laws are valid 'until further notice', and so prediction based on these laws with absolute certainty seems somewhat premature; (ii) the fundamental laws of quantum physics are actually probabilistic, not deterministic; (iii) many complex systems exhibit chaotic behaviour, meaning that the qualitative features of the future state of a system depend very strongly on the *exact* initial conditions. This is the well-known 'butterfly' effect: a butterfly flapping its wings in Brazil can cause minuscule changes in the local air flow, leading eventually to a tornado in Texas. Since we can never know the initial or present conditions with absolute precision, we cannot really predict the future in the narrow sense above; (iv) predictability also raises questions about the position of man in the world. For the future to be predictable, one argument goes, the future has to be predetermined. If the future is predetermined, there is no room for free will because we cannot choose a different future and alter its predetermined course. Thus, paradoxically, in a deterministic world there is no value in knowing the future or predicting it: it is inevitable and there is no way of changing it. We will do what we have to do. Fatalism ensues. Therefore we should be extremely careful when using the word *prediction*.

Let us then turn to forecasts. According to the Oxford English Dictionary (OED) a *forecast* is 'a conjectural estimate or account, based on present indications, of the course of events or state of things in the future.' Tomorrow's weather is the prime example: the weather forecast is not always reliable, so it is not a prediction.[1] Nevertheless a plausible reaction to a rainy forecast is to take an umbrella. Though not explicit, a forecast often addresses the very near future, that is a few days in the case of weather forecasts, yet the term can also be used in the context of longer time horizons.

The Latin origin of the term *projection* (*pro-icere*) literally means to 'forecast'. The relevant definition in the OED actually derives from geometry: a 'projection [is] the drawing of straight lines or 'rays' according to some particular method through every point of a given figure, usually so as to fall upon or intersect a surface and produce upon it a new figure each point of which corresponds to a point of the original figure.' This is exactly what happens when you project a slide onto a screen: the visual elements on the slide are enlarged, but the spatial relations between them, the proportions and the colours are preserved. Thus the emphasis in the concept of a projection is the preservation of relations, or, speaking in temporal terms, the continuation of past and current trends. For example, if the oil price has increased by, say, three percent per month for the past year, then a plausible projection of the oil price for the next year would be an extension of this trend. In the short-term such projections are useful tools, though often it is not obvious which indicator can actually be projected, what is fundamentally responsible for the trend, and thus how long observations can be extrapolated, in particular when there are time lags between cause and effect.

Finally, a *scenario*, in the original sense of the word, is a sketch or outline of the plot of a play, giving particulars of the scenes, situations and so on. A scenario is not bound by considering past or recent trends, and it does not need to specify details of how exactly the future unfolds. A scenario is a kind of 'what-if' narrative that is only bound, as far as it concerns the real world, by plausibility and the demand for some coherence. The lyrics of the John Lennon song 'Imagine' would qualify as a scenario story line. A scenario can start and end at any point in the future and can go to any level of detail. What if tomorrow there are two metres of snow? What if the government steps down? What if you could transplant brains? What if time travel were possible? Scenarios can be used to explore the possibilities of the future. Scenario analysis is not bound to look into futures that we like or we do not like. Each scenario represents a plausible future, and there are whole families of scenarios. That is why today the future 'is spoken about in the conditional, and should be used exclusively as a plural' (Nowotny, 2006). This emphasises the fact that the future is not just happening to us, but that to a certain extent we can create it.

In assessments of the future environment all of the above four terms are being used, unfortunately often interchangeably. This leads to unnecessary confusion, as can be seen in public discussion of climate change. We will return to this in a later section. Let us first turn to risks.

Recall that risk is an expected damage, that is it involves negative consequences and our ignorance of the future. If we could *predict* an event with certainty, a risk would turn into a certain damage, and so we would not speak of predicting a risk, but rather predicting a certain damage. If we are *forecasting* or *projecting* an event (say, tomorrow's rain and thus our getting wet) we may assign a probability for the event and quantify the damage for the event. In a full-fledged *scenario* risk analysis one would have to consider all possible futures and assign probabilities to them. Whether this is an adequate procedure depends very much on the problem at hand and the question being asked. We will return to this issue below.

A number of potential issues warrant clarification at this stage. *First*, in practice we often do not quantify probabilities of events when we describe them as risks. We are comfortable talking of risk when we mean that there is a non-zero probability for something bad to happen. It is only when we want to compare risks or put a price tag on a risk – such as the insurance business or the financial markets do – that we need to estimate probabilities explicitly. But even the quantification tools widely used by practitioners may fail, because they sometimes ignore correlations of events or – understandably – do not take into account things that are not known. Also, quantification tools often cannot help us in situations for which we do not have an intuition, as is the case when probabilities are low but losses are disastrous, such as nuclear accidents.

Second, not only may the occurrence of negative consequences be uncertain, but also the extent of the damage. The risk definition above assumes that first all information about uncertainties can be evaluated and then combined with definite values for the ensuing damage. So if you live in an area that is at risk of being flooded, and the value of your property is uncertain, then you combine the uncertainty of being flooded and the uncertainty in the property valuation by asking: what is the probability that I will lose €10,000, 20,000, 30,000 and so on, rather than, what is the probability of losing the grand piano, the bookshelf, the washing machine and so on?

Third, we may say that we *identify* a risk, but we do not really *predict* it. This is not a deep epistemological insight, but again can avoid confusion. When I find today there is a risk that I might die in a car accident next Tuesday, then already today there *is* a risk that I might die on Tuesday – because today I know the bad outcome and I know that it is possible, but I do not know whether it is going to happen or not. Naturally on Tuesday there is still the risk that I might die on the very day, but today I do not *predict* the risk. I already *know* about the risk today – it does not suddenly appear on Tuesday. Also, we *avoid* or *reduce* risks, but we do not prevent them. We may prevent bad outcomes (by staying in bed on Tuesday), and we may reduce probabilities (by belting up), but we do not *prevent* expected losses.

Finally, defining probabilities, let alone quantifying them, is a complex subject on its own that we do not have enough space here to discuss (Gillies, 2000). Suffice it to say that in the context of repeatable controlled experiments, such as tossing a coin or measuring a quantum spin, probabilities can be motivated by relative frequencies of outcomes. But for large and complex systems, such as the earth's climate system, we do not have the luxury of performing long series of experiments or simulations, because too many parameters are uncertain and each simulation just takes too long. In such a situation, only a partial assessment is possible, for example the sensitivity to a single parameter is estimated, or a small number of simulations are used to estimate probabilities.

If it is difficult to assign probabilities, can we at least estimate the damages while quantifying risks? For climate change this is also an extremely challenging problem, not least because climate models by definition tell us something about large scale trends, but often the devil lies in the detail. An increase in probability for drought can be factored into an estimate of potential crop losses, but whether there is a drought every five years or in three consecutive years (which may still be consistent with the laws of probability), can make a significant difference for local farming, national economies and world food markets, not to speak of changes in migration patterns and the potential for conflicts. While some of these impacts can be assessed with quantitative tools, the fundamental question is whether a partial impact assessment can be useful in guiding decisions.

Another challenge for quantifying impacts from a changing climate is that many of these will only be felt over decades or, to put it more aptly, over the lifetime of our descendants. This raises questions of intergenerational equity, and is related to the question of discounting in economic assessments (Sen, 1984). Point estimates may be misleading, as they potentially ignore important impacts later on. To assess the risk of climate change on the basis of climate model runs until the year, say, 2030 is myopic and underestimates the scale of the risk. Finally, some of the impacts may unfold rather rapidly and cannot be reversed. The Intergovernmental Panel on Climate Change (IPCC) has identified a number of such possible 'tipping points' beyond which new challenges could lurk.

It is one thing to identify and to quantify risks; it is an entirely different matter deciding how to act on this information. How should one deal with environmental risks? Is there an objectively 'right' way? If there was a generally accepted procedure that anyone could follow, then there would be no need for decisions: scientists would simply compile risk information for all possible choices, negotiating parties would have no difficulty in agreeing what the issue is and how to act on it. But, alas, there is no such procedure in environmental management: different actors have different risk perceptions and there is no universally accepted strategy in the presence of risk. Let us discuss these two issues in turn.

It has long been observed that when decisions in environmental management need to be taken under uncertainty, those who take the decisions often act as if they assumed that nature behaves in a certain way. A useful typology by Schwarz and Thompson (1990)[2] distinguishes four 'myths of nature', beliefs about the fundamental behaviour of nature:

1. *Nature benign*: Nature is predictable, stable and forgiving. Nature can look after itself, returns to stable equilibria and does not need to be managed. The appropriate management style is non-interventionist or laissez-faire. In the context of climate change this translates not into generic scepticism, but rather the belief that even if we pull the system out of equilibrium temporarily, self-regulation will eventually bring us back into equilibrium.
2. *Nature ephemeral*: Nature is fragile and unforgiving. Human behaviour can lead to catastrophic impacts and therefore needs to be kept in check. In the context of climate change there is the danger of a 'run-away climate change', a series of self-enhancing climate-change effects that move

us further and further (and possibly with increasing speed) away from an equilibrium of climatic conditions in which we have been living. The appropriate management style corresponding to this myth is the *precautionary principle*.
3. *Nature perverse/tolerant*: This is a combination of (1) and (2) in that, to a certain extent nature is stable and does not suffer from small impacts. However, once a threshold is passed, the system behaves as in (2). The appropriate management style is termed *interventionist*: regulation is needed to prevent major excesses, while nature can be left to itself to take care of minor disturbances.
4. *Nature capricious*: Nature is unpredictable, there is no point in managing the system, and the motto is *que sera sera*.

Schwartz and Thompson align this typology of 'myths of nature' with their typology of human nature and construct four different rationalities (individualist/hierarchic/egalitarian/fatalist). This typology is too simple to capture all the subtleties and inconsistencies in human perception of the world. However, within this framework you can quickly see that the same information about uncertainties can lead to very different environmental policies, depending on who is deciding. For example, the individualist and fatalist will see no need to impose any policy. Myths of nature and their associated rationalities are self-sustaining and new information on risks and uncertainties is likely interpreted as supporting one's own position.[3]

The second issue we need to address is strategy in response to risks, and we mention three examples in passing. (i) Risk minimisation: minimise the causes of potential losses, that is of pollution and polluting behaviour. In the short run, this could only be achieved if the underlying activities were discontinued, that is the burning of fossil fuels would have to be stopped immediately, with renewable sources taking their place, because emissions cannot be filtered down to zero.[4] (ii) Cost-effective risk reduction within a given budget. An alternative approach is to not specify a budget in advance, but to find a solution that minimises the cost-benefit ratio. There is a large critical literature on the viability of cost-benefit analysis that we cannot fully engage with here. Suffice it to say that the critical issues are the valuation of non-substitutable goods and the question of completeness. (iii) Avoid extreme losses. Extreme events (think of a nuclear accident or the shutdown of the Gulf Stream with its implication for agriculture) are events with such low probability that they do not contribute much to the statistically expected loss, but which are – if they do occur – devastating. No insurance company would cover such a loss and therefore, one may argue, extreme events deserve special consideration: they need to be avoided at almost all costs.

All three of the above strategies have their merits and could be linked to the myths of nature. The point here is that there is no unique, 'best' way of dealing with risk – risk management strategies are matters of choice, and choices are strongly influenced by worldviews and ideologies.

5.3 Models as organs for sensing the future

A simple narrative of a plausible future becomes complex rather quickly; worse, it runs the danger of becoming inconsistent as it unfolds. Models are used to structure our thinking of what we know about the world, what is persistent and what is changing, and how this change comes about. Models are tangents to reality in the sense that within a range of specific circumstances there is a correspondence between elements of reality, and elements of a model: within this range one can translate one into the other (cf. Chapter 2). The future is not directly accessible to us; but just as other media allow us to extend our sense organs to connect to remote areas otherwise not accessible directly (e.g. the telephone, see McLuhan, 2001), so models allow us to access the potentialities of the future.

Models can be classified in many different ways: there are quantitative and qualitative models; there are simple and complex models; there are models in every conceivable field of knowledge, every discipline, every twig on the tree of knowledge. There are models of the world economy, models of genetic drift, of the human brain and of bird migration. A model suggests a method, and a method relates to a set of priorities. Thus, different models use different techniques to produce their results.

Here I would like particularly to draw a distinction between two types of models used in environmental sciences, though the line drawn between them is rather fuzzy. Roughly, the purpose of the *first kind of model* is to *explain* (the relationship between) observed data and to *discover* new phenomena. Newton's Law of Gravity can be thought of as a model of how planets and stars interact and it explains quite a wide range of celestial phenomena. It has even been used to predict (indeed this time to predict!) the existence of a planet previously unobserved. In climate change science general circulation models (GCMs) simulate the physical systems of ocean and atmosphere over periods of decades or even longer. They can explain the Gulf Stream, long-term temperature changes and precipitation patterns.

This first class of models – let us call them 'pure' models – is used to explore a piece of unknown territory, to solve puzzles, to push the limits of knowledge. In a realist reading of science the purpose of such models is to reveal the truth. They can be used to perform thought experiments, which are useful when actual experiments are expensive or, in the case of complex earth systems, if repeatable experiments cannot be carried out with the real thing. Most models of this kind are disciplinary, in that they are expressed in the language of a specific discipline.[5] But as there are 'splitters' and 'lumpers' in science,[6] so there are models of different levels of aggregation, and some cut across several disciplines.

The *second class of models* puts less emphasis on knowledge generation than on *decision support*. These are IA models. An IA model is a tool that combines 'knowledge from diverse scientific disciplines in such a way that the whole cause-effect chain of a problem can be evaluated from a synoptic perspective' (van der Sluis, 2002). The integrated model should 'have added value compared to single disciplinary assessment; and it should provide useful information to decision-makers.' Implicit in this definition is that there is something in the cause-effect chain that a decision-maker can influence. For example, emission policies may influence the level of pollution, whereas no model of nuclear fusion in the sun will ever be an IA model, as there is no room for a decision-maker.

In the next section I shall focus on the GAINS integrated assessment model, viewed widely as one of the most successful examples of a scientific IA modelling tool that has been used to aid policy makers in addressing a transnational environmental problem. In the remainder of this section, however, I would like to highlight what can reasonably be expected from the above two types of models.

State-of-the-art 'pure' models are the best we have to answer very specific questions in science. Pure models are used to explain the properties of semiconductors, the folding of DNA, the formation of clouds. Pure models can be used to explore territory previously inaccessible, and thus new phenomena can be discovered. Some of these newly discovered phenomena may have bad consequences, so pure models may reveal new risks we were not aware of, they may even allow us to estimate some of the relevant probabilities – for example, a model that describes how nano-particles enter our lungs and bloodstream can indicate increasing risks of inflammation and heart attack. Similarly, long-term climate modelling tools can tell us about the risks looming in the distant future.

But even though pure models can tell us about risks, they cannot be expected to be used on their own to guide policy makers in developing robust risk reduction strategies – in particular when the risk is man-made. Decisions on risk and risk reduction typically involve stakeholders with conflicting objectives, and an understanding of potential trade-offs and synergies is essential before decisions are taken on the what, who, how and when.

This is where IA models enter. IA models are designed to aid decision-makers, hence they focus on two tasks: (i) identifying possible options for action, and (ii) estimating the consequences of these decision options. These consequences can be both in terms of environmental effects as well as in economic, social or technological terms.

In contrast to pure models, which are used by specialist scientists, IA models are designed to be used by policy makers and their staff, and this requires the models to be accessible to them, both conceptually (they cannot be too complex mathematically) as well as physically (decision-makers need to have access to input and output data). Good IA models are combinations of simplified versions of complex pure models that capture the important features of the full disciplinary models. But IA models need to be transparent, accessible and able to deliver results fairly quickly.

There are some trade-offs between demands for accuracy and simplicity, but some of these trade-offs can be addressed. The GAINS model, for example, uses so-called source-receptor matrices that approximate much more complex atmospheric-dispersion models that require high computational power to solve. These source-receptor relationships hold only within a certain range of pollution levels, but the model can be calibrated so that this range just coincides with the range of interest, that is the actual current level of pollution and just below it.

In summary, what we have called pure models can be expected to give us new insights and information on future risks. Pure models operate at the forefront of science, and as such are subject to normal scientific debate, where answers lead to new questions. In contrast, IA models are not used to simply reflect an objective reality, but also they help us to understand how we relate to it. They can be used to frame risks and make information available to stakeholders and decision-makers in a compact and 'closed' format, with the focus on options for policy intervention. How this can work in practice we will see in the next section, with a focus on the observation that a model can be thought of as a language in which stakeholders can communicate.

5.4 The GAINS experience

Air pollutants, such as fine particles, sulphur dioxide (SO_2) and nitrogen oxides (NO_x), when released into the atmosphere, can cause local and regional environmental problems, such as acid deposition (commonly known as 'acid rain'), eutrophication (excess nitrogen) and health problems (increased risk of heart attack, respiratory diseases, etc.). Since the atmosphere knows no national borders, air pollution is a prime example of a transboundary problem, meaning that it cannot be tackled effectively by domestic measures alone and requires the cooperation of actors at the international level. Here IA models can help.

The GAINS model, and its predecessor RAINS, has been used extensively in policy processes leading to air-pollution legislation in Europe.[7] In Europe the European Commission (EC), in consultation with stakeholders, has decided (i) to take an effects-based approach and (ii) particularly to focus on cost-effective ways to achieve given sets of targets. This means that the objective is to reduce environmental *impacts* at lowest possible costs and that emissions are reduced only as a means to reduce these impacts. Thus, for example, a uniform emission reduction target for all member states (MS) may not make sense, because the emission reduction in some MS may be more effective for reducing overall impacts than in others.

Questions that arise in such a setting include:

- What are the likely air-pollution impacts in the future if no policies were to be imposed in addition to what are currently in place?
- How much could these impacts be reduced, and at what costs?
- How can we be assured that both costs and environmental benefits are distributed in an equitable way among MS, and also within MS among different economic sectors (e.g. industry, households, transport)?

The stakeholders, in this case the EC, representatives of MS, and representatives of industrial organisations as well as environmental NGOs, use the GAINS model to address the above questions, thereby taking into account information on projected economic development, air pollution and related policies, technology (costs, efficiencies and potentials), as well scientific knowledge of the atmosphere and ecosystems (location and vulnerability).

In many ways the GAINS model serves as a language that allows communication between stakeholders, with obvious parallels: the model, like a language, is a rule-governed system for recording significance and for communication. A language can be used to describe thoughts in order to understand oneself and the psychology of others. Similarly, the GAINS model can be seen as a tool for understanding a set of inputs and assumptions, and to generate outputs as means for communicating the implications of these rules and inputs, as well as of the assumptions built into the model. Languages are organs of the mind, to use an expression by von Humboldt, and so are models: for example the GAINS model can be used to explore hypothetical future air-quality regimes.

Models and languages share some important structural elements that justify that comparison: both are characterised by a vocabulary, a grammar, and a user constituency.[8]

5.4.1 Vocabulary: words and their meanings

A vocabulary is a mapping between words and meanings. It is a dictionary or lexicon, a set of definitions. Broadly speaking, the more entries there are in the vocabulary, the higher the resolution and the higher the information content. The more different words you can use the more specific you can be. In its entirety the dictionary defines the limits of the language and therefore the limits of the world describable in this language. In the context of models we speak about the system boundaries, the delineation between what is considered inside the system and what is outside, i.e. in the system environment.

In the GAINS model, for example, we represent countries by a number of economic *sectors* (e.g. power plants, steel production, a national fleet of heavy-duty trucks, etc.). In each of the sectors a set of *activities* may occur (the combustion of coal/oil/gas in the power plants sector), and this will lead to the emissions of a set of *pollutants*, which in turn can be reduced by certain *technologies*. The use of effective control technologies is associated with lower emissions but also higher *costs*. *Environmental impacts*, such as *acidification* and *eutrophication*, affect various ecosystems, and the extent of the pollution can be expressed as the *exceeding of critical load*. Human health is impacted by exposure to different pollutants, the most prominent ones being *fine particles* and *ozone*.[9]

As the words in the dictionary do not have to refer to reality (e.g. 'unicorn'), so the vocabulary of a model may not have counterparts in reality. What counts for a modeller is whether a concept is useful, not whether it is real. For example, GAINS only works with the 'average' person, neglecting individual behaviour and exposure.

5.4.2 Functional relationship: the grammar of models

A model connects concepts through functional relationships, such as equations and rules. For example, in GAINS the emission level from a given activity can be calculated from the activity level, the emission factors and the extent to which control technologies are in place. Other model equations describe how the emissions of air pollutants actually lead to environmental impacts. When policy makers consider alternative policies for the future, they need to be aware of certain *constraints*, both in the real world and in the model. For example, certain emission-control technologies cannot be applied under all circumstances, so their *applicability* is restricted. Also, while technologies can reduce the emissions, they often cannot completely suppress them. Hence, even through the use of the most *effective* technologies, there will often remain *residual emissions*, and hence *residual effects*. Decision-makers need to be aware of these limitations in assessing the full range of options available to them.

Model equations and rules constitute the equivalent of a 'grammar', a codified structure of rules on how to form sentences using the vocabulary. They provide the logic by which the model elements, and therefore the data, fit together. Grammar and vocabulary are intricately linked.

Naturally, a model needs to be furnished with data, and a model looking into the future needs to be *calibrated* or *validated* with data of the past and of the present. Without data a quantitative model is empty. Worse than being empty, a model filled with the 'wrong' data (e.g. inappropriate or outdated data) can appear to be functioning, but can deliver misleading results. Model maintenance and update is therefore an integral but often underestimated part of good IA modelling practice. Probably more than 70 per cent of the manpower in my research department is spent on data maintenance, including stakeholder consultation, data exchange with other modelling teams, and database management.

5.4.3 The community of users

One of the basic tenets in this paper is that in order to manage risk, information needs to be shared in a technical language that everyone speaks and understands. To agree on such a language can be difficult when the group of stakeholders is inhomogeneous, such as negotiators representing different national governments, industry organisations, NGOs and scientists. Typically all of these stakeholders will have their own sources of data and quantitative tools, and since interests are often conflicting, there is always an element of suspicion that the other parties are using biased data.

So a *common* model can serve several functions. First, it provides a database each stakeholder has equal access to, that is no stakeholder has an information privilege. Second, stakeholders can control the data update and thus act as peers for each other. Third, the use of a common model forces stakeholders to reflect on their own methods and to compare, possibly to improve their own assessments. Finally, results from a common model can help negotiators to explain to their own communities the 'deals' they have agreed to, possibly highlighting where other parties have made concessions.

Stakeholders will typically ask the IA modeller three basic questions. First, is the model representation adequate to the problem at hand, that is have all relevant aspects been taken into account? Second, are the latest data available taken into account? Third, will the model help me take a decision, that is will the model help me in assessing and comparing alternative options for action? The GAINS/RAINS model has been developed over a period of more than 20 years to address these requirements efficiently.

In general, one of the obstacles that potential users of complex scientific models face is accessibility, both intellectual and physical. Above we have already referred to this potential barrier when we introduced IA models: in the present context GAINS covers multiple disciplines, ranging from macroeconomics and chemical engineering to non-linear physics and ecosystem vulnerabilities. We overcome such barriers by patiently building capacity through dialogue, training and project work. A significant amount of our time is spent presenting at stakeholder meetings, lecturing at workshops and international courses, and documenting the model.

Naturally the model dictionary and the grammar need to be accessible in order to make the model a useful tool, and many complex models fail in this respect. Physical access to model inputs and output is of paramount importance; at IIASA this has been understood early on, and for almost a decade the GAINS model has been openly available through the Internet, so that all input and output data can be accessed free of charge. What is often not appreciated by modellers is that it is not the model *results* that are the most important aspect of an integrated assessment, but rather the process, and part of that process is to make transparent the *assumptions* in the analysis to all stakeholders. In GAINS we have even gone a step further and have given MS experts writing privileges in parts of our centrally stored database.

In 2005 more than 20 MS each sent a team of experts to IIASA for several days at a time to review the current set of assumptions, a process that kept the modelling team at IIASA busy for about six months. In 2007 representatives of European oil and gas industries hired a consultancy to check on the GAINS model. They downloaded all input data and recreated the model structure from scratch, only to find that they were obtaining the same results as IIASA, thus confirming the integrity of the approach. Making all the information available required a large effort in terms of software development and manpower, but it gave the whole process a boost in credibility.

The GAINS model as a language develops as we modellers and the stakeholder community move along. The model is extended and modified (i) in consultation with our scientific peers as new scientific data become available, (ii) in consultation with the user community to improve accessibility and transparency, and (iii) initiated by ourselves to improve the manageability and in anticipation of future requests for analysis. In one sense our modelling team acts as a gatekeeper, not unlike the editors of the German Duden, the authoritative source for correct spelling. However, we also noticed recently that those peers whom we provided with stand-alone versions of the model have actually transcended the original structure and have adapted the model to their own purposes – not unlike a local dialect of a language.

'Hot media are, therefore, low in participation, and cool media are high in participation or completion by the audience', writes McLuhan (2001). Thus, while models in cutting-edge science typically rely solely on the experience, skills and knowledge of expert scientists and are therefore hot media in the above sense, decision models for the real world, in particular IA models, must be supplemented with input by the stakeholders to turn them into cool media – and to keep them ever fresh.

Decision-makers are well aware of the difference between reality and models. In 2006 I attended a stakeholder meeting on future air-quality strategies in Brussels. The chairperson explicitly reminded participants that the results of our modelling exercise were pertaining to the 'GAINS world' and not to the real world, but that stakeholders had also agreed to use results of this model as the basis for negotiation on emission limits for the individual MS. To provide such a 'world' is all that can be expected from a good scientific tool for policy purposes.

5.4.4 Translation, style and dialogue

There are a number of other similarities between models and languages worth noting. A model can be thought of as a metaphor, either in the bland sense of a representation of reality, or as a genuine translation of experience from one mode into another (McLuhan, 1962; Ravetz, 2003). A metaphor is an abstraction that also helps to distance us from the world as we usually see it, and therefore allows us to appreciate the unexpected or surprising.

Models can be used to translate a narrative into a coherent whole, or a grand schema into detailed implications.

As there is no *lingua universalis,* there is not *the* model of the world. There are different models for different purposes, as there are different technical languages. As linguists, writers and literary critics engage in debates on translation problems (Steiner, 1998), so do modellers debate the meaning and relevance of features in one model expressed in the language of another. Each model, each language, slices up reality differently, from a different perspective, and therefore reflects a different conception of the world. This may be called a 'style'. Different styles lead to different information, information that may be incommensurable. But incommensurability does not mean incomparability.

Finally, a model needs to be taught and learned, just as a language needs to be taught to, and learned by, a community that shares values and that communicates to reach a common understanding of its values. It takes time for a student to take in a set of new concepts, to understand the rules of the game, to reach the level of fluency required to base informed decisions on model results. Over time technical experts in different countries have learned to use the GAINS model, partly because the model is considered a useful tool and partly because there is peer pressure. Naturally this fluency in the model does not necessarily extend to board rooms, but that is not required in a negotiation process that refers technical details to expert committees. The GAINS model is publicly accessible, but experience shows that neither journalists nor the general public use it widely for their purposes, perhaps because results look comparatively dull to an audience used to the spectacular.

For Lacan, language is a gift. But he also cautions: language is as dangerous as the horse for the Trojans – once accepted it will colonise us (Zizek, 2007). Similarly, we have to acknowledge that models, understood as metaphors, can easily become ideologies that can creep in and are difficult to be consciously aware of. Keynes found that 'practical men, who believe themselves to be quite exempt from any intellectual influences, are usually the slaves of some defunct economist.' (Keynes, 1997: chapter 24).

5.4.5 The treatment of uncertainty in the GAINS model

Castells and Ravetz (2001) have identified a number of elements that led to the success of the GAINS (then RAINS) model in supporting policy processes through IA in Europe in the 1990s. First and foremost, at the time there was a common willingness in different countries to define international policies on air pollution, and the process was largely driven by those who were affected by the pollution. Structural elements of the success of the modelling include the relentless emphasis on quality control, the focus on specific questions the model was designed to answer, and the combination of a very pragmatic modelling style, with the use of the best available scientific information. Procedural aspects of the success included the dialogue-like interaction between stakeholders and modellers (and amongst stakeholders) that also led to a differentiated awareness of the limitations of the model; the fact that data provided by individual country experts were evaluated and included by the modellers; and a clear definition of the task at hand.

Finally, it has certainly helped that GAINS is operated out of IIASA, an internationally recognised, scientifically credible research institution that is specifically dedicated to addressing global environmental and social challenges of the future. IIASA is a non-governmental organisation (NGO), sponsored and governed by National Member Organisations (NMOs) in 17 countries on four continents, including the United States, Japan, Germany, Russia, China, India, Pakistan, Korea and South Africa. These NMOs do not represent governments, but are scientific organisations, typically National Academies of Science. Founded during the cold war to build bridges and to confront growing global problems on a truly international scale, IIASA's mission is to conduct policy-orientated research into problems that are too large or too complex to be solved by a single country or academic discipline. IIASA has a long track record of developing and assessing scenarios in the fields of population, energy, air pollution, forests and agriculture.

My personal sense is that another factor in the success of this model has been its treatment of uncertainty, and by implication, of risk. We have seen above that uncertainty (or probability) estimation is an element of risk analysis, but I have also argued that 'pure' models can identify risk in a wider sense without explicitly addressing the issue of probabilities. Also the GAINS model always works with best estimates of parameters and avoids using probabilities for uncertainty and risk estimates. This procedure is an outcome of our observation that decision-makers do understand that the future is uncertain, but are confused by probability distributions, confidence intervals and so on. Even when they are given uncertainty intervals, they often end up choosing the mean value. Decision-makers prefer to be presented with discrete decision options, fully aware of the fact that these represent aggregates that are uncertain. Our approach to uncertainty is pragmatic, in that we identify potential biases in our analysis and eliminate them as much as possible. Focused sensitivity analysis is likely to lead to deeper understanding of the issues by the decision-makers and to more confidence in their joint decisions, thus avoiding the danger of being bogged down in irresolvable uncertainties.

Is there a danger that our model results are described (by others) as more certain than they really are? Of course there is, in particular when the distinction between prediction, forecast and scenarios described above is not taken seriously. The GAINS team is working with sets of scenarios, and the business-as-usual scenario (or as we call it, the 'current legislation scenario') only has the role of a forecast in the narrow sense of the word described above, without any reference to probabilities. Our task is to assemble what is considered known and what are agreed reasonable assumptions. Naturally all of these can turn out to be wrong and assumptions may change, but in reality decisions need to be taken at some point in time with incomplete information.

Compared to the relevant timescales in flood warning (Chapter 9) our 10-to-15-year outlook stretches far into the future. This has a variety of implications. On the one hand, there is always time for policy adjustments that can be made over time as new information becomes available, time that you do not have when faced with an immediate risk of being flooded. On the other hand, the further you project into the future the less specific you can (and would wish to) to be. Only because in aggregation many of the uncertainties cancel each other, can a reasonable projection be made at all.

Are we comfortable that our model results are used to justify policies? In general, yes, this is exactly what IIASA's mission is: to provide scientific insight for policy making. Imagine a world in which environmental policy is made by gut-feelings, popularity votes or dictated by industrial polluters. These are the grim alternatives. But again readers should not overrate our role in this game: we are catalysts who supply the tools for stakeholder dialogue, we are not driving the policies. I should also emphasise again the importance of the iterative aspect of the decision process. When we engage in a project we seek to be in close contact with the stakeholders over the whole period of the process (which can take several years). We write reports, attend stakeholder meetings, hold workshops and invite country experts to review the tools. Only through these close contacts can we ensure that the model results are neither misjudged nor misinterpreted. Yet we cannot prevent them from being misused.

5.5 Conclusion

Scientific models can help us to identify environmental risks, in particular risks that are beyond the horizon of our direct senses. Under certain circumstances, models designed to support decision-making can also facilitate the dialogue between stakeholder groups with conflicting interests, by describing causes and effects in a structured way, ideally also indicating potential trade-offs and synergies in a wider context. In many ways a model works like a language, a rule-governed system for recording significance and for communication.

In Europe, existing international air-quality policy is largely the result of integrated assessment, understood as an iterative process that generates knowledge and common understanding among high-level stakeholders on scientific, economic, technological and ethical issues. As we have seen in the last section, a number of favourable factors have contributed to the success of the GAINS/RAINS model in such a process, including the model's transparency, its modelling style and the fact that IIASA is perceived as an independent scientific advisor. Educating decision-makers is an important aspect of successful IA modelling.

It is also important to conceptualise issues of uncertainties. We all take decisions under uncertainty in our daily lives and we can do this without having exact numerical estimates of what the risks are. Thus, the key lesson for public decision-makers is not how to understand, say, a probability of 43.7 per cent for a stock market meltdown over the next 58 days, but that the objectives as long-term public planners are often and should be different from those of short-term orientated individuals. A risk I am personally willing to take may not be one a society as a whole should be willing to take. This is particularly prominent in counting the costs and benefits of air-quality mitigation (Broome, 1993). So my plea is for a deeper conceptual approach that highlights the causal relationships (as well as correlations and possible time lags) rather than a climate-change quantitative approach to uncertainty and risk.

Can we learn from the GAINS experience for other environmental risks, for example climate change? Yes and no. Yes, we can learn how to build a transparent IA model and how to operate it in a multi-stakeholder context. There are, however, a number of crucial differences between air pollution and climate change. For one, causes and effects of climate change are further separated, in space and time, than in the case of air pollution. Second, the reduction of greenhouse gases requires that we save energy, and use cleaner energy, but we also need to change some of our behaviour: in contrast to air pollutants, greenhouse gases cannot just be filtered out.[10] Finally, the group of stakeholders is much larger and more diverse. There is no central political body that can exert significant pressure on negotiating parties, as the EC and the European Parliament can in EU legislation. Most significantly, there is currently no real political will for significant action on greenhouse-gas mitigation.

GAINS is not a fully-fledged integrated assessment model of climate change, that is it does not represent the full cause-effect chain of climate change. But in the run-up to Copenhagen, we have developed the *Mitigation Efforts Calculator* (MEC) tool based on the GAINS model, for the very specific task of estimating the cost of greenhouse-gas-mitigation in the industrialised countries and for comparing the results across countries (IIASA GAINS). This allowed us to focus only on one of two negotiation tracks under the United Framework Convention on Climate Change (UNFCCC), the so-called 'Ad-hoc Working Group under the Kyoto Protocol.' The idea here was to provide a publicly available tool that would allow a comparison of the proposals for emission reductions that the industrialised countries were bringing to the negotiation table.

The IPCC has identified and characterised the risks of climate change to the extent possible. What is still lacking is a joint vision of a sustainable future and of the path leading there. It will take utopians, like Plato and

More, to spell out possible designs for the future. The most important insight is, however, that the future not only holds risks, but also opportunities.

Notes

1. Ironically, the German term for weather forecast, Wettervorhersage, literally means 'weather prediction', a certain case of hubris.
2. Extending work by Holling (1979, 1986), described lucidly in Adams (1995).
3. In the field of climate change, see Hulme (2009).
4. To avoid also the risks from air pollution, in particular health risks from fine particles, also the combustion of biomass and the production of livestock would have to be stopped. In the field of climate change immediate remedies have been proposed in the form of geo-engineering. However, possible side-effects - such as changing monsoon patterns - are not well understood, and other problems associated with the accumulation of greenhouses gases–such as the acidification of the oceans - would not be addressed by this technology either. Thus, these options appear to always involve some Faustian bargain.
5. It is useful to think of a model as a language to describe a scientific problem in, see below.
6. Or, with Archilous and Isaiah Berlin, 'foxes' (who know many things) and 'hedgehogs' (who know one big thing).
7. The acronym GAINS stands for Greenhouse Gas and Air Pollution INteractions and Synergies, RAINS for Regional Air Pollution INformation and Simulation. A brief history of the model, its uses in negotiations until the late 1990s and current applications can be found at IIASA's website (Cleaner Air for a Cleaner Future).
8. Morphology and phonology do not have equivalents in the world of modelling.
9. To be more precise, it is *tropospheric* ozone, that is ozone in the lower layers of the atmosphere where people live, that poses a health risk to humans. In contrast, the *stratospheric* ozone layer protects us from harmful radiation from space (cf. 'ozone hole').
10. Carbon Capture and Storage (CCS) technology seems to violate this rule, but carries unexplored risks of leakage, thus involving yet another Faustian bargain.

6 Risk, Uncertainty and the Assessment of Organised Crime

Tom Vander Beken

6.1 Introduction: organised crime as a transnational threat

Organised crime is not a 'natural' crime phenomenon that can be observed, counted and classified like other crimes. More than most other types of crime, organised crime is a social construct that strongly reflects policy choices and beliefs. Organised crime is something – it is not a coincidence that organised crime is very often pictured as an active creature – that is considered threatening or dangerous to society and therefore serious in itself. The distinguishing feature is that it is 'organised' (Finckenauer, 2005), suggesting that the threat and seriousness of the phenomenon only stem from the way that such crimes are committed.

From that perspective, a concept like organised crime is only functional in an environment in which the organisation of crimes has taken a visible form and is challenging, because of this form, to traditional law-enforcement strategies and results. Initially, there were originally few countries in that situation. Organised crime was something specific and exceptional. Something for a country like Italy with its mafia problem, rooted in the nineteenth century. Or for the specific environment of the United States, far across the ocean.

From the 1970s, most European states did experience problems with various forms of serious crime and growing professionalism on the part of perpetrators, it was only in a few countries, however, that 'organised crime' was recognised. This was a slow but steady process. In Germany it took about 20 years for organised crime to move into the criminal-policy debate (von Lampe, 2001). But once there, it was there to stay, even when it became clear in the early 1970s that what was happening in Germany did not fit the American mafia paradigm. The Netherlands, a bit later, was the next country to 'discover' organised crime. What organised crime conceptually was remained rather unclear. But it certainly was something threatening and serious (for further details and background on other countries see van Duyne and Vander Beken, 2009).

Until the beginning of the 1990s, organised crime remained mainly a national concern, hardly taken up at the European or international level, and with little attention paid to its potential transnational aspects. The murders of the judges Falcone and Borsellino in 1992 changed that situation in Europe, shining a spotlight on what was happening in Italy. Fear that something similar would cross the Alps and infect other European states brought the issue to the European (and global – see for example the 2000 UN Convention Against Transnational Organized Crime and its Protocols) agenda as part of its growing focus on crime.

From then on, organised crime and its transnational potential became one of the key concerns for European policy, as a reaction to different forms of serious crime. Definitions, including legal ones, depict organised crime as a transnational threat requiring transnational action. Organised criminals thereby represent a set of people who are 'really dangerous' (because they commit offences in groups, use violence, corruption, influence and commercial structures to shield their activities) to the essential integrity of the state and international community, and who necessitate special investigative powers because of this threat (Levi, 2002).

The recognition of this new, international transnational threat coincides with transformations within European law-enforcement and security policies, moving from reaction and coercion to pro-activity and risk assessment and management. In law-enforcement theory in general, and policing in particular, the Weberian perspective on contemporary western policing, that focused on order maintenance and coercion as the defining-capacity of law enforcement (Bittner, 1970), was challenged. Ericson and Haggerty (1997) provided a comprehensive theoretical alternative beyond coercive policing (Brodeur, 1998, Sheptycki, 1998), situating police in a postmodern, complex and diverse environment orientated towards the detection and management of all sorts of risks. They argue that police are only one of the institutions engaged in monitoring and managing risks and therefore they need to communicate and exchange information with others. As a consequence structures, strategies and intelligence requirements have been profoundly influenced by this risk orientation and developed into institutions with an insatiable demand for data on all sorts of activities and events. In such an environment, traditional intelligence models, that are focused on 'knowing' what has happened in order to be able to respond, are challenged (Kessler and Daase, 2008). A clear shift can be discerned in that respect: reports describing past criminal (and law-enforcement) activities are being replaced by assessments that have much more forward-looking and future-orientated ambitions. Prevention and multidisciplinary action are keywords in this discourse. Policy makers no longer focus on repressive aspects, but want to be informed about upcoming challenges and threats to anticipate, to take appropriate preventive action, and to target their reactive response better (Zedner, 2007). It is not the (retrospective) crime *situation* that is considered of interest, but the possible *risk* or *threat* a phenomenon poses to society (Levi and Maguire, 2004: 401–402). Similar to other transnational, the question is if, or to what extent, it is possible to know all what is relevant and understand what will, or could, happen, with a view to developing (preventive) responses.

This chapter discusses this transformation towards a more forward-looking discourse in the European security arena, applied to the case of the assessment of organised crime. As there is no consensus on what can be known and said about organised crime from that new perspective, different views coexist. First, the position and discourse of those who believe that it is possible to collect relevant data about all sorts of issues and use this to assess and manage contemporary security risks in an objective manner (Innes et al., 2005). This *believer approach* has led to the introduction of more technocratic and expert-based forms of risk calculation, generating quantitative estimates of the probabilities and impacts of crime events. Such analyses seek to make estimates of probabilities, using various conceptual models, known past cases and available historical data. There is, however, a second *non-believer* approach in which it is accepted that not everything can be known or predicted and that not all risks can be known or calculated. Especially since 2001, uncertainty and unpredictability seem to have found their way into discussions on crime assessments (Gill, 2006). How should or could law-enforcement agencies and policy makers in the security arena think and respond to risks whose contours can only vaguely be known? In this chapter it is argued that the uncertainty approach has many merits but has seldom been developed consistently in the area of (organised) crime analysis and intelligence.

6.2 The believers: organised-crime assessments about the future

6.2.1 A risk-based approach

Traditional organised-crime assessments contain data and statistics about perpetrators and criminal activities. This information is mainly retrieved from what has been collected in specific investigations. A major critique of such assessments is that they report on law-enforcement activity rather than on the phenomenon itself. Indeed, enhanced activity to fight organised crime may lead to more investigations and more data about perpetrators and activities, and thus a thicker annual report the following year. Such organised-crime assessments risk becoming self-fulfilling prophecies, in which the assumptions and definitions of what the real threat is lead to targeted actions and, accordingly, specific results of that action in terms of crimes and suspects. The usefulness in policy terms of such assessments is questioned. What does quantified information about the number of criminal groups or offences and their nature contribute to the decision-making process about the seriousness of the phenomenon and the priorities to be taken? And are police or law enforcement best placed to prepare such assessments, given the influence they have on their own activities and resources (van Duyne, 2006)? The consequence of this is that simple questions – so obvious to an outsider – have hardly been answered: Is there much organised crime? Is the situation serious? Is it bad that there are more criminal groups now than in the past? Which criminal groups are the most dangerous? (Vander Beken, 2004).

As a reaction to this, risk-based approaches to the assessment of organised crime have been developed. Their purpose is twofold: (i) collecting and systemising existing data about criminals and activities in a way that better allows priority setting; and (ii) identifying new sorts of data that can be relevant to the assessment of organised crime. In this context, concepts like risk, threat, harm and vulnerability are used. Risk is then defined as *the chance of something happening that will have an impact upon objectives and can be measured in terms of likelihood and consequences.* In the context of crime assessments, the likelihood of crimes being committed can be evaluated by looking at the intent and capability of the perpetrators, that is the 'threat' posed (Brown, 1998; Vander Beken, 2004). Given the fact that the consequences of a crime are generally considered negative for society – especially from the law-enforcement point of view – crime assessments use the terms 'harm' as *the damage occurring should a threat be realised,* and 'vulnerability' as *those aspects of the environment offering opportunities to the threat to cause harm.* In such an approach, we consider risk as the combination of *threat* (focusing on the abilities and willingness of *offenders,* linked to the *likelihood* of crimes being committed) and *harm* (orientated towards the negative *impacts* or consequences of criminal activities on society in general and victims in particular) (Black et al., 2001). This is in line with Tusikov and Fahlman (2009) who describe threat as the nature and magnitude of specific phenomena that can pose harm, and refer to risk as the probability that an adverse event may occur, and the impact of that event in terms of nature and severity. As a third concept, vulnerability can be considered as a factor to be placed between threat and harm as it encompasses the weak points in the legal environment that allow criminal intentions and capabilities to cause harm to society (see Figure 6.1).

6.2.2 Threat assessments

In a threat assessment, the likelihood of a threat can be considered as *a function of the intent and capability of identified actors to achieve specified aims,* where intent refers to the '*likely desire of a subject to engage in activities... and*

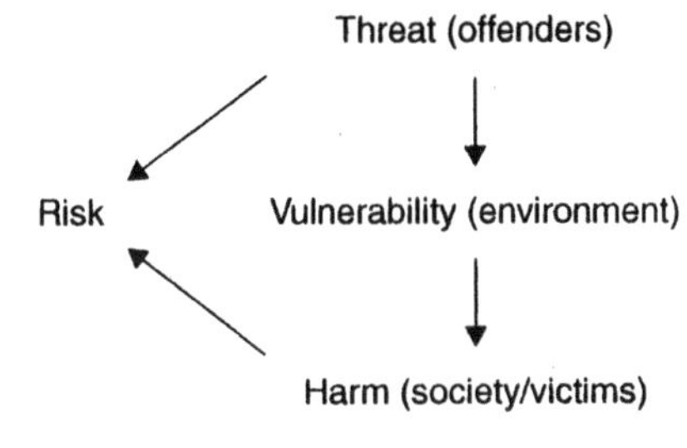

Figure 6.1 Relationship of risk, harm, threat and vulnerability

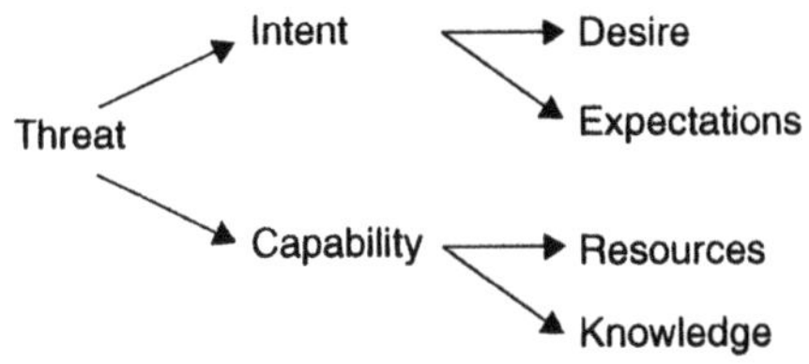

Figure 6.2 Threat assessment scheme, based on Brown (1998)

their confidence that they will be successful' (Brown, 1998). Likewise, capability can be seen as *the function of the resources and knowledge available to the subject in this pursuit* (Figure 6.2). To each of these elements in the sets of relationships described above, can be attributed a value – either quantitative or qualitative.

There are various ways in which the threat of organised-crime groups can be assessed. Most approaches, however, are inspired by what has been developed in the Canadian *Sleipnir* project (RCMP, 2000). In this project the development and ranking of salient attributes of criminal groups is combined with the use of a four- or five-point qualitative scale for each attribute. Comparable exercises have been developed elsewhere (Klerks, 2000; Black et al., 2001) and applied in practice. Such an approach is advocated by the EU in its Organised Crime Threat Assessment (OCTA) (Europol, 2008). A closer look, however, shows that the nature and methodology of this report is far too hybrid and diffuse to be labelled a threat assessment (van Duyne and Vander Beken, 2009).

6.2.3 Harm assessments

Some assessments focus on the consequences of organised crime, in attempting to rank phenomena, groups and vulnerabilities in order of the harm they (might) cause. An accurate evaluation of this 'cost' of organised crime, however, poses similar difficulties. Considering that organised crime exists, at least to a large extent, to supply the demand for goods and services that are either illegal themselves, or whose production and/or supply is illegal and thus hidden, the ability to assess these areas accurately is considerably reduced. Thus, while it seems appropriate to use broader descriptors of effect, the actual application of a value is difficult. As a concept, harm can cover economic, emotional, physical, intellectual and political damage. Further, costs of anticipation of crime, as a consequence of crime and in response to crime, can be taken into account (Dorn and Vandebunt, 2010). Others (Kopp and Besson, 2009) distinguish between tangible harms (primary damage to the society), intangible consequences (direct emotional and physical impacts upon a victim's wellbeing) and systemic effects (social destabilisation inflicted on society) (Savona and Vettori, 2009). For the determination of harm a variety of sources are suggested: court adjudications, audits of the accounts of public and private entities, insurance companies decisions, losses directly reported to the authorities and anonymous surveys (Levi and Dorn, 2008).

The determination of harm is not something that can be done in isolation. Ideally, in determining the impact of organised crime on society, it needs to be defined by as broad as possible a range of interests, and must depend upon the offences being committed in the various markets. Nevertheless, it always implies policy choices about what harm is or should be. As a measure for harm, attempts have been made to convert all harms (including non-monetary harms) into monetary costs (see e.g. Brand and Price, 2000) and have even been applied to the harm of organised crime (Dorn and Vandebunt, 2010). Many difficulties remain, however, in this approach. How can all these costs be evaluated in a credible way? As the response of crime and the costs associated with it do not necessarily depend on the level of criminality, how can they be said to flow from organised crime?

6.2.4 Vulnerability assessments

The first to realise the importance of analysing the context in which organised crime operates was Smith (1980), who partially abandoned the traditional approach embraced until then (which concentrated on the characteristics and the activities carried out by organised-crime groups) to move towards a wider approach where attention was paid to the same markets in which such groups operate. In his 'spectrum of enterprises', Smith (1980) concentrates on the structural forces that determine the logic of organised-criminal forms and activities, and theorises that legal and illegal activities do not operate on parallel and distinct levels, but rather that they are connected and interdependent. Following this reasoning, the next step is to acknowledge that there is a point where the two businesses – legal and illegal – necessarily meet. This point is profit, which is the main driver for both activities. Smith's theory was picked up by Albanese (1987), who made 'an exploratory attempt to predict "high-risk" business conditions', rendering businesses vulnerable

Table 6.1 Predictors of low-risk and high-risk businesses, from Albanese (1987: 109)

Predictors	Low risk	High risk
Supply	Few available small, financially weak businesses.	Readily available small, financially weak businesses.
Customers	Elastic demand for product	Inelastic demand for product
Regulators	Difficult to enter market	Easy to enter market
Competitors	Monopoly/oligopoly controlled market	Open market with many small firms
Patronage	Entrepreneurs are professional, educated managers	Entrepreneurs are non-professionals ill-equipped to deal with business problems
Prior record	No prior history of organised-crime involvement in market	Prior history of organised-crime infiltration in industry

to organised-crime infiltration (Albanese, 1987: 103). Albanese stresses that his model is designed to predict an intermediate condition (i.e., high-risk business), rather than the ultimate behaviour of concern (organised crime). In other words, the predictive variables that he identified in his study can be understood as variables that once again attempt to define vulnerability, rather than predicting organised criminality (see Table 6.1).

Recognising that there are probably going to be some necessary refinements, Albanese cautions that the model serves as a starting point rather than a comprehensive analytical tool. Possible problems identified included concern that the study may have been based on atypical examples, thus skewing both the model and its subsequent utility.

The idea of a vulnerability study has explicitly been taken up in research on a risk-based approach to the assessment of organised crime (Black et al., 2001, further specified in a Method for Assessing the Vulnerability of Sectors (MAVUS) road map (Vander Beken et al., 2005) and applied to specific economic sectors such as the diamond sector (Ibid., 2004), the European transport sector (Bucquoye et al., 2005), the European music industry (Brunelli and Vettori, 2005), the European pharmaceutical sector (Calovi and Pomposo, 2007), the fashion industry (Calovi, 2007) and the European waste management industry (Van Daele et al., 2007)).

In identifying the weaknesses of those sector that could be exploited for criminal purposes, MAVUS embraces both an economic (e.g. Porter, 1990) and a social and criminological perspective (Smith, 1980), leading to an analysis carried out on different levels. The methodology developed comprises several steps grouped in two broader phases, a descriptive phase and an analytical phase. This description takes place on various levels and provides information on the sector itself (meso-level), the cluster surrounding it (macro-level) and the business activity within the sector (micro-level).

Building on some specific criminological models, especially Albanese (1987) and – for business process vulnerabilities – Rozenkrans and Emde (1996), some vulnerability indicators have been developed (Vander Beken and Van Daele, 2008).

Besides vulnerability studies as such, environmental scans are conducted to gather and subsequently process information about the external environment of organised crime. It is a process that requires limited dedicated resources, to identify major trends affecting an entity and to enable analysis to define potential resultant changes. As such it contributes to the development of a proactive focus and clarifies the relationships between identified trends (convergence, divergence, change in speed, etc.) and the posture of the organisation. The goal of environmental scanning is to alert decision-makers to potentially significant external changes before they manifest, so that decision-makers have sufficient lead time to react to the change. Consequently, the scope of environmental scanning is broad (Morrison, 1992). There are numerous ways in which environmental scanning is done and its success depends predominantly upon providing a structure that reflects the broader environment. The most common method for examining the macro-environment capable of affecting organisational interests (directly and indirectly) is to consider its theoretically discrete components or sectors. This generally means scanning for developments that fall under the broad headings of the political, economic, environmental, social and technological sectors.

Williams and Godson (2002) suggest that – as opposed to prediction – anticipation of organised-crime developments is possible using such an approach. They state that anticipation stands for analysis based on an effective knowledge base, the use of underlying warning indicators, and intelligence that is timely and actionable. As believers in the risk paradigm, they argue that while the future of organised crime cannot be predicted, 'careful use of models and extrapolations from past experiences enable us to contend that if certain conditions are present then there is a serious probability that particular kinds of developments will occur' (Williams and Godson, 2002: 314).

6.3 The *non-believers*: assessing organised crime in an uncertain world

6.3.1 Accepting uncertainties

The belief that it is possible to collect all relevant data (of past situations) to assess the organised-crime situation of tomorrow is not shared by all. Even Beck argues that, where the logic of private insurance disengages, where the economic risks of insurance appear too large or too unpredictable for insurance concerns, the boundary that separates predictable risks from uncontrollable threats has obviously been breached (Beck, 1992: 130). From that perspective the limits, of a specific style of reasoning about risk, challenge the limits of rational assessment in general and the ability to use present and past data for future assessment. This links in with the criticism of the idea that (social) evolution is underpinned and determined by laws. This 'historicism' is, according to Popper (2002: 2–3, 149) nothing more than a misunderstanding of the methods of physics. Historical prediction, which would have to be attained by discovering the 'rhythms' or the 'patterns', the 'laws' or the 'trends' that underlie the evolution of history, can and should not be the aim of the social sciences. In his essay 'Describing the Future' (1998) Luhmann argues that we can neither learn from history, nor can we hope to anticipate the future: '*We can only be certain that we cannot be certain whether or not anything we remember as being past will in the future remain as it was*' (Luhmann, 1998: 67). According to Luhmann, modern societies can only describe their future in the present. The future is not predestined but rather the uncertain, contingent outcome of human action and decision-making. We can only make decisions in the present about an uncertain future. Modern societies therefore experience their future in the risk of deciding. Anticipating or preparing for possible directions in organised crime is then no longer about calculating probabilities. It is about making decisions, which may have unintended outcomes, in light of an uncertain future. The future of organised crime is the outcome of human action and decision-making.

The consequences of such a position of disbelief on the assessment of organised crime cannot be underestimated. While some argue that the fundamentally uncertain nature of our contemporary environment can be overcome by new methods to collect more and other information about the environment (see e.g. 'neighbourhood policing' (Innes, 2006), 'third party policing' (Ransley and Mazerolle, 2009)), we believe that the acceptance of uncertainties implies a fundamental reshuffle of the methods for (organised) crime assessments or even challenges the possibility rationally to make future-orientated reports. The application of scenario techniques, enactment studies or a resilience approach might be examples of that.

6.3.2 Uncertainties for believers: scenario techniques and enactments

Schwartz and Ogilvy (2004: 2) describe scenarios as 'narratives of alternative environments in which today's decisions may be played out. They are not predictions. Nor are they strategies. Instead they are more like hypotheses of different futures specifically designed to highlight the risks and opportunities involved in specific strategic issues'. Scenario thinking is not new (see e.g. Ringland, 1998). Even though scenarios remain a much-debated issue, they have proven to be valuable in the context of corporate-strategy building, catalysing change and action, stimulating collaborative learning and creating a shared vision and increased alignment around strategic direction (Verfaillie and Vander Beken, 2008a).

Scenarios have their origins in the military-planning process, where they are used to imagine what the opponent might do, and subsequently to help organise a more rapid and efficient response to enemy strategy. It was not until the 1960s, under the impetus of Herman Kahn, that scenarios were introduced to the corporate world. One of the first companies to accept the development of scenarios as part of its strategic-planning process was Royal Dutch/Shell, which had scenarios that allowed them to anticipate the oil embargo, and anticipate and prepare for the dramatic drop in oil prices in the 1980s. Since then, scenario thinking has become a popular tool for the development of strategy in the private sector.

Applied to the field of organised-crime assessments, these considerations give new meaning to anticipating or planning for organised-crime developments. Instead of trying to assess what organised-crime developments will occur, it is wiser to reflect on what has the potential to change significantly or have an impact on economies, societies, or public services or organisations. Scenario planning thus deals with strategic risks and opportunities in a very different manner from traditional organised-crime assessments. It shifts the focus from historicist reflexes, from making estimations or calculating probabilities about the future of organised crime, towards imaginative and flexible reflections on the consequences of public (criminal) policies and social or contextual developments. Scenarios are thus more than arbitrary, imaginary stories about future organised-crime developments, and can therefore stimulate policy makers to reflect on the foundations of their choices, make choices based on more than law-enforcement data alone and reflect on issues which are vital to societies (Verfaillie and Vander Beken, 2008a).

Scenario exercises indeed have the interesting feature that they allow for (organised crime) assessments to accept uncertainty and move away from analyses in which the likelihood of certain events is addressed. In practice, however, the belief that the future (of organised crime) cannot be known or predicted is not completely overturned. The purpose of scenarios remains anticipation of multiple but plausible futures. Scenarios therefore only accept and use uncertainties for some of the driving forces used. Some elements of the scenarios are considered predetermined and thus stable over a given future timeframe. They are used as 'certain' building blocks of the story. Other forces are labelled as uncertain, volatile or highly dynamic and have the potential to change the issue at stake in significant ways. Only driving forces of the latter nature that are 'critical' to the issue at stake, are the uncertainties used in scenario work. This implies that scenarios about the future of criminal markets in Europe will, for example, accept that it is uncertain to what extent globalisation will impact on dualisation (thus allowing for scenarios on the two extremes of the continuum of possibilities), while globalisation as such is considered as a certain building block supporting each of the scenarios developed (Verfaillie and Vander Beken, 2008b).

Scenario work shows similarities to applications of enactment theory in order to assess security-related issues (Collier, 2008). In this approach enactment-based knowledge, in contrast to archival-statistical knowledge, is produced by acting out certain future threats (like catastrophes) in order to understand their impact. The central point in this is that the limits of a specific knowledge form do not necessarily mean that a rational assessment in general is impossible (Collier, 2008: 229).

6.3.3 The real non-believers: resilience and the focus on uncertain high-impact events

Since the events of 2001, further stimulated by the 2008 credit crunch, attempts are being made to move the uncertainty approach in (organised) crime assessments one step further. Rather than trying to evaluate the likelihood of events (risk) or to make statements about uncertain but plausible future situations (scenarios or enactments), the future is seen as fundamentally uncertain. In such an approach, the focus is turned to the worst imaginable events, not only including the 'known unknowns' (events that are known to exist but whose timing or magnitude is not predictable) but also the 'unknown unknowns' (what is not imagined until the moment they cause impact) (Longstaff, 2005: 13). These highly unlikely or even unimaginable events stay out of the radar of all risk-based (organised crime) assessments or scenario work. Assessments focusing on such high-impact Black Swans (Taleb, 2007) have a *resilience* purpose (how to recover from a serious attack), rather than the ambition to calculate the likelihood and impact of criminal events. Especially in anti-terrorist policies, as in financial-market developments, an enhanced awareness of the uncertainties attached to systemic turning points and use of the concept of resilience can be seen (see, e.g., Cabinet Office, 2008).

This new approach, developing alongside the more traditional risk approach, opens interdisciplinary debates between scholars from different disciplines like natural science, environmental studies, disaster management, business, and markets (Klima, 2009). It is clear, as shown in anti-terrorist policies, that precautionary interventions taken to forestall possible future, uncertain, but big-impact events may carry with them their own risks. How can such interventions, and their costs, be evaluated since nobody actually knows what would have happened if the action had not been taken? A precautionary approach indeed widens the focus from specialists (whose risk techniques cannot quantify systemic uncertainties) to society as a whole. Justification for precautionary measures is then to be found in a democratic negotiation about the price a society is willing to pay, especially in terms of individual rights and freedoms, to prepare for high-impact events. This high-impact focus drives precautionary approaches into the direction of harm studies. Potential harms to (critical) infrastructures are indeed related to the seriousness of events or crimes and the impact they have (had) on society. Resilience approaches are, however, much more forward-looking than traditional harm assessments.

6.4 Conclusion

The nature, purpose and methodologies of organised-crime assessments have changed significantly over the last decades. We have seen that the traditional situation reports, listing numbers of criminals and criminal activities, are being replaced by risk-based assessments, in which concepts like threat, harm and vulnerability are used. Forecasting exercises, and warnings issued on this basis, assume that it is possible to find and manipulate the requested data and to make accurate and reliable assessments with sufficient transparency. Since September 2001, however, assessments that start from the assumption that is useful to prepare for the probable have become the subject of criticism as well. Calculating probabilities and risks in relation to activities like terrorism and organised crime in order to prepare for future events, is considered more and more as an impossible mission (see Chapter 2 on this in general). The uncertainties of the contemporary society, and criminal activities it induces, push the assessments on organised crime in new directions. Some still believe it is possible to engage in rational future-orientated assessments by reconsidering the methods to achieve that goal. As Wagner illustrates in Chapter 5, scenario and enactment exercises accept that uncertainties exist and play an important role in how (multiple) futures might look. Yet, they do not consider this as a sign that the risk paradigm and rationale has reached its limits. Organised-crime assessments to address and prepare for the future(s) may be different in form, but not impossible or irrelevant. Some believe, however, that transnational security threats, as posed by organised crime, are essentially unpredictable and highly uncertain. This shifts the focus to the ability to bounce back (resilience) from especially high- impact events and to the protection of critical infrastructures in society to all sorts of (even yet unknown) security attacks.

So far, all these changes in concepts, methods and paradigms have not had significant implications for the way organised-crime assessments are made. Indeed, situation reports have been renamed and reshuffled into threat, harm or vulnerability assessments to keep up with the requirements of a risk-driven society and some modest steps have been taken to introduce uncertainty into approaches and assessments of organised crime. Most of this, however, is still in its infancy and lacks conceptual clarity. It is time for the security community in general, and those responsible for warnings and responses to organised crime in particular, to open their eyes and see that others are engaged in comparable challenges. And to learn.

Part II

Communicating and Learning from Warnings

7

Mediatised Warnings: Late, Wrong, Yet Indispensable? Lessons from Climate Change and Civil War

Chiara de Franco and Christoph O. Meyer

7.1 Introduction

Why should we expect the news media to play an important role in warning about transnational risks? After all, governments have their intelligence services, regulators their scientific experts, and companies their in-house or external risk-consultants, each charged with identifying relevant risks and bringing them to the attention of decision-makers. Why should the news media have any role at all? We tend not to notice the dog that did not bark, and in fact prevention of drug trafficking, terrorist attacks, or conflict escalation is good news to most, but usually not newsworthy. Nonetheless, this chapter contends that the news media still play a crucial role, for good and for bad, in amplifying or muffling warnings.

In modern knowledge societies, and within pluralistic democratic systems, warnings are often mediatised, although in very different ways and to different degrees. The news media, for example, have diffused warnings about the impact of future migration flows, peak oil and increasing energy dependency, violent religious extremism, proliferation of WMDs or the rise of antibiotic-resistant superbugs and the implications of new technologies such as GMO food or nanotechnology. These threats are not just discussed on political and science pages of quality papers or magazines, but have also spread to products of popular culture, including a number of recent dystopian movies such as *The Day after Tomorrow, The Age of Stupid* and even *The Simpson Movie*.

However, it is not simple to evaluate the quality of media's role in the warning-response process, and even more difficult to identify best practices journalists should follow to ensure that their publications do not hinder but help effective prevention. The problem is that once a warning enters the media a number of things happen that are relevant to the acceptance of the warning as accurate, and to the probability that preventive or mitigating measures will be taken to address it. When mediatised, a warning is not just disseminated across various recipients and audiences, but also transformed through selection, amplification, framing, commentary, etc. What makes the picture even more complex is the fact that no general rule seems to apply: while in certain circumstances warnings are more effective if they remain hidden from the public and circulated only among those tasked to respond to the threat at stake, at other times reaching and mobilising the public is essential to the very success of prevention. Moreover, detached and rational messages can be appropriate for some kinds of warning, whereas emphasis on the emotional elements of threat can be the right strategy for other types of risk communication.

These issues have not been overlooked by scholars, but their research is still fragmented across a number of different disciplines. In the intelligence literature, an increasing number of studies have looked at the role of the media as a source of information as well as an instrument of policy and political power struggle (see, e.g., Gover and Goodman, 2009). In the area of foreign policy, authors have investigated the role of the media in bringing crises abroad to the attention of domestic audiences, prompting international organisations and third countries to act, as well as influencing the behaviour of different conflicting parties (see, e.g., Wolfsfeld, 1997; Robinson, 2002; Gilboa, 2003; Bahador, 2007). In the area of risk governance, the media are seen as playing a crucial role in how risks are perceived by the public, stakeholders, regulators, and policy makers, particularly in areas related to hazards arising from technological and environmental issues (Wahlberg and Sjöberg, 2000; Breakwell and Barnett, 2001). Apart from a number of primary empirical studies in the area of risk governance, usually in the form of case studies, the literature tends to draw on generic insights about news values, professional routines and organisational culture from media studies. However, these writings are often unclear about the yardsticks and criteria used to make judgements about media performance in communicating warning, and often downplay the role of communicators and regulators.

Therefore, this chapter aims firstly at better grounding the analysis of warning communication in theories about the way the news media work when dealing with warnings and what effects they have on policy, particularly in a transnational context. Secondly, it reflects on the performance of the news media in risk communication and on what the right benchmarks might be. To underpin this approach empirically, the chapter uses two different kinds of transnational risks, namely climate change and civil war, as exemplary cases illustrating and clarifying the interplay of various factors that condition media performance in communicating warnings.

7.2 Climate change and civil war news as mediatised warnings

Sharing some similarities, but also relating to very different spheres of knowledge, professional competence, policy formation and political action, climate change and civil war are well-suited case studies to advance our understanding of warning mediatisation through comparative analysis. Both climate change and civil war require coordinated international action because of their transboundary effects. Yet they both involve a substantial degree of uncertainty about the timing and scale of the expected harm. Macro-environmental issues such as climate change are 'characterised by uncertainty over consequences, diverse and multiple engaged interests, conflicting knowledge claims, and high stakes' (Lorenzoni et al., 2006: 65). Civil war remains a particularly difficult object to forecast. Even if researchers like Barbara Harff (2003) insist they can assess the risk of genocide through quantitative models, a high level of dissatisfaction remains over the capacity of both quantitative and qualitative methods to deliver sufficiently accurate and timely warning (Matveeva, 2006; Nyheim, 2008). Moreover, warnings about climate change and civil war are also difficult to communicate because individuals have problems visualising (Tonn et al., 2006) or imagining future periods. This is particularly true in the case of climate change, as research has shown that individuals consider scenarios describing events developing in the next 20–50 years to be so far into the future as to be almost completely hypothetical (O'Neill, 2009: 362). In the case of civil war, in contrast, spatial distance often adds complexity and makes the predicted events remote both geographically and temporally from the individuals to whom the warning is most probably directed (Ibid.: 361).

However, two substantial differences exist between the two cases. First, while climate change builds on the natural sciences, civil war is subject to a social-scientific epistemology. Arguably socially constructed, the distinction between 'natural' and 'social' has been applied to knowledge production in order to distinguish, and at the same time assimilate, the study of 'natural' and 'social' phenomena. In particular, the study of nature has offered a model epistemology which, grounded on empiricism, has become synonymous with 'science' (see Chapter 5). A necessary dialectic has therefore been established between this model and non-natural sciences willing to recognise their specificity, but at the same time to be treated as 'scientific.' While the resulting tension between refusal and adoption of empiricism is still present in the social sciences, and is indeed at the very basis of the existence of so many 'social sciences' and readings of the social, the epistemology, methodology and ontology of physics remain the scientific 'standard.'

As a consequence, natural sciences enjoy a social recognition that makes their claims more credible and trustworthy, while the social sciences still struggle for authority. On the one hand, 'the social' is popularly perceived as the domain of chaos and not completely knowable, while on the other hand physical nature – 'the natural' – is believed to be the domain of regular and universal laws and to be knowable 'scientifically.'

So strong are these popular perceptions that they reinforce each other, affecting both recognition and communication of social risks. With respect to social recognition, scholarly knowledge of conflicts is rarely used by policy makers, who often believe they possess better information, contacts and understanding of the conflict context than any forecasting system. On the contrary, scientists are an unavoidable point of reference for any policy makers willing to address environmental risks. Moreover, while only few resources are allocated to academic institutions and non-governmental organisations (NGOs) working to advance our understanding of violent escalations, the apparently direct usability of research in the natural sciences makes it a relatively rich sector.

In terms of risk communication, this means that risk attaching to a natural phenomenon communicated by the credible language of mathematics is considered more trustworthy than any 'social' risk, precisely because recipients do not consider themselves competent to judge these risks. Journalists, in particular, share a highly sceptical view that forecasting conflict is a science at all, and rarely report about scholarly predictions concerning violent conflicts. A second difference between the two cases lies in the scope and nature of their consequences. Climate change is a global risk threatening in the long-term everyone on earth, although in the medium term some more than others, whereas intrastate conflicts have usually regional consequences. The level of impact matters because it conditions policy makers' acceptance of a warning as relevant, but also news media's attitudes regarding the potential story. In the case of a civil war, we can expect governments and media to engage with warnings about a conflict developing in a region in which they have some sort of interest, whereas it less likely to see any diplomatic or military involvement by a third country with no strategic interest in the area. This contrasts with climate change as the geographical spread and level of harm facilitates a closer connection between the political responsibility of democratic governments to take action and of media outlets to inform and mobilise citizens.

Starting from the above-mentioned characteristics of climate change and civil war, how can we understand the process by which warnings about these matters are mass-communicated? Peter Weingart et al. (2000) identify the rationalist-instrumental model of science communication as a naive starting point for many debates: 'scientific research helps to discover an environmental problem; it identifies options for the problem's potential solution; scientists inform politicians of these findings; and, as political decision-making can always be expected to suffer from some inertia or be distorted by interests that run counter to (scientific) concerns, scientists can also try to create public awareness to foment political pressure' (Weingart et al., 2000: 262). According to this framework, if the information fails to engender action, this is because of misrepresentations of scientific information by the media, or 'miscommunication' between experts and members of the media of the kind experienced in intercultural encounters (Peters, 1995: 44–45). Following this argument, the solution to the problem of unsuccessful communication of risks involves more and better information and mutual understanding for all the parties involved.

Even if very detailed, this explanation misses a crucial point: it is the news media that produce the news, not simply the journalists, and, as any other organisation, the news media have their own rules for determining if and how a given issue must be covered. This, in turn, can be compatible or incompatible with the political or scientific criteria of relevance. A mass-mediated communication process is led by notions of authority, entertainment, newness, and so on, which can cause some communication failure and cannot be simply dismissed as miscommunication, misrepresentation or misunderstanding. When depicting the world, the media produce their own narrative, which may vary also substantially from other social discourses, the political and the scientific in particular. Particular ideas and worldviews are produced, reproduced and transformed in media discourses; others are excluded from them (e.g. Bennett, 1988; Fairclough, 1995; Allan et al., 2000). Indeed, operations of codification of the issue into media discourses are directed by organisational cultures and professional rules and routines.

In the next sections, the most important factors determining how warnings about climate change and civil war are mass-mediated will be analysed systematically by focusing on the role of news values, journalistic routines, and news cycles. Finally, an examination of the possible effects of mass-mediated warning over policy making will follow to evaluate media performance and assess the compatibility of warning mediatisation with both democratic and scientific processes.

7.2.1 News values and frames

News values, a term coined by Walter Lippmann (1922–1965), are the criteria by which media outlets choose stories and attach relevance to them. Lippmann named relevance, proximity, sensationalism, facticity and unambiguity to be the most important news values, and the concept was further developed over time to comprise references to elite nations or people, negativity or conflict (Galtung and Ruge, 1965; Gans, 1979; Harcup and O'Neill, 2001). News values determine both news gathering and news making, because they not only discriminate between newsworthy and non-newsworthy events, but also between newsworthy and non-newsworthy editing of those events. As the media are essentially story tellers who construct plots and create characters by following the universal characteristics of narratives (Propp, 1928; Greimas and Courtés, 1982), news values can also be seen as 'story values.' These can favour stories coming from a certain country, about certain people, and regarding certain actions, but they can also favour the use of some specific 'frames' in which to tell those stories. When telling stories, in fact, the media select 'some aspects of a perceived reality and makes them more salient in a communicating text, in such a way as to promote a particular problem definition, causal interpretation, moral evaluation, and/or treatment recommendation,' which is what is usually called 'framing' (Entman, 1993: 52).

What is crucial to understand is that a complex mix of internal and external, cultural and organisational conditions determine news values and shape what is known as 'news making.' The latter, therefore, is a result of the relations and interactions between journalists, editors, managers, owners, politicians, spin doctors, and advertisers in a chain of actions and reactions which is very difficult to untangle.

As any other portion of the reality that is being mediatised, knowledge claims are also transformed by the application of the news criteria. In particular, a few relevant phenomena occur. First, as the vagaries of scholarly hypotheses fail to sell experts' opinions as 'interesting news,' the media translate hypotheses into certainties. In the case of climate change, early scientific warnings, although characterised by many reservations, were taken seriously and translated into the certainty of an impending 'catastrophe' (see Carvalho, 2007). This transformation was achieved by changing what climatologists described as gradual, and hidden beneath seasonal and yearly fluctuations, into an alarming sequence of events and into concrete, everyday experiences. The manifold scientific uncertainties and methodological problems remained almost completely unnoticed, while policy makers were accused of having ignored early scientific warnings for far too long.

Further problems arising from the transformation of uncertainties into certainties have emerged in the last months when the enormous body of scientific evidence produced in the last 30 years by different scientific communities was scrutinised and re-examined by climate sceptics. The latter have questioned the scientific trustworthiness of warning about climate change by referring, not to the proper scientific theory and evidence, but to its mass-mediated version. Reference to mediatised warnings also caused the events following the online release of hacked emails sent by respected researchers at the University of East Anglia that seemed to confirm the sceptics' conspiratorial views. Thus, although scientists insisted that the content of their emails was not in conflict with their official predictions about climate change, an investigation had to be launched and the data supporting the science had to be made publicly accessible. At the same time, the scientists' long-term refusal to release the data in response to a freedom-of-information request, on the basis that 'the data doesn't really change the analysis at all', left a bad impression in media coverage. In this case, despite having been at the forefront of the man-made climate argument, the media worked as an amplifier of the sceptical view and gave room to the challengers of the dominant thesis about climate change.

The media's appetite for certainty makes them also reluctant to cover claims or warnings that a potential conflict could escalate in the near future: a conflict is usually only reported if it is already in full-swing, not when it is predicted by various sources. This principle is further strengthened by another news value favouring stories that can be illustrated by images. Unless accessibility of the region for journalists is an issue, conflicts that have already escalated into a civil war are usually highly newsworthy because they can be accompanied by graphic footage. On the contrary, events developing in the future are not only difficult to imagine or visualise, but they are also events without pictures. Translated into warning communication, this means that warnings of civil wars will be inevitably late: 'unless you have a situation that has come to carnage point it is difficult to obtain coverage; and carnage is very tricky, because it can't be so systemic and regular that it ceases to be newsworthy. And yet, when it becomes newsworthy, it tends to happen so quickly that you have difficulty moving the machine and getting there in time to cover the killing' (Power, 2004: 4–5).

On the other hand, conflict is the almost perfect media story as well as the ideal frame for any kind of report. Most hypotheses about the role of the media in escalating conflicts are based precisely on this insight, and media logic is said to favour stories about conflicts over those about cooperation, agreement or peace. The same mechanism can impact on the mediatisation of science warnings. Science news often ends up being about the politics behind science and the tensions dividing different scientists' communities or politicians. Paradoxically, for example, the widespread consensus surrounding the science of climate change pushed journalists at the Barcelona and Copenhagen summits to focus on the dispute over the appropriate political response and the political conflict between developed and developing countries. Instead of reporting about science, journalists emphasised the 'red-blooded cut-and-thrust of negotiation – even if all it leads to is the Copenhagen Accord' (Kirby, 2010: 1).

Finally, tensions also arise between essentially national media and the transnational character of the risks we are analysing, which call for a collective responsibility transcending the borders of the nation-states (see Olausson, 2009). The news media, indeed, are essentially national organisations, sensitive to national audiences more than to anything else, globalisation notwithstanding. In the case of civil war, this means that conflicts with a regional or strategic proximity to the nation the news organisation belongs to will more easily become news than those developing far away in a region of no or little strategic relevance. This also means that the international organisation in charge of collective security, the UN, and the world superpower, the United States, will be the most frequent addressee of mediatised warnings about civil war, notwithstanding the appropriateness of their intervention and the existence of other actors with stronger interests, will or capabilities to act.

In the case of climate change, the fact that the responsibility for mitigation is primarily delegated to international institutions, whereas responsibility for adaptation is left to the local or national spheres, has led the media to use two distinct frames: the collective action frame of adaptation (that is, action intending to adapt society to climate change), and the collective action frame of mitigation (that is, action aiming at reducing greenhouse gas emissions). Instead of being presented as two sides of the same coin, the two frames exist in parallel to each other, hardly ever appearing in the same news items (Pielke, 1998; Adger et al., 2004; Tol, 2005).

7.2.2 Journalistic routines and norms

In addition to news values, professional routines and norms can also affect the way news is collected and edited. In particular, the credibility of the individual or organisation issuing the warning is central in the news-gathering process, as journalists will usually not be able to verify the knowledge-claim underlying a forecast themselves. As journalists are afraid of being wrong, they tend to use either official sources they can blame for not having been accurate, if needed, or sources they trust because of previous experiences or existing professional relationships.

However, they do not necessarily choose the scientifically most trustworthy sources, but those who are best at tailoring the story in a way that maximises its news value and minimising the additional work required by time-scarce journalists: 'The great thing about that sort of story is that the journalist can never be wrong: so much is going on at a COP that there is always something you can write without fear of contradiction. But don't try that with the science, or it is liable to blow up in your face' (Kirby, 2010: 3).

In the case of climate change, Trumbo (1995) has identified three distinct phases in the media coverage based on a shift in sources. In the beginning, the media started reporting about environmental risks by using scientists, and then turned to policy makers and special interest groups. This was clearly due to the fact that the latter were ultimately better than the former at pushing their scripts into the media, which has in turn led scientists to change their language and behaviour in order to adapt to the media and finally make their voice heard by the public.

With regard to warnings about civil war, reporters are usually dependent on official sources, especially in the early stage of the issue being covered and even more if they do not have any other source to obtain some specific information. Upon arrival in a conflict zone, reporters start relying on official sources because they usually need to get a press pass. Then, only rarely do they receive from their editors the resources they need to get alternative information, not to mention ensuring physical security and access to the areas where the fighting is taking place. Moreover, following the norms of balance and objectivity, journalists usually wait for the official version of the story before using problematic labels such as 'genocide.' In Rwanda, for example, the killing 'looked like genocide to them, it looked like an intent to exterminate...every last Tutsi. But journalists refrain from stating what they know to be true' (Power, 2004: 6).

Journalistic routines determining the way news sources are selected can interact with other professional norms, especially those aiming at objective and balanced reporting. Boykoff and Boykoff (2004), for example, have argued that in the last years, as climate-change sceptics have started to be more active in the public sphere, the journalistic norm of balance has led to biased depictions of knowledge on climate change in the US prestige press with an excessive weight given to those that deny its anthropogenic origins or that the problem is scientifically provable. Interacting with the value favouring news about conflicts and negativity, the norm of balance has eventually emphasised scientific divergences to the detriment of an existing large scientific consensus. Similarly, Antilla (2005) has analysed the frames constructed by a large number of US newspapers and wire services in relation to climate-change science, and contrasted the growing consensus in the scientific community with a media-generated image of controversy and a disproportionate attention being given to a handful of climate-change sceptics.

Of course, the norm of balance can short-circuit the rules governing the selection of news sources. The recent move of the BBC from a balanced account of both mainstream and sceptic positions on climate change to a much more politicised narrative, distinguishing between an overwhelming scientific consensus and a small minority of sceptics and framing climate change as a security issue, can be, in fact, explained as a consequence of the BBC's ultimate preference for the British government as a source. Journalistic norms and routines also vary in different national and cultural settings: balance, for example, is particularly salient in the US context, whereas in Germany it is considered much more acceptable for journalists to take stance about who is considered to be most trustworthy and what is right.

Shanahan and Good (2000) have also advanced a hypothesis emphasising the relevance of journalists' subjectivity. In fact, they suggest that variations in actual temperature can function as what social psychologists call the 'availability heuristic' and play a role in journalists' attention to the issue of climate change. In fact, although it should be obvious that a broadly and generally increasing global temperature defines the phenomenon of global warming and, therefore, attracts coverage, it is also true that personal perceptions about daily temperature abnormalities may well play a role in what journalists think about global warming and in how they report it.

7.2.3 The news cycle

The news cycle, as the temporal rules about when news should be released, has also an impact on the form that warnings assume when mass-mediated.

There is a noticeable structural discrepancy between the news cycle on one side and science or conflict cycles on the other: while the timeline for 'news' is hours to a day, the development of science or of a conflict takes at least months and usually years. In the case of climate change, numerous studies have examined problems related to the cyclical nature of issue coverage. Such studies have sought to explain why coverage fluctuates severely. Ungar (1995), for example, has identified three distinct phases of global climate-change reporting: a first peak in 1988, then a decline in the early 1990s, finally to resurface on most news agendas in late 1997. He explains this as the inability of the topic to sustain constantly the status of a dramatic crisis. After the issue decline in the early 1990s, events such as the Kyoto Summit and El Niño's dramatic return may partially explain the re-emergence of climate-change reporting. Fluctuation in coverage could also result from what Downs (1972) first identified as the issue-attention cycle of reporting about environmental issues: constituted by five stages: pre-problem; alarmed discovery and euphoric enthusiasm; realising the cost; gradual decline of interest; and post-problem.

In the case of conflict, instead, the 24-hour news cycle introduced by cable news channels, as opposed to the day-by-day pace of the earlier daily newspaper cycle, has produced what is known as 'media fatigue' or 'compassion fatigue' (Moeller, 1999). It has been found that, after a first immediate shock that can trigger action, the broadcasting of images of famine, fighting and death, usually linked to an escalating conflict, no longer produce compassion in their audience and can lead to a consequent decline in the public's interest for the covered conflict. Indeed, the continuous use of the same type of images and the parallel definition and re-definition of the image, can change its efficacy over time. After an initial stage, when it 'attacks' (Magli, 2006) its reader because it is unexpected and emotive, the image can persist and be subject to a continuous erosion of its meaning until a final loss of sense and obsolescence (Ibid.). The images coming from Palestine picturing the second Intifada are probably the most graphic example illustrating this phenomenon which clearly diminishes the media's ability to build the public agenda and ultimately influence foreign-policy making. Besides, media fatigue can start a negative trend, causing a conflict to disappear from the public sphere, at least till the next escalation stage.

A cycle can also be detected in the way the media frame certain issues. In particular, the problem definition and its moral evaluation can change over time in the media coverage of a political issue. In the case of environmental risks, a radical shift occurred in the last ten years from the reductionist 'global warming' to the more comprehensive and explanatorily powerful 'climate change', and from a merely ecological issue to a security issue. Similarly, civil wars are usually reported first as an 'incoming humanitarian disaster' that subsequently becomes either a security issue, revolving around the threat of refugees fleeing across national borders, or a moral issue, based on the re-framing of the humanitarian emergency into genocide. This process of framing and re-framing which follows the events, but also public, political and scientific debates, is the result of a complex interaction between the media and all interested sectors of society, at the national and international levels.

7.3 Possible media effects

Having clarified the way the mediatisation process transforms warnings, this section aims at advancing our understanding of the effects mediatised warnings can have on the political process. In fact, before evaluating media performance, it is essential to recognise what the possible effects of mediatised warnings are, as well as what factors condition their occurrence. Focusing on news making alone has often led analysts to reductionist conclusions, describing media performance but not clarifying it. Understanding the media starts with the analysis of news making, but remains incomplete unless the effects of reporting are explored as well.

7.3.1 The 'CNN Effect' and the Agenda Setting

Two concepts developed in media studies can be used to understand how exactly preventive policy making can be affected by the mediatisation of warning: Agenda Setting and the CNN Effect. While the first has a wide range of applications to different policy areas, the second is rooted in studies about foreign-policy making and humanitarian crises in particular.

The term 'CNN Effect' attaches to the hypothesis that when media coverage exposes human suffering and atrocities, public pressure to respond forces governments to do something (Cohen, 1994; Hoge, 1994; Robinson, 2002; Bahador, 2007). Applied to other policy areas, the CNN Effect suggests that the media are able to change political behaviour and force politicians to do what they would not otherwise do (de Franco, 2010). This effect rests on a sort of empathy the media establish between their audience and the issue at stake, whether actual or potential, human or animal, suffering due to conflicts, pandemics, GMO, or other environmental risks. Moreover, the CNN Effect presupposes that the media are able to suggest a solution either independently or taking the side of an advocacy group. According to this hypothesis, it is not the accuracy of the information provided or the analysis of the situation which convinces policy makers to intervene, but the eruption of emotions in both the public and policy makers, given the emotional power of images and live coverage of events. Moreover, following Entman (2000), this process gives power to the media because it raises the salience of alleged public feelings as depicted by the news.

When applied to the warning discourse, the CNN Effect becomes an hypothesis about the way the media becomes a warner itself and attracts attention to an impending crisis while asking decision-makers to adopt measures which can mitigate or solve the problem. Media pressure can change decision-makers' calculation of political expediency (when the reputation of the US President and hence his ability to lead is endangered through inaction) or touches them at an emotional level – the 'not on my watch' reaction. Through 'priming' one particular issue, the media may affect the importance organisations and decision-makers attach to the crisis in question. Moreover, the media can support advocacy coalitions of NGOs and parliamentarians in favour of a problem-solving approach, and delegitimising political opponents and bureaucratic resistance.

In any case, the CNN Effect seems possible only when a crisis is mature or a disaster has already occurred, as in the case of Kosovo (Bahador, 2007), which does not mean that there can be no media effects at an earlier stage. According to the Agenda Setting theory (Lang and Lang, 1981; Cohen, 1963; Shaw and McCombs, 1979), in fact the media determine which elements of the public discourses the audience notices or ignores, and consequently emphasises or neglects. This effect is clearly not the outcome of the choices made by a single journalist or newspaper, but the result of the complex functioning of news organisations and of the media system as such.

Applied to the early warning discourse, Agenda Setting underlines that the media can have an important role in the warning-response dynamics because they can focus public discourse on a certain issue and frame that issue as a problem that has to be solved. In this case, the media put that issue on the political agenda and finally determine the agenda itself, without influencing the outcome of the final decision (which is what the CNN Effect argues instead). In the case of foreign-policy making, Nye (1999) has argued that the Agenda Setting function of the media forces politicians to intervene in certain international crises and to neglect others that are even more serious. In the 1990s, for example, the media favoured humanitarian interventions in situations, 'which regard indirectly the western security, but which do not menace directly western interests, such as Kosovo, Bosnia, Somalia, and Rwanda crisis,' (Nye, 1999: 14), to the detriment of strategically more relevant threats, like 'vital threats to the West comparable with that which the Soviet Union has represented,' (Ibid.: 13–14) or 'imminent, but not vital threats to the western interest, such as that coming from Iraq in 1991' (Ibid.: 14).

An early application of the Agenda Setting model to environmental issues is provided by Atwater (1985). Atwater's interest was in the environment as an example of an 'unobtrusive' issue, in which most audience members have little direct experience. Unobtrusive issues such as the environment can be distinguished from 'obtrusive' issues such as the economy, which people experience directly and viscerally. Atwater found that the media set environmental issue agendas; he also found that this extends to the 'sub-issue' level. These considerations are of course under revision, because it is no longer possible to think of the environment as an unobtrusive issue. In fact, people are now so used to 'experiencing' environmental phenomena that members of the public as well as media professionals may erroneously believe that a long-term global issue like climate change is manifest in particularly hot, dry or otherwise unusual weather. Such beliefs could impact not only on how the public and the media understand and 'create' the issue, but also on how policy makers frame their solutions.

7.4 Mediatised warnings: an evaluation

A comparison between warnings about climate change and civil war can illustrate both the challenges and opportunities of mediatised warnings. In particular, it highlights that we cannot decouple news making from media effects. An evaluation of mediatised warning, which starts from idealised models of news making, scientific and the political processes, has no added value if it is not combined with the analysis of the short- and long-term effects of media coverage. Media translation of scientific warnings is neither automatically positive nor necessarily negative. None of the discussed characteristics of mass-mediated warnings are *per se* problematic in terms of their effects on preventive policy. The transformation of hypotheses into certainties, the use of a conflict frame, even the 'sensationalisation' and dramatisation of risk, can lead to both misguided action and badly designed policy, but also to public mobilisation and political support for an issue that would have been otherwise disregarded. Similarly, even if a journalist or a particular media outlet was able properly to evaluate a risk and publicise this risk without exaggeration, the net effect could still be negative if secrecy was essential to finding a compromise between conflict parties.

Moreover, assessments about media performance can change substantially as soon as the focus shifts from the short to the long-term. It is apparent, for example, that the media have greatly contributed to public awareness about climate change by framing it as a certain catastrophe and by evoking fear in the public at large. Journalists have no doubt quickly understood their role in mobilising people to take action and reduce the impact of their consumption habits over the environment, but can instilling fear be the right strategy for facilitating climate-change mitigation policies? Fearful representations of climate change appear to be memorable and may initially attract individuals' attention, but they can also act to distance and disempower individuals in terms of their sense of personal engagement with the issue. According to O'Neill, fear does not pay out as climate-related fear appeals are very difficult to sustain in the long-term (O'Neill, 2009: 362). Moreover, increased concern for one risk may decrease concern for other risks given that individuals only have a certain capacity for worry. So it could be posited that communicating particularly fearful messages about certain climatic phenomena (e.g., dramatically rising sea levels because of ice-sheet melt) might desensitise individuals to concern about other potentially more salient concerns they could act on constructively (O'Neill, 2009: 363). The same research shows that there are other types of visual imagery, icons and combinations of messages involving some degree of connection with 'the everyday,' in both spatial and temporal terms, that can be engaging and can specifically help to make climate change a personally salient issue for people and one that they feel able to do something about (O'Neill, 2009: 372–373).

In the case of civil war, even if journalists are sincerely interested in making a positive contribution to preventing or managing a conflict, the use of emotional frames may backfire. When the media reports about a violent clash, they tend to transform the multitude of contrasting stories constituting that conflict into a single and certain narrative. Not only do nuances disappear, but also the tone of the report escalates: the violence on the ground easily becomes 'ethnic cleansing' or even 'genocide,' while politicians are criticised for standing idly by and are called to do 'something', which is never specified but nonetheless described as necessary and obvious. As a result, the so-called journalism of attachment (Bell, 1998) and the frame of compassion fill newspapers articles every time an armed conflict becomes the subject of coverage. One can doubt that using emotions to communicate warnings is the best option available, especially because the public at large cannot do anything to stop the conflict, apart from exercising pressure on their governments. In the Balkan Wars, for example, most western journalists supported the Muslims and vehemently advocated military intervention against the Serbs. Even if this was arguably the right thing to do then, doubts have emerged about journalists' practice of playing favourites instead of reporting from all sides, running the risk of neglecting historical and political contexts of violence and setting themselves up as judge and jury (Hume, 1997: 4–5). Indeed, the same mechanism can lead the media to become an actor in the escalation of a conflict, especially when it contributes to further polarisation of the conflicting parties, formulates conflict as zero-sum, and/or delegitimises parties on one side or the other (Reuben, 2009).

Similarly, the unintentional consequences of mediatised warnings can be equally functional or dysfunctional with regard to preventive policies. Some communications about climate change or civil war can be *functional,* if they highlight transnational threats at a time when risk governance and preventive policy have only partially become internationalised as well as *dysfunctional,* if they cause quick disengagement due to an excessively emotional coverage of the issue and consequent detachment or 'compassion fatigue.'

Choosing a media-effects focus, it can be said that the impact of the media is highest in the cognitive realm, when they set public and political agendas and frames issues in a certain way. Whereas news values can obscure a warning that is judged as not newsworthy in some instances – in which case the impact of the warning depends on its being communicated through bureaucratic and scientific advisory channels – they can equally lead journalists to pay attention to other warnings.

With respect to the framing of political responses to risks, the news media are generally less influential, particularly in the short-term and particularly when preventive policies depend on an internationally coordinated response. In the medium and long term, however, the news media may affect the emergence and strengthening of political movements in support of preventive action in particular fields, such as preventing climate change and genocide. Whether the impact of the news media is positive or negative will depend to substantial degree on all actors' ability to recognise that the scientific and the political processes as well as the news making need to preserve key elements of autonomy.

The CNN Effect, for example, is a Janus-faced phenomenon, especially as it functions on the basis of images and emotions. The media's demand for a certain preventive policy is not necessarily a good thing: it can be based on a superficial and ultimately inaccurate analysis of the situation; it can propose a solution which is not appropriate; it can be a mere alarm which is not followed by any policy advice. In particular, the media's ability to address a certain problem proposing an appropriate solution seems to vary according to different policy areas. A missing link between the news and the kind of policy to adopt is particularly frequent in cases where a technical understanding of the problem is required. Whereas this is not really an issue in the case of civil war, news about environmental issues frequently faces this problem (see, e.g., Wilson, 2000).

Another aspect of assessing the news media's performance is whether it manages to convey the transnational dimension of risks, meaning not only the degree to which other countries and communities will be affected by a threat, but also the extent to which the perception of the 'threat' will differ according to worldviews and values held, and how this then reflects on international problem-solving efforts. With respect to this, what is lacking most is a vertical debate about cross-border risks between primarily nationally-focused news media. Such a debate could help to illuminate the extent to which risk perceptions are culturally contingent, related to beliefs and views about technology, trust in authorities and collective memories related to similar occurrences. Without this kind of discussion, it will be difficult to mobilise political pressure for transnational solutions to cross-border problems, advance an equitable distribution of costs and benefits, and hold national decision-makers accountable for failure.

7.5 Conclusions

This chapter has aimed at providing an overview of how the news media cover risks and impacts on public opinion and political response to warnings about such risks. Insights from studies about foreign-policy making and climate change reveal that the news media can influence both negatively and positively the process of translating expert warnings into political action within democracies. On the one hand, they can force politicians to take notice of an issue and undertake appropriate preventive policy, but, on the other hand, they can favour snap decisions with disproportionate effects, the exclusion or distortion of expert advice and high public expectations and fears. The challenge remains one of finding the appropriate normative yardstick, or combination of yardsticks, to judge the appropriateness of mediatised warnings. In retrospect, it is easy to assess media performance, but what are the best journalistic practices that work, without the benefit of hindsight? When should experts overrule public concerns about risks, which, as we know from various studies (Renn, 2008), operate quite differently from scientific assessment about risk probability, consequences and the cost-benefit distribution? What we have is in essence, a clash between the logic of the scientific process, the logic of news making and the logic of majoritarianism within democracies. Is it reasonable to expect the media to judge who is right in scientific debates and refrain from coverage of international negotiations? Is it reasonable to expect journalists to portray risks in a way that will be misunderstood or ignored by audiences? Is it reasonable to expect policy makers to ignore previous electoral promises to address a new risk through costly measures, to stand-up to media criticism after things go wrong, to argue that some risks cannot be eradicated, or to take measures they will be unlikely to get credit for when successful, but will be surely blamed if they fail?

A first, almost impossible option would be that media professionals make accurate assessments about the nature of the risk at stake and the scope of its communication. A very basic decision could then be taken about how necessary risk communication is and what its style should be. The choice of communicating a warning is, in fact, usually taken by media professionals on the basis of a social function the media has and wants to exercise: social mobilisation. Described as 'campaigning for societal objectives in the spheres of politics, war, economic development, work and sometimes religion' (McQuail, 1983: 99) mobilisation exists in autocratic societies all the time, in new nations during the nation-building phase, and in democracies in times of crisis and warfare. Mobilisation may result from a governmental initiative or from the media's own initiative. In the case of climate change, mobilisation was attempted by creating fear, while compassion is the vehicle to mobilise in the case of civil war. However, the assessment of how necessary public mobilisation is for different risks remains a crucial point. Sometimes, for example, publicity can spoil diplomatic activities in the context of conflict mediation. Media professionals should therefore develop a higher awareness of the public (dis)utility of mediatised risk communication and take these into account when making decisions whether and how to cover a given risk. Unfortunately, this would be strongly in contrast with other rules and criteria which favour competition among media outlets as well as commercial standards. No newspaper could afford renouncing to cover an issue that other outlets could scoop and no media company can be asked to act on the public interest first, as most of them are private corporations looking primarily for profit. No doubt, non-publicity would in some cases advance the public good, but whom can we trust to be the judge of this? The news media's role can never be evaluated by their impact on policy alone, given the crucial role they play in pluralistic democratic societies. Inappropriate publicity, overreaction and distortion are the price we pay for freedom of speech and vigorous debate.

A second, more feasible, way would be changing the conditions of the media's information gathering. A critical issue is how the media select their sources, as they can be pushed by various advocacy groups to take sides and eventually become biased in how they frame different solutions or even simply represent the scientific state of the art or the conflict situation. In particular, questions arise over the possibility of preserving norms of scientific as well as democratic processes when scientific knowledge becomes politicised and scientists mobilise the populace by using the news media, which may spread fear and ask for extraordinary measures for preventive action against a deadly threat. Warnings may thus 'securitise' a given referent object to an extent that normal scientific and democratic debate is short-circuited and persuasion turns into propaganda.

As spin doctors and news management professionals take the lead when journalists do not have the necessary expertise to judge different positions, and create an autonomous narrative as well as an independent agenda, two strategies become necessary. On the one hand, journalists should be able to understand complex scientific issues concerning both 'the natural' and 'the social.' Even though a specific education either in the natural or social sciences cannot possibly become a necessary condition for access to news-media professions, at least continuous training should be provided by employers in order to facilitate a science journalism that is better able to understand and convey complexity, uncertainty and trade-offs. On the other hand, scientists should become better communicators. Not only should they stop delegating to professionals the communication of their research, but when they do speak to the media they need to be aware of how they operate. In addition, there should be more interchange between both worlds, allowing more scientists an entry route to journalism.

Having said this, we do not advocate 'understanding the media' to mean necessarily 'adapting to the media.' The mediatisation of the scientific process has neither improved the communication of scientific warnings nor led to better control of scientists over the impact of their warnings. Science mediatisation has to date brought scientists to look for media visibility and therefore to make public the results of their research by simply adjusting their language to that of the media. However, this has only reinforced the existing limits of mediatised warnings (Weingart, 1998), which may undermine scientific credibility for short-term effect. The 1997 ICCP report's overestimation of the rate at which Himalayan glaciers were receding can be considered a telling example of this phenomenon (see, e.g., Webster, 2010). The unmediated communication of science can have an added value precisely because it employs a different language and can engage the public, which is too often depicted as needing spoon-feeding.

The ongoing professionalisation of scientific risk communication is a symptom of an increasingly tighter coupling of the three communities: experts, media and legislators. As there is evidence of scientists packaging and targeting their discoveries to the media (Weingart et al., 2000), similarly decision-makers seem to have undertaken media training to produce successful sound bites and adjusted decision-making to fit news cycles (Mazolleni and Schulz, 1998). Clearly, problems arise when this coupling leads to bad science, bad journalism and bad policy, rather than to more self-critical, informed and differentiated professional practice in each of three areas. It remains to be seen whether the current crisis in the commercial viability of the conventional media will have only negative effects for quality journalism or whether it opens up new ways for experts to become engaged directly in debates about risks without professional intermediation.

8

Do They Listen? Communicating Warnings: An Intelligence Practitioner's Perspective

William Shapcott

8.1 Introduction

This short chapter seeks to examine, from a practitioner's perspective, some of the elements that contribute to successful and unsuccessful communication of warnings to policy makers. For this purpose, it assumes that accurate and timely warnings are available and focuses on the communications aspects of the warning process. It does so by drawing on experience of the last seven years from within the European Union (EU), looking primarily at our processes and experience. That said, some of the examples mentioned are not of course just of warning interest to the EU but also to a wide range of other international actors.[1]

As discussed elsewhere in this book, warnings can take many forms and come via many channels. This chapter focuses more on warnings delivered in formal or semi-formal frameworks, from bodies delivering warning products to policy makers. It also treats warning as an exercise in assessment and evaluation rather than the delivery of physical intelligence to consumers who then make their own judgements (consistent with Chapter 3). With the increase in ease of access to large volumes of generally available information this evaluation process is open to a much larger group of actors. This group extends well beyond classical intelligence agencies, and now includes policy makers themselves, the media, lobby groups and other non-governmental organisations (NGOs), all of whom are now in the business of making and communicating warnings.

The chapter focuses on the communication of warnings and not the quality of the warnings themselves. It examines the extent to which concepts, doctrines and frameworks contribute to the communication of warnings, as well as the manner and style of the communications themselves. The chapter also recognises that the EU context for warning is both new and rather complex. For while national machinery may well be complicated by the need to bring together a potentially wide range of warning actors and policy makers, in the EU it is rendered even more complex by the fact that we have 27 Member States (MS), most with their own *warners* and all with their own policy makers, as well as the EU institutions themselves. Finally, by way of preamble, it must be borne in mind that while much of the discussion around this subject includes the role of intelligence agencies in the warning process, the EU itself has no intelligence agency of its own, no secret intelligence assets, and that therefore many of the features of the traditional intelligence cycle are absent or only present in a very distorted form.

8.2 How structures and frameworks affect the communication of warning

Firstly, to what extent does a framework or a structure contribute to the warning function and the effectiveness of communication within an organisation? There is often a tendency amongst students of government to overstate the degree of organisation that exists within governments. Or put another way, governments are often more disorganised than they appear. In the UK, the Assessments Staff and the Joint Intelligence Committee (JIC) would claim, with some justification, that they have a clear early-warning function, able to give both strategic notice and on occasion more precise tactical warning. But the UK is a rarity in having such a solid and developed structure. In many other countries there is a range of ministries or agencies, all largely ploughing their own furrows. In the better organised countries there will be much information sharing. Only occasionally though is there a body charged with collective analysis for the production of early warning.[2]

So it is no surprise that the EU is little better organised. The Council of Ministers does dispose analytical structures, particularly the EU Situation Centre (SITCEN) and the Intelligence Directorate of the EU Military Staff (EU MS) that are charged with analysis and assessment, and indeed with early warning. There has however never been a proper discussion of the organisation of warning, no concepts developed, no doctrine and no agreed terminology. The idea that an early-warning function is a good and necessary thing is *acquis*, but how it should work is not well defined. There is an assumption that the issue is fully understood and therefore needs no further discussion or definition.

Sometimes of course, in the early stages of an organisation, it is a good thing to not have too many concepts or doctrines to tie you down. They take time to agree, especially in a multinational framework, and they can be restrictive. We have developed our own ideas of how to do the general situation assessment work that is our primary function. This work is of an estimative nature, drawing on assessed rather than current intelligence provided by MS. Whilst it is not current intelligence, it certainly has warning value and is delivered as such to our clients. Our experience shows, though, that this organic development process contributes quite quickly to a failure to communicate properly. It is my firm conviction that having properly understood and shared concepts and doctrine is an important element in ensuring proper communication between *warner* and warned.

Having said the EU Council has no written early-warning concept or doctrine, I have also related that it has developed some early-warning processes, together with mechanisms for identifying the information needs of decision-makers. Before looking into communication, I should like briefly to describe these processes. The first peculiarity for the EU, and a big complication, is that no one is in charge and therefore no one is solely responsible. Anyone, MS or institution, can announce a warning. Nevertheless, certain elements of the Council Secretariat (SITCEN, Policy Unit (PU), EU MS Intelligence Directorate) plus the Commission (DG RELEX) collaborate in one formal element, which is the development every six months of a 'Watchlist' of countries in crisis or at risk of crisis. This list of 40 countries is put to MS for approval, after which it is used as a trigger for further assessment work, work which may contain more detailed warnings. The Watchlist seeks to look ahead 18–24 months and to identify those countries in, on the verge of or at risk of crisis.

The Watchlist is, though simple, the first tool at EU level that goes some way to identifying the priorities of decision-makers. Before the Lisbon Treaty, the Presidency had an important role in refining the Watchlist, tasking the SITCEN and EU MS Intelligence Directorate with a six-month programme of work that takes the areas of concern identified in the Watchlist, refining them by giving them a sense of priority and adding additional elements, particularly horizontal and thematic issues not captured by a geographically based Watchlist.

The regular assessment work that follows, done by us and our military partners, may include warnings as situations develop. This is where we begin to find that the lack of conceptual foundation begins to intrude. There being no concept of early warning or of early-warning communication, we have invented the process above. MS have come to expect regular assessments of Watchlist countries, but without necessarily regarding these as explicit early warnings. It should be borne in mind that many MS take the view that it is the responsibility of the Brussels structures simply to describe situations and for the MS to judge whether the situation so described merits a reaction. In other words, it is for them to decide whether the description constitutes a warning and warrants a reaction. Whether they feel warned and motivated to react is down partly to a judgement on their part as to how the situation affects their interests. Notwithstanding this notion of MS primacy, as the Brussels bodies have grown in competence and confidence, and as perhaps their judgement has improved, they have become more explicit or strident when it comes to announcing warnings.

8.3 Understanding the interests of the clients

This leads us to the second problem that complicates warning and the communication of warning, which is the absence of agreed notions of interests. Firstly, some MS affect to not have national interests, preferring to talk of values instead. This has a tendency to produce a view that potential crises are of equal importance – a coup in Fiji is as important as a coup in South Africa, making Fiji as important as South Africa. A further problem with the absence of agreed notions of interests is that, even when MS accept they have their own national interests, we have not progressed far in identifying common interests. The effect of these two facts is that the Watchlist makes no distinction between potential crises in terms of likelihood or impact on interests. This of course distorts early-warning work as it creates noise, which can drown out the most vital warnings.

With clients within the institutions, it is possible to develop an idea of their priorities, only drawing to their attention the developments most likely to impact on perceived EU interests. This is done by producing a variant of the Watchlist that looks at the likelihood of crisis and its impact on what we collectively, within the early-warning bodies, perceive to be the EU interest. We then concentrate our follow-up work on those countries where there is an intersection of strong likelihood and high potential impact. If MS were to study our output they would divine our priorities, but this slightly underground approach avoids actually having to try to agree those priorities. Doing this in the open would probably not work, given the absence of agreed interests. So the absence of interests and the absence of a solid discussion on concepts means that some of the work is less visible, to a certain extent less legitimate, and a part of the communication process is either absent or implicit, the latter carrying the risk that it is also misunderstood.

8.4 The means of communication

Having established that we have in our processes a certain vagueness about why we concentrate on some areas and that this compromises communication we now look at how to compensate. Before describing our own model, it is worth considering some of the issues relating to communication in all organisations. A number of questions arise. What are the channels for communication? Paper, electronic, human? Communication as a physical process – does the stuff reach the right people? If not, why not? How do you define 'reach'? Does it arrive in their building? Their department? Their office? Their in-tray? Or their brain? Are the flows understood? Are they one-way or two-way? Are warnings implicit or explicit? Is there standard terminology? Is the terminology understood? Might it be ambiguous? How responsive are the feedback loops, that is how easily can the *warners* refine judgements, particularly in the light of comments and questions by policy makers? Is the warners' work central or peripheral to policy makers? Do policy makers have other sources of warning? Do they contribute this to the central process or at least the Brussels discussion? Are staff familiar with the organisation of assessment and warning, particularly at the interface?

To get perfect answers to all these questions would help a lot but would probably not be possible, even in a small but efficient state structure that might have had the time and will to build a proper framework. Clearly therefore, in a big, complex, new, multinational context, quite a lot of these questions cannot be answered adequately.

So, with an inadequate framework, how do we compensate? Having said there are areas where we have to be indirect, there are also occasions where we have to be direct. Some of this is banal but necessary. We announce that a warning product is on its way. We announce on the product, in large red letters, that it is a warning product, and we draw attention to the elements of papers where those warnings are concentrated.

8.5 How communication makes a difference

We must look carefully at the style of communication. It has to catch the attention. Even so, it must not be undervalued by being gaudy or overly colourful. The language must be clear and understood by non-English speakers. Nuance and ambiguity, the refuge of many intelligence analysts, should be avoided anyway, but are even trickier for non-English speakers to write and to understand.

The perceptions of the warned have to be understood, including the extent to which styles of communication and forms of words can influence this. In some cultures and some administrations the words 'intelligence indicates' are an 'Open Sesame', a phrase that gets your information noticed and registered. That said, there are others for whom the phrase is a complete turn-off, or a warning. Phrases such as 'we assess that' can be read by some to mean 'we have a mountain of intelligence which, when carefully considered, leads us to the following conclusion in which we have a high degree of confidence.' It can be read by others to mean 'we have very little intelligence, so we are making an inference that...' (see Chapter 3).

Hence the importance, if it can be agreed, of terminology. In the absence of proper frameworks and concepts, a well-developed and agreed lexicon is not feasible. At EU level, we have at least agreed certain terms relating to a subset of products known as Risk Assessments, which are developed to judge the risk to the EU's crisis-management missions. Here we have agreed terms giving meaning to phrases such as High Risk or Medium Risk. Not only has this helped make the warning much clearer when it entails a change in risk to a single mission; it also greatly facilitates the tasks of comparing risks between missions and prioritising resources.

Another powerful tool is the illusion of precision, or what I would call pseudo-precision. All policy makers want to be able to distinguish the relatively unimportant warning from the highly important. Organisations with a global or near-global view, such as the EU, the United States or the UN, have to deal with a significant number of important crises. Without getting into the relative quality of warnings for such crises, the decision-maker will be looking for expressions of precision, of relative probability and especially for any use of language that implies high degrees of confidence. Use of non-standard communications styles can wrongly allow the reader to infer the clarity that they seek. A famous example of inappropriate precision that springs to mind is: 'Intelligence indicates that the Iraqi military are able to deploy chemical or biological weapons within forty five minutes of an order to do so' (JIC, 2002). Since 2001 a number of intelligence services, recognising this problem, have sought to provide explicit descriptions of what certain phrases mean. The US intelligence community, for example, has a glossary that goes with its estimative intelligence products, defining the meaning of certain set expressions, especially those dealing with degrees of confidence.

The reader is influenced not only by the manner of the communication but also obviously by the content, and the extent to which it presses that reader's hot buttons. A warning that the situation in Somalia is at risk of deteriorating further, with a dreadful impact on the local population, will get less attention in certain capitals than a warning that the same deterioration risks creating a lawless zone that could be exploited by extremists for the preparation of attacks against western interests in the region or in Europe. An intelligence service or warning body that has a close interaction with its clients will have a good idea by observation of the clients' hot buttons. We all know this and I suspect consciously or unconsciously we all exploit it from time to time, notwithstanding the departure it represents from true objectivity.

I would observe that in a multinational environment we will have, taking the example above, some MS for whom the hot button would be the risk of terrorist attack on the EU MS, and for others for whom it would be the impact on the local population. This has the positive effect of enforcing a greater degree of objectivity. I wonder, for example, if the Iraq dossier would have got past first base if it had had to be prepared jointly with a couple of other European services.

So far, I have concentrated on whether warnings get noticed and whether they are understood. There are also the questions of whether they are accepted or acted upon (see de Franco and Meyer, chapter 1).

Acceptance obviously depends on much more than just the communication. In a national structure it depends on issues such as the track record of the *warner*, whether they enjoy the confidence of the policy makers. This can mean right down to the personal level and the interrelationship between briefer and briefed. I spoke earlier about the channels. The dynamics of the US President's daily intelligence briefing delivered personally by the Director of National Intelligence (DNI) is very different from a JIC assessment for the Cabinet. Each presents different opportunities and dangers.

When examining acceptance, we also need to recognise that today warning is a competitive business. We also need therefore to take into account the extent of resonance or dissonance between official warning and non-official warning, especially bearing in mind the impact of the latter on public opinion. A high degree of resonance may be more persuasive, but it could also be counter-productive if there is a sense on the part of decision-makers that the official *warners* have tuned their warning to seek this resonance effect in the hope of more effective persuasion.

This question of resonance and dissonance does not just crop up when comparing official and non-official warning. In the EU, we have our warnings and we have the warnings produced within the national structures. For many, the starting point is that their national assessment is *ipso facto* more correct and more legitimate. The track record needed to challenge this self-belief takes years to acquire (and minutes to lose).

As others have pointed out, warning will often challenge policy makers. How organisations process this cognitive dissonance is very important (see Chapter 11). Individuals and states vary in their cultural receptiveness to alternative lines of thinking. Organisational structures, leaders and historical experience all make a difference. Communication can help too. To warn effectively in a multilateral environment requires a degree of tailoring, partly to identify the arguments most likely to convince on merit, and partly to identify the arguments most likely to overcome the resistance coming from cognitive dissonance. In theory at least, the crowded warning terrain that exists in a multinational structure, such as the EU, and the fact that the warned are less able to fire the warners, means that there is probably more scope for a warner to move away from the mean. That said, it is also necessary to recognise that the EU's warning structures are still new and relatively immature, which mitigates against bold warning.

8.6 The interrelationship between warning and advocacy

There is then the question of whether warnings are acted upon and the role of communication. Here I must declare that I do not subscribe to the idea that warning is a discourse aimed at persuasion (see Introduction). Our goal is less lofty. We are not omniscient. We are not driving in a particular direction. The EU model separates collection, assessment and policy. Collection is generally the business of MS and their intelligence services, with a small portion of this harvest being made available to the EU. In the EU, assessment stands apart from policy, which is for a wider circle. With such a structure, the success of a warning body is thus not measured in terms of the number of recommendations for action that are followed. Rather it can be seen in the credibility accorded to the work, which in itself derives from a retrospective comparison of assessment with outcome (indeed, a comparison that is easier to make when there has been no reaction to a warning).

The EU model, with its stark separation between policy and assessment, is not unique, but neither is it universal. Some states bundle assessment with collection, that is assessment is an activity of intelligence agencies. Others have free-standing assessment bodies, and a third category bundle assessment with policy, or more commonly have no formal assessment body, with this task left to officials and high-level policy makers themselves.

If you accept that assessment must be policy neutral, then the way warning is communicated has to respect this. We must of course on occasion identify the most likely scenario, but also identify alternative futures, some of which will have to take into account actions contemplated by us. Obviously, this is fraught with danger, as the way in which alternative futures dependent on certain policy options are described gives a tremendous power to shape the choices.

Warners need close relations with policy makers, to know their thinking, to know their priorities, to know what tools they have at their disposal and are contemplating using, and to establish relationships of trust. Warners should be present at the policy discussion and be invited to give their assessments of the likely impacts of certain policies. To an extent, they need distance too. They must not try to shape policy with their warnings and they must not appear to be trying to shape policy, even if they are not, if they are to remain credible. Again, a multilateral clientele with a range of views can be a benefit in policing this fine line between warning and interfering in policy.

8.7 Examples of warning communication

Clearly nothing above is based on scientific analysis. It is based instead on a number of years' experience and observation, enriched particularly by cases where respectable warnings have been produced but not heeded. Three examples that spring to mind are Iraq, Darfur and Georgia. In the case of Iraq I have certain knowledge of warnings indicating that weapons of mass destruction (WMD) were not likely to be present, that inter-ethnic strife was likely to occur after invasion and that the conditions would be created for the terrorist organisation al Qaeda to prosper. These were not possibilities mentioned for the sake of completeness at the end of long reports, but warnings made at the outset by certain European services. In some capitals, these would have been dissonant, missed key hot buttons and led to a breakdown in trust between *warner* and policy maker. You can certainly see though that certain elements could have been communicated differently and had a greater impact, particularly the element on the likely development of a safe haven for al Qaeda, and that if skilfully done this could at least have induced some changes to the plan.

Darfur is another example where good warnings were available perhaps 12 months before the gravity of the situation was widely accepted. The reasons for inaction, or delayed action, are many, and go well beyond the issue of communication. Here I think resonance with non-governmental warning hindered rather than helped. Warnings emphasised the humanitarian consequences and echoed too much the NGO warnings. Humanitarian consequences can indeed be a hot button, but only under certain conditions. It also needs to be borne in mind that the EU's warning culture was in its early days, and the whole international community had much of its attention on Iraq.

My last example is Georgia. A review of warning material shows that quite a lot of what happened was to be expected. Warning failed for two reasons. Firstly, it was simply not strident enough. And, in my environment at least, we neglected to communicate to, or remind, policy makers that for the 45 years of the cold war we had always thought that exercises offered a good opportunity to concentrate forces for offensive action. We knew it, but we neglected to communicate it.

8.8 Conclusion

The journey from new information to warning to action has its pitfalls. As others have indicated, there are many reasons why may not even be possible, with the best systems available, to navigate this path reliably. Sometimes though, good warnings are developed, but many factors intervene to ensure that not all of these will result in action, and there are many reasons for that too. Effective communication can only help. To have good communication requires well established patterns of communication, well established processes, properly understood terminology, high levels of mutual trust and experience.

As Goldman states, warning is not intelligence (Chapter 3). And as Omand (Chapter 2) points out, new technology means that abundant information is no longer the monopoly of intelligence services. Taken together, these mean that good warning is available from a far wider range of sources than before. At the same time, national security structures that have invested heavily in intelligence collection will take some time to accept that new structures, be they government supported multinational assessment centres such as SITCEN, or quite simply NGOs such as International Crisis Group, can match their own judgements. This plays into the earlier discussion on the acceptance of warning, and to a large extent will only be settled over time, as the track record of the new warning sources emerges.

As an official in a multinational organisation, I have to recognise that there are peculiarities that apply in a multilateral context that make warning and its communication more complicated than in a purely national context. It is perhaps no surprise that the EU, with its relatively small membership and the breadth and depth of its competencies and inter-relationships, has made more progress in building an assessment and warning structure than NATO and the UN. Even so, the complexities of the multinational context apply to all: the competition with national warning, little or no central role in collection of intelligence, incomplete convergence of interest, a more diffuse policy-making partner, and differing national understandings of the language of warning. But multinationality can also bring benefits: a range of inputs and perspectives, a range of motivations and interests, with few dominating hot buttons, and the moderating effect that this brings. A warning structure that adapts to these positives and negatives, and that is insulated from the interests and policy considerations of a single state, can be a 'motiveless warner'. It may thus have a better chance of having its warnings heeded than those fed in individually by MS which, even if they are neutral, may not be seen as such.

Notes

1. Please note that the chapter reflects the status-quo before the coming into being of the European External Action Service, provided for by the Treaty of Lisbon.
2. For the purpose of this chapter, 'warning' is meant in the relatively limited sense relating to the warning of a conventional security threat to a country and to its overseas interests. This relatively narrow definition, which serves the purpose of this chapter, is a reality also in that most government warning structures focus on this activity and rarely look at the wider range of warnings, such as of pandemic, climate change or systemic risks such as those related to sub-prime lending, credit default swaps and leverage in general (see Introduction).

9

Responding to Early Flood Warnings in the European Union

David Demeritt and Sebastien Nobert

9.1 Introduction

The first warning of the severe flooding that would afflict Romania, Moldova and the Ukraine in the summer of 2008 was issued by the European Flood Alert System (EFAS) on 20 July 2008.[1] With soil moisture levels already high from an unusually wet summer and heavy rainfall forecast for the week ahead, this experimental, pan-European early-warning system was predicting a significant probability of river flows exceeding the 'severe', or very highest, EFAS alert level on all the major river basins in Romania from 25 July onwards. Seeing a strong flooding signal persist over consecutive forecast simulations, the scientific team working on the pre-operational development of EFAS at the European Commission's (EC) Joint Research Centre (JRC) in Ispra, Italy felt confident enough to issue a formal alert to the Romanian National Institute of Hydrology and Water Management (INHGA). INHGA is the national body with operational responsibility for flood forecasting and warning in Romania, and in 2006 it signed a formal Memorandum of Understanding so as to receive medium-term (3–10 days) EFAS alerts to complement the weather forecasts, real-time river monitoring systems and short-term (0–48 hours), largely statistical, flood-forecast models it uses to provide flood forecasts to the General Inspectorate for Emergency Situations in the Interior Ministry and the national water authority, Apele Romane, who in turn is responsible for issuing catchment-scale forecasts and warnings to local civil protection authorities (CPAs) and the public at large in Romania. Over subsequent days, further EFAS alerts were issued for the River Tisza to VITUKI, the Hungarian hydrological institute responsible for flood forecasting in that country, to the Slovak Hydrometeorological Institute for the River Bodrog, and to the State Hydrometeorological Service of Moldova for the Prut and Dnester river basins, but not to Ukrainian authorities, who have not signed the Memorandum of Understanding authorising the JRC to send them early warnings from EFAS. As a matter of course, all EFAS alerts are also sent to the EC's Monitoring and Information Centre (MIC) in Brussels, which coordinates the European Union's (EU) response to natural disasters under its Community Civil Protection Mechanism (Council of the EU, 2001, 2007).

Unlike conventional deterministic forecasting systems that produce a single 'best guess' prediction of what is thought most likely to happen, EFAS is based on a new method of 'ensemble' forecasting (Cloke and Pappenberger, 2009), which generates a suite, or ensemble, of predictions, designed to cope with chaos and sensitive dependence on initial conditions (see Figure 9.1; Chapter 5, for a discussion of its implications in climate modelling). While the most extreme, outlying values forecast by the ensemble offer an indication of potential worst-case scenarios, the ensemble as a whole can be converted to a probability-distribution function. This mathematical equation can then be used to estimate the probability of any future system state, and optimise risk management responses to them by balancing potential losses against the costs of precautionary action to avoid them (i.e. Palmer,

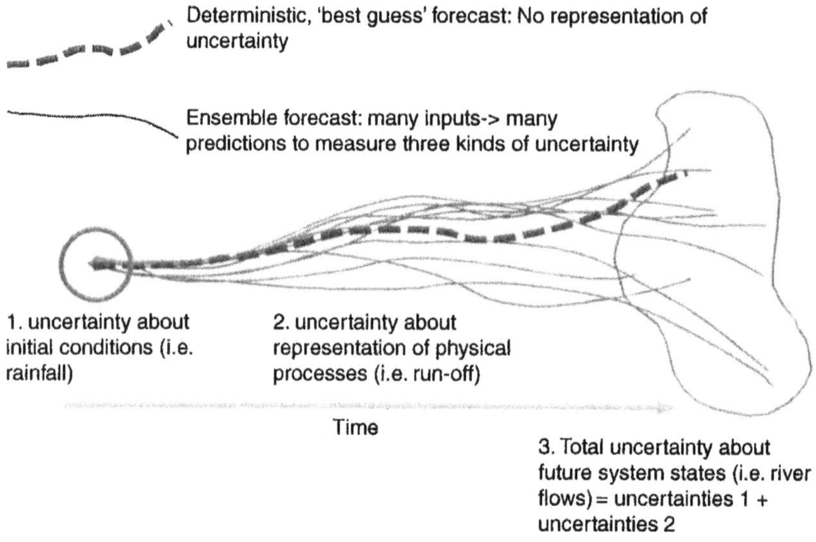

Figure 9.1 Deterministic v. ensemble forecasting methods (In deterministic modelling, systems use a single input is used to generate, or determine, a single best guess prediction. In ensemble-forecasting systems a suite, or 'ensemble', of predictions is generated so as to sample the uncertainty about (1) initial conditions and the errors to which those lead over time, (2) model parameterisation or physical processes, or (3) the total uncertainty caused by both. This figure is based on a schematic originally produced by Dr Ken Mylne of the UK Met Office.)

2002; Altalo and Smith, 2004; Buizza, 2008). Used regularly for operational weather forecasting since the mid-1990s (Gneiting and Raftery, 2005), such ensemble methods are only now being developed for use in other hydrometeorological domains, such as storm surge and seasonal forecasting and climate-change assessment. Applied to fluvial-flood forecasting, ensemble methods are often said to show 'greater skill than deterministic ones', particularly over the medium term of 3–10 days (Roulin, 2007: 736). As de Franco and Meyer (Chapter 1) note, a number of different dimensions of forecasting skill can be distinguished, including increases in forecasting scope, certainty, specificity and temporal horizon. Ensemble methods promise to deliver both more specific forecasts – of the precise quantitative probability of different water levels – and to do so over longer time horizons than is possible with comparable deterministic methods.

These technical capabilities were central to the decision to incorporate novel ensemble methods into EFAS. However it is also important to recognise the wider institutional implications of this scientific decision. The use of ensembles served to differentiate EFAS both functionally and technologically from existing national flood-forecasting systems, which did not have the same medium-term forecasting horizon or probabilistic content as EFAS. By providing these additional, complementary capacities, the use of ensembles thus helped to dispel political concerns arising in some member states that the development of EFAS was somehow 'intend[ed] to replace national or regional forecasting systems' (WDEU, 2003: F9). At the same time, however, the novel application of ensembles to an operational flood-alert system then created a series of new challenges for the communication, learning and action phases of the warning-response framework outlined by de Franco and Meyer (Chapter 1).

Flood forecasting is an uncertain science, and warnings, particularly those issued more than several days in advance, are not always followed by actual flooding. But in this case, the July 2008 EFAS alerts proved to be all too accurate. As EFAS had warned some six days beforehand, heavy rain over the Carpathians led to severe flooding in eastern Romania, western Ukraine and Moldova, where the rivers Siret, Prut and Dniester reached some of their highest levels since records began in the mid-nineteenth century. Thousands of homes and hectares of farm land were flooded, roads and bridges washed out, and critical infrastructure such as water treatment facilities and power supplies disrupted, before the flood waters finally abated in mid-August. Direct damages for Romania alone were estimated at €471 million, for which Romania later received €11.785 million from the EU Solidarity Fund to help with costs of reconstruction (EC, 2009). All told, 47 people were killed and more than 40,000 temporarily displaced from their homes (IFRC, 2009; WHO, 2010).

Early warnings issued by EFAS played an important, if differentiated, role in the emergency response to this disaster in Europe's least-developed region. At the national-level flood forecasters regarded EFAS alerts as a 'very welcome "pre-alert" just to tell your country, "pay attention, there could arise dangerous phenomena"' (2009 interviews). In terms of the warning-response framework, EFAS alerts led to learning and greater vigilance within INGHA and Apele Romane, but such early warnings were not enough, by themselves, to prompt more concrete actions, such as issuing a formal 'yellow' or 'red' alert. In Romania's highly codified system for dealing with emergency situations, such warnings trigger a cascade of other actions by the Ministry and CPAs following pre-determined plans (2010 interviews with Romanian CPAs), and the decision to issue them is based on:

> our own forecasts and having inputs in all gauging stations and procedures to provide forecasts sometimes or not sometimes. Very often our data are in real time better than this long range forecasts which was planned to be provided by EFAS. (2009 interview)

In making decisions about whether to issue flood warnings, the Romanians place great importance on real-time rainfall and river-gauge measurements. Such 'nowcasting' provides greater certainty and local detail than EFAS, which is instead designed to offer greater temporal scope and specificity, in terms of spelling out the probability of given levels of flooding. There are inevitable trade-offs between these different dimensions of forecasting skill, which this forecaster has failed to acknowledge in declaring that his own real-time data are 'better' than the medium-term forecasts provided by EFAS some 3–10 days previously.

The preference of Romanian authorities for certainty over timeliness is conditioned by a strong institutional aversion to false alarms. As one Romanian forecaster explained, emergency response protocols are fixed by statute to the three alert levels, and if an alert is triggered this 'means even if I have 1 per cent of probability to having a significant flood over this certain threshold let's say, I have to evacuate the people. So that's the problem.' Romanian CPAs were loath to order an evacuation of an area unless flooding was certain to occur there, and so this forecaster saw the only 'alternative is to decrease the time you need to take the action. Anyway, I don't think we'll be able to provide very accurate forecasts even 1, 2 days.' Romanian forecasters were similarly fixated on certainty and the importance of avoiding false alarms. While they acknowledged the skill of EFAS in extending the lead time for reliable flood forecasting on the main rivers of the Danube, and welcomed the early warnings it provided them, they insisted that EFAS and ensemble methods more generally were 'not to be used as forecasting tools at the level of the country' but were instead 'another concept' altogether. Such medium-term forecasts were said to be 'well detailed at the European level' but to lack the local detail and certainty required for issuing flood warnings to CPAs and the public. Having received the first EFAS flood alert on 20 July 2008 warning of potential flooding on all major rivers in Romania, INGHA did not issue the first 'yellow' alert for the upper Siret and Prut Rivers until two days later and when they did so based them on real-time 'hydrological data from our stations in Romania and from Ukraine, during the flood period, regarding levels and discharges already recorded... as well as meteorological forecasts and nowcasts from the National Administration of Meteorology'.

By contrast, EFAS early warnings were much more influential in triggering action at the international level. With advanced warning from EFAS, the MIC is able to begin its own internal preparations for relief efforts in advance of receiving a formal request for assistance from the affected countries. By the time the first formal requests for assistance were received in the 2008 floods, the MIC had already determined which European expert teams and other resources were available and had made a head start on the paperwork needed to deploy them to Romania. In all, some 22 countries contributed resources to the relief effort, either through bilateral donations or coordinated through the MIC and United Nations Office for the Coordination of Humanitarian Affairs (MIC, 2008; IFRC, 2009).

Focusing on EFAS in particular, this chapter is about the development and dissemination of such early flood warnings within the EU. A perennial local hazard managed by regional and national authorities in Europe (Mitchell, 2003), flooding has begun to attract the attention of the EU as a risk of regulatory interest, in the contexts both of precautionary environmental protection and of security and civil contingencies. Whereas the recently enacted Flooding Directive sets out an EU-wide framework for reducing the frequency and impact of flooding, EFAS is one of a number of early-warning systems now being developed by the EC to enhance its capacity to anticipate and manage at a European level the incidence of such civil contingencies. Drawing on more than 65 semi-structured interviews with various forecasters, CPAs, and policy makers involved in operational flood management in 17 countries from across Europe,[2] we highlight a number of barriers to overcoming the warning-response challenge in operational flood management. After placing the origins of EFAS in the wider policy context of the EU Civil Protection Mechanism, we turn to the challenges of communicating and interpreting EFAS alerts. But beyond these cognitive challenges to acting on EFAS alerts, we also highlight some institutional and political difficulties associated with the delivery and response to early flood warnings by the EU.

9.2 The EU civil protection mechanism

Recent years have seen the management of natural disasters and other civil contingencies emerge as an area of increasing concern for the EU. In the immediate aftermath of the 9/11 terrorist attacks on the United States, EU member states hastily agreed to establish a legal mechanism 'to provide, on request, support in the event of such emergencies and to facilitate improved coordination of assistance intervention provided by Member States and the Community' (Council of the EU, 2001: Article 1.2). Over time, the scope of EU involvement in security and civil contingencies has steadily expanded (see Chapter 8), though as Ekengren et al. (2006) note the process has often been ad hoc and contested. The Community Civil Protection Mechanism formalised a long, if patchy, record of EU cooperation in response to transboundary environmental disasters, such as the Sandoz chemical spill of 1986 in which more than 30 tons of pesticides were accidentally discharged into the Rhine, near Basel, Switzerland, turning the river red in places and extirpating aquatic life as the toxic plume flowed 900 kilometres downstream through France, Germany, Belgium and the Netherlands before finally issuing into the North Sea. As well as promoting cooperation in training and other emergency preparedness activities, the Mechanism committed member states to identify and make available for rapid deployment 'intervention teams' that could be dispatched at short notice 'in the event of a major emergency' (Council of the EU, 2001: Article 3). It also established the MIC to 'react immediately' to requests for assistance from member states, to 'mobilise and dispatch as quickly as possible small teams of experts responsible for assessing the situation ... facilitating ... coordination of assistance operations on site, and liasing ... with the competent authorities of the State requesting assistance.'

The initial emphasis was on developing the capacity to respond to emergencies and to do so more efficiently by coordinating and sharing resources at the EU level, as this Commission official explained:

> We think the European response is the best way to do it because we can share better. Imagine a country has to prepare for 100 year flood and every country has to do that. While it happens only once in 100 years, if you have let's say a reserve capacity in Europe at several levels, say you have the mechanism, so you can get assistance from other countries. ... Then actually you have a much more cost efficient system. Rather than everybody buying 20, we buy somewhere, we lease somewhere a capacity of 20 and then we move it around over and above. That's cheaper and more efficient. (2008 interview)

The EU Civil Protection Mechanism, and the MIC in particular, was soon put to the test by the central European floods of August 2002, which devastated Germany, the Czech Republic, Slovakia, and Austria and caused an estimated €15 billion in damages in what is still the largest single natural disaster to have struck the European Union since its establishment (EEA, 2003; RMS, 2003; Barredo, 2007). Floodwaters in the Czech capital of Prague crested at nearly 8m above their normal levels, flooding parts of the

Old Town and much of the Metro system before reaching Dresden four days later and inundating more than a quarter of its residential area (Kreibich and Thieken, 2009). Faced with this rapidly unfolding disaster, the MIC did not wait to be asked for assistance, but initiated contact with Czech officials. Once the formal request for assistance was then received, Commission officials tried to work with French, Italian, Greek and Belgian authorities, some of whom had already been in touch with the Czechs themselves independently, to deliver the pumping and water purification equipment needed for the emergency response to the flooding (EC, 2002). But despite the MIC and the existence of the Mechanism to coordinate civil protection cooperation within the EU, many states continued to offer bilateral assistance directly to the Czechs, leading to confusion, duplication and wasted effort, and ultimately to the Czech interior minister announcing that while his country was grateful for emergency assistance much of what was being offered was not needed (Ekengren et al., 2006).

One lesson drawn by the MIC from the 2002 experience was the need to be more proactive and to anticipate needs rather than just sit back and wait to be asked for assistance. As one Commission official explained:

> We try to be proactive. We do not wait until we get a request. But we screen and monitor and ... get it validated by our colleagues, our human network that we have with the member states. (2008 interview)

Adopting this kind of anticipatory, proactive approach is just one way in which the activities of the MIC have moved beyond those initially envisioned when the Civil Protection Mechanism was first established in October 2001. The original focus for the Mechanism was on responding to emergencies within the territorial bounds of the EC, but this was quickly adapted to respond to the needs of the 2002 flooding in the Czech Republic, which had not yet formally joined the EU. From there it was then a relatively small step from monitoring and coordinating the EU response 'in the event of a major emergency *within* the Community' (Council of the EU, 2001: Article 2.1, emphasis added), to doing the same internationally in support of DG ECHO and the increasing role of the EU in international humanitarian aid, disaster relief, and civil conflict (Chapter 4). The 2004 Asian tsunami disaster led to the establishment of the Global Disaster Alert and Coordination System (GDACS), which is now run by the JRC on behalf of the MIC and the UN Office for Coordination of Humanitarian Affairs.

While proposals by the Commission to establish a standing rapid reaction Civil Protection Force have been rebuffed by member states, the Civil Protection Mechanism has now been recast to give an explicit mandate for 'the development of detection and early-warning systems for disasters' by the Commission (Council of the EU, 2007: Article 2.7). This gradual expansion of the role of the EU into forecasting and the development of its own early-warning capacity has advanced, largely unplanned, through various ad hoc responses to events, as the development of EFAS clearly demonstrates.

9.3 Developing Europe's early flood-warning capacity

The 2002 flood opened a window of opportunity for the development of EFAS and a pan-European early flood-warning capacity. At the political level, EC President Romano Prodi was keen to demonstrate the effectiveness of a European-level response to civil contingencies and other disasters. On 15 August, with flood waters having just peaked in central Prague and the flood wave heading downstream to Germany, Prodi pledged a series of emergency measures, including proposals to divert EU structural funding to create a European Solidarity Fund to help support reconstruction and to accelerate agricultural subsidy payments to farmers in the affected areas (EC, 2002), prior to accepting an invitation from German Chancellor Gerhard Schroeder to attend a summit in Berlin on Sunday 18 August, along with his Czech, Austrian and Slovakian counterparts to discuss the response to the unfolding crisis (AFP, 2002).

Meanwhile, at the policy level, the skeleton staffs left on duty within DG Environment and DG Research during the traditional summer holidays were scrambling around to assess the capability of the Commission and assemble a response to the emerging crisis. While flood-incident management was not formally within its legal competency, the Commission had, nevertheless, begun to take an interest in flooding as 'a true European problem, which do[es] not stop at administrative borders' and in the wake of two severe floods on the Rhine in the early 1990s provided €58 million to 'some 50 multinational projects related to flood research' (EC, 2003). Among the beneficiaries of that largesse was a small research team at the JRC. Initially established to do scenario research to 'assess the influence of land use on flooding' and identify 'focus areas for land-use change policies' (de Roo et al., 1999), the JRC team was winding down its involvement in an experimental Framework V funded research project, European Flood Forecasting System (EFFS), to explore the possibility to extend the lead time of the flood-warning process up to ten days into the future (Gouweleeuw et al., 2004: 11). Several scientists involved in EFFS recounted how, at the height of the 2002 floods, the JRC team had scrambled to reconfigure their experimental system, which was being tested with historical hindcasts on the Oder and Meuse, to generate a rough-and-ready real-time forecast for the flood afflicted Elbe and Danube, which Prodi was then able present to Schroeder at the summit. Within days, almost as an addendum to the Communication establishing the Solidarity Fund to release structural development funds to finance disaster relief and reconstruction, the EC formally pledged 'to provide scientific support for a European flood-warning system containing information on the main European basins and with real-time access to medium-term meteorological forecasts' (EC, 2002).

One way to understand this sudden change in Commission policy, from supporting research to developing an operational forecasting capacity, is in terms of Kingdon's (1995) model of policy windows. In Kingdon's model, shifts in the policy agenda occur when the normally independent and parallel 'political', 'problem', and 'policy' streams of policy making come into alignment to open a 'policy window' through which entrepreneurs or advocacy groups can advance new policy agendas. Whereas the political stream embraces the political desire of Prodi and other proponents of greater European integration, the problem stream refers to competing issue framings and interest group perceptions of whether alternative solutions available in the policy stream, such as structural flood defences or European-level flood forecasting, can address or mitigate the problem. Although there had previously been large transboundary floods, most notably the 1995 Rhine floods, which had caused some €5 billion in damages and had led to the precautionary evacuation of 200,000 people from low lying areas of the Netherlands threatened by a potential break in the levees (Meijerink, 2005), the response to that crisis was framed in terms of the need to make more 'room for the river' (Klijn et al., 2004; Wiering and Arts, 2006). That framing in the problem stream, in turn, spurred an interest in the policy stream in local flood-risk mapping and reducing development on flood plains as responses to what was framed as the inevitability of flooding. It was still possible for the Commission to play a supporting role through INTERREG support for cross-border cooperation in spatial planning and Framework programmes of research, but flood forecasting at the EU-level was not on the policy agenda in the 1990s. Indeed, suggestions made in 2000 by the EFFS team, that they could start work developing an operational system to build on their Framework V research testing the feasibility of medium-term flood forecasting, were met with indifference, both within the Commission and cooperating national forecasting services (2009 interviews JRC and EFFS scientists). By contrast with the post 9/11 establishment of the MIC there was both a stronger appetite in the political stream for a more active, European-level role in managing civil contingencies and a constituency within the Commission for whom the lack of a pan-European flood-forecasting capacity was an obstacle to that ambition. At the same time, research funding for the experimental EFFS project was running out, and when the 2002 floods occurred, a policy window opened the idea of developing a pan-European flood-forecasting capacity. EFAS was born.

The Commission's snap decision to create EFAS raised a number of questions about how this new European-level forecasting capacity would relate to existing agencies responsible for forecasting, warning, and civil protection in the Member States. Some national forecasting agencies worried that EFAS 'might take away their work from them' (2008 interview EC official).

Beyond mere institutional rivalry over 'turf', there were also practical concerns about accountability and the potential for confusion – 'if you have two forecasts being issued for the same area' – by different forecasting agencies (2008 interview national forecaster). JRC officials were very sensitive to these concerns and have worked closely with EFAS partners to address them. With initial consultations showing that 'dissemination directly to the general public is controversial' (Thielen et al., 2003: 6), the EFAS team dropped early suggestions about the potential for creating public access 'via an internet website' (Ibid.: 15) and devised strict protocols to keep real-time access to EFAS alerts 'restricted to National and Regional Forecasting Centres and the EC' (Ibid.: 6). As well as responding to concerns from national-level forecasting agencies that 'civil protection will ring me and ask for an interpretation of an [EFAS] forecast I didn't prepare' (2009 interview national forecaster), such restrictions on the dissemination of EFAS alerts also helped fulfil the licensing terms under which EFAS receives real-time ensemble rainfall forecasts from the Reading-based, European Centre for Medium-Range Weather Forecasting (ECMWF), which made it impossible to share experimental products developed by the EFAS team through its participation in several Framework research programmes.

From the outset, JRC officials have been careful to emphasise how EFAS 'complements the work of the existing national forecasting centres' (Thielen et al., 2003: 24). Central to these efforts at institutionally differentiating EFAS from existing national forecasters was the scientific commitment to using ensemble methods of prediction. Although ensemble forecasting is now well established in operational weather forecasting (Gneiting and Raftery, 2005), its application to flood forecasting and warning is still in its infancy (Cloke and Pappenberger, 2008), and this has allowed EFAS to be positioned as 'a research project and not an operational service' (Thielen et al., 2006). EFAS was in some senses the first test of the operational feasibility of real-time ensemble flood forecasting, and as well as making steady improvements to the skill and capacity of EFAS itself over the first few years of its pre-operational testing and development (Pappenberger et al., 2011), the success of the JRC in developing and running the EFAS prototype has also inspired 'the adoption of an ensemble hydrological prediction approach also in national and regional flood forecasting systems in Europe' (Thielen et al., 2009: 138). But it is also important to recognise the institutional significance of describing the EFAS project in terms of further research and development of ensemble forecasting – as a 'pure' model in Wagner's terms (Chapter 6). So long as EFAS remains in the pre-operational 'development and testing phase' (EC, 2007), it is possible to defer some unresolved political questions about who might actually run it when it goes operational and whether a fully operational EFAS would represent an expansion of EU competencies into national areas of responsibility for providing decision-support for operational flood-incident management.

By using ensemble methods EFAS complemented existing national capacities in other ways as well. National flood forecasting and warning systems across Europe are largely still based on deterministic forecasting methods, though the success of EFAS in demonstrating the operational feasibility of ensemble flood forecasting has encouraged a number of European forecasting agencies to begin developing their own ensemble systems (Cloke et al., 2009). Given their historic concern with public safety and flood warning, national flood-forecasting systems typically focus on providing detailed predictions of flood inundation over comparatively short (0–48 hour) timescales with models set up at high spatial resolutions. By contrast, EFAS operates at a much coarser (5×5 km^2) spatial scale, in essence sacrificing the local specificity needed for predicting exactly where local inundation will occur so as to free up the computational resources needed to forecast over a longer time horizon by producing many different model iterations, each with slightly different rainfall inputs, so as to account for the uncertainty about them and the propagation of error to which they lead over time.

In addition to its very real scientific advantages in terms of generating more specific, probabilistic forecasts over longer time horizons, the use of ensemble methods also served functionally and technologically to differentiate EFAS from existing national flood-warning centres using deterministic models. At the same time, however, it created a series of practical problems about how probabilistic forecasts based on novel ensemble methods should be communicated to, interpreted by, and acted upon by national flood forecasters and CPAs accustomed to deterministic forecasts.

9.4 Making sense of early flood warnings

The operational flood forecasters we interviewed were not always comfortable working with ensemble forecast products. The novelty of their use in flood forecasting means there is not, as yet, any agreed international standards for communicating them (Lumbroso and von Christierson, 2009; cf. Aikman et al., 2010; Bruen et al., 2010). Forecasters across Europe are experimenting with different ways of visualising the uncertainty information they contain, including 'spaghetti' hydrographs (Figure 9.2), box and whisker diagrams, and plume charts (Demeritt et al., 2010).

For most flood forecasters in Europe, medium-term ensemble predictions of rainfall and flooding represented a supplementary source of information, rather than a central part of in-house operational routines, and there is, as yet, no established consensus about the best way to interpret or use them in operational flood-risk management. Some flood forecasters recommended focusing on the statistical mean of the ensemble. Compared with the 51 individual members of ECMWF ensemble weather forecast, or a 'spaghetti' diagram of the 51 EFAS river-flow predictions derived from it, the ensemble mean is easy to understand and communicate to others. Moreover, the mean is sometimes also said to represent the 'best guess' forecast, in much the same way as statistician Francis Galton famously found the weight of an ox at a county fair to be more accurately estimated by averaging many guesses made by members of the crowd than by any one guess made by an expert (Surowiecki, 2004). Indeed, there is scientific research to suggest that comparing different model predictions – sometimes called a '"poor man's ensemble" distinguish it from a formally designed ensemble system in which different ensemble members are perturbed to reflect key input or process uncertainties – can provide more accurate predictions than simply relying on a single deterministic model' (Arribas et al., 2005). For these various reasons, a few flood forecasters suggested that the statistical mean was the most important piece of information to extract from an ensemble forecast, while others insisted, 'if you use the mean it's not too much value' (2009 interview).

While forecasters welcomed the prospect of ensemble forecast methods providing more specific information about forecast uncertainty, there was a wide variety of opinion about how well the number and statistical dispersion of ensemble members reflects total forecast uncertainty. Some forecasters were quick to use the ensemble spread as an operationally useful summary of total uncertainty. As this forecaster explained:

> So if there's a big spread, there's a lot of uncertainty and we would not be able to give forecasts with big, big lead-times. And if there's a very small spread then we are a little bit more certain about the forecast and we might enlarge the, the lead time of the forecast for this occasion. (2008 interview)

To this way of thinking, the ensemble spread is a useful heuristic that summarises, at a glance, the degree of total forecast uncertainty. Others were even more bullish about the potential for ensemble flood-forecast systems not simply to give a broad indication of the likelihood of any given event but with appropriate 'post-processing to give you a [quantitative] probability' of any given forecasted event (2009 interview).

Other forecasters, however, rejected any simple equation of ensemble spread with total forecast uncertainty. Many were deeply sceptical of efforts to convert the ensemble to a quantitative probability distribution from which the probability of given levels of flooding could be calculated:

> No, I don't believe because if you make a spaghetti plot and 5 of the 51 lines are higher than the threshold value, you can't say the probability is 10%. Maybe it's a special case... it might be 5% or 50%. I don't know. I can't estimate it. (2009 interview)

This forecaster is picking up on a complicated technical debate about the adequacy of post-processing routines to correct model outputs and to simulate the full range of hydrological system responses, given the well-recognised tendency of models to underperform in predicting extreme events at the statistical margins of the observed values they have been calibrated to reproduce (Bogner and Pappenberger, 2011). Moreover, in the particular case of ensemble flood-forecasting systems, the initial scientific focus has been on the propagation of error over the medium term due to initial-conditions uncertainties about rainfall inputs (see Figure 9.1). Much less effort has been devoted to dealing with uncertainties about runoff, water routing, and other model processes (Cloke and Pappenberger, 2009), which some flood forecasters we interviewed saw as being as great a source of forecast error as the rainfall uncertainties addressed by EFAS (cf. Zappa et al., 2011). For these reasons some flood forecasters were sceptical of the ability of the current generation of ensemble-forecasting systems to quantify correctly the risk of extreme flood events, which at least some of the operational flood forecasters we interviewed regarded as essentially unknowable.

In addition to these generic questions about ensembles, EFAS recipients also sometimes struggled to understand the specific meaning of EFAS alert thresholds. Although 'flow dynamics are well captured by the model', EFAS 'is not able to reproduce hydrographs quantitatively well in all river basins', because difficulties in securing access to consistent, pan-European data meant the EFAS team 'had to work with a limited amount of hydrological data for calibration and validation, and entirely without information for reservoirs and lakes' (Thielen et al., 2009: 129, 132, 129). While the EFAS team has made steady progress in overcoming them, these limitations have had important implications both for the definition of EFAS alert levels and for how the EFAS team represents them graphically in the EFAS alerts. 'In the absence of exhaustive discharge data' for local calibration and validation, or information about the height of flood defences and other operationally significant local thresholds, alert levels for the EFAS rainfall-runoff model are not defined in terms of empirically specific river level predictions. Instead they are defined nominally in terms of their statistical relationship to a reference period of simulations, initially 14 years long (1991–2004), but since extended to 16 (Thielen et al., 2009) and now 20 years, 'performed with the same hydrological model set up for the operational forecasting system and with observed meteorological data as input' (Ramos et al., 2007: 114). In this 'model-consistent' approach the EFAS 'severe' threshold corresponds to forecasted values exceeding the maximum seen in the entire reference period of simulations for that pixel, whereas the 'high' alert was initially defined as forecasted values exceeding 99 per cent of all simulated discharges in the reference period (Ramos et al., 2007; Thielen et al., 2009).[3]

The tacit assumption here is that the response space of the virtual rainfall-runoff model closely corresponds to that of the actual hydrological system. In hydrology (Beven, 2002), as in climate change more generally (Demeritt, 2001; Edwards, 2010), there is an important debate about the degree to which the virtual response space of computer models adequately reflects that of the actual systems they simulate (Oreskes et al., 1994; Sismondo, 1999). Whereas an empiricist tradition of hydrological modelling operates inductively and uses regression and other statistical techniques to make predictions based on historically observed relationships between rainfall and runoff (Demeritt and Wainwright, 2005), EFAS 'simulates surface process using physically-based algorithms... [that] require little additional calibration for individual catchments' (Gouweleeuw et al., 2005), and in this physics-based epistemic culture, mathematical formalism and physical theory are prioritised as the grounds for truth (Brown, 2004; Odoni and Lane, 2010).

EFAS users did not always appreciate these philosophical assumptions or their implications for how EFAS alert levels were calculated or what exactly they were representing:

> [...] the question is how EFAS thresholds are established. This is our big problem since the thresholds of our two models are tailored to our data bank. [...] They have simply taken the 20 years of flow simulation since 1995-98. Thus, because these years were relatively dry, their thresholds are very very low. (2009 interview)

In contrast with their own empirically calibrated thresholds, EFAS alert levels are nominal – they measure 'the relative difference of simulated discharges to simulated thresholds, but not the actual values' (Thielen et al., 2009: 132). EFAS recipients, however, often failed to appreciate this distinction. They assumed that EFAS alerts were providing specific forecasts of the precise flow levels to be expected from given volumes of forecasted rain, rather than broad intelligence, in the sense of Goldman (Chapter 3), based on the relative magnitude of the response of the virtual EFAS system to those forecasted inputs. Consequently, they were frustrated that EFAS forecasts are displayed in tabular form, listing the number of ensemble members exceeding various nominal threshold levels, rather than in hydrographs displaying river discharges in cubic meters per second ($m^3\ s^{-1}$) over time, such as that in Figure 9.2:

> The problem with EFAS particularly is that... they do not show hydrographs, but they only tell you that there is a chance of serious flooding... But they don't say what the level will be. They only say there is a chance of serious flooding or extreme flooding, but you don't know what it means. (2008 interview)

Hydrographs are the traditional form in which flood predictions are displayed in hydrology, and without them this forecaster struggled to relate the EFAS alert levels to his own operational thresholds for triggering local risk management responses. This was a common problem. Indeed, the

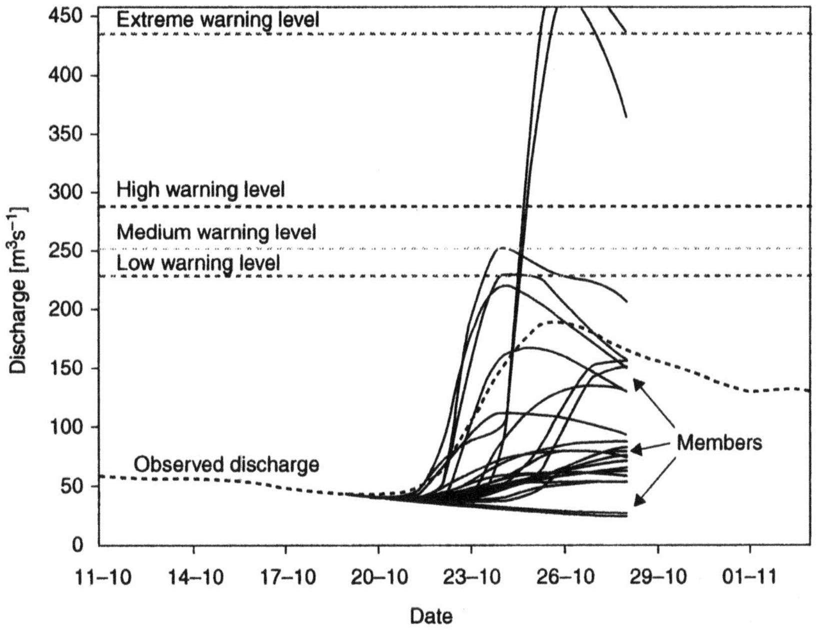

Figure 9.2 An example of an ensemble 'spaghetti' hydrograph for a hindcasted flood event (The plot shows the discharge predicted for each ensemble forecast (solid lines), the observed discharge (dashed lines) and four flood discharge warning levels. Taken from Cloke and Pappenberger (2009: 614)

most consistent complaint made by national-level flood forecasters was that there was no access to a complete, spaghetti-style representation of the EFAS ensemble hydrographs: 'If they would give a hydrograph, forecast with hydrograph, that would be... fantastic, yes in addition to [the summary tables]' (2008 interview). To satisfy that demand the EFAS team recently began a pilot project, initially involving the Czech and the Bavarian water authorities, but now expanded to other discharge stations across Europe where the necessary historic and real-time data are being provided, to post-process the model output so that its quantitative flow forecasts closely match empirically measured values and a meaningful hydrograph can be provided for key discharge stations (Salamon and Feyen, 2009; Bogner and Pappenberger, 2011).

One of the reasons EFAS recipients were so keen on receiving a hydrograph was so that they could more easily use the EFAS ensemble forecast to validate their own deterministic flood forecasts. Ensemble prediction systems are not designed for this purpose, and EFAS training sessions specifically advised against the practice, but it was still quite common for operational forecasters in the member states to confess that in practice they looked to EFAS alerts to confirm their own local deterministic flood forecasts:

> *Interviewer*: Let's say you're using your model and then you look at what EPS model is predicting...
>
> *Forecaster*: Yeah, we can compare and we can decide and we can strictly express that it's true or not... [whether] our statements are right or wrong... (2008 interview)

There are two potential problems with this way of using EFAS. First, it is prone to a 'confirmation bias' whereby forecasters search out those members of the ensemble that confirm their preconception and to discount those who do not (Demeritt et al., 2007). Second, like using a feather to scratch an itch, looking to an ensemble forecast to confirm a deterministic forecast is more likely to frustrate than relieve. Operational forecasters are most likely to feel the need to confirm their local deterministic forecasts in situations of high uncertainty, but it is at these moments, when the physical system is approaching a bifurcation point between possible different system states, that the spread of the ensemble members is likely to be at its widest, denying the forecaster the desired confirmation for any particular a deterministic forecast (Buizza et al., 2005). Of course displaying the uncertainty associated with its early warnings is precisely what EFAS is designed to do. But this is not typically what operational flood forecasters were hoping for when they turned to external forecasting products like EFAS. Their desire was to reduce uncertainty, rather than confirm it, and as this flood forecaster noted ruefully, 'It doesn't make your life easier if they have EPS. It's a bit more work. A little bit more interpretation' (2008 interview).

9.5 Acting on early warnings

Notwithstanding these difficulties in interpreting their probabilistic content, operational flood forecasters were generally still eager to receive EFAS alerts and other ensemble-based early-warning products. In an operational context where there are typically many more computer screens than on-duty flood forecasters, another source of information was always welcome (Fine, 2007). Echoing the Romanian response to EFAS quoted at the start of this chapter, several forecasters described the utility of EFAS early warnings in terms of raising awareness internally within their own forecasting service:

> It is useful because these warnings came to our office let's say 4 or 5 days before.... it's useful for us to raise the preparedness of our staff a few days before. (2009)

Another value of EFAS alerts was as supplementary confirmation of information available to forecasters from other sources, as another east European forecaster explained:

> Yeah. We also get EFAS reports. For us, it's a useful pre information, but normally 2 or 3 or 4 days before a flood, we normally know from the weather forecast that we should be aware of this... (2008 interview)

As the window for taking actual operational decisions approached, this forecaster was confident that he and his team would already be aware of an impending flood from their own in-house models and monitoring data. Picking up on that essentially supplemental value of EFAS, another forecaster echoed a sentiment that seemed widespread, particularly in wealthier parts of 'old' Europe with well resourced national flood forecasting systems:

> It is useful. But we could easily live without it. (2008 interview)

Beyond helping to inform their own in-house work preparing local flood forecasts, operational flood forecasters saw relatively little scope, given the uncertainties associated with current levels of forecasting skill over the medium term, for such early warnings to lead directly to them issuing earlier flood warnings or to precautionary action by CPAs. At most, EFAS provided national forecasting agencies with a pre-alert to spur greater vigilance within the forecasting team itself. This, of course, was precisely the sort of complementary role EFAS had been designed to serve. Not one of the 27 operational flood forecasters we interviewed saw EFAS early warnings as leading directly to them issuing earlier warnings to CPAs or to the public at large. For that specific purpose they looked to their own short-term, locally-detailed models rather than to the longer term but more uncertain early warnings from EFAS and other ensemble prediction providers like ECMWF.

There were several reasons why national flood forecasters did not act immediately on these early warnings. First, as implied by the comment above about how easy it would be to live without them, there were concerns about the accuracy and precision of such medium-term forecasts. Asked about EFAS, another western European forecaster replied:

> Yeah, I've heard of it. But the colleagues... said it's not so good than our model. (2008 interview)

Implicit in this forecaster's assessment is a tacit idea of what makes a model 'good'. But in flood forecasting, as in other forecasting domains, there are trade-offs between the different dimensions of skill outlined by de Franco and Meyer (Chapter 1). Since EFAS was not designed for locally-precise, short-term forecasting, it is not surprising that this aspect of its performance compares poorly with models that were. EFAS was instead designed for medium-term forecasting at a European scale and so sacrifices the local detail for multiple iterations necessary to assess initial conditions uncertainties and generate skilful forecasts over a longer time horizon. While flood forecasters consistently welcomed receiving early warnings from EFAS, they have not always had enough confidence in their geographical specificity and certainty to take much action on the basis of those pre-alerts alone. For example, in November 2008, EFAS issued an alert five days before flooding occurred on the upper part of the Loire basin in France, but because the 'forecasts were thought to be unstable', the alerts were not 'sufficient to convince them of the usefulness of the information' (Thielen et al., 2009). The extra lead time provided by EFAS was lost because local forecasters delayed sending out warnings to local CPAs until the EFAS alert could be strongly corroborated by local sources of information.

Second, the tendency for national flood forecasters to wait for local confirmation of medium-term ensemble forecasts of rainfall and possible flooding also reflects some deeper institutional concerns for the reputational and other consequences of false alarms. Historically, one of the reasons that European flood-forecasting agencies have sometimes set quite high thresholds for issuing flood warnings is that their statutory focus has been on public safety.

> [They are] primarily concerned with issuing short-notice flood warnings, you know 2 hours, with as a high level of certainty about that as they can manage... so normally, unless they are absolutely certain that there is going to be a flood, they are not going to issue a warning, even if there is a fair chance of flooding. And this is because their primary customer for flood warnings is the general public. So they think that's what they have to do. (2009 interview)

Institutional concerns about the effects of false alarms on public confidence in and responsiveness to flood warnings reinforce a bias in the epistemic culture of flood forecasting against type 1, false positive errors (Demeritt et al., 2007). Faced with a trade-off between earlier warnings and more certain ones, flood forecasters consistently chose certainty over timeliness. The concerns of national flood-forecasting agencies with the potential for error are magnified, in the case of EFAS alerts, because of their external provenance. If the EFAS alert proves to be wrong, it is the national agency that will be blamed, and this lack of clear accountability was the cause of anxiety about the very existence of EFAS and of a European-level flood forecasting capacity that might compete with national-level competencies.

> If you have a European Agency [EFAS] with an unclear mandate that does not have a national responsibility, providing such a service, then we would be very nervous about this. (2009 interview)

Finally, the reluctance of flood forecasters to act on early warnings from EFAS alone also reflects beliefs about how CPAs would respond to probabilistic flood warnings. There was a widespread belief that even trained CPAs would be confused and frustrated by probabilistic forecasts rather than iron-clad predictions:

> Okay, we can train our end users... to understand what prediction in the probabilistic way means, but even if they might intellectually grab it they don't want to know what it is. They want a yes or no because probabilistic means they have to live with uncertainty. (2008 interview)

This response was typical of the way flood forecasters described the likely response of CPAs to the kind of warnings generated by ensemble-forecasting systems. As well as questioning whether CPAs would be able to understand a probabilistic forecast, there were also widespread doubts about their operational utility for CPAs. Flood forecasters from across Europe repeatedly complained that CPAs demanded precision and would not be interested in forecasts couched probabilistically:

> At the very end, I think everything must be a kind of deterministic forecast because I had one experience in the 2005 flood. I was in operational service. The police officer responsible for the city called and said ok, we have this lake level of 435 cm, 10 cm more and we have to evacuate parts of the inner city. Does the lake exceed this threshold, yes or no? It's always... at the very end, it's always a yes or no decision. (2009 interview)

Though common, particularly in Germany, where as Rothstein et al. (Chapter 12) note 'risk-based approaches to policy making and enforcement fit uneasily with entrenched institutional arrangements and practices', such views are not universal. In Sweden, for example, the national meteorological agency now successfully provides CPAs with its own probabilistic flood forecasts. Partly this reflects the 'proximity principle' of Swedish natural-hazard management, which makes local CPAs responsible for flood response and creates an appetite among CPAs for assuming greater ownership of the associated uncertainties. But it is also supported by effective training programmes that assist Swedish CPAs both in understanding the ensemble products they receive and in identifying various hedging and optimising strategies that make probabilistic flood forecasts more useful to them than deterministic ones (Nobert et al., 2010). Sweden, however, was unusual. In most European countries, the tendency is for forecasting agencies to wait for local confirmation before acting on early warnings, and this ingrained conservatism points to important institutional challenges to the idea of preventive policymaking.

9.6 Probabilistic forecasts and precautionary policy

Beyond the cognitive and communicative challenges associated with making sense of new ensemble flood forecasts, this chapter has also highlighted some institutional and political difficulties associated with acting on early flood warnings. As well as providing earlier and more skilful predictions of potential flooding, ensemble-forecasting methods also promise to facilitate preventive policy by making their uncertainty more transparent, so as to empower forecast recipients and enable them to make better decisions. But the technical shift from deterministic to probabilistic forecasting is not politically neutral. It also entails a shift in the institutional liability for decisions taken in the face of uncertainty, as this forecaster explained:

> You're putting the onus on the people that receive that probabilistic warning to make a decision what to do with it themselves. (2009 interview)

The first-order scientific uncertainties about whether or not a flood will occur comprise only part of the wider 'decision' uncertainties faced by those charged with flood-risk management. They must also consider questions such as how the warnings they issue will subsequently be interpreted and what will happen if they are wrong. By making those first-order scientific uncertainties more explicit, ensemble forecasting can sometimes complicate the second order decision uncertainties they are supposed to clarify. Another flood forecaster put the dilemma even more starkly:

> EPS also means dumping responsibility onto forecast users. By forcing forecasters to provide deterministic predictions, the accountability remains entirely on the shoulders of forecasters. If a forecaster provides a probabilistic forecast, they give the import for the decision to forecasts users.... [By contrast] asking for a deterministic prediction is also a way for the person in charge of taking a decision to avoid decisional problems and blame. (2009 interview)

Error and blame are rather different risks to the substantive first-order one of flooding. If ensemble forecasting has not entirely lived up to the very high hopes invested in its capacity for earlier and more skilful warnings of potential flooding, it is at least partly because of the institutional tensions between those very different risks.

Notes

1. The opinions expressed herein are those of the authors alone and are not necessarily endorsed by the UK Economic and Society Research Council, which funded

this research, or by the EFAS team at the Joint Research Centre of the European Commission whose cooperation the authors gratefully acknowledge. The authors take sole responsibility for any errors of fact or interpretation.

2. These data were collected in 2008–2010 as a part of a wider project, funded by the UK Economic and Society Research Council (RES-062-23-0913). Our interview sample focused largely on those concerned with flooding on the Rhine and the Danube, though we also draw on interviews with forecasters working in France, Sweden and the UK as well those working at the EU-level. Interviews were recorded, transcribed and coded. To protect the confidentiality of our informants, we identify the sources for individual quotations in broad, non-identifying terms.
3. To make these alert thresholds easier for EFAS end users to understand, this statistical ranking of threshold exceedances has recently been redescribed in terms of the more hydrologically familiar concept of return periods, with the high alert level 'correspond[ing] to a simulated flood event with a return period of >5 yr. and <20 yr.' (JRC 2011).

10

Dark Secrets: Face-Work, Organisational Culture and Disaster Prevention

Marc S. Gerstein and Edgar H. Schein

> *All the world's a stage, And all the men and women merely players: They have their exits and their entrances; And one man in his time plays many parts.*
>
> Shakespeare, *As You Like It*

10.1 Face-work and other forces preventing reporting

Shakespeare had it right and sociologist Erving Goffman went further: men and women play many parts at the same time, each representing his or her 'self' in different ways in different settings as well as at different times. These differentiated representations of self are called *faces* and the work we do to create and maintain them is called *face-work* (Goffman, 1959). Organisations, too, reveal different faces, perhaps aggressive in some dealings and compliant in others. They may treat their employees, customers, suppliers and regulators similarly, or with great differentiation. Yet this facile summary is a vast oversimplification – the variations in any organisation's face are far more subtle and just as variable as our own – especially when it comes to matters of risk.

Since an organisation is not alive it is the behaviour of its people that animates its faces. Nevertheless, there is often great commonality in the way organisation members behave and in the faces they present to each other and to outsiders, when playing their organisational roles. This commonality is a key aspect of the organisation's *culture*, the pattern of assumptions, beliefs, practices and behaviours that define what it is like to live and work within a particular setting.

Through assumptions that are widely shared – even if they are not always visible to its members – an organisation's culture imprints its common ways upon its community even across generations as people come and go. This imprinting is particularly important when it comes to matters of safety and ethics, because organisational expectations and incentives sometimes encourage behaviour that people might otherwise avoid or even find repugnant.

One of the most fundamental aspects of any culture is the set of rules by which its members maintain face and self-esteem. They are all trained early to believe that the social order will not survive if they say to each other exactly what they feel. Instead, they have learned to grant each other what they claim, so that life can go on smoothly. Weaknesses, errors, and sometimes behaviours that are far worse, are overlooked unless they specifically set out to criticise them.

This same tendency to uphold each other's positive self-images, and the social order that depends on them, occurs within government, the military, and industry, even among organisations that compete with one another.

In consequence, organisation members not only avoid reporting the worrying and unethical things they see, out of fear, greed, or social pressure, but because they do not want to acknowledge things that are wrong and do not want to upset themselves, their bosses or colleagues by pointing them out, even though grievous harm may be done or laws broken.

We may all love to criticise jokingly what others do wrong, or complain about how awful things are in our workplaces. But we then rationalise it away with a smile and a shrug of the shoulders (Weeks, 2004). Taking our observations seriously by reporting them might be too anxiety-provoking and disruptive, even if we were not punished for doing so. In this sense all groups, organisations and societies have faces just as individuals do, and we learn not to destroy these collective faces, just as we learn not to destroy those of individuals.

An insider exposing organisational secrets is thus a 'social revolutionary', and it should not be surprised at receiving a violent response from the establishment. From the vantage point of most leaders, it is better to have one's wrongs discovered by an outsider than to have them revealed by one's own members. People who do so – whistleblowers – are considered disloyal and are usually severely punished. From this perspective, insider-reported misbehaviour should not really be expected unless law-makers, regulators, auditors, leaders and managers make special efforts to create the structures, incentives and requisite sense of safety to counterbalance the powerful drives of face-work that keep embarrassing secrets from getting out.

People also have other reasons not to speak up. We show in Table 10.1 the extensive list of reasons why risks are not reported by insiders. The length of this list is testament to the ubiquity and strength of the forces that maintain silence. After the table, we will focus in greater depth on the particular cultural role of face-work and its implications for solutions.

Table 10.1 Reasons why insiders do not warn about risks

INDIVIDUAL	**Self-interest**	Concrete rewards discourage the reporting of facts or judgments concerning risk because it might affect employment, bonus payments or chances for promotion. (Also see 'Fear', below.)
	Ignorance	Lack of awareness or understanding of the relevant conditions and warning signs.
	Carelessness or indifference	Too much trouble to bother – need or desire to remain aloof and uninvolved.
		Lack of energy or motivation to see it through if not initially listened to.
		Complacency, indifference to problems – 'who cares if they screw up, it doesn't affect me.'
	Machismo	Visible signs are considered trivial, and to report them would appear to be a sign of weakness.
	Resignation/ apathy	Belief that 'they never listen anyway' or 'I've tried before and they did not listen then so they won't listen now.'
	Overload	Too much is visible that could be reported, so nothing is reported. The truly important becomes lost in the clutter of the mundane.
		Unwillingness to expend the extra energy required to look into an abnormal condition and fix it if something is found.
		Just as the subordinate may be unwilling to 'rock the boat', 'make waves', or 'turn over rocks', the boss also does not want to dig too deeply over concern about what might be found.
	Fear	Fear of being punished for bringing bad news (shooting the messenger).
		Fear of personal embarrassment or criticism from higher-ups that something may not be right in one's own area of responsibility whether or not the source of the problem is beyond one's control.
		Fear that what I see may not be valid leading to embarrassment or perception of self as having poor judgment or lacking in expertise.
		Fear that what I report may be denied (making me look foolish) or I may be asked to prove it by mustering more proof than I have (making me look unprofessional for being unprepared).
		Fear of reprisal arising from raising a point of view counter to prevailing dogma or in opposition to policy or operational decisions concerning the nature of risks being faced.
		Fear of legitimising the presence of 'undiscussable' risks or conditions whose presence higher-ups wish to deny.
		Fear of getting a reputation as a trouble-maker, complainer, or worrier, and therefore less likely to be considered loyal and team-spirited. More instrumentally, concerned that pointing out problems will reduce chances of being re-hired (as in the case of merchant seamen), given choice assignments or promoted.

Continued

Table 10.1 Continued

GROUP/INTERGROUP	**Unwillingness to challenge, disrupt, or embarrass one's group, department, or the organisation**	Unwillingness to challenge the ideal self-image because it is too threatening to consider that things are not working properly. (This leads to an initial attitude of scepticism toward any negative feedback and asking for escalating levels of evidence or proof, that is, defensively ignoring 'weak signals' as defined by Igor Ansoff (1976: 133, also see Schwartz, 1991; Tsoukas and Shepherd, 2004; Schoemaker and Day, 2009) Reluctance to 'make waves' by upsetting the social order. Fear of being ostracised by the peer group for reporting something bad that is going on in the group. Loyalty to buddies or to one's superiors who might be hurt or embarrassed by the new information.
	Hostility to others laterally or upward	Not reporting something in order to let others get into trouble, or not reporting something soon enough, knowing that it will get worse if left alone. Anger – 'they deserve to fail', and so on. Passive-aggressive complacency – 'who cares if they screw up'.
	Intramural rivalry and competition	Cutting corners and not reporting known risks in order to save time and money or to make one's own group look better.
	Structural/ cultural barriers to systemic-risk identification and team-based diagnosis	Organisation design or cultural factors encourage stove-piped views of the enterprise and inhibit the identification of potentially dangerous interaction effects.
ORGANISATIONAL	**Productivity pressures**	Unwillingness to report hazards or attend to potential risks due to perception and/or reality that doing so will reduce productivity and efficiency.
	Normalisation of deviance	Unacceptable levels of risk persist without incident and thus become acceptable conditions that do not merit special attention. Lax regulatory or other enforcement redefines the de facto meaning of rules and regulations.
	Weak or compromised safety, compliance, audit and risk management functions	Formal risk-control groups lack the power, motivation and resources to compel action or set demanding safety, risk control and ethical standards. Incentives and rewards for risk control and compliance groups encourage greater risk-taking or strongly motivate 'pleasing the client' rather than ensuring high risk-control standards.
	Weak protections for truth-tellers	Personnel wishing to raise concerns lack adequate advice, counselling, legal assistance and protection from management or peer group retaliation. Lack of meaningful punishment (and sometimes rewards) for retaliators.
	'No-win' demands for managers and supervisors 'in the middle'	Supervisors and managers are caught between pressures simultaneously to meet production, quality and financial targets vs. safe/ethical standards. Faced with unavoidable real-world trade-offs, instead of help and support they are told, 'You take care of it, that's what you are paid for.'

10.2 The role of leadership, outside forces and regulation

Beyond the factors listed in the previous section, further erosion of safety and ethics often occurs when actions are undertaken in the name of desired organisational outcomes initiated from the top. Cost cutting, in particular, gives rise to all manner of risky actions: delaying inspections; skimping on upgrades, maintenance and training; increasing staff workloads; and other commonplace expense reduction initiatives all tending to increase danger by subtly changing the probability of an adverse outcome over time.

For example, training and equipment cutbacks contributed to the mistaken 1994 shoot-down by US Air Force F-15s of two US army helicopters carrying a contingent of twenty-six high-level allied dignitaries, soldiers and air crew on a tour of the no-fly-zone in northern Iraq after the first Gulf War. This shoot-down is considered by many to be the most serious friendly-fire accident in US military history (Snook, 2000).

The inability of the fighters and the helicopters to communicate with each other, and the failure of the airborne warning and control systems (AWACS) to identify the helicopters and notify the fighters – especially since the extra wing tanks made them look more like the Iraqi-enemy helicopters – is perhaps as attributable to the cost-cutting efforts that had been occurring over several years as it is to human error. For example, financial pressures and budget cutbacks precluded the rewrite of AWACS pre-mission training simulator software to conform to the actual mission's requirement to manage routine helicopter flights. In addition, limited funds precluded radio equipment upgrades that would have allowed the helicopters to communicate with the F-15s' more advanced combat radios,[1] and also eliminated a liaison role between the army helicopter and air force commands that might have improved coordination between the two services.

Although only a small minority of leaders would wilfully harm their organisation's members, customers or the public, most of them (like the rest of us) are nevertheless likely to focus on their own priorities rather than those of others. Some people of power, however, are willing to take self-interest considerably further. Daniel Ellsberg helps explain their possible motives:

- A potentially disastrous gamble offers the possibility of avoiding loss altogether, coming out even or a little ahead; and the alternative to the gamble is certain loss in the short run, a loss that impacts the leader personally.
- The certain loss that is rejected may appear small or even trivial to an observer, -compared to the much greater damage, perhaps societally-catastrophic, that is risked. This damage, however, may be to 'other people', outside the leader's organisation or even nation, and inflicted in 'the long run': thus, less easily attributed to this leader, who may well have moved on by the time of the disaster. In effect, the leader acts as if a sure,

short-term loss to his own position – a perceived failure, risking his job or re-election or his influence – were *comparably* disastrous to a possible social catastrophe that costs many lives: an avoidable war, a widely-used drug that proves to have lethal side effects, a dangerous product or the explosion of a nuclear plant or space vehicle.

- In the leader's eyes, both of these outcomes are 'disasters.' One of them, resulting from a particular course of action, is sure to occur. The other is uncertain, a possibility under another course of action, though perhaps very likely; and it is combined with the possibility, not available with the other course, of coming out even or perhaps ahead, winning or at least not losing. In choosing the latter option, he sees himself as accepting the possibility of a loss – in hopes of coming out even – rather than accepting a *certainty* of a failure, defeat. It seems – and it is so presented to him by some advisors – a simple, inescapable decision, 'no real choice': the possibility of winning, or at least of avoiding or postponing defeat, versus a 'no-win' course of action, or worse, a sure loss in the short run. He, and these advisors, simply ignore the fact that the scale of the respective losses, and who it is that mainly suffers them, are vastly different in the two courses (Ellsberg, 2008).

Many of the major disasters we have researched – Bhopal,[2] Space Shuttles Challenger and Columbia, Chernobyl, Thailand's preparations for the 2004 tsunami (PBS, 2005), Vioxx (US Senate Committee on Finance, 2004; Loudon, 2005), Xerox's extensive accounting fraud (described below), among others – fit Ellsberg's description: the taking-on of a significant risk in order to avoid the guaranteed failure of a major financial loss, political embarrassment, or personal humiliation.

Beyond imprudently taking large risks, leaders may also contribute to harm by engaging in 'damage control': covering up or otherwise seeking to minimise the negative impact of organisational errors, misjudgements or acts of malfeasance about which they may or may not have been aware but which nevertheless occurred on their watch and for which the organisation will pay a price and current leadership may well be blamed.

For example, in the 2005 BP Texas City Refinery explosion of vent-stack gases, which killed 15 and injured 180, the company first blamed employees by firing the accused responsible parties, and then it claimed that it could not have anticipated the complex interaction of events that led to the explosion. As the government-led investigation and legal cases unfolded, however, it was revealed that the plant had previously sustained a number of 'near miss' incidents related to vent-stack over-filling, had failed to fix faulty instrumentation linked to the accident, had repeatedly postponed major equipment upgrades to save money, had violated its own rules concerning the safe location of employee work trailers on the site as well as the explicit restrictions on the use of motor vehicles in the vicinity of explosive vapours, and had ignored repeated union safety complaints. Not only had leadership deliberately, and over many years, put their employees and the facility at considerable risk to keep costs down, they had tried to shift the blame for one of the US's most serious industrial accidents onto the victims. While preventing and mitigating disasters are our clear priorities, the exposure and punishment of those who directly contribute to harm by their actions would be likely to aid such prevention. Unfortunately, it occurs far too rarely even when thousands die.

10.3 Organisational culture and 'dark secrets'

Let us now look more closely at the cultural impacts on reporting. Through an understanding of face-work, we realise that the representations that individuals and organisations make to the outside world are not always consistent with all the known facts in their possession. We all 'put our best foot forward' when making a presentation, selling ourselves or our organisation, or writing advertising copy. In fact, many common communication techniques allow us to 'profit from lies without, technically, telling any' (Goffman, 1959: 62). Furthermore, as humans we are prone to a variety of self-serving distortions and biases that operate below the conscious level to help us achieve our objectives while maintaining our self-image (Hastie and Dawes, 2001; Bazerman and Watkins, 2008: 71–94).

Representing one's self and one's organisation in the best light is not the exception, it is the rule, and most organisational leaders have learned that projecting a positive self-image eventually leads to more effective performance. Naturally, once we develop a positive self-image and express it to others, we work zealously to preserve it. Taking some liberties with the facts – or at least not revealing all that we might know or suspect – is not only natural, it very much appears necessary when others do the same.

We all know this, of course, which is why claims such as 'Brand-X detergent gets your clothes "whiter-than-white"' are not always taken literally, or even seriously.

But what if, hypothetically speaking, as a 1960s-era employee of a big soap company you had known of research that showed that phosphate-based so-called whiter-than-white detergents contribute to the growth of algae in lakes and rivers, a process known as eutrophication that results in the premature aging of those waters. Would you have gone to your bosses? Or to the environmental authorities or the media if the company had not heeded your warnings?

While the US Environmental Protection Agency did eventually break this story in 1970, thus sparing would-be whistle-blowers from possible company sanctions arising from their public disclosure, it is not much of a stretch to say that most employees would keep silent, bystanders to potential harm. While phosphate pollution may not appear to affect health and safety in a big way (although it is arguable that water quality is an important environmental issue), the difference between phosphate contamination of surface waters and tobacco's injurious impact on cancer and health, cold remedy ingredient PPA's relationship to haemorrhagic stroke,[3] and gasoline's tetraethyl lead (TEL) pollution of the air and soil is one more of extent than of kind (Hamilton, 1997; Kitman, 2000; Bryson, 2003: 149–160; ATSDR, 2007).

In particular, TEL's toxicity was known by its manufacturers since the 1920s, and its widespread environmental effects were publicly known since the 1950s. Nevertheless, it took another 45 years – over 50 years from the initial rash of TEL manufacturing deaths – for it to be banned as a fuel additive in the United States. Today we know that lead is extremely dangerous, even in minute quantities.

During the 60 years TEL remained in widespread use, the powerful lead lobby promoted doubt, funded self-serving research and prevented the leading expert on atmospheric lead, Clair Patterson, from participating in the 1971 US National Research Council investigation of lead poisoning, among other delaying tactics. Patterson also found his research funding withdrawn, and the trustees of his university were pressured to fire him or keep him quiet. Merck used the same methods against Vioxx critics Stanford Medical School professor Dr Gurkipal Singh (US Congress, 2004) and Cleveland Clinic provost Dr Eric Topol (Topol, 2004).

While such tactics appear extreme, the harm done by a relatively small number of institutions is startling: the tobacco industry kills 5.4 million people every year from lung cancer, heart disease and other illnesses, a number that will increase to more than eight million a year by 2030, according to WHO (2009a, b); TEL has demonstrably lowered intelligence (Canfield, 2003) and increased antisocial behaviour for many children who were exposed to lead poisoning from vehicle exhausts; the Union Carbide (now Dow Chemical) Bhopal, India chemical plant explosion killed 7000 people and injured 555,000, of whom 100,000 suffer from untreatable chronic conditions and 15,000 have died over the years from lung cancer, kidney failure and liver disease (Amnesty International, 2004); and Merck's Vioxx is estimated to have killed between 26,000 and 55,000 people and caused well over 100,000 heart attacks, before it was withdrawn from the market in 2004, according to testimony by Dr David Graham, senior drug safety researcher at the US Food and Drug Administration (FDA) (US Senate Committee on Finance, 2004).

Although many organisations do not make, use or trade in products that can produce grievous harm even in worst case scenarios, there are a surprising number of industries in which massive harm is possible. These include: food production, distribution and retailing; health care; pharmaceuticals and medical devices; automobiles; air travel; transportation; natural resources and mining; marine shipping and passenger transportation; energy; heating equipment; home products and construction; toys; banking and finance.

To these industries we must also add the governmental and non-governmental regulatory or watchdog organisations that exist to protect us. Failures there, such as the subprime crisis that went unrecognised by the entire spectrum of the United States and international financial regulators and credit-rating agencies, eloquently underscores the watchdog's critical role.

While some of the risks to members and the public posed by some organisations are obviously larger than others, to sustain their self-image all organisations engage in protective behaviour to some degree. They may:

- Repress and deny bad news, or the possibility of bad news. (Cases include Enron, BP Texas City refinery, Merck's Vioxx, NASA, BP's Deepwater Horizon).
- Promote doubt, hide data, and support biased, self-serving research in pursuit of financial gain and avoidance of blame for harm. (Cases include asbestos, tobacco, PPA, TEL, Vioxx, Columbia University Medical Center (Gerstein, 2010)).
- Take advantage of scientific uncertainties and political debates to promote their own interests, continuing their traditional business models for as long as possible, even when there are viable alternatives. (The most visible case is tobacco, but cases also include beryllium, lead, mercury, vinyl chloride, chromium, benzene, benzidine, nickel and many other toxic substances (Michaels, 2005)).
- Deploy legal, public relations and political options after a tragedy or disaster to avoid blame and liability and to minimise compensation to victims and their families. (Cases include asbestos, lead, PPA, tobacco, Merck's Vioxx, BP Texas City, Columbia University Medical Center).

And to some degree all organisations expect their members to demonstrate *immoral loyalty* by:

- Abandoning their escalation of concern if those in charge accept the identified large-scale risk or deny it in spite of the evidence. (This applies to government agencies, NGOs, regulators, and watchdogs, as well as to commercial firms.)
- Minimising the relevance (or simply concealing the existence) of compromising research or evidence, especially when results are known by superiors.
- Remaining silent about known dangers or acts of malfeasance. If necessary, equivocating or lying to authorities to conceal the transgression to protect the organisation and their superiors.

These characteristics sound melodramatic, and perhaps they are when stated this baldly. Yet there seems little doubt that having *some* secrets increases one's chances of success as well as helping to preserve the existing social order upon which one's success so often appears to depend. Inevitably, however, this means that among these secrets some organisations will have what Goffman (1959: 123) calls *dark secrets* – those harmful or unethical aspects of organisational practice whose revelation would deeply threaten the external faces that any organisation, public or private, presents to its constituents – members, customers, investors, regulators and the public. When dark secrets exist, one's own external face cannot be wholly truthful.

In addition, since dark secrets tend to engender cover-ups to contain them, there are additional rounds of secrets to be kept and increasingly more people who must keep them. Faced with evasive responses from their bosses, most organisation members learn that certain topics are 'undiscussable', and it is best to keep one's questions and criticisms to oneself. The near-universal and often ruthless retaliation against whistleblowers is a convincing argument that keeping your head down is usually wise.

As human beings have confronted such situations over millennia, it seems likely that we have evolved not only to create secrets but to be 'loyal', by protecting those of our family, clan, village, and tribe. Betrayal by ancient man almost certainly meant ostracism and, with it, the likelihood of suffering and death. We have carried this ancient fear of banishment into the present day, extending our loyalty to the workplace. Such loyalty helps explain why so many of us remain bystanders, even in the face of unambiguous harm to others or ethical transgressions we know to be wrong. To permit us to live with ourselves, we have developed a psychological capacity to deny or rationalise our complicity. Denial and rationalisation are virtually universal human characteristics.

An interesting question is whether organisations follow these same practices. We know that to maintain the social order we work to maintain each other's faces, and avoid exposing faults or embarrassing facts unless we wish to cause harm. Do organisations also protect one another, preserving their dark secrets and expecting others to do the same? History suggests that when an industry or government body shares a common but questionable practice, such as unregulated lobbying, or a profitable but dangerous raw material, such as lead, asbestos, tobacco or PPA, it is likely that they will support one another by going to great lengths to protect their shared secrets for as long as possible. In the United States, special interests have been with us since the dawn of the Republic (Bazerman and Watkins, 2008: 132).

10.4 Some possible ways forward

The challenge we face as shapers of organisations is how to harmonise the unavoidable need for secrets and the loyalty they command with the equally important need to protect the public interest and create a safe, moral and just society. While the preservation of the social order – or at least its orderly

Table 10.2 Specific suggestions for committed organisations

Leadership and governance	Explicit main board-level responsibility for safety and risk supported by regular external audits and reviews in finance, safety and risk by truly independent firms. Clear executive leadership policy position regarding safety and risk. Political and financial support for government and NGO regulators and other watchdogs to set standards, provide oversight and critique and impose sanctions. Top management reinforcement actions to ensure that safety and open communications are genuinely rewarded (praise, financial rewards, responsibility taking, consistent promotion practices, etc.) Policy of fair compensation for whistle-blower retaliation consistent with the true harm done (loss of long-term employment, psychological harm, etc.)
Education, training and review	Top management education regarding the inadvertent risk-seeking incentives they create for the levels below them. Training for managers about the appropriate responses to employee worries, concerns, and reports of danger or abuse. Employee education on the possible negative consequences of silence. Real-world practice/simulation, especially of unusual conditions (i.e., 'flight simulator' approach to training for potentially catastrophic rare events). Formal 'after-action reviews' for both good and bad experiences to build on success and identify areas for improvement in areas of safety, risk and ethics. 'Intergroup' interventions, such as membership exchanges between interdependent or rival teams to reduce dysfunctional intergroup competition and add multiple perspectives to diagnosis and problem-solving.
Measurement, reward, discipline and incentive systems	Organisation-wide risk-reduction goals/priorities. Improved reporting of risks, identified risk conditions, and near misses. Measurement and reward/incentive systems at all levels to better balance productivity/financial objectives and risk, especially positive incentives to make communication of dangers and concerns worthwhile. Redesign of financial reward systems to incorporate long-term risk/reward provisions. Rewards and recognition for risk-prevention activism. 'Zero tolerance' approach to truth-teller/whistle-blower retaliation.
Organisational structure and process	Truly independent internal safety/audit units reporting to knowledgeable and sympathetic senior executives. Disciplined reporting and follow-up of 'weak signals'. Anonymous truth-telling reporting mechanisms via independent outside parties and independent, anonymous legal counsel and advice for truth-tellers if necessary.

Continued

Table 10.2 Continued

Culture	Reinforcement for danger/ethics reporting by employees from supervisors and rank-and-file opinion leaders. New heroic myths and positive role models (with formal and informal rewards/recognition to reinforce them). Redefinition of 'loyalty' under conditions of risk or malfeasance. New norms of supervisory and work group behaviour concerning matters of risk and malfeasance.
Budgets/ funding practices	Special resource pools to deal with unbudgeted risks. (Note: It must be culturally valid for such pools to be tapped and considered a violation for them to be abused.) Adequate budgets/staff for risk control, safety and audit functions. Funding for outside counsel/advice for truth-tellers/whistle-blowers.
Staffing, selection, and careers	Selection criteria and financial compensation of key safety, risk and audit functions consistent with other high importance organisational activities. Staffing of -, safety and audit with high potential individuals who then go on to significant senior positions. Attractive career paths for functional alumni who spend time in safety, audit and so on (In other words, these functions are not 'dead ends' or second class careers.)

change – is arguably essential for stability, it must not come at the cost of ethical conduct or result in grievous social harm.

Two major challenges must be met and surmounted. First is the obvious need to transcend the rules of the social order to keep secrets, particularly in the workplace where the drives toward conformity and bystander behaviour are unusually potent because of the normative power of these cultures and the rewards and punishments available to ensure compliance. The second and far more difficult challenge is dealing with those risks and unethical practices instigated by leadership itself. Such initiatives typically harness the full power of the organisation's structures, systems and rewards. Over time, they also co-opt and poison the culture itself.

Fortunately, the most numerous and straightforward cases involve preventing the potentially dangerous or unethical acts committed by employees outside the purview and against the wishes of their leaders. Such actions inevitably run counter to the organisation's safety protocols and ethical standards and are simply undesirable by any objective standard. Unfortunately, however, most organisational remedies are conceived and implemented piecemeal, when a systemic approach is actually necessary because organisational behaviour tends to be over-determined, the product of many overlapping forces, and thus largely immune to simple solutions such as policy statements, rule-making, and training. While the more routine actions listed in

Table 10.2 will address many of these undesirable behaviours, simple fixes will not address dismantling the rewards for risky behaviour, eliminating the social benefits of remaining a bystander, or reduce the freedom of most public or private-sector managers to arbitrarily punish 'disloyal' subordinates.

Beyond these already formidable obstacles, history has shown that some of the greatest harm is created as a side effect of misguided leadership polices[4] or as a set of deliberate acts conceived to save money, make money, or achieve other legitimate organisational objectives, albeit by questionable and sometimes illegal means. Considerably stronger medicine is needed to address such transgressions.

10.5 Creating a robust context for safety and ethics

As the chapters in this book reveal, many factors affect the creation and ultimate effectiveness of warnings. Clearly, however, to change toward organisations in which information about hazards and malfeasance are routinely reported from within, one must overcome the cultural rules that encourage us to maintain the social order irrespective of the larger costs. Put this way, it should be clear that only a force that is partly *outside* the existing organisation's or industry's culture can initiate and sustain such change.

The most important changes needed to create the proper incentives are:

1. Strengthening the responsibility, independence and power of external oversight.
2. Ensuring that internal whistleblowers and truth-tellers are free from the retaliation that serves as both a punishment for 'disloyalty' and as a warning to others.

Creating such change is a burden that clearly falls to each organisation's top leadership, to its employee representatives or union (if it is more than a 'company union'), and to law-makers, regulators, auditors and external watchdogs.

On both counts, many will claim that changes are unnecessary because an extensive web of laws, regulations, and professional practice-support systems are already in place. While a considerable infrastructure certainly exists, there is extensive evidence that it often fails when it is most needed.

For example, virtually all of the major US accounting-based frauds – Waste Management, Enron, Xerox, among others – involved collusion on the part of the firm's audit firms (Bazerman and Watkins, 2008: 43–67). Similarly, according to many critics the US FDA's Office of New Drugs played a complicit role in the Vioxx crisis. Dr Sidney Wolfe, Director of Public Citizen's Health Research Group, has argued that many re-labelling compromises negotiated by the FDA, such as that affecting the use of Vioxx at the high doses known to increase the risk of heart attacks five-fold, effectively sustain dangerous drugs on the market even when there are safer alternatives (Molotsky, 1987; Wolfe, 2006).

At the root of these and other regulatory failures is a combination of political influence, inadequate regulatory funding or misaligned priorities, and industry-level structural and financial arrangements that compromise independence by encouraging regulators, auditors and credit-rating agencies to identify too closely with industry – which even some regulators define as their 'clients.' There seems little doubt, for example, that Moody's and Standard & Poor's pursuit of commercial objectives exacerbated the build-up of risk that culminated in the subprime crisis. Such commercial or political conflicts of interest make it effectively impossible to report dark secrets. One is expected – in fact, required – to adopt the client's point of view and to be 'loyal' in the manner the client defines.[5]

In addition, the frequent criticism that private-sector boards of directors are often too close to their CEOs appears valid, and that their involvement in matters of risk is often too distant and indirect to be effective protectors of shareholder value, especially when auditor or regulator independence is compromised.

After Merck announced the withdrawal of Vioxx in September 2004, for example, its stock price dropped precipitously and did not return to its prior relationship to the S&P index for approximately three years. Since dramatic stock price drops in the wake of a crisis tend to 'reset' market price levels, and such resets effectively deprive shareholders of a significant return on their investment, it is the board's fiduciary responsibility to try to prevent them.[6]

While Merck has continuously defended its actions in the Vioxx case, court papers and congressional testimony reveal that well before the drug's withdrawal the company was in possession of worrying clinical-trials data, it had systematically intimidated critics, violated its own rules regarding the professional staffing of its clinical trials, and published positive research results that were based upon questionable research protocols (Gerstein et al., 2008: 126–142). In light of these facts, Merck's board arguably failed in its responsibilities in not having put in place systems to detect such widespread transgressions in a drug that was such an important engine of company revenues and shareholder value.

Like other 'insiders', board members are expected to keep secrets when, in fact, their larger responsibilities demand that they sometimes do exactly the opposite.

Similarly, the late 1990s Xerox accounting fraud was characterised by the US Securities and Exchange Commission (SEC) to be one of the most blatant because of its duration, the company's lack of cooperation with the government investigation, and the complicity of company executives including board chairman and former CEO Paul Allaire.[7] KPMG, Xerox's auditors, paid a large fine for its role, as did a number of company executives, including

Allaire, all of whom were barred from being an officer or director of a public company for a period of time.[8]

However, when the possibilities of wrongdoing prompted an SEC investigation in the summer of 2000, an in-depth internal investigation by the board's audit committee would probably have revealed the lies Xerox was feeding the media. In fact, by that time James Bingham, a Xerox assistant treasurer, had written a scathing memo and presented his conclusion to Xerox's CFO and other executives that there was a 'high likelihood' that the company had issued 'misleading financial statements and public disclosures.' Bingham was fired immediately – which should itself have been an important red flag for the board.

In spite of the seriousness of the fraud, and despite the symbolically 'large' fines, none of the participants was required to admit guilt, and no criminal penalties were involved. One must wonder whether the relatively modest sanctions for both Xerox staff or KPMG will dissuade others from similar acts (Bander and Hechinger, 2001: C1).

As much as a governing board can and should do, however, it remains the responsibility of an organisation's operating head and its top managers to specify and reinforce the behaviours that will lead, in time, to a change in culture. We assume, of course, that management will issue the proclamations and establish the policies that appear, on paper at least, to require high standards of behaviour and encourage truth-telling. While policy statements are necessary and useful, the difficulty arises with the practicalities of achieving them, especially when people are under time and financial pressure, or are encouraged by performance measures or incentives to engage in risky practices.

Unfortunately, there are no simple answers to conflicts between the drive toward organisational success, and safety or ethics. In the infamous B. F. Goodrich (BFG) A7D Corsair II attack aircraft-brake scandal, the company won an important contract on the basis of an innovative but unproven low-cost brake design. Unfortunately, the new design did not work. Rather than redesign the brake system after internal tests failed (as eventually occurred), BFG chose to falsify test data, a step that only delayed the inevitable (as well as violating US federal law). In a subsequent real-world test, the brake overheated and fused causing the test aircraft to skid dangerously 1500 feet down the runway upon landing. A Senate investigation followed, but no one at the company was indicted and the managers who ordered the falsification were promoted, a surprisingly common occurrence. Unfortunately, Kermit Vandivier, the BFG whistleblower who brought the fraud to FBI and Senate attention fared much less well (Vandivier, 1972).

10.6 The plight of whistleblowers

As with Vandivier and Xerox's Bingham, much has been written about the severe punishment whistleblowers receive after revealing dark secrets

(Glazer, 1983; Alford, 2001). The US Federal Government is perhaps the most striking example of failure to support dissenting employees, despite superficially good intentions.

The various attempts to protect US Federal Government whistleblowers in law have all had limited effect in practice, because the legislation excludes certain groups, such as intelligence services, and provides inadequate protections against retaliation, specifically limitations to access to trial by jury in federal court as an escalation to existing bureaucratic administrative procedures.

While the situation is arguably somewhat better in the US private sector, the retaliation against corporate truth-tellers is much the same – and perhaps more arbitrary because of near-universal employment-at-will and the enormous expense and time involved for restitution through the courts that, in any case, place the burden of proof on the employee. Even professional associations, such as those for engineers, which might be expected to stand up for their members on matters of safety and ethics, may fail to defend them. Although members must often sign their association's ethical code of conduct, experience suggests those who abide by it by speaking out are often on their own if they are punished or dismissed, especially when onerous legal expenses are involved.

In contrast to such iniquitous results, one might think that employees revealing the truth in areas in which management *wants* visibility – primarily safety and malfeasance – would be free from retaliation. That is incorrect. While there are certainly cases of danger or individual misbehaviour that can be safely reported, as the BFG, BP Texas City and Xerox fraud cases illustrate, many dangerous or unethical acts are performed with tacit or explicit management permission in order to accomplish a sanctioned organisational objective by dubious means. Management's desired response to an employee's discovery of the dark side of such an initiative is to go along with it and to keep his mouth shut. Any alternative behaviour is seen as disloyal and often grounds for reprimands, sanctions or dismissal.

10.7 Conclusion

Since organisational culture is formed primarily through the pattern of leadership actions rather than through words alone, it must be these actions that counter the 'normal' range of individual, group and organisational phenomena that act in concert to preserve the social order and the organisation's dark secrets. This means that the successful reporting of hazards and ethical violations requires that behaviour typically considered countercultural must be transformed to become culturally acceptable. In particular, conditions must be changed so that truth-tellers are confident that they are not putting their careers and families at risk by speaking out. Counterintuitively, this is much less about protecting the rights of those few who may be forced by an unresponsive management to 'go public' than it is about creating an organisational culture that values dissent and protects *all* truth-tellers from punishment, even those whose concerns ultimately prove ill-founded.

Therefore, one must view the recommendations summarised in Table 10.2 as intended for those leaders who are dedicated to greater transparency and dissent. Even for such committed leaders, however, achieving success will be difficult. External oversight and strong sanctions for truth-teller retaliation should therefore be considered 'critical success factors' (Rockart, 1986). For the reasons we have described in this chapter, while progress can be made, we believe that changes in voluntary reporting cannot be sustained over time by either internal or external actions alone. Unless we concurrently alter internal organisational culture and the larger societal context that contains it, our struggle to prevent disasters will ultimately remain a losing one.

Notes

1. While the F-15s had the capability to talk to the Army helicopters using conventional radios, it was their practice to rely on their secure and highly sophisticated HAVE QUICK II radios that utilised both encryption and frequency hopping. Some but not all of the Army helicopters had HAVE QUICK II capabilities but the Army's helicopter command had decided not to enable them (a task that required the loading of daily codes) because not all the helicopters in use were so equipped.
2. The material on the Bhopal disaster is voluminous. For an excellent overview see (Wikipedia, Bhopal disaster) and particularly the extensive references therein. An important point, as well as Union Carbide's primary defence, is that the proximate cause of the accident was employee sabotage, a conclusion contested by others. In any case, a widely shared view is that many other factors contributed to the release of the poisonous gas, including the basic design of the plant, especially the raw materials used and the decisions made about the storage of hazardous materials, and safety systems. There is also a clear consensus that many critical safety systems were not operational at the time of the accident. Union Carbide's (Dow Chemical) position is articulated on their dedicated web site (Union Carbide, 2001–2009).
3. Phenylpropanolamine (PPA) was a widely used over-the-counter ingredient employed since the 1930s as a decongestant in cold remedies such as Alka Seltzer Plus, Dimotapp and Contac, and as an appetite suppressant in so-called 'diet pills'. Before it was withdrawn in the United States, six billion doses of PPA were consumed annually by approximately seven and a half million people in the United States. (PPA is still sold over-the-counter in the UK and Europe, although it is a different isomer of the molecule with a different side-effects profile. Appetite suppressants ('diet pills') containing PPA are not sold in these markets.) Starting in the late 1970s, scattered reports of haemorrhagic (bleeding) stroke began to surface in the United States among young women who had used diet pills containing PPA. Although substitutes for PPA were available (and have successfully replaced it

since the FDA's decision that the drug be withdrawn), PPA manufacturers rejected the FDA's concerns, employing scientists and lobbyists to pressure for continued PPA use in their over-the-counter (OTC) preparations. The delays were successful: it took nearly 20 years from the initial reports for a systematic epidemiological study to be undertaken. Prior to PPA's withdrawal, the FDA estimated that between 200 and 500 strokes per year among 18- to 49-year-old women were caused by the drug. Although these are small numbers in percentage terms, viewed through the lens of public health the deaths were unnecessary since effective alternatives to PPA were available. Curiously, while the industry sponsored and approved the Haemorrhagic Stroke Project (Keman, 2000), a five-year study conducted during the 1990s by the Yale Medical School with FDA approval, industry defence lawyers attacked its conclusions in a series of victims' lawsuits filed after the FDA's decision to withdraw the drug.

4. Arguably the mistreatment of detainees initiated under the banner of the US 'War On Terror' provides a vivid example.
5. Carl Bass, a member of auditors Arthur Andersen's Professional Practice Group, and the firm's expert on audit rule interpretation, was removed from the Enron account at the request of CFO Andrew Fastow because he objected to a number of Enron's more aggressive accounting practices. See Eichenwald (2005: 426).
6. Gerstein's analysis of stock market data was performed for Merck, Xerox and BP. One should note that since each stock trade involves a buyer and seller – and the vast majority involve institutional investors and market-makers – all stock movements reset prices to some degree, and significant changes in price levels often (but not always) do so for an extended period. Contact the author for more information.
7. For the SEC documents concerning the Xerox accounting fraud, see SEC (Various documents concerning the late 1990s Xerox accounting fraud). In addition, *The New York Times* and *The Wall Street Journal* extensively covered the story from 2000, when the first signs of the fraud emerged, to 2006 when final settlement was reached.
8. Since Xerox executives were not convicted of a crime or required to admit guilt, under the by-laws of the corporation the company repaid their lost stock sale profits and bonuses for all but the one million dollars-per- person fines imposed by the SEC. In Allaire's case, this means that the company repaid his disgorgement of $5.2 million he received from selling shares of Xerox during the fraud, $500,000 in bonuses he received for meeting profit goals the SEC determined were met because of the fraud's earnings impact, and $1.9 million of interest payments on these amounts. Xerox's shareholders, therefore, paid bonuses for profits never earned and provided restitution to Allaire for stock prices inflated by these fraudulent profits (Norris, 2003).

Part III
Responding to Warnings

11
Transnational Risk Management: A Business Perspective

Corene Crossin and James Smither

11.1 Introduction

In our work as risk consultants, we provide clients with analysis and consulting support to enable them to better understand the political, operational and security risks their investments and operations may encounter. Through analysis of the contextual background and the immediate and longer-term importance of unfolding political events and developments, we map the vulnerabilities of specific investments or projects – with the aim of forecasting potential events. In this chapter we provide an explanation of our approach, and discuss the challenges faced by risk consultancies when providing risk assessments and forecasting on behalf of companies seeking success in a broad range of complex environments and sectors globally.

This chapter is designed to provide an explanation of a business-risk practitioner's approach to risk management and forecasting as a potential point of contrast from other chapters in this book. While we draw on well-known international risk-assessment frameworks, and have adapted them to develop our own approaches and methods to deal with the challenges of forecasting and managing risk, forecasting complex scenarios is challenging. This is particularly true in the context of doing business in new markets amidst ever evolving global, regional, national and local trends and dynamics.

In this chapter we seek to share some of our experiences. In particular, the chapter will outline some key lessons learned from conducting risk assessments and forecasting for clients with investments and operations in emerging markets. We discuss how our clients' appetite for risk affects their expectations and attitudes towards risk assessments, and conclude with a summary of key lessons learned.

11.2 Risk consulting

Control Risks is an independent business-risk consultancy that provides political, operational, reputational and security risk analysis and forecasting to corporate, governmental and non-profit clients. Through risk consulting we aim at enabling our clients to understand the contextual background and the immediate and longer-term importance of unfolding events and developments. We also aim at facilitating our clients to anticipate future incidents and monitor evolving trends, where necessary adapting their business strategy to accommodate forecasted change.

Risk management is a comparatively new discipline for business, and is growing in importance for many companies as regulators, host governments, shareholders, insurers, financiers and other stakeholders seek to ensure companies are managed in a manner that complies with law as well as globally-recognised standards of corporate governance. At the same time, there is increasing pressure on companies to strengthen practices to obtain early and rigorous identification of risks (cf. Chapter 13). Consultancies providing support to companies expanding their portfolios in new markets are thus seeing sustained levels of business from companies seeking to extract value from new opportunities.

The oil-and-gas industry is a case in point. Pressures on oil and commodity prices, and constraints on supply from the most established producer markets, combined with projections of 'peak oil', have created a powerful dialectic that has seen political and security risk return to prominence. Multinational companies are increasingly travelling to new locations to exploit previously marginal deposits; and at the same time host governments and disrupted host communities they encounter there are also seeking to extract the maximum benefit from this growing desire to tap into their natural resources. Competition to secure access to reserves thus must be balanced against the need to protect investments from governmental interference and community opposition. Companies must closely weigh up the value of potential opportunities against the myriad risks associated with operating in complex political and social environments.

It is not only extractives companies that are increasingly broadening their horizons into new zones. Numerous other sectors are facing similar dilemmas – whether in search of new customers away from more saturated markets (such as telecommunications and retail banking firms), cheaper inputs-sourcing, manufacturing and back-office functions (food and beverages, automobiles and customer-service call centres) or new centres of research and innovation or unpenetrated populations for product development purposes (pharmaceuticals). It is in this sphere that specialist risk-management expertise is called for.

11.3 Identifying and assessing risks: methodology

There are a number of methodologies for identifying and evaluating risks, including those set down in national and international standards including: the *Risk Management Standard* (2002) published by the Institute of

Risk Management (IRM), the Association of Insurance and Risk Managers (AIRMIC), and Alarm (The Public Risk Management Association); the UK's *BS 31100 Code of Practice for Risk Management* (2008); the United State's *NIST 800-30* (NIST, 2001) – with a primary focus on IT security; and the *ISO/FDIS 3100: Risk Management – Principles and guidelines* (ISO, 2009).

Our approach to assessing risks on behalf of our clients is broadly on the methodology set down in the *AS/NZS 4360 Risk Management Standard* (AS and NZS, 2004), though frequently our clients will have developed their own approaches and standards for assessing and managing risks – in which case we adapt our assessments to suit these other methodologies where appropriate. This methodology has recently also been captured by the International Organisation for Standardisation (ISO) in its ISO 3100 *Risk Management Standard*. Thus our approach is in line with that adopted by many international clients. The framework is also useful as in allowing for flexibility in applying recommended risk-assessment stages. As risk assessments need to be tailored specifically to clients' industrial sector, business operations and risk appetite across different markets – clearly a hedge fund or commodities trader faces different risk questions from a gold-mining company – flexibility in approach is essential.

Our approach is based on a qualitative (as opposed to quantitative) assessment of risk – though we do assign numerical values to 'score' various constituent elements of a risk analysis once a qualitative assessment has first been conducted. The methodology provides guidance on the stages to be followed when conducting an assessment. However, the approach set down in the methodology is as much about drawing out information from appropriate stakeholders and sources as it is in following these steps. We provide an illustration of each stage, and how it applies to our assessment of risk on behalf of clients (see Figure 11.1).

11.3.1 Context

Risk management is an integral part of all business processes. Thus before commencing a risk assessment, we first seek to understand the external and internal context of the client organisation in order to ensure the assessment is appropriately tailored to the client's business. The more we can understand those processes the better we are positioned to ensure risk assessments provide a valuable contribution to strategic planning, project management, change management and other decision-making processes. This is by definition a consultative process, and includes examining the following areas:

- The external context for the risk assessment, and the drivers behind the assessment, including for instance requirements set down by insurers, project partners, lenders, host or national governments or other stakeholders.

- An organisation's appetite for a range of political, operational and security risks. Risk appetite, or risk tolerance, is a particularly difficult concept to define and apply yet it is crucial the concept is explored before conducting a risk assessment, in order to begin framing organisation-specific understanding of the overall level of risk that is acceptable. This in turn informs definitions of impact and the resources available to mitigate risks.
- The goals and objectives of the assessment, including an understanding of the client's wider objectives in relation to how the risk assessment will be used.
- Identification and understanding of any pre-existing internal risk management processes, policies and practices.
- Agreement on the process or programme for the assessment, including how information from previous assessments should be used, and how we will be able to consult with appropriate stakeholders (such as local law enforcement authorities).
- Identification of any constraints, including the need to establish a thorough understanding of any potential sensitivities with regard to confidential security arrangements.
- Confirmation of any evaluation criteria that the client will require to ensure the assessment and any subsequent mitigation plans are fit for purpose.

The context-setting phase is fundamental to ensuring the following stages are accurate. To that end, client openness and engagement are crucial: we

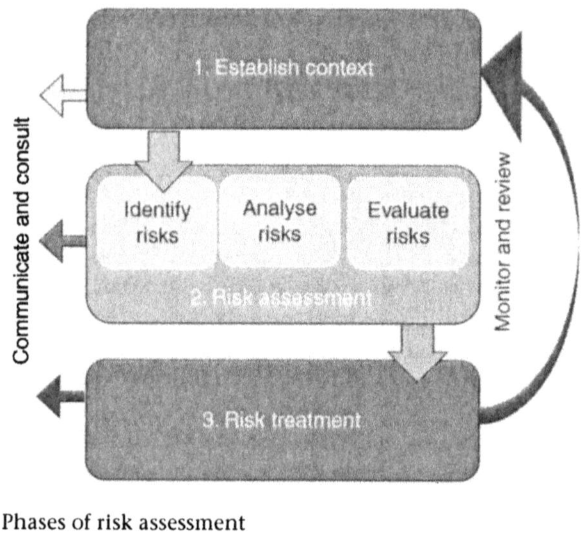

Figure 11.1 Phases of risk assessment

need to build a relationship with the client so that the assessment speaks to their business – and also to ensure they are able to learn from the assessment. A weakly-defined context or underdeveloped client relationship may mean that an assessment misses important nuances and consequently results in inaccurate findings.

11.3.2 Identifying and assessing risks

When carrying out a risk assessment, we first examine threats. We identify the range of sources (individuals, groups, institutions or objects) that may have the capability and necessary intention to carry out an event that may have an impact on our client's objectives. This is crucial: to identify risks, we must first consider the full range of potential sources of those risks.

Threats are different from risks. Threat is defined by the ISO/IEC as *a factor that could lead a source to cause an event*. It refers to a motive or condition. Risk, on the other hand, is defined as *the likelihood of an event and its impact on objectives*. Risk is thus more specific than threat (cf. Chapters 5 and 16).

Terrorism provides a useful example to understand the division between sources, threats and risks. There are many different domestic and international groups that may be described as terrorist organisations. These groups may be defined as the source of the threat of terrorism in any given context. Depending on the overall modus operandi, tactics, capability and intent of each group, a number of different terrorist events may occur. For example, suicide bombing is one of many possible threats that may be carried out by a terrorist organisation. It is only when we assign values for likelihood (or probability) and impact (or consequence) of that threat that we can say what the risk of a suicide bombing will be in a given context. To get to the point where we can provide values for likelihood and impact, we need to conduct in-depth, careful analysis of intention and capability and other factors – as is discussed further below.

Establishing the overall threat context is particularly important when assessing exposure to political risk. Too often, the views of the insurance industry and segments of the financial and business community narrowly drive an organisation's view of its political risks. Risk classes defined in advance by underwriters – expropriation, strikes, riots and civil commotion (SRCC), non-payment, and so on – dominate considerations of the events that may be confronted, and the exclusion-crammed policies to transfer the liability created by such an event offered by those same underwriters in turn dictate the corporate response. This is both an incomplete and a short-term approach: risk conditions in a market can change rapidly, and can often manifest at a non-sovereign level where policy coverage may not apply.

A broader definition of political risk is one that evaluates the likelihood of a *variety* of state *or non-state* political actors negatively affecting business operations in a country through regime instability, or direct *and indirect* interference. State actors can include domestic (central and local) as well as foreign governments, parliament, the judiciary and the security forces. Non-state actors can include insurgent groups, secessionist movements, lobbies, other companies, organised criminal groups, and ethnic and indigenous groups in the project vicinity, as well as international organisations.

In taking this broader view, investors can begin to assess in a comprehensive way the specific political, economic, social and security threat environment they confront at a national, regional and local level. As part of this process, it is crucial to consider how the full spectrum of political stakeholders (at every level) view the investment: for example, their prior opinion of the industry sector where the investment is to be placed, local perceptions of the nationality of its owners and operators, and the precise physical footprint of its assets and supporting infrastructure on the ground.

11.3.3 Stakeholder analysis

Since the core of good political-risk management is developing a plan to influence political stakeholders, when assessing threats the stakeholder identification process needs to be as comprehensive as possible – and to recognise that different stakeholders can be providers of support as well as sources of risk to a project. The next step is therefore to identify and map stakeholders and understand how their objectives may affect the investment in positive and negative ways. To map stakeholders fully involves:

- Identifying the full spectrum of political stakeholders who may have an interest in, or influence on, the investment: this can include international actors, as well as national and local players in the project country.
- Conducting detailed research to identify each stakeholder's interests, motivations and position vis-à-vis the investment: these may not have emerged yet, or may be incoherent or contested.
- In each case, identifying areas where there is overlap between the aims and objectives of the investment and those of the stakeholders.

11.3.4 Intent and capability

There is a lack of guidance in existing international risk-management standards on how best to measure threats, and so we have developed our own approach to fill that gap. In particular, we consider whether a source (such as a terrorist group) has an expressly stated intent, the history and modus operandi of identified sources, as well as that source's capability to carry out an event. To assess capability, we examine the degree to which a source has the requisite access to the resources that would be required to carry out an event. In the case of a terrorist organisation, therefore, we will examine the extent to which a group has access to requisite technical expertise, financing, training and ideological support to carry out a terrorist attack. Finally, we also look at whether there are internal or external constraints (e.g., the effectiveness of a country's security forces and intelligence apparatus) that would prevent a source from carrying out an event.

Analysis of intention and capability is also useful when forecasting, and in particular in developing, future scenarios and identifying triggers that may influence a change in threat environment.

It should also be noted that we adopt a dynamic approach to examining threats. Underpinning our threat analysis is a recognition of the importance of the changing, two-way relationship between a client's project and the political, security, operational and social environment in which the project is located. Thus assessments do not focus only on threats and risks to the particular client emanating from the threat environment, but also examine the potential influence of the client's activities on other stakeholders arising from the manner in which the project or business activity interacts within the wider environment.

11.4 Vulnerability: a key determinant of likelihood and impact

A thorough risk assessment considers both the likelihood and impact of the full range of possible risks on an investment stemming from all stakeholders identified, and anticipating all credible changes in the underlying circumstances. To measure the likelihood and impact of a range of political risks accurately, it is first necessary to consider the vulnerability of the investment to a range of threats (issues and problems) posed by stakeholders (or sources of threat). In other words, a risk assessment asks what specific problems or issues could arise as a result of the investment's interaction with these stakeholders, and also considers whether the investment has sufficiently robust risk-management processes in place to address those problems or issues. The weaker an investment's ability to manage political and other types of threats, the higher the probability (or likelihood) that those issues will have a negative impact on the investment.

Therefore, the objective of a vulnerability assessment is to examine the client's position vis-à-vis the overall threat environment, and to see whether the client has in place measures that will either prevent an event from occurring, or that will reduce the impact of an event once it has occurred. We also examine potential actions or inactions that may lead to *unintended* exposure to threats. This is a comparatively straightforward exercise when examining a client's vulnerability to security threats. Our security consultants will look to examine security policies, procedures and how they are implemented, to determine exposure to threats – and to assign values for likelihood and impact. However, the task is considerably more complex when considering a client's vulnerability to political, operational or reputational threats.

A critical further aspect of risk assessment is the acknowledgement that things will rarely remain static, either in the host context and amongst the various stakeholders located there, or in the actions and progress of the investment itself. Holistic risk management therefore requires the development and constant updating of scenarios to identify how the current national and local risk environment may change, and how these changes will interact with changes during the life of the investment itself: for example, as a gold mine transitions from a construction phase (where local-employment requirements are traditionally highest), through an operational phase (when its physical and fiscal output will probably be most attractive) to potentially its closure. These should include worst-case as well as best-case scenarios: unanticipated regime change, be it through coup, incapacitation or the ballot box, is a classic source of political risk as the new leadership often seeks to 'renegotiate' the business deals concluded by predecessor administrations on terms deemed more 'preferential' to the host country, and less 'exploitative' of its inhabitants.

To understand this dynamic fully, the organisation needs to audit the investment's own risk-management structure and approach, and identify whether this is sufficiently well structured and implemented to manage identified threats effectively. This involves the recognition that steps taken, or not taken, by a project, even if in good faith, can themselves create risks – especially involving local-community stakeholders – as well as providing a perfect pretext for the imposition of other (political) risks by authorities with an already hostile agenda.

Assessing vulnerability opens the gateway to values for likelihood and impact to be assigned to specific risk events. Both the likelihood and impact of the risks are examined so that steps may be taken to identify them as early as possible, and then ideally prevent them from occurring (reduce likelihood) or, failing that, implement strategies to ensure that the consequences of the risk are as benign as possible for the investment (reduce impact). Assigning values for likelihood and impact enables priority risks to be identified, and thus facilitates decision-making when developing plans to manage risk. Recording the likelihood and impact of events assists in prioritising the allocation of resources to reduce a client's exposure to those risks.

In order to apply a value for impact, consideration first needs to be given to how impact is categorised and ratings developed. For instance, when conducting political risk assessments, commercial organisations will require impact to focus on the potential reputational, operational, legal, and financial ramifications of identified risk events. For other, security focused risk assessments, impact categories may focus on the potential consequences of an event on personnel, assets and management.

Once categories of impact have been identified, it is then necessary to consider sub-definitions for levels of impact. That is, an organisation must consider how a 'major' impact on personnel may be defined as opposed to a 'minor' impact. This is necessarily a function of an organisation's tolerance for particular kinds of risk, and thus needs to be tailored to reflect that tolerance.

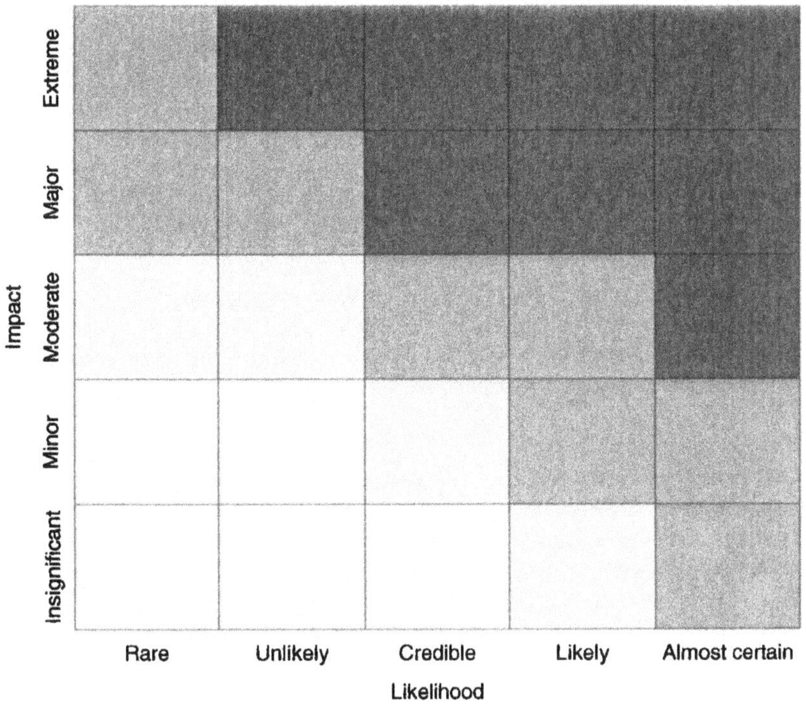

Figure 11.2 Impact-likelihood-matrix

Likelihood, on the other hand, is comparatively easy to define and is generally independent of an organisation's risk tolerance. Values for likelihood can be described using qualitative statements (for instance, 'almost certain,' 'likely' or 'unlikely') and may be further qualified by percentages indicating the range of probability.

Taken together, likelihood and impact provide a useful framework for distinguishing between those risks which may be able to be managed through routine risk management measures, and those more critical risks which require additional risk-mitigation measures. In this vein, Impact-Likelihood Matrices can be a useful tool to illustrate overall levels of risk severity – as in the example shown in Figure 11.2 – where each colour gradient illustrates the overall severity of the risk.

11.5 Mitigation

The aim of a risk mitigation (or treatment) strategy is to identify measures that can reduce the client's exposure to assessed risks. In simple terms, this means identifying measures that may reduce the likelihood and/or the impact of risks to a level that is acceptable to the client. In this respect, the vulnerability assessment is again useful as it can provide an indication of key points of weakness in a client's approach to risk management. In summary, the following risk-treatment options are generally open to clients:

- Avoiding the risk by deciding not to do something that contributes to the risk
- Taking or accepting a risk in order to pursue an opportunity
- Removing the source of the risk
- Putting in measures to reduce the likelihood or impact of an event
- Sharing the risk with other parties

Finally, a key part of risk management is ongoing monitoring – both of the overall threat environment, but also of the implementation of risk-treatment measures. Control Risks assists in both aspects of monitoring. The following section provides an explanation of a number of different ways in which we assist clients in the monitoring of the threat environment.

In terms of political-risk assessments, for example, stakeholder engagement is frequently a key risk-mitigation tool. That is, identifying risk-mitigation measures requires consideration of how relationships with stakeholders need to be adjusted or bolstered to both support objectives and to lower an organisation's exposure to identified risks.

Having therefore identified key threats and risks, and having closely considered the stakeholders who may affect the investment's exposure to such risks, a framework risk-management strategy (or a risk-mitigation strategy) can now be built. Those stakeholders whose objectives and motivations are in opposition to the investment will need to be closely and actively managed to achieve a greater area of mutual interest. Those whose objectives are closely aligned with the investment will need to be engaged and their shared objectives cemented. The importance of mutual self-interest cannot be overstated in this context: the company that seeks to 'get one over' on its host government when the playing field is tilted in its favour at some point during the lifespan of an investment project, is invariably the same party that finds itself most enthusiastically pressurised whenever the balance of power shifts in the opposite direction. Ebbs and flows in commodity prices regularly catalyse exactly this kind of tit-for-tat exchange between an extractives company and its host government.

The specifics of a risk-management strategy will always vary according to individual context: company, sector, geography, status of project. From the company perspective, community grievances with a mining project entering production phase may involve conflict over persistent levels of fuel or equipment theft from sites and vehicles. Resentment may, however, be building among the community over a perceived reduction in employment opportunities, escalating environmental contamination, or the slow delivery, or non-delivery, of anticipated social and physical infrastructure improvements such as new roads, power provision, hospitals and schools. Instead of attempting to address each problem in isolation, an integrated risk-management strategy would recognise that theft and protest problems are likely to stem directly from prevailing socio-economic conditions, and a perception that the local community is not benefiting from the project as much as had been hoped or promised. A heavy-handed security-focused solution to the theft problem is therefore likely to exacerbate all of the issues being confronted. Dialogue followed by demonstrable actions is key to achieve recognition and shared understanding of where jobs can be created. This may not be possible in the project itself, since positions may be too specialist; however, there may be employment creation opportunities in the supply of services and logistics to the project's daily operations – where the infrastructure enhancement can be achieved to all parties' benefit in a cost-effective, sustainable and non-polluting, as well as job-creating, manner.

Similarly, at the national level, disputes over a project's fiscal contribution to its host country are also best addressed in a collaborative rather than conflictual framework. A solution that maximises tax revenue by having the project run as efficiently and profitably as possible is in everyone's best interests – but may involve compromises and sacrifices on both sides. Similarly, investments that use as many local rather than foreign suppliers and partners as possible, and add as much local value as possible through the refining, processing or manufacturing of raw materials unearthed from the country's soil, achieve multiple positive outcomes in terms of greater fiscal income, job creation and local-infrastructure enhancement.

11.6 Ethical considerations in project-risk assessments

Our clients request political, security and operational risk assessments for a variety of reasons. They may be driven by routine internal processes that require routine project-risk assessments before capital is committed to a potential investment. Some may have a low appetite for potential risks inherent in certain jurisdictions, and need an objective opinion on the likelihood and impact of potential events – as well as advice on whether it will be possible to lower exposure to identified risks to a level that is acceptable. Other clients commission forecasting and risk assessments at the behest of external stakeholders (such as insurers or financiers) to provide third-party reassurance that a project will not be derailed by significant level of risk.

The consultancy we work for (Control Risks) is an independent company that is majority employee-owned. In our work we strive to be as objective as is possible while also appreciating the client's short- to long-term aims and objectives. Part of this means we must be prepared to present results of assessments that may not present a positive picture for an investment project. Indeed, it is our professional responsibility to be clear in our assessments and forecasts about what risks may be potentially mitigated, and what may need to be tolerated, should the client wish to proceed.

Further, particularly when conducting risk assessments for projects in high risk jurisdictions, we strive to clarify for the client how their investment will interact with the risk environment. We consider both risks to the project as well as the *impact* that the project (through its lifetime) may have on local, regional and national social, economic, political, environmental, security and other factors. We encourage clients to see projects as active participants in the risk environment that, through their activities, will – by the very presence of the investment – have an influence on that environment. To that end, we are driven by a commitment to encouraging our clients to adopt a sensitive approach to developing and managing projects, to reduce negative impacts on local stakeholders, and at the same time to maximise opportunities to make a long-term positive contribution to society. This entails providing detailed advice on best practice on managing corruption, human rights, community engagement, governance, security, managing relationships with local security forces and other complex issues. While our advice may not always be taken, we continually draw on examples of what can go wrong in the short, medium or long term to encourage clients to learn lessons from others.

11.7 Transnational risks

The foregoing analysis has focused predominantly on the assessment of risks for specific projects or investments. When conducting analysis a multi-layered approach to analysis is particularly important in order to capture the risks posed by transnational threats. For example, when considering a project's vulnerability to terrorism, it is necessary to go beyond traditional state boundaries to consider the intention and capability of domestic and international terrorist groups. Sophisticated and internationally-connected organised criminal groups – ranging from those trafficking illegal narcotics to those engaged in more subtle activity such as counterfeiting or confidential data theft - similarly require a more nuanced transnational understanding by companies seeking to avoid entanglement in their activities. A cocaine operation could potentially be encountered equally or indeed simultaneously at its point of production in Latin America, via its supply chain in the Caribbean or west Africa, or at the point of sale where it may be trying to launder its money in the main cities of western Europe or North America.

The degree to which our clients ask us to examine transnational risks will therefore tend to be driven by the client's sector and type of investment, business activity and organisational culture. For instance, for companies with their own complex international supply chains, these business processes may themselves necessitate a more global or holistic understanding of risk – be it piracy on the high seas or unethical labour practices at a supplier factory site. Whereas for companies with a limited portfolio of current or prospective international projects, or whose investments are more financial than physical, a more local focus will be required. That said, there is growing recognition among clients working in a variety of sectors, of the local consequences of transnational issues such as global warming or the recent global economic crisis leading to a growing need to include consideration of global and cross-border issues when conducting risk assessments.

There are several drivers of increased demand for transnational risk analysis. The international media have played a clear role in highlighting transnational risks. Employees and managers alike have access to information which will generate concerns about the impact of an issue. Legislation can be a further driver of enhanced transnational risk awareness: even if corruption is seen as an unavoidable way of life in many of the countries where a company may be actively operating, if that company has a formal footprint in the United States then it is liable to investigation and prosecution for extra-territorial crimes of integrity under the increasingly actively used Foreign and Corrupt Practices Act - a trend likely to be replicated in the UK under the new Bribert Act (2010).

As risk consultants, we also have a role in highlighting the full range of issues of which a client may need to be cognisant. From monitoring global issues such as a growing move towards extra-territorial prosecutions for corruption ourselves, we highlight potential areas of transnational risk for our clients that they may otherwise not have considered. For instance, in conducting a recent review of the risk management structures of a major international company with involvement in a range of high risk markets, we highlighted their potential exposure to the activities of non-governmental organisations (NGOs) and other campaigning groups at local, national and transnational levels. The company hitherto had only considered the potential impact of NGO activity at a local level and had not considered the potential outcomes of complex networks of NGOs focusing on their activities across a number of jurisdictions simultaneously and criticising the company's 'brand' as a whole.

11.7.1 World-views

We work for clients with a wide variety of industrial and national roots, and national background has a clear influence on the questions we are asked as well as the acceptability of different types of information contained within risk assessments.

For example, in negotiating the scope of work for a recent risk-assessment project for a Japanese corporate client considering an investment in west Africa, there was heavy emphasis placed on the need for statistical data to demonstrate levels of political instability and insecurity. The client was insistent that historical analysis of data outlining the type, frequency and scale of criminal and insurgent activity would be the best premise for projecting the likelihood and impact of future militant attacks, criminal and community incidents on their project.

The challenge for us was to alert the client to inherent weaknesses of relying on historical data to predict future events, especially in the context of conducting analysis in a country where such data was inconsistent and inherently unreliable due to systemic under-reporting. We had to explain these weaknesses and at the same time provide reassurance that in-depth analysis of *qualitative* data on the intention, capability and historical security context of the country in question would nevertheless provide a clear picture of the range of risks they were likely to face.

This raises an important wider question about uncertainty. Many of our clients would like us to provide them with concrete answers on fundamentally uncertain topics: for example, the likelihood that terrorists will target their particular building in a city, or the likelihood that a populist president will expropriate their operation. Here, our role contains a number of elements. The first is to place the threat in context: as previously outlined, considerations of the assessed intent and capability of the actor(s) behind the threat are especially important here alongside statistical analysis of precedents of similar targeting of asset type in the past. Expectations need to be managed that where a risk is the direct result of a (potentially irrational) individual's personal whim, the degree of certainty in predicting it is axiomatically small. Clients also need to be reminded that we are unlikely in most situations to have access to classified intelligence material to inform such analysis, as well as that such intelligence may in any case itself be inaccurate. Perhaps equally valuable is a reminder that fixating on the most dramatic and at the same time the most uncertain classes of risk is a commonplace fallacy for risk management: across the business world, far more projects or companies incur losses or even fail due to what we would class lower-impact, higher-likelihood – and generally more certain or predictable – risks (e.g., difficulties importing critical material through a port's bureaucracy or problems imposed by highly restrictive labour regulation) than those that incur loss or fail through classic extreme-impact but very low-probability risk events like terrorist attack or expropriation.

Often such requests for quantitative risk analysis are driven by the need to estimate the potential financial impact of risks accurately. The impetus to predict the financial consequences of a risk will be partly driven by the nature of the investment and the sector the client operates in. Mining companies need to estimate the probable costs of operational downtime caused by political interference or community protests; construction firms need to build in the costs of possible delays related to weak supply chains when building and operating large-scale projects in emerging markets; companies that provide temporary electric power solutions need to know the probability of a state-owned utility company defaulting on payment.

At the same time, a client's risk appetite will vary considerably depending on the national origin of the client, the sector the client operates in, and is also closely tied to internal corporate culture. For instance, experience shows that Chinese companies are aggressive in their search for investment opportunities in Africa and other regions, and have a comparatively high appetite for a range of risks. These companies tend not to be concerned about political risk as they generally feel assured that they will be shielded from undue political interference abroad by the Chinese state's direct bilateral relations with the host authorities in the countries where they are undertaking conduction exploration and production. In some of these cases, in particular where state-owned companies are involved, even profitability may not be a dominant concern either, with the overarching need to secure long-term natural resource income being instead the driving force. Both tendencies have led to complaints of unfairly tilted playing fields from such companies' commercial rivals. Chinese extractive companies are, however, increasingly concerned about the potential impact of security threats in regions such as sub-Saharan Africa on their ability to operate smoothly and safely. This concern – indicating a lower risk appetite for security risk - has partly been driven by a range of security incidents resulting in Chinese employees being kidnapped, killed or injured while operating abroad.

In contrast, companies from across the Nordic region tend to have a low appetite for political, security, integrity and operational risks, leading to frequent requests for in-depth, carefully considered risk assessments. Nordic companies across a wide range of sectors (from paper manufacturing, pharmaceuticals, oil and gas, telecommunications and shipping) are partly responding to shareholder and home-country media demands that they invest and carry out their operations internationally in a responsible, sustainable manner. Perhaps it is also the overall openness of Nordic society that encourages more frank examination of the upside and downside of opportunities. That is, there is a general and clear willingness to uncover and understand issues that may adversely affect overall business objectives. While not all Nordic companies have the same outlook, we have seen an overall willingness to engage in self-criticism, to question prevailing wisdom and to seek external views on risks.

11.7.2 Objectivity

Risk-advisory companies are constantly 'damned if they do and damned if they don't' when it comes to the quality of their advice and analysis, being simultaneously accused of being too cautious when hedging their bets with a forecast, or being excessively inaccurate or even 'doom-mongering' if a daring projection fails to materialise.

Control Risks' culture encourages debate and critical and creative thinking about risks. Project-risk assessments are generally conducted by small teams, with oversight from senior colleagues often cast in the role of devil's advocates to encourage full consideration of potentially contrarian thinking or potentially unforeseen new dynamics (sometimes called 'Black Swans', cf. Introduction, Chapters 15 and 16). Recruitment deliberately emphasises diversity in both personal and professional background to aid original thinking. Once hired and trained, these analysts are trusted to advance their own opinions, and are deliberately kept separate from (albeit informed by and debated with) the opinions in other parts of the business with a potential interest of their own in the recommendations and advice being offered.

A further constituent element of objectivity is the salient importance of 'on the ground' corroboration for all analysis issued: we believe that risk assessments and forecasting should not be conducted in an academic vacuum far away from where the risks themselves may be manifesting. As such, wherever possible, assessments include on-the-ground research.

Thus, while risk assessments are tailored to a client's sector and investment, and take into consideration a client's risk appetite, they are built nevertheless upon rigorous and emphatically independent risk analysis. We make it clear that our analysis is independent, we are very rarely asked to adjust our findings to suit a client. In those rare circumstances we strongly resist suggestions that our view be adjusted if we disagree with the client's opinion.

This structure is critical when the audience for our output is almost entirely composed of businesses for whom a decision to divest or temporarily evacuate project cannot be taken lightly, given the accompanying disruption and financial impact. Given that our company's stated mission is to enable its clients to succeed with their activities in complex and hostile business environments, the focus is always on rational advice that will enable business to continue in a manner in which risks are both identified and minimised to the greatest possible extent.

As discussed above, we occasionally need to present unexpected or unpalatable findings to clients. The twin clichés – 'absence makes the heart grow fonder' and 'familiarity breeds contempt' – can both be relevant when a project champion within an organisation disagrees with a less emotional evaluation of the risk profile of an investment in a country that he or she has potentially been championing and dedicating efforts to advance for months or even years (*especially* if they happen to be a national of that country). Similarly, we have encountered clients who have formed close personal relationships with planned political or business partners for investments who have found it very hard to accept 'red flags' we may have identified about the personal integrity or prior operational track record of such individuals.

Ultimately, if our conclusions and recommendations do not directly match our clients' own perceptions or hopes, it is their decision whether to absorb or ignore our advice. Given the fundamental assumption that returns can be higher for riskier investments, the broad guiding principle is always how best to protect the business and enhance its success prospects than it is how to prevent the move at all. What is certain is that we cannot compromise our objectivity in order to win friends – while the short-term benefits in terms of direct client satisfaction would be greater, the longer-term ramifications for the company's reputation and potential to do repeat business either with that same company or with others in its sector were a subjective and ultimately inaccurate opinion on our part to be revealed to have been offered at the client's behest, would be highly damaging.

Another related area, where objectivity can in theory be compromised and risk consultancies stand accused of an in-built conflict of interest, is where they also provide ongoing risk-management services. Such a business model creates a potential inherent bias, either to exaggerate risk in order to sell expensive follow-on products, or instead to downplay risks in order to encourage a client to proceed with an investment for which follow-on services can then be offered, or more widely to promote greater investment in a country where the company has a corporate presence. Objectivity is again the watch-word here. An independent risk consultancy is, for example, in theory less 'conflicted' in the advice it provides on prevailing insurable-risk conditions than a seller of insurance products who also offers 'risk-advisory services'. For example, reputational due diligence conducted by a niche provider of business-intelligence services may be more objective than a similar service offered by a law firm that is also hopeful of financially more significant work on contracts should a mooted joint venture proceed as planned.

A risk consultancy 'piper', who always plays the tune its pay-master requests or its wider business interests tempt it to do may win a fair amount of business in the short-term; however, such conflicts are likely to unravel quickly and expose the fundamentally self-interested shortcomings that underpinned its inaccurate advice from the outset. With losses of cash, property, corporate reputation and potentially human life, the 'wages of sin' in the contexts where business risk is concerned, such operators are unlikely to sustain that business model in the long run.

11.8 Conclusion

This chapter has provided an overall explanation of our approach to providing risk analysis and forecasting. Drawing on widely used international risk management standards, we have developed our own approach to dealing with the challenges of forecasting and managing risk. Particularly by developing an in-depth understanding of the context of our clients' business and their risk appetite, we are able to tailor our assessments to indicate priority areas of risk that will need to be managed in order for objectives to be met. When engaging with clients, we are conscious of, and sensitive to' potentially different world-views, but nevertheless strive to provide objective analysis of risks – even where the results may not sit comfortably with the client.

Done well, risk assessments are time-and-resource intensive process that involves rigorous and critical analysis of threats and a client's vulnerability to those threats. While predicting the likelihood and impact of future events – particularly those that may arise as a result of transnational threats – is an intrinsically difficult exercise; the more risk analysis is conducted in an atmosphere where critical and creative thought is encouraged, and the earlier it is built into the business-planning cycle, the better the end result is likely to be.

Risk management is all about helping companies avoid the pitfalls and problems that can be encountered doing business in the world today (and tomorrow): from identifying threats the business may not have imagined it might face to begin with, to addressing them before rather than after they manifest; from providing efficiency and coherence to internal organisational structures where ownership of risk may be spread far and wide across different business units and functions, to identifying cheaper and more effective tactics for risk mitigation than what may previously have been relied upon (such as insurance, or expensive physical security). Far from undermining foreign investment and limiting a company's ability to expand and diversify, when delivered properly risk management provides businesses with a competitive advantage.

While many companies and organisations have internal resources of varying size and cohesion dedicated to risk management, and others rely most heavily on information available in the public sphere, these entities can nevertheless often additionally benefit from external assistance and from incorporating the views of specialist risk consulting firms. Indeed, many of our clients most appreciate the flexibility and customised service they receive from us – tailored as it is to their precise operational requirements.

This makes the output of specialist consultancies a valuable addition to the range of risk-related analysis available to practitioners. An out-sourced private-sector provider usually offers a more responsive, objective and broader range of expertise and geographical experience than an in-house team can provide; it can also synthesise lessons learned from multiple clients' experiences, across different sectors in a wide array of investment contexts into its recommendations. It is also comparatively unencumbered by narrow policy or research focus and frequent budgetary constraints that can afflict the public intelligence community, academia and think-tanks. In conclusion, we feel the consulting area has as much to teach those other areas as it has to learn from them in what should ideally be a symbiotic process and ideas-exchange and sharing of innovations in research methodology between the three communities in recent years.

12

From the 'Neurotic' to the 'Rationalising' State: Risk and the Limits of Governance

Henry Rothstein, Olivier Borraz and Michael Huber

12.1 Introduction

During New Labour's third term in office in the UK, risk-based regulation and management came to form a major plank of public policy. In 2005, the then Prime Minister Tony Blair argued in a well-publicised speech that there was enormous pressure on decision-makers 'to act to eliminate risk in a way that is out of all proportion to the potential damage' and called for a 'sensible debate about risk in public policymaking' (Blair, 2005). 'Something is seriously awry', he argued, where '...health and safety rules across a range of areas is taken to extremes', and when the Financial Services Authority is 'seen as hugely inhibiting of efficient business by perfectly respectable companies that have never defrauded anyone'. Arguing that we need to 'replace the compensation culture with a common-sense culture', the prime minister committed the government to ensuring regulatory action is 'risk based' to help ensure that creativity in the private and public sectors is not stifled by overly risk-averse cultures.

The examples were controversial – especially in the later light of the financial crisis – but the speech signalled a change in the way that risk was perceived in UK governance. Historically, risk regulation in the UK has largely been regarded as a matter for technocrats managing conventional health, safety and environmental threats to society. Yet the speech captured a drive to inculcate the language and methods of risk analysis – in particular, probability-consequence frameworks – as a way of thinking about and addressing problems across much wider domains of public policy and corporate governance, such as the environment, finance, education, mental health, housing and charities (see, e.g., Cabinet Office, 2002; de Goede, 2004; Black, 2005; Hampton, 2005; Hutter, 2005, Rothstein et al., 2006). In particular, risk is no longer simply just a policy instrument for setting acceptable levels of harm, such as cancer risks from exposure to ionising radiation.

Increasingly, risk concepts are now used to frame information about adverse events, as well as the allocation of scarce enforcement resources to ensuring regulatory compliance across policy domains.

The UK has not been alone in promulgating 'risk-based' approaches to regulation. In recent years, risk has become a central organising concept for regulation in many countries such as Australia, New Zealand, Canada, Sweden and the Netherlands. Risk has even emerged as a central tool for supranational governance regimes, such as the Organisation for Economic Cooperation and Development (OECD), the European Union (EU), and the World Trade Organisation (WTO), in domains as diverse as food safety, media regulation and flood management (see, e.g., OECD, 2010). The WTO, for example, forced the EU to adopt risk assessment as the basis for import restrictions of meat containing artificial beef hormones following a successful complaint by the United States over the EU's prior ban. It seems that the regulation *of* risk is turning into regulation *by* risk.

The ostensible rationale for risk-based regulation is that it can maximise the benefits of regulation while minimising the burdens on those regulated by offering 'targeted' and 'proportionate' interventions. By taking account of probability as well as potential damage, risk-based regulation has been promoted as an economically rational decision-making instrument for managing the uncertainties that are inherent in any regulatory intervention. As such, 'risk-based' decision-making appears to offer a universal foundation for the governance of collective dangers.

Yet cursory observation suggests that 'risk-based' logics of regulation provide a far from universally accepted rationale for decision-making across policy domains and national settings. Instead, the spread and practice of risk-based approaches appears to be institutionally patterned, across countries, and between and within regimes, in at least two ways. *First*, as this chapter will show, risk-based approaches to regulation have become institutionalised across a wide array of policy domains in the UK, yet in France and Germany the language of risk tends to be confined to traditional policy domains such as the environment, nuclear energy and health-and-safety. And *second*, different regulatory logics can coexist within different parts of the same regulatory regime; for example, risk-based logics may inform the framing of evidence, but policy making and rule enforcement may be shaped by entirely different rationales.

Such patterns suggest that there is a need to consider the factors shaping the emergence and spread of this supposedly rational and universal organising concept for regulation. For example, increasing international efforts to create 'risk-based' frameworks for governing harms that cross-national boundaries are predicated on the idea that 'risk' provides a common set of concepts, tools and approaches for negotiating different national philosophies of regulatory intervention. Indeed, the very term 'transboundary risk' is one that constructs governance 'problems' as amenable to analysis through universally applicable 'probability-consequence' frameworks, irrespective of national setting. Yet a growing body of research – both at the organisational and national level – suggests that such assumptions may be misleading. Far from risk being a universal foundation for governance, understandings of, and responses to, ideas of risk are processed and filtered through established institutional rules, settings, instruments and cultures of governance. As will be discussed in this chapter, this can generate variety rather than convergence in the governance of harms, be they country-specific or transboundary (see Chapter 9).

Building on a growing body of work on the emergence of risk as a central concern of regulation, this chapter takes as its focus the emergence and spread of risk-based logics of regulation within different national settings. In particular, it focuses on the way in which institutional contexts can facilitate or constrain the emergence of risk-based regulation, paying particular attention to the way in which regulators are called to account for their decisions and actions. In order to do so, it considers the cases of the UK, France and Germany.

12.2 The emergence of risk-based regulation

A review of the broad risk-and-regulation literatures suggests a number of reasons why risk has emerged as a central concern of regulation and governance more generally. For some, such as Beck (1998) and Renn (2008), there is a growing global convergence towards risk because of a change in the type and scale of the actual risks confronting society, and the difficulties they pose for traditional governance systems (see also Chapter 15). They argue that the interrelatedness of contemporary risks – from finance to climate change – which cross organisational, system and national boundaries with potentially devastating effects, point towards a global convergence of the ways in which regulatory problems are framed and solutions sought. Beck, for example, echoing the dystopian fears of the Frankfurt school, argues that a new global-risk technocracy is emerging, presenting a veneer of legitimacy for the doomed management of the catastrophic downsides of late modernity.

Other perspectives on the relationship between risk and regulation suggest that there is a growing convergence towards risk as an organising principle for governance for very different reasons. From a Foucauldian perspective, for example, risk frames the ideas and approaches of governance in ways that extend neo-liberal notions of rationality into ever more domains of economic, political and social life (Rose and Miller, 1992; O'Malley, 2000). Power (2007), in contrast, argues that the growing significance of risk is a further iteration of what he has termed the 'Audit Explosion', in which bureaucracies are adopting risk-based decision-making as a form of protocolised defence in the face of increasing challenges to their activities and legitimacy. Such kinds of numerical rationales, as Porter (1995) has argued, have a peculiar power to augment the legitimacy of decision-making, irrespective of their methodological validity (see also Heintz, 2010).

Power's argument draws on neo-institutional approaches to understanding the 'isomorphic' pressures driving the spread of risk-based decision-making. Power points, for example, to the normative power of risk ideas, to increasing legal and regulatory mandates that demand risk-based approaches to decision-making, and to risk consultants selling risk-management tools to organisations competing in uncertain environments. Such vectors of transmission have been evident in regulatory contexts, where a mixture of mandate and ideas of 'better regulation' are slowly diffusing risk analysis throughout organisational, national and supranational contexts.

At the same time, there are a number of reasons why risk may be evolving as an organising principle of regulation in a more institutionally-varied pattern. After all, the well-known powerful driving forces that shape the often discussed variety and inconsistencies of risk governance, can be aligned with, or against, risk-based approaches to regulation (see Hood et al., 2001). For example, risk issues that attract the attention of the public and non-governmental organisations (NGOs) are often argued to drive politicians and regulators towards risk-averse policies in the face of electoral and other legitimacy pressures (see, e.g., Brennan, 1991; Chapter 7 in this book). It is not hard to see why politicians find it difficult to argue publicly that the prevention of deaths and injuries has to be balanced against costs, especially after tragedies such as rail crashes, child deaths at the hands of abusive parents, or a fatal animal disease outbreak such as Bovine spongiform encephalopathy (BSE).

Conversely, risk-based approaches to regulation are often advocated by business groups seeking to lighten regulatory burdens. One does not have to look far to see campaigns to relax regulatory standards, such as restrictive rules on pesticides in drinking water, or overly zealous enforcement of regulation, such as occupational health and safety rules. At the same time, business groups can also profit from safety rules that restrict competition, such as pharmaceutical regulation, or that create new markets for the supply of 'safety', such as vehicle-safety checks.

Risk governance regimes, however, are rarely simply mirrors that reflect the preferences of public demands and organised interests. Rather they comprise varyingly complex and entrenched institutional cultures, traditions and styles that serve to filter and reframe demands to manage risks in ways that fit with internal institutional and professional values, beliefs and worldviews. For example, commentators on the politics of risk regulation in the 1980s noted how the United States' adversarial legal culture and sympathy for regulatory cost-benefit analysis favoured the emergence of numerical risk-based regulatory decision-making rationales, such as the US National Research Council's (NRC) landmark 'red book' (NRC, 1983; Brickman et al.,

1985; Vogel, 1986). Likewise, in the UK, the strong tradition of using cost-benefit analysis in the context of occupational health-and-safety and road safety, has fitted well with the emergence of risk-based approaches in those domains.

A final set of explanations suggesting that the spread of risk-based decision-making is likely be institutionally patterned, focuses on accountability demands on regulators (Rothstein et al., 2006). Risk is often used as a synonym for hazard, and there is a considerable literature on the way in which popular understandings of risk focus on impact rather than probability. The formal probabilistic aspect of risk, however, frames the goals of regulation not in terms of harm prevention, but in terms of acceptable levels of potential harm to which individuals, organisations or the environment can be legitimately exposed. From this perspective, risk-based regulation emerges where regulators need to account for their own limits; from the need for policy makers to balance the costs and benefits of interventions to manage the impact of potential future harms, to the cognitive, resource, and institutional constraints on inspectors that limit their ability to spot or prevent compliance failures.

It is, of course, nothing new to recognise that regulation is constrained by inevitable difficulties, conflicts and trade-offs, but from this institutional perspective, risk-based philosophies have been argued to 'colonise' regulation in response to an increasing need to justify these constraints (Rothstein et al., 2006). For example, the limits of government have become more visible because of 'good governance' trends towards greater accountability and transparency, the emergence of 24/7 media, and the new internet army of 'armchair auditors' (see Chapter 7). Equally, the emergence of the 'regulatory state' has been accompanied by enhanced systems of scrutiny and accountability to compensate for the democratic deficits posed by the delegation of policy making to non-majoritarian institutions. These processes have transformed behaviours and outcomes that previously went unrecorded or were considered acceptable within bounded organisational settings, into recorded successes and failures that can threaten the legitimacy of governance organisations themselves, posing what might be termed 'institutional risks'.

Framing regulatory problems in the probabilistic terms of risk, as Luhmann (1991) has argued, resolves the dilemma of imperfect control by explicitly anticipating the limits of government and the possibility of failure within decision-making. Indeed, from that perspective, risk-based regulation is an attempt to reframe governance problems in ways that define the boundaries of acceptable and unacceptable regulatory outcomes. As such, the concept of 'risk-based' regulation is less related to a change in the threats facing society than to threats facing regulation itself. From this perspective, it might be expected that the spread of risk-based approaches in domains far removed from traditional policy domains of health, safety and the environment, will reflect changing accountability structures and governance philosophies that demand the rationalisation and justification of the limits of regulation.

These different perspectives on risk-based regulation, therefore, suggest that there is a need to study the institutional settings that encourage or hinder its colonisation of policy domains. In order to do so, this chapter studies the role of risk as an organising concept of regulation in the UK, France and Germany – three advanced European democracies but with different institutional arrangements and traditions for governing risks. The following section will describe these different institutional settings in the three countries and the factors that have been driving or resisting the emergence of risk-based approaches to regulation.

12.3 Case studies

12.3.1 UK

Regulatory standards have long been risk-based in a number of policy domains in the UK. For example, in road safety, the cost of measures that could save lives, in probabilistic terms, is explicitly set against the monetary value of preventing those fatalities (currently a little more than £1 million). Risk analysis has also increasingly been used as the basis of regulatory inspection and enforcement, as a way of rationalising the delivery of an often diverse range of regulatory responsibilities with only limited resources. The Health and Safety Executive, for example, which regulates 750,000 workplaces, uses a risk-rating system to rank inspection priorities for its 4000 staff. Equally, it uses the concept of As Low As Reasonably Practicable (ALARP), which dates back over 50 years, to judge how much resource should be devoted to avoiding potential harm.

The use of probabilistic methods for determining levels of regulatory intervention, however, is by no means universal. There is no shortage of anecdotes about the creation of regulatory regimes that owe more to knee-jerk reaction to events than cool-headed risk analysis. Equally, some regimes deploy enforcement practices that, look at best, like an irrational use of resources, and at worst, like regulatory overkill, such as the tradition of permanently stationing meat-hygiene inspectors in abattoirs irrespective of the risks posed by individual businesses. Striking variety can even be seen within a single policy domain, such as transport safety. For example, following a series of rail crashes in the late 1990s, the then Minister of Transport, John Prescott, proposed introducing an advanced but expensive train-protection system that would have implied a cost of £14 million per life saved – 14 times greater than the value of saving a life on the roads.

In recent years, however, there has been an explicit move away from the idea that government is in the business of ensuring public safety, towards the idea that government is in the business of managing risk. As part of that process, the language and tools of risk analysis have colonised core functions of regulation and governance in the UK. Increasingly, information about adverse events are framed in terms of risk, be it the Bank of England's projections for UK Gross Domestic Product, side effects of pharmaceuticals, or terrorist threats. Equally, regulatory compliance, inspection and enforcement activities across policy domains are expected to be risk-based in the way that they set their priorities and allocate their scarce resources in meeting their regulatory objectives, from the regulation of higher education to child protection.

Risk-based approaches to policy making have emerged more patchily. Much of the active use of risk-based rationales falls within domains where policy is dominated by regulatory agencies, such as food safety and finance. Risk-based decision-making rationales, however, have penetrated less far in government departments led by elected ministers, but even in those governance contexts, there is increasing interest in such approaches. For example, the UK environment ministry – DEFRA – recently appointed a chief risk officer and is actively trying to manage formally what it terms 'policy risks' (Rothstein and Downer, 2012, forthcoming).

There are at least three factors shaping the emergence of risk-based regulation in the UK. *First*, and perhaps simplest, the emergence of risk-based regulation in the UK is driven by an ideological commitment to an economically rational decision-making process that can maximise the benefits of regulation while minimising the burdens on those regulated by offering 'targeted' and 'proportionate' interventions that balance costs and benefits. As such, risk-based approaches to appear to be a nuanced descendant of long-running UK government programmes to cut regulatory burdens on business; holding out the promise of checking bureaucratic creep and inefficiency, countering vested interests, and mitigating risk-averse tendencies within government.

Indeed, Prime Minister Blair's speech followed a stream of reports, initiatives and guidelines within UK government promoting risk-based approaches to regulation as a core strategy of the modernising government and better regulation agendas (see, e.g., ILGRA, 1996, 1998, 2002; UK Cabinet Office, 1999; RRAC, 2009). The Hampton review (2005), for example, set out a vision for risk-based approaches to regulatory inspection and enforcement across policy domains, which was further embedded by the requirements of the Regulatory Enforcement and Sanctions Bill (2008) to ensure that businesses and individuals are not unnecessarily burdened by regulation. Equally, the UK Cabinet Office demands for all 'Impact Assessments' of new regulations to involve an explicit assessment of risk have institutionalised risk assessment in central-government departments. Initiatives such as these, paralleled by similar moves within the private sector, have meant that there is no shortage of management consultants rebadged as risk consultants eager to market their latest risk-management wares.

A *second* driving force has been the increasing need in the UK for decision-makers and those who implement policy to account explicitly for decision-making processes and outcomes (Power 1997; Hood et al., 1999). In recent years, for example, the UK has seen a rapid growth of audit and target cultures inside government associated with New Public Management philosophies. Central-government decision-making has become more closely coupled with the behaviour of extended delivery networks, making the traditional culture, of central ministries 'throwing policy problems over the fence' to be picked up by delivery agents, less tenable. Likewise, front-line delivery services have been forced to think more about how they allocate their scarce resources in implementing regulation, as they become more widely held to account for regulatory outcomes. Equally, decision-making and practice have been exposed by the Freedom of Information Act, public disclosure of performance indicators on the internet, and various experiments in participative decision-making.

Greater accountability and scrutiny have forced decision-makers to find ways of rationalising decision-making in front of wider audiences. For example, regulators have been forced to set and justify aims and trade-offs of regulation in more public arenas without recourse to the political manifestos of elected politicians or the opaque cloak of administrative procedures beloved of central ministries. Reframing regulatory objects in terms of risk has proven attractive for rationalising the inevitable trade-offs of governance decision-making. For example, the UK's Health and Safety Executive developed its well-known Tolerability of Risk model for regulatory action in order to justify its decision-making processes to the Public Inquiry into the Sizewell 'B' nuclear power station in the 1980s (HSE, 1998).

Third, and closely related to the context of greater accountability, risk-based decision-making in the UK has emerged as a way of shifting, or perhaps more accurately, 'absorbing' blame for failure. Greater scrutiny and accountability have amplified the 'institutional risks' of governance, as 'failures' that can threaten the legitimacy of governance organisations themselves are routinely recorded. Indeed, as the UK Cabinet Office argues, 'in relation to its own business...government has a responsibility to identify and manage risks' (Cabinet Office, 2002).

The application of risk-management solutions to regulatory problems acts to absorb failures by redefining the limits of governance as the boundary between acceptable and unacceptable risk. For civil servants in central ministries, risk-based decision-making offers a new procedural defence for failure by helping steer a path between enhanced accountability and blame. For front-line services, increasingly in the media spotlight, or ministers seeking to deflect blame, risk-based decision-making serves to redefine the limits of their ability to manage problems. A striking feature of recent child-abuse scandals in the UK, for example, was the way in which social workers defensively invoked the language of risk management, arguing that it is impossible to eliminate tragedies in the absence of certain knowledge and limitless resources. Indeed, risk-based regulation is part of a broader discourse that seeks to persuade the public that there is no such thing as zero risk – not just in the design of regulation, but also, critically, in its implementation. It is perhaps no surprise, for example, that New Labour's market-led focus on individual 'choice' and 'responsibility' in the provision of public and private services, has resulted in the public being bombarded with 'risk' information both to help inform those choices, but also limit blame for information error.

Risk-based regulation in the UK, therefore, is a way of managing expectations of regulatory performance, by redefining what constitutes acceptable regulatory goals and actual outcomes. Regulation may prohibit particular behaviours, such as the sale of food that is injurious to health, but the ideas and application of risk-based enforcement helps mitigate the *blameability* of enforcement authorities for failing to ensure that people never get food poisoning. Indeed, attempts to redefine the limits of governance in this way have seen 'risk' discourses displace the traditional policy discourses of 'defence', 'safety' and 'security'. For example, preventive 'flood defence' has become adaptive 'flood-risk management', under the banner of 'making space for water' (Defra, 2005). As the security services have increasingly become accountable for their behaviours and performance, so terrorism is talked about less in the language of national security but more in the language of 'risk management' (de Goede, 2004; Chapter 2 in this book). Even the UK is itself being framed as a risk-management project, with the recent creation of the National Risk Register. If the value of risk is in displacing the idea of failure, it is perhaps no surprise that it has become such a popular mantra.

12.3.2 France

Like the UK, France has been going through a process of regulatory reform. Indeed, far from the entrenched image of a country stuck in its ways, France has changed profoundly in the last two decades under pressure from the cumulative effects of decentralising power to local government, Europeanisation and economic globalisation. This has prompted a number of economic, social and labour reforms, with often discreet but far-ranging effects (Culpepper et al., 2006). Yet at the same time, the French state has strived to maintain throughout this period an image of stability, enshrined in an institutional arrangement and a policy style that resists pressures for change. As a consequence, a few ministries (Industry, Finance and Agriculture in particular) continue to wield a great deal of influence, working closely in private with organised interests to regulate policy fields that are regarded as strategic for the French economy, whilst relying on regional field services to monitor and enforce regulation across policy domains.

Since the mid-1980s, however, a number of health scandals have revealed the limits of these institutional arrangements. In 1986, for example, government officials claimed that the radioactive cloud from Chernobyl stopped at the French borders (Liberatore, 1999). In 1999, a former prime minister and several of his ministers were put on trial for negligence in permitting haemophiliacs to be given blood-plasma products contaminated by HIV. Then came BSE, which imposed a high economic toll on French farmers; an asbestos scandal in which little was done to prevent exposures that are expected to result in 100,000 deaths; and more recently, the 2003 heat wave that claimed 15,000 lives and led to accusations of government inadequacy in warning the public. These crises became public symbols of the state failing to protect the health and safety of its citizens.

These scandals took their political toll and prompted parliament to reform regulatory arrangements in 1998 to provide greater protection against a host of health and environmental hazards. The reforms were ostensibly designed to deal with what officials perceived to be a lack of reliable scientific evidence, with the creation of four new agencies to provide scientific advice to government in the fields of food, pharmaceuticals, environment, workplace safety and disease control (Borraz, 2008). Furthermore, following international best practice, French authorities adopted the NRC's 1983 'red book' model of separating the processes of risk assessment and risk management, putting agencies in charge of the former, whilst leaving central ministries in charge of the latter (Joly, 2007).

The French reforms to risk governance were designed to restore trust in the state's capacity to protect citizens against hazards to their health, by introducing risk-based scientific assessment. The introduction of risk, however, remained limited to domains in which crises and scandals occurred; it did not extend to a wider set of policy domains. Moreover, the reforms were restricted to risk assessment: central ministries remained in charge of policy making, enforcement and inspection. Hence, in view of the UK case, this raises two questions. First, why were risk-based approaches limited to scientific advice, and why did they not extend to policy making and enforcement? Second, why have risk-based approaches not colonised a much wider range of policy domains? To answer these questions, it is worth considering four features of the French state.

The *first feature* has to do with the culturally-established commitment or 'promise' by the French state to provide security to its population, i.e. to ensure that regulation *and* its implementation provide a large degree of protection for the public. Security has always been a key concern of the French state, but the health crises and scandals demonstrated clear failures at a time when the role of the state was being questioned. Accordingly, French authorities pinpointed security as one of the remaining core tasks of the state, with health issues offering a case in which they could demonstrate their will and capacity to act.

As a consequence, there was an extensive political emphasis on the state's role in providing security against a wide range of hazards, initially starting with health but rapidly working its way through the entire political agenda. An unintended effect of this 'promise', however, was that security became defined as non-negotiable (Borraz and Gilbert, 2008). For example, while France was a forerunner in applying cost-benefit analysis to public-infrastructure projects such as roads, bridges and dams (Porter, 1995), the idea of valuing life remained a cultural anathema. This feature of the French state works against risk-based approaches that explicitly eschew absolute principles such as security or safety.

The *second feature* of the French state that works against risk-based approaches to governance is the priority given to maintaining 'public order'; a principle that is defined in administrative law, has been interpreted by the courts, and is given great significance by state officials (Worms, 1966). Indeed, a core role of state officials is to prevent any form of disorder that could imply the Republic is not able to maintain control. As health concerns have become a source of public controversy, they have become a central issue on which the state has attempted to reaffirm its capacity to govern and to avoid conflicts becoming crises. From this perspective, the problem of risk-based approaches to regulation is that they explicitly recognise and reveal limits to state intervention and create the potential for controversies and disorder. For example, in the early 2000s, the French Ministry of Agriculture refused to provide its food-safety agency with information on the performance of its field services, because it neither wanted the agency to supervise its activities, nor run the risk of having the results published in the press (Besançon et al., 2006).

A *third feature* that works against risk-based regulation is the Republican interpretation of 'equal rights'. In France, the law must apply to all citizens in the same way; in other words, every individual or organisation must get equal treatment in both the law and its implementation. This constitutional principle is strongly upheld by the *Conseil Constitutionnel* and administrative courts. Here again, risk-based governance is problematic, because of the tension between the principle of equal treatment and risk-based approaches to setting priorities and allocating scarce resources. For instance, during the 2009 H1N1 flu pandemic, the Minister of Health had to choose between following expert advice to vaccinate everyone, or just 30 per cent of the population – the minimum needed to provide herd immunity. She opted for the first option, having no legal or political grounds to decide which two thirds of the population would be left 'unprotected'.

Finally, a *fourth feature* of the French state that works against risk-based governance relates to the notion of the 'general interest', which civil servants are expected to represent and defend. In essence, this notion precedes any type of ideological or private interests, and relies on civil servants and elected officials working for the 'general good' on the basis of their personal ethics and use of rigorous evidence. Yet, risk-based approaches, as modes of accountability, conflict with the French tradition of a paternalistic elite working behind closed doors for the general good; particularly in the absence of freedom-of-information legislation and difficulty of accessing government documents. Indeed, civil servants and elected representatives have resisted pressures to introduce more open and deliberative styles of decision-making because it undermines their privileged role in defining the general interest.

These entrenched institutional philosophies and cultures have limited the extent to which risk-based regulatory reforms are likely to take root in France. Such reforms have best fitted expert advisory processes in those domains where there have been crises, but any attempt to establish them more widely will need to resolve conflicts with pre-existing institutional approaches to decision-making, enforcement and inspection. Given the limited applicability of risk-based approaches to regulation, how are the inevitable limits of governance dealt with? At least three different kinds of approach can be observed.

The *first approach* is secrecy. Rather than acknowledge the inevitable compromises and trade-offs between security, economic, social, and organisational concerns in implementing regulation, officials prefer to keep their actions veiled in secrecy. Cases of non-compliance or failure in the implementation of regulation are discussed behind closed doors and never made public. In so doing, the state can maintain the illusion that it is offering security, as long as failure to deliver on that security never becomes public. The same holds true at the level of policy making: opacity simply obscures the trade-offs that a risk-based approach would make transparent.

A *second approach* is to acknowledge failures, but then to identify individuals who will be held politically or legally accountable to protect the integrity of the state. Examples range from the trial of ministers for their role in the contaminated blood scandal, to the dismissal of the head of the general health directorate after the 2003 heat wave, followed closely by the Minister of Health. But there are other many other less-publicised cases where local *préfets* or heads of administrative services have been demoted after mishandling a crisis or not preventing an event from taking place, such as the 1999 storm that swept through France or a house bombing in Corsica. In other words, institutional dysfunctions may account for the crisis, but the focus is on finding public officials accountable for either tolerating these dysfunctions or not preventing the failures becoming public.

A final *third approach* is reactive crisis management, where the clear objective is to maintain or restore public order and manage the reputation of ministries. In an age of increasing media attention, ministries from Health to Education have installed early warning systems to catch weak signals of impending crises or controversies, and contingency plans in case crises occur. In situations of uncertainty or under pressure from social movements, ministries will prefer to be risk averse, invoking the precautionary principle rather than undertaking a thorough risk assessment, even if it means facing later criticism for overreaction. So far, no public official in France has ever been sanctioned for being too cautious.

12.3.3 Germany

'Risk' is certainly no stranger to German political debate, figuring as a central concern of debates in many policy domains, such as nuclear safety, food safety, the environment, biotechnology and financial services. Beyond being an object of governance concern, however, risk-based ideas have also started to play a greater role in framing governance processes. For example, risk assessment plays an important role in climate-change policy, following the similar probabilistic, scenario-based approach that has been championed by the Intergovernmental Panel on Climate Change (IPCC). In food-safety debates, risk assessment plays a key role in informing food-safety decision-making, drawing on risk assessments from the European Food Safety Agency and corresponding national agencies. Indeed, in 2002, a new agency was created – the Federal Institute of Risk Assessment (BfR) – whose task is to provide risk-based scientific advice to the public, government and other stakeholders on consumer-related issues, ranging from BSE to toys and lipsticks.

Like the UK and France, risk is also an implicit central concern of decision-making. Indeed, risk-based approaches to setting the limits of government intervention are implicit in the necessary trade-offs between the rights to economic activity and protection of human health and safety that are enshrined in the German Constitution. For example, thresholds of acceptable risk were pivotal in a long-lasting and complex legal conflict throughout the 1970s–1980s when the anti-nuclear movement challenged the authorities over the risks from nuclear radiation or accidents. More recently, biotechnology was similarly caught up in adversarial legal battles over levels of acceptable risk.

However, risk-based approaches have only colonised the core functions of a few regulatory regimes completely – that is the processes of risk assessment, policymaking and implementation, principally because of international demands. For example, the two Basle Accords turned the previously opaque world of financial-services regulation into a risk-based approach that followed international norms of accountability. This development resulted in the establishment of the Federal Financial Supervisory Authority (BaFin) as one of the few fully-fledged regulatory agencies in Germany. BaFin was created as an image of the UK Financial Services Authority, institutionalising risk management as the central control mechanism and applying it to information gathering, decision-making and enforcement across the financial sector.

Instead, in most domains, risk-based approaches to policymaking and enforcement fit uneasily with entrenched institutional arrangements and practices. In particular, at least four structural features of the German state help constrain the emergence of risk-based approaches to governance: fragmentation of the federal system; the *juridification* of risk related decisions; the broad involvement of stakeholders; and the precautionary principle.

The *first factor* constraining the emergence of risk-based governance is the fragmented federal system that distributes policy competences across at least three levels of political decision-making: Communities, Länder and the federal state. Such multi-level political processes pose problems for risk-based decision-making because of the number of decision-makers with varying philosophical approaches to governing risks and often contradictory interests. For example, the distribution of risks, costs and benefits can vary across Länder, triggering distributional conflicts over levels of acceptable risk within and between Länder. Such problems can occur with conventional environmental problems, such as water pollution, as well as more traditional areas of social policy, such as the control of dangerous dogs, on which different Länder have developed an array of distinct and often conflicting regulatory approaches (Lodge, 2001).

Fragmentation is also a feature of the German legal system and can inhibit the establishment of common understandings of acceptable risk. For example, according to the Industrial Code (*Gewerbeordnung* GewO §24 IV), conditions for licensing industrial plants should normally involve experts and stakeholders (Huber, 1998). Consensus over what constitutes acceptable risk, however, is not always easy to achieve and disputes can readily spill over into regional courts that can reach inconsistent decisions. The nuclear power programme, for example, reached an impasse because of the conflicting views of regional courts of what constituted an acceptable risk.

Such legal conflicts emerge from the centrality of the law and, in particular, of administrative courts in decision-making, and pose a *second* serious constraint on risk-based approaches to regulation. In particular, courts have found it difficult to base their decisions on probabilistic concepts of risk, or even to reach a view on what is meant by concepts of 'risk' and 'acceptable risk'. Caught between conflicting rights to economic activity and health protection enshrined in the constitution, even the federal constitutional court has had difficulty in defining acceptable risk, having attempted to define it in terms of being 'practically unimaginable' and 'irrelevant' (Proske, 2008: 469). In the absence of clear legal definition, proceedings can readily fall prey to intractable adversarial conflicts between stakeholders, on which judges are ill-equipped to adjudicate. Indeed, the federal constitutional court has decided that it should abstain from decisions on scientific conflicts or disagreements. Moreover, these legal constraints are reinforced by the traditional domination of the civil service by lawyers who are professionally and culturally poorly disposed to such approaches. From this perspective, risk has proved a problematic concept when policymaking becomes juridified.

The *third factor* constraining the emergence of risk-based approaches to regulation is the limited transparency of the German system – which is roughly situated between the UK and France – and the political emphasis on consensus and negotiation. Whilst there is freedom-of-information legislation, there is a strong emphasis on 'data protection' and privacy, which limits the pressure on decision-makers to account for decision outcomes, and hence the need for risk-based rationales for decision-making. Where social movements have challenged decision-making on risk issues, it has become customary since the 1980s to hold public hearings on risk issues, which have attempted to bring scientific expertise – latterly in the form of the BfR – and stakeholders together. In such public contexts, however, the political acceptability of risk assessments has become sorely tested, thus reinforcing the preference of decision-makers to reach negotiated political solutions.

Fourth and relatedly, the emergence of risk-based approaches to governance is also constrained by the German emphasis on the precautionary principle (*Vorsorgeprinzip*), which started as an axiom of environmental law, but has become a principle in much wider fields of social regulation. Bora (2004) has argued that the adoption of a precautionary philosophy, which sanctions the introduction of regulation in the absence of scientific certainty, is a reaction to a growing number of risks that societies seek to control. Having to react to challenges before clear evidence is gathered has increased the importance of political negotiation in decision-making at the expense of ever more elaborate risk assessment processes.

These considerations suggest that, while risk is a familiar concept in Germany, a set of institutional factors have impeded the extent to which it has become an organising principle of decision-making. These factors have less to do with ideological or cultural factors, as is often argued when British neo-liberalism and the Continental provisional state are compared (Ewald, 1986), but more to do with horizontal and vertical fragmentation of policy responsibilities and accountabilities and a rule-bound legal system that struggles with defining the concept of *acceptable* risk. Consequently, policies to manage risk are harder to devise and implement than those concerned with prevention and precaution. The governance of risk in Germany, therefore, may involve probabilistic approaches to information gathering, but the need to negotiate outcomes amongst a wide range of stakeholders appears to constrain the emergence of risk-based approaches to policy making and implementation.

12.4 From the 'neurotic' to the 'rationalising-state': examining the institutional logics of risk-based regulation

The last section has provided a brief overview of the varied emergence of risk-based regulation in three countries, and in so doing has attempted to discern patterns in the way that risk has 'colonised' regulation in different institutional contexts. In particular, the overviews suggest that the widely held view that government is no longer in the business of ensuring public safety but in the business of managing risk has nationally specific dimensions. Whilst the chapter relies on broad-brush evidence, it provides a basis with which to test a number of emerging hypotheses about the varied salience of risk within different national contexts.

The case studies provide some evidence that risk-based regulation is being spread by isomorphic pressures across the three countries. This can be seen, for instance, in the adoption of international standards of risk analysis by the three governments when they reorganised their regulatory regimes in the field of food safety. The adoption of standards initially defined by the NRC and later diffused by the OECD, Codex Alimentarius and European Commission, served two purposes: to legitimise new organisational forms of knowledge production in the aftermath of crises and scandals; and to help countries uphold national interests within wider international negotiations and forums such as the WTO. In both cases, institutional mimetism was a strong driver in achieving policy credibility. Risk-based regulation, as advocated by the OECD, seems also to have made some progress in the three countries, although this diffusion is most notable in the UK. More generally, as policy issues from pharmaceuticals and chemicals, to global warming, financial regulation and even security threats, are increasingly framed as risks on the international agenda, so national authorities are likewise under pressure to adopt similar organisational forms and operating procedures to tackle them.

Most strikingly, however, it appears that risk has emerged as an organising principle of regulation in response to pressures for greater transparency and accountability, because of the way in which it defines the boundary between acceptable and unacceptable outcomes across different functional-control components of regulation. To start with, the growth of risk-based approaches to gathering information about potential harm across all three countries has coincided with institutional contexts in which there is heightened accountability for information error. Just 20 years ago, scientific advice to European governments was regarded as opaque and secretive, permitting considerable room for discretion and 'professional' judgement (see, e.g., Brickman et al., 1985). Yet the last two decades have seen a wide range of reforms, such as: the creation of dedicated risk agencies across Europe that have accountability and transparency built into their guiding missions; transparency initiatives, such as the Arhus Convention on freedom of access to environmental information; and regulatory regimes that demand disclosure of information to the public and the adoption of deliberative procedures. Under these circumstances, framing advice to the government and the public within the language of risk serves to emphasise the limits of expert knowledge and deflect liabilities for information error, such as financial products that fail to deliver hoped for returns, terrorist threats that fail to materialise, or medical interventions that cause more harm than good.

Such pressures have also promoted the use of risk as a means of framing policy decisions. Risk, of course, is a familiar concept for policy making across all three countries as an implicit basis for decision-making. The case studies suggest, however, that for those regimes led by regulatory agencies – most notably in the UK – risk can provide a rationalising logic for policy making in the absence of electoral mandate. However, it is interesting to observe that even in traditionally opaque UK central-government departments where policy outcomes are shaped by ministerial political priorities, civil servants are taking a nascent interest in risk-based decision-making as a way of responding to accountability demands whilst trying to avoid blame for failure.

Equally, such pressures help explain the emergence of risk-based implementation and enforcement in confronting the inevitable problems that limit their ability to meet policy goals, such as constrained resources for wide remits, inherent uncertainties and ungovernable actors. In the UK, constraints on the abilities and behaviour of delivery agents have become more salient in the context of increased emphasis on scrutiny, performance and accountability. As a consequence, risk-based logics of enforcement and service delivery have served to justify the limits of policy implementation in domains far removed from conventional risk domains.

The case studies, however, also suggest that the varied emergence of risk-based approaches to regulation across the three countries is dependent on their particular administrative and accountability structures and demands. For example, in France, the lower salience of risk as an explicit principle for policy making can be partly explained by central-government departments retaining policy making responsibilities, having only delegated risk assessment responsibilities to regulatory agencies. As a consequence, there is less need for explicit rationales to justify the limits of state intervention by opaque central-government departments, where accountabilities are less pronounced and where politics can readily trump principles.

Likewise, public disclosure of the results of centralised routine monitoring and enforcement performance is also rare in France. As a consequence, cases of implementation failure or non-compliance are kept outside the scope of public scrutiny, and indeed, attempts at scrutiny, such as by the food safety agency, have been actively resisted by successive governments. Again, under such circumstances, there is little need for risk-based rationales.

In Germany, the emergence of risk-based policy making, implementation and enforcement is also constrained by limited openness, but also by the fragmented nature of the state. Risk-based rationales for policy making sit uneasily with the political autonomy of the Länder in many domains of social policy, and the strong role of decentralised administrative courts in decision-making make it difficult to reach common agreement on acceptable risk thresholds. Such fragmentation can lead to wide inconsistency in approaches to policy making, implementation and enforcement and can constrain the emergence of risk-based approaches to governance.

Moreover, risk-based approaches to regulation can conflict with entrenched political cultures and philosophies. The deeply-rooted expectation in French political culture and institutions, that the state will provide security, works against risk-based philosophies that explicitly eschew such absolute principles. The same holds true of other features of the French state, such as equal treatment of all citizens by the law, and the notion that civil servants work for the 'general interest'. Such processes are even stronger when it comes to implementation and enforcement in France, because of the constitutional DNA of the French state that demands the preservation of public order and the protection of its reputation; that is, the state cannot be seen to fail.

Ex ante risk-based logics of failure are problematic, therefore, because they would explicitly entail an acknowledgement of the limited ability of the French state to meet policy goals. Instead, individual officials take the blame for any failure that could undermine the integrity of the state, or the fiction that the state provides security. It is perhaps no surprise that in an age of 24/7 media and the internet, great effort is put into horizon scanning for weak signals of failure to forestall reputational damage to the state and officials, and crisis management to attenuate the impacts of an accident or controversy.

In Germany, risk-based approaches to governance come into conflict with entrenched philosophies of governance differently. The externalisation of decision-making conflicts over acceptable risk to administrative courts has proved problematic because their rule-based culture has no ready solution to resolving tensions between conflicting constitutionally-enshrined rights. Indeed, the ready displacement of political conflict over risk into the legal arena has led to judicial resistance to defining levels of acceptable risk, inconsistency and an emphasis on precaution. Instead, solutions have been sought through negotiation and bartering with stakeholders, which sit uneasily with risk-based approaches to regulation.

Such differences have significant implications for understanding the different ways that countries handle potential threats and warnings of harm, which are sometimes thrown into sharp relief when those harms cross-national boundaries. For example, the French government's reaction to the Chernobyl gas cloud may reflect more than a simple failure to assess risks, but reach deep into the 'psyche' of the French state in its attitude towards the protection of the public from ionising radiation. Likewise, the inability of the German legal system to agree on what constitutes an acceptable risk from nuclear radiation in Germany stemmed not just from political mobilisation of environmental groups but also from an apparently irresolvable constitutional tension.

Put in psychoanalytic terms, if the UK's solution to the problem of accountability is an *ex ante* rationalisation of the limits of the possible, the French solution is to deny that failure is possible whilst neurotically searching for signals of failure that could damage the reputation of the French state. By contrast, Germany appears to be more uncertain or 'mixed-up', with accountabilities too diffused through a highly fragmented administrative and legal system for there to be consistent agreement on what constitutes acceptable and unacceptable failure. Such categorisation may verge on crude humour, but it does suggest that if we want to explain the varied adoption of risk-based approaches to regulation across these three countries, we need to go beyond a simplistic argument that there are inevitable leaders and laggards with any reforms to the tools of government. Instead, we need to examine the institutional contexts in which risk can do more than simply serve as a synonym for hazard, but also serve as a way of reframing the limits of regulation itself.

12.5 Conclusions

While risk-based regulation has attracted considerable interest as a major instrument of regulatory reform, much of the discussion has been normative in orientation. This chapter, by sketching the varied emergence of risk-based regulation in three countries, is just a first step towards greater reflection on the factors driving or hindering its emergence in different national contexts. The chapter has not sought to provide a systematic description of the emergence of risk-based regulation across policy domains; such a study is clearly needed if the hypotheses discussed in this chapter are to be fully tested. Nonetheless, notwithstanding the admittedly limited and general focus of this chapter, the country overviews suggests that whilst the emergence of risk-based approaches to regulation is institutionally patterned across countries, policy domains and regulatory regimes, it is possible to discern a distinct set of institutional factors shaping or constraining its emergence. In particular, the analysis permits us to draw five, albeit tentative, conclusions.

First, the chapter has shown that far from being a universal phenomenon, the emergence of risk-based regulation in the three countries varies in at least two dimensions across policy domains and the functional-control components of regulation. In the UK, risk has both come to dominate a wide range of policy domains that seem far removed from traditional risk concerns, as well as shape regulatory information gathering, policy making and implementation processes. In France and Germany, the language and tools of risk analysis have been constrained to traditional policy domains associated with risk, and have in general been confined to processes of risk assessment rather than to policy making and implementation. The implication for the theme of this book is that warnings related to transnational risks are likely to be institutionally processed and responded to in different ways in different countries.

Second, the analysis provides some insight into the way in which objects of regulation are constructed as risks, and why. We have become so familiar with the language of risk that it is easy to forget the important way in which its probabilistic dimension anticipates and legitimates the limits of governance. The spread of risk-based philosophies to policy domains beyond conventional threats to human health and safety reflects the way in which those conventional threats were themselves framed as risks in order to rationalise the limits of societal attempts to manage them. The analysis suggests that the emergence of risk-based ideas in governance is not simply a universal feature of late modernity, but is shaped by the institutional contours of contemporary cultures of blame and accountability. Where demands for accountability and laying blame are heightened, risk acts as a way of reframing or redefining the limits of the possible, whether it is in the contingency of expert advice, the limits of goal setting, or the constraints on regulatory implementation. In the case of transnational risks, therefore, we might expect the profile of responses across countries to be shaped at least in part by the extent to which the concept of risk provides an acceptable rationalisation of the limits of government action.

Third, and building on that argument, we argue that the specific emerging patterns of risk-based regulation across the three countries can be closely related to the extent to which risk concepts fit with institutional patterns of accountability and other constraining institutional factors. In the UK, the heightened salience of potential failure, in the context of increasing cultures of scrutiny and accountability across all control-dimensions of regulation has focused attention on the concept of risk as a means of redefining the goals and expectations of governance. In France, however, the concept of risk challenges the self-understanding of the state; that it cannot, or at least be seen to, fail in providing security for its citizens. Instead, there is greater emphasis on maintaining opaque policy processes that make failures harder to identify, and on searching for warning signs of failure to avoid dramatic consequences for officials and politicians. In Germany, by contrast, risk has only limited salience because of the diffusion of accountabilities through a highly fragmented administrative and legal system that cannot reach agreement on what constitutes acceptable and unacceptable failure. Hence, framing potential threats and warnings as risks is not a neutral decision: it carries heavy implications for the accountability of decision-makers.

Fourth, whilst we have tried to develop a strong institutional argument for the emergence of risk-based philosophies of governance, we also recognise that the trends we have identified are slow, complex and often contradictory. In-depth studies of risk-regulation regimes always reveal highly differentiated philosophies and practices across institutional settings that could not be captured in a short chapter (see Hood et al., 2001). We could not hope to capture complex national philosophies of accountability and develop a cross-national 'theory' of risk governance given our limited evidence base. We do believe, however, that the chapter captures a set of underlying themes that might help explain an institutionally patterned emergence of risk governance that would be hard to explain in other ways.

Fifth, and finally, there is a need for national comparative case studies to study how far the emergence of risk-based logics of governance is related both to the self-understanding of the state in providing safety or security to the public, and institutional cultures and philosophies of accountability and blame for failure. This chapter suggests that the shifting emphasis in the UK from the provision of security to the management of risk is not universal across countries. Indeed, even the common framing of advice to government in terms of risk that we have detected in all three countries may not prove universal, as may be the case in regimes or countries where certainty is (unrealistically) expected or even demanded. Such possibilities suggest a new avenue of research in the political economy of knowledge production. Moreover, it suggests a new dimension of study for those interested in transnational risk management, if the very use of the term risk clashes with entrenched national policy practices, cultures and philosophies. If it is the case that the very concept of risk is tied up with the self-understanding of the purposes of the state, then more thought needs to be given to the widely held belief that the international governance of transboundary risks and international standards of good governance will induce greater convergence between different national polities and policy styles. Indeed, further study may elicit that in the psychoanalytic spectrum between the 'rationalising' and the 'neurotic' state, there may well be other national 'personality' types that are revealed by the logics of risk regulation and governance more generally.

13
Silos and Silences: The Role of Fragmentation in the Recent Financial Crisis

Gillian Tett

13.1 Introduction

Why did the financial crisis of 2007 and 2008 explode with such vehemence? Why did so few people see this crisis coming – or prevent the credit bubble from growing so large, before it turned into a bust? These are questions which have been asked numerous times by policy makers, journalists, investors, risk managers and bankers since the financial turmoil of 2008. And dozens of different explanations have been offered.

Some economists, for example, blame the crisis on the lax monetary policy implemented by Alan Greenspan, former Federal Reserve chairman, in the early years of the twenty-first century. Others point to a savings glut in China, which exemplified a broader pattern of global macroeconomic imbalances, or cite the problem of excessively loose regulation in the western financial system. Many politicians have blamed the crisis on unfettered financial innovation or warped incentives inside the banking system. Meanwhile, in the eyes of most ordinary voters, the biggest culprit of all was greed – or excessive banking pay.

Looking at these explanations from the perspective of a journalist and former anthropologist – as opposed to that of a banker, regulator or academic – it seems that most of those explanations have a grain of truth. Lax regulation, loose monetary policy, excessive innovation and naked greed, in other words, did collectively fuel the disaster (see also Chapter 14). However, in addition to this long list of culprits, I would cite another factor that has hitherto received far less attention: namely the problems created by 'silos' in the modern financial world.

Most notably, in the last couple of decades, the banking system has become increasingly fragmented, not just in a tangible, institutional sense, but in a cognitive sense too. Tunnel vision and tribalism have come to shape how finance is both organised *and* conceived, on at least three levels: inside the banks; within the government agencies which were supposed to be monitoring the financial system as a whole; and in terms of how finance functioned within society as a whole.

That fragmentation – or 'silo-isation', as some might dub it – has made it hard for bankers to look at their own craft within a wider context (or to even conduct effective risk management inside their own banks.) However, it has also made it hard for non-bankers, such as regulators or politicians, to see where risks were developing in the system as a whole. This fragmentation, in other words, has undermined the ability of bankers and non-bankers to 'join up the dots'. And one tangible consequence of that is that risk managers and regulators alike generally failed to spot the looming financial disaster before 2007, let alone take steps to actually prevent it.

13.2 Silos inside banks

Nothing illustrates the 'silo problem' more clearly than the story of what happened with the so-called 'super-senior' activity pursued by some of the world's largest investment banks from around 2004 to 2007. In late 2007 and early 2008, news broke that the three mighty investment banks UBS, Citigroup and Merrill Lynch had suffered massive losses on 'super-senior' tranches of collateralised debt obligations (CDOs). These are essentially complex financial instruments that effectively bundle together different mortgage-backed bonds, and the 'super-senior' tranches were supposed to be the safest parts of these debt bundles, commanding a credit rating of AAA.

When the news of these losses was first announced, it came as a huge shock to most non-bankers. The total scale of the write-downs was over US $50 billion. However before the crisis of 2007, there had been very little indication that the banks were sitting on assets which could potentially produce such big losses; indeed, most of the investors who owned shares in groups such as UBS, or Merrill Lynch, had little idea that these banks were dabbling in 'super-senior' investments at all, or even what the term meant.

But if that blow was striking for the non-banking world, what was doubly startling was that the news about the 'super-senior' disaster came as a complete shock to *to the vast majority of employees inside these banks too.* Before late 2007, most bankers – like investors in banks – had only a hazy idea of what a 'super-senior' security might be, and even fewer knew the degree to which banks such as UBS or Merrill had amassed these instruments on their balance sheets. Indeed, even at the senior echelons of the bank, there tended to be considerable ignorance about these products. Or, as one senior board member of UBS confessed in 2008: 'We never even talked about super-senior securities really, until the summer of 2007.' What was causing such devastation, in other words, was an activity that was practised by few dozen people – at most – operating within a tiny silo inside a giant bank.

In retrospect, it is tempting to conclude that this pattern was down to a deliberate strategy of wrong-doing or concealment. Perhaps some employees were deliberately setting out to 'hoodwink' the bank, the argument goes. In reality, though, the pattern was more subtle than that; the reason why so few non-bankers – or even other bankers – had peered into the activities of the CDO desks before 2007 was that the structure of these desks was not particularly unusual. On the contrary, within the operations of many large, modern investment banks there are numerous pockets of knowledge, or silos of activity, that are poorly understood and usually ignored by all but a tiny handful of players – at least, until disaster strikes.

Why? Part of the explanation can be attributed to issues of size, complexity and specialisation. In the immediate post-war years, banks were considerably smaller in size than in the later years of the twentieth century, and many bank employees entered banking with a fairly generalist education. Advanced specialist academic qualifications were not always required, since 'on-the-job' training was considered the norm. And once employees entered a bank, they were then often expected to spend a large part of their career inside the bank, learning their craft on the job. Moreover, at prestigious banks, such as JPMorgan, there was a strong tradition of rotating their staff through different departments, to give them a wide experience, and thus good understanding, of different bank functions.

However, in the last two decades of the twentieth century and early years of the twenty-first century, at least four key changes took place in the financial system that fuelled the silo problem. Firstly, the largest banks swelled dramatically in size, due to a wave of cross-border and cross-sector consolidation. This was partly triggered by the growing integration of the European, Asian and American markets. However, another key factor which accelerated the consolidation wave was the abolition of the American Glass-Steagall reforms in 1999, which had previously separated commercial lending from securities activity. In the aftermath of that reform, banks were effectively allowed to combine a host of different functions within one organisation and, as they became larger, that raised the competitive pressure on rivals to follow suit.

A second key trend was that the financial operations of banks became more complex due to financial innovation and technological changes. One of these changes was the advent of the handheld computer in the late 1970s, which suddenly made it possible for financiers to perform significantly more complex mathematical calculations, in order to value or price financial products. However, a second, crucial technological 'leap' was the arrival of the Internet in the 1990s, which removed many of the capacity constraints that had previously limited bankers, and further fuelled geographical integration and mathematical complexity. By the end of the twentieth century, in other words, banking had moved from being a relatively simple craft that could be tracked with pencil and paper, into a new world of 'cyber finance'.

That, in turn, led to a third shift: the growing specialisation – or 'silo-isation' – of financial professionals. As the banking business became more complex towards the end of the twentieth century, the type of all-round generalists who had been recruited into finance in the post-war years were replaced with more 'experts', who tended to develop their careers in one or two fields. Banks also started deliberately to recruit academics trained in advanced mathematics or the hard sciences. That created growing differences in the levels of technical knowledge, between a tiny minority of financial experts who understood the more esoteric areas of banking – and the vast majority who did not. A sense of intellectual elitism and tribalism took hold inside many banks, as these technical experts took control of certain pockets of knowledge, and, by default, those silos of activity.

Meanwhile, a fourth factor further exacerbated the silo trend: the highly hierarchical power structure and incentive system of many banks. In the closing years of the twentieth century and early years of the new decade, the world's largest investment banks became increasingly large and complex. As a result, their operations became ever-more marked by internal divisions and subdivisions, within a vast bureaucracy. In theory, all these different units were supposed to cooperate, within a single structure that was monitored by the banks' senior managers and risk departments. However, in practice, the different departments of banks such as UBS, Merrill Lynch and Citi often appeared to operate more as rival units, competing with each other for resources rather than collaborating.

At any one time, whichever unit was reaping the biggest profits tended to wield most power. And that effectively meant that the 'dominant' unit was able to prevent other areas of the bank from controlling its activities, or even getting much information, not least because power and information tended to flow up and down the departments in a very vertical manner, with little cross-departmental scrutiny. And while the risk departments of the big investment banks were supposed to provide this horizontal scrutiny, the risk departments of banks such as Citi or UBS often wielded limited power (partly because they were viewed as cost centres, and not producing profits).

All of this contributed to the 'silo' problem – and helped to explain why so few players either inside or outside the banks knew much about the activity of the CDO desks, or the potential for 'super-senior' investment to produce losses. During the early years of the twenty-first century, the CDO desks of banks such as UBS and Merrill Lynch appeared to be creating large profits for the banks, and thus wielded huge power; however, very few financiers outside these desks actually knew what the trading strategy entailed or how values of these CDO products were calculated. Even fewer observers inside the bank were in a position to challenge these activities, or to spot the wider risks that these activities could pose for the bank as a whole. Thus, while risk officials inside Merrill Lynch, say, would periodically raise questions about the CDO book of that bank, their enquiries were easily fobbed off; similarly, at UBS, the CDO department was so powerful and savvy that they effectively persuaded the bank's risk department to remove any detailed description of the CDO positions from the risk reports that were presented to the board.

However, it was not just those sitting outside the CDO department which found it difficult to 'join up the dots'; the limited information flow meant that even the CDO traders tended to suffer from tunnel vision, of sorts. Although the bankers who were creating CDOs at UBS, say, had a keen sense of how their activities were generating reported profits, they did not often worry about how their activities might affect other parts of the bank, such as the need to settle trades via the back office. Those tasks had been delegated to another department, in another corner of the bureaucracy. Similarly, CDO traders at one bank never had a particularly precise idea of the overall size of the marketplace. Because CDOs were created in the so-called 'over-the-counter' market – or away from any public exchange – there was no overall data showing precisely how many deals were being created each month from all the banks. And the fragmented, competitive nature of banking meant that individual CDO desks tended to be relatively secretive, not just from other departments inside their own bank – but also in relation to other banks.

This pattern was not present to quite the same degree in all the investment banks. During the early years of the twenty-first century, the senior management of some groups, such as Goldman Sachs or JPMorgan Chase, self-consciously tried to take a more holistic view of their banks' operations, and to rein in the activities of, say, the CDO 'experts.' The risk departments of those banks also tended to wield more power. However, that approach was the exception, not the rule; inside many banks, the activities of the CDO desks remained hidden in broad sight; until, that is, the vast losses suddenly appeared – seemingly out of the blue.

13.3 Silos and regulators

In theory of course, there were some players within the financial system as a whole who were supposed to be looking out for those types of risks within the banking world: regulators and central banks. Those, after all, are the bodies which have historically been charged with 'joining up the dots' in terms of financial stability – and spotting when danger loomed.

In practice, however, regulators and central bankers mostly failed to do that in relation to the banking crisis of 2007 and 2008. And while there were a number of reasons for that failure, one of them was this same 'silo problem.' For just as the private sector banking world was marked by fragmented structures and thinking, so too the public sector had fragmentation and tunnel vision too. 'Joining up the dots' was thus almost as hard for regulators as for many bankers.

Fragmentation partly stemmed from institutional history. In the United States, for example, regulatory responsibilities have historically been divided between numerous different institutions, such as the Federal Reserve (Fed), to the Office of the Comptroller of the Currency and the Securities and Exchange Commission (SEC) (to name but a few.) Like the different departments of the banks, these institutions were supposed to collaborate; in practice, though, they often competed for influence and survival, hampering the flow of information around the system. And the fragmentation was further exacerbated by a woeful lack of cross-border communication between different regulators in different countries (notwithstanding the fact that many banks straddled borders.) To make matters worse, financial institutions deliberately exploited these gaps; AIG financial products, the arm of AIG insurance group which traded CDOs, deliberately chose to be regulated by the Office for Thrift Supervision (OTS), instead of the SEC or Fed, knowing that the OTS had fewer technical skills. However, it also placed many of its operations in London and Paris, to further enable it to fall between the supervisory cracks.

Cognitive fragmentation further intensified the problem, even in countries which tried to create a more unified institutional structure. In the late 1990s, for example, the UK government created the Financial Services Authority (FSA), by consolidating several different regulators into a single body. The theory behind this move was that the act of combining different prudential and consumer protection functions would enable the UK to create a more 'joined-up' approach towards regulating the financial system. But while this produced more coordination in some senses, it also created other types of fragmentation. Before the birth of the FSA, some of the responsibility for banking supervision had sat with the Bank of England, which had often tried to take a fairly holistic approach to assessing credit conditions. However, after the birth of the FSA financial supervision was left firmly separated from overall monetary policy (which remained under the control of the Bank of England). And while the Bank retained a vague mandate for maintaining financial stability, inside the bank there was little serious attempt to combine the analysis of monetary policy and macroeconomic conditions with a detailed examination of what was happening inside banks, or the shadow-banking world. The antics of the CDO desks, in other words, were rarely connected in any conceptual sense to the macroeconomic debate – either inside the bank or the FSA. And that not only prevented the FSA from spotting just how dangerous all this CDO activity was becoming, when combined together – but it also prevented the bank from seeing how the creation of CDOs was fuelling a bigger (and highly unstable) credit boom.

13.4 Finance as a silo

In retrospect, these failings seem very obvious; so much so, in fact, that it is tempting to ask why they went so unnoticed by wider society, for so long. However, the explanation for that partly lies in another, subtle twist on the silo problem: namely the fact that in recent decades finance as a whole had increasingly turned into a cognitive silo, semi-detached from the wider society around it. Precisely because banking became shrouded with a sense of technological elitism, and academic specialisation, it became harder for non-bankers to monitor the activities of banks; and since there was so little external scrutiny, there was less pressure than ever for financiers to be prodded out of their silo mentality.

The CDO desks of the big banks, once again, illustrate the problem. Before 2007, there was minimal coverage of the CDO business in the mainstream financial press, and most politicians (let alone ordinary voters) were almost entirely unaware of the degree to which banks were bundling together mortgage securities in that way. Once the crisis broke, many observers assumed that was because the banks had been deliberately hiding these activities, or because some bankers had been conducting a nefarious plot. In reality, though, the truth was more subtle. Before 2007, some bankers on the CDO certainly were determined to keep much of their activity relatively discrete; the banks, as I have noted above, rarely published detailed figures about what these operations were doing. However, though specific detail about the CDO trades was hard to get, there was plenty of data available in the public sphere that indicated the *general* scale of activity that was underway. By 2006, for example, the Bank for International Settlements had published estimates for the entire market in its annual June report.

Thus the lack of external interest in these activities – or limited level of enquiry – appears to have reflected cultural factors and prejudices, as much as any tangible barrier. Most notably, before 2007 there was a widespread assumption in most of the mainstream western media and political world that the activities of complex finance were best left to the financial experts; the business of creating CDOs, in other words, seemed dull, technical or excessively difficult for non-bankers to understand. That was an assumption that suited many of the bankers fine: after all, being perceived as a technological elite put the CDO geeks into a position of power. However, it was not an assumption that was ever presented as a *deliberate* strategy, created by the financiers; instead, by 2006 it had come to appear almost natural that finance should be treated as a mental island of its own. Financiers did not expect non-financiers to delve too deeply, or see any reason to 'join up the dots' for society as a whole; and non-bankers did not see any reason to peer into the financial island; or not until it was far too late.

13.5 Joining up the dots

This problem of fragmentation has big implications for how policy makers and bankers try to reform finance for the future. In the aftermath of the 2007 and 2008 banking crisis, there has been extensive public debate about how to build a stronger financial system, and a plethora of tangible reforms have been proposed, many of which are very sensible. However, what is clear from the last decade is that it will be crucial to address the problem of cognitive and institutional fragmentation, if the reform effort is to produce sustainable change. 'Silo-busting', in other words, should be at the forefront of reform, not just inside banks but across the system as a whole.

The good news is that many bankers and policy makers appear determined to engage in this 'silo-busting' (even though they rarely phrase it in quite that way.) Since the credit crisis, most large investment banks have taken steps to empower their risk management departments, and are now seeking to introduce ways to promote better cross-departmental information flows. The new mantra among risk managers and senior bank management alike is that they need to strive for more 'joined-up thinking'. And on a macro-level, it is now widely accepted that national and international regulators need to coordinate much better. In 2009 in the United States, for example, efforts started to create a systemic-risk regulator, with an oversight function. At the same time, supervisors and regulators from the leading western nations created a new entity known as the Financial Stability Board, with the goal of promoting more cross-border coordination too. At the same time, during the course of 2009 and 2010, regulators and central bankers started calling for more 'macro-prudential regulation', or a policy approach which attempts to take an holistic view of how the real economy and banking systems are interacting throughout the cycle.

Last but not least, the crisis has also helped – at least temporarily – to undermine the prior assumption that it was natural to treat finance itself as a self-contained silo within society. During 2009 and 2010, politicians, journalists – and even voters – started to ask hard questions about the operations of complex finance, often for the first time; meanwhile, bankers were forced to engage with a new level of external scrutiny – and give more consideration to the wider implications of finance. The idea that banking should be left to bankers – or that the geeky part of finance would always be safe in the hands of geeks – was no longer taken for granted. Once-obscure terms such as 'CDOs' began to enter the mainstream press.

But while these moves are welcome, nobody should pretend that it will be easy to overcome the 'silo problem.' After all, the question of how to deal with growing complexity and fragmentation is a problem that is baked into twenty-first century life, extending well beyond finance. As innovation spreads in the modern world, the level of complexity spreads too, the sense of technological elitism and tribalism is spreading too, in areas as diverse as medicine, science, government and energy – as well as finance. And while modern communication technology could theoretically help to reduce silos, by allowing information to circulate more freely, in other senses this is actually reinforcing – not reducing – the problem. By linking the world more closely together, the Internet might have undermined geographical boundaries, but it is also creating online communities which can become equally tribal, and inward-looking too. And as communication technologies become more complex, and innovation gathers pace in many fields, the gap between the technological elite (or those with the skills and education to understand a particular field) and everyone else can potentially grow. The type of silo problem seen on the CDO desks, in other words, is repeated in numerous other pockets of activity today – and will not be easily eliminated. Or to put it another way, the question of how to 'silo bust' is truly a key challenge of our age, not just in finance but the non-financial world too. Financiers and non-financiers alike have much to learn from the first banking crisis of the twenty-first century – most notably, because this was a crisis that revealed a social problem that goes well beyond the financial world.

14

Forecasting, Warning and Preventive Policy: The Case of Finance

Thomas F. Huertas[1]

14.1 Introduction

Crisis or problem prevention and mitigation are central to many disciplines, including defence, homeland security, nuclear energy, chemical engineering and the handling of natural disasters such as earthquakes and floods. As is evident from the contributions to this book, a rich literature has developed a framework for analysing the factors that determine whether crises can be prevented and/or their effects mitigated. The framework used in this book (Chapter 1) highlights four specific challenges to successful crisis prevention/mitigation: risk recognition, warning about risks, prioritisation of risks vis-à-vis other demands, and preventive/mitigating action. This chapter attempts to apply this framework to finance and to the problems that we are facing in formulating a new financial system – one that will be more resistant to crises, so that we will not face another economic calamity on the scale of the downturn that started in 2007.

In finance, risk recognition, warning about risks, prioritisation of risks vis-à-vis other demands, and preventive/mitigating action constitute a continuous loop. That is effectively the way that financial markets work. Market participants identify risks and make some assessment of their impact if they were to manifest, as well as some estimate of the probability that the risks will in fact manifest. Market participants communicate the results of their analysis to other market participants through offering to buy or sell assets or assume liabilities at certain prices. In effect, the prices of financial assets contain the warning of market participants to each other about the risks that may lie ahead for those who hold the asset. For example, the spread on a corporate bond contains a signal about the probability that the issuer will default. These warnings should induce market participants to take preventive measures, such as portfolio diversification and hedging. However, such portfolio decisions create potential movements in the demand for and supply of assets, causing potential price movements and risks that in turn need to be identified.

14.2 Why risk recognition and prioritisation failed

The markets' warnings will only be effective if market participants anticipate the possibility that they may suffer a loss. Two factors dulled that perception and muted the risk warnings that the market might have given.

The first was the extraordinary success that macroeconomic policy achieved in taming inflation and producing steadier economic growth – something economists called the Great Moderation. This created the expectation that good times were here to stay – that the business cycle had to a large extent been mastered. As Federal Reserve Chairman Greenspan (2005) remarked in testimony to Congress in February 2005:

> Over the past two decades, the industrial world has fended off two severe stock market corrections, a major financial crisis in developing nations, corporate scandals, and, of course, the tragedy of September 11, 2001. Yet overall economic activity experienced only modest difficulties. In the United States, only five quarters in the past twenty years exhibited declines in GDP, and those declines were small. Thus, it is not altogether unexpected or irrational that participants in the world marketplace would project more of the same going forward.

The state of the economy is the dominant external risk to which financial markets are exposed, and how market participants expect the economy to develop has a dramatic effect on the availability of credit and on the prices of assets. If the economy slides into recession or sinks into depression, this will reduce cash flows at firms and reduce incomes of consumers. The ability of creditors to repay debt will be compromised. Risk will increase, and the prices of assets such as equities, bonds and houses will fall. Conversely, if the economy exhibits steady, positive growth, creditors will be more able to service debt, risk will decrease, and the prices of assets such as equities, bonds and houses will rise – this was exactly the situation prior to the crisis (Huertas, 2010a: 9–19).

The second factor dulling risk recognition was resolution policy (Huertas, 2010d). Resolution effectively determines risk to the private creditor. If the authorities always intervene in a manner that protects the creditors of the bank, loss given intervention is zero. The risk to the creditor is also zero, no matter what the probability is that the bank will require intervention. If the authorities do not protect creditors of the bank, then the creditors can expect to suffer some loss given intervention, and risk to the creditor will be the loss given intervention multiplied by the probability that the bank will require intervention.

Over the years market participants had come to expect that there was a high likelihood that governments would come to the assistance of large, complex financial institutions if they were to get into difficulty. Rating agencies even went so far as to factor this expected support into their ratings of major financial institutions. There grew a belief in the market that some institutions were 'too big to fail,' or that some institutions' failure would be 'too complex to contemplate'.

Such an implicit guarantee blunts the market's incentive to impose higher funding costs on large firms that take excessive risks. If the government stands behind large, complex firms, then the private investor need not worry about placing his money with such firms, no matter what risks the large firm takes (Huertas, 2010b).[2]

This belief was considerably strengthened in March 2008 when the US authorities rescued Bear Stearns. To facilitate the acquisition of Bear Stearns by JPMorgan Chase, the Federal Reserve extended a non-recourse loan of $30 billion secured only by distressed and illiquid assets in the Bear Stearns portfolio. If the assets defaulted, JPMorgan Chase would be responsible for the first $1 billion in losses. Anything over that amount would be for the account of the Fed and, effectively, the US taxpayer.

This step created the impression in the markets that the US authorities would act in a similar manner if any institution larger than Bear Stearns were to get into similar difficulty. For private creditors of major financial institutions the message seemed loud and clear: a firm might require resolution, but the loss given resolution for creditors would in all likelihood be zero. This expectation of government support reduced the spreads on bonds and other liabilities issued by large financial institutions and muted the risk warning contained in such spreads. Thus, the low expected loss given resolution masked and muffled the signal that the market might have given regarding the probability that the firm would require resolution or actually default.

Although macroeconomic policy and resolution policy blunted the risk recognition and prioritisation that the market might have provided, a separate question is why neither the authorities (governments, central banks and regulators/supervisors) nor market participants recognised the risk that the financial system would implode and that the global economy would go into free fall.

Some officials did not recognise the risk of implosion at all. They did not believe that there was an asset-price bubble at all, but contended that the productivity surge in the economy created a basis for permanently faster growth and thus created a further fundamental factor for asset-price increases. Others acknowledged that the Great Moderation could lead to an asset-price bubble, if the expectations of market participants ran ahead of what the economy could conceivably produce, but were doubtful that one could identify an asset-price bubble prior to its having burst.

Even if policy makers had recognised that there was an asset-price bubble, the prevailing wisdom was that such bubbles would burst without significant adverse impacts on output and employment. That had been the experience after the dot-com bubble and earlier episodes. Finally, policy makers saw no means to prevent an asset-price bubble from developing apart from starting a recession – a cure that would be worse than the disease. So asset-price bubbles may have reached policy makers' risk registers, but they never made it to the risk-reduction agenda.

The ultimate cause for this may have been the assumptions that central banks used to model the operation of the economy and the effect of monetary policy. Although these models were staggeringly complex, they basically ignored the financial system. The financial system played little or no role in the models that policymakers employed to decide changes in the interest rate. Although the financial system is the transmission mechanism for monetary policy, central banks' macroeconomic models generally ignored default risk, counterparty risk, and the possible changes in the financial system that changes in monetary policy could cause. Although central bankers acknowledged that monetary policy would affect prices and output with a long and variable lag, they generally regarded the financial system as a straightforward pass-through mechanism. The dynamic stochastic general equilibrium models used as the basis for economic policy discussions and decisions generally ignored the possibility that the monetary policy could affect the transmission mechanism provided by the financial system as well as the possibility that changes in the financial system could affect output, employment or prices.[3]

Essentially what central banks and governments ignored was the possibility that a reversal in one segment of the market (securities backed by sub-prime mortgages) could generate a debt-deflation spiral. As the market fundamentals and market liquidity of securitised assets declined, this created the potential for capital losses at institutions that held those securities, and cut off securitisation as a source of new funding. That in turn created funding difficulties at financial institutions and threatened to turn the financial crisis into an economic crisis in which the real economy would decline.

The second failure in official risk recognition and prioritisation concerned resolution policy. The US authorities failed to recognise that forcing Lehman's into bankruptcy on 15 September 2008 would push the financial system and the world economy toward meltdown.

The decision to let Lehman's fail on 15 September 2009 rudely ruptured the market's expectation that loss given resolution would be zero or close to it. Over $600 billion of liabilities were suddenly at real risk. Creditors stood to experience severe losses. In addition, investors found their assets tied up in the Lehman's administration. Consequently, the failure of Lehman's had severe knock-on effects on other firms and other markets, and the decision of the US authorities to impose losses on unsecured creditors and uninsured depositors in Washington Mutual compounded the shock unleashed by Lehman's.

Following the failure of Lehman's the world economy went into free fall, with output falling at a rate as fast as or faster than the rate experienced at the start of the Great Depression. With the benefit of hindsight one can perhaps say that the authorities did not fully appreciate the risk that their resolution policy had created, and this may have contributed to their error in assessing the impact caused by a sudden reversal of that policy.

Market participants were generally no better than officials in discerning the risk of implosion. To some extent this may have been due to the silo mentality in the financial sector (see Chapter 12). Market participants broadly accepted the prevailing wisdom about the general macroeconomic environment, assumed the ongoing stability of the financial system, and sought (and for many years captured) significant financial rewards via ever more complex financial innovations. Only with the benefit of hindsight and extensive forensic research (Poszar et al., 2010) has it become apparent just how extensive – and dangerous – the shadow banking system had become during the years 2004–2007. At the time the innovations were widely heralded as reducing, rather than increasing, systemic risk.

14.3 Measures to prevent a recurrence

Following the bankruptcy of Lehman's, economic activity began to collapse. To arrest this decline, governments acted promptly to introduce massive fiscal and monetary stimulus and to stabilise the financial system. In particular, governments boosted fiscal deficits to levels unprecedented in peacetime. Central banks not only slashed interest rates to zero, but in some cases (United States, UK) supplemented this with huge purchases of government and/or private sector securities. In addition, in October 2008 – in the wake of the panic that gripped financial markets following the failure of Lehman – governments promised that no systemically-important institution would be allowed to fail. Governments backed up that promise through recapitalising major institutions. Providing this backstop was just as important as monetary and fiscal stimulus in arresting the slide in the real economy. Instead of the Great(er) Depression, the year 2009 turned into the Great Recession.

But it is widely acknowledged that these emergency procedures are not a long-term cure. We need an 'exit policy', not only from fiscal and monetary stimulus, but also from the policy of 'too big to fail'. Attention is now turning to what should be done to prevent a crisis of this magnitude from ever happening again.

There is broad agreement that preventive measures must be strengthened – that the dykes of the financial system must be reinforced. This means higher capital requirements for banks, especially with respect to the trading book, and it means higher quality capital, with more focus on forms of capital, such as stockholders' equity, that can absorb losses whilst the bank remains a going concern. It also means tighter controls on the liquidity risks that banks are allowed to run, as well as greater buffers to absorb the liquidity shocks that could arise, such as the closure of certain funding markets (BCBS, 2010). Finally, it means greater attention to risk management and governance, including the design of remuneration policies, procedures and practices, so that they are consistent with and promote effective risk management (FSB, 2009).

This is a very significant reform agenda. Taken together the measures will assure that banks are stronger and more resilient. But will that be enough to stem future crises? That depends on two still open issues: resolution and macro-prudential supervision.

14.3.1 Exiting 'too big to fail'

The first open issue is resolution. The experience of Lehman's demonstrated to the world community the peril of abruptly reversing the market's expectation that some firms would be too big to fail. Consequently, governments committed to sustaining systemically-important firms during this crisis.

But for two reasons this is not sustainable. First, it removes market discipline from such institutions. That increases the probability that systemically-important institutions overstretch themselves such that governments will be required to perform on their guarantee. As outlined above, that contributed to the crisis. Second, the promise is unsustainable simply because of the potential expense involved. Even if countries were willing to stand behind these liabilities, they may not have the means to do so and/or they may not secure the political authorisation that would be required in order to meet such commitments of support. If they suddenly reverse course, as the US authorities did in the case of Lehman's, the financial system and world economy would again be at risk. Consequently, the world needs an exit strategy from 'too big to fail'.

So the right answer is to get to a position where there is *no* guarantee, implicit or explicit. We have to move to a point where the market does not expect institutions to be bailed out. That requires an effective resolution regime. That will restore market discipline, so that banks will pay a risk premium in line with the risks that they take rather than the government support that they might obtain.

We therefore need to map out what our long-term resolution policy should be, and consider how we will take steps to move from where we are today to where we need to be. Ideally, we want a resolution policy that allows governments to resolve failing institutions promptly without recourse to taxpayer funds, but at the same time avoids the social disruption that could occur from widespread interruption to deposit, insurance and/or securities accounts. This would allow for maximum continuity in customer-related activities, whilst assuring that capital providers remain exposed to loss and avoiding the need to give widespread or long-lasting guarantees of the bank's liabilities.

Progress is being made. The UK and other jurisdictions have introduced special resolution regimes for banks. Regulators have demanded that major banks prepare recovery and resolution plans (a.k.a. living wills) (Huertas, 2010c). Finally, regulators and banks are working to develop the concept of 'bail-in' as a replacement for 'bail-out'. Bail-in would effectively amount to a pre-pack recapitalisation of a bank so that, if it failed, its capital could be quickly restructured without interruption to its customer activities. This would in turn permit either the solvent wind-down of the institution, its sale to a third party, or possibly even its revival as an independent entity (Huertas, 2010e).

However, much remains to be done before one can say with certainty that bail-in can replace bail-out. Should it not prove possible to do so, attention will in all likelihood turn to more structural solutions, such as limiting the activities in which banks may engage and/or establishing a strict limit on the size to which a bank may grow. The first does not solve 'too big to fail' at all, for 'too big to fail' encompasses, as Bear Stearns, AIG and Lehmans amply demonstrate, more than just banks. Nor does limiting the activities of banks eliminate the risk that they will fail. Indeed, traditional lending remains the primary cause of bank failure. Restricting the size of banks may also fail to make the financial system more stable, especially if no size limits are placed on other financial institutions, such as money market mutual funds, that exercise bank-like functions. And, such a solution is only practical, if deposit-guarantee schemes are truly robust and truly able to pay out insured deposits promptly in the event of a bank failure.

14.3.2 The role of macro-prudential supervision

The second open issue is risk identification, the issue of risk warnings and the design and implementation of risk mitigants. What we need is a broader look at the vulnerabilities or fault lines that may exist in the system as a whole, as well as a means to overcome these vulnerabilities. The former is the task of systemic-risk boards; the latter comes under the heading of 'macro-prudential supervision'.

In response to the crisis systemic-risk boards have been created at the global, EU and national level. The Financial Stability Board has tasked its Committee on Vulnerabilities to identify threats to the global financial system. The IMF has taken on a similar task. The EU has created a European Systemic Risk Board. The UK has created a Financial Policy Committee, and the United States has created the Financial Stability Oversight Council. All these boards are to identify systemic risks, issue risk warnings and develop tools for macro-prudential supervision that supervisors and/or monetary/ fiscal authorities could use to assure financial stability.

This is a daunting task, and the mere creation of the bodies to assume it carries no guarantee that such bodies will be able to accomplish the task successfully. The new entities may identify a risk to financial stability, but underestimate the probability that it will occur or the impact of failing to mitigate the risk. Such, after all, was the case with asset-price bubbles. Chairman Greenspan clearly identified an asset-price bubble as a risk to financial stability, but pointedly declined to do anything about it on two grounds. First, he thought the only way to puncture the bubble was to raise interest rates to the point where a recession would start, and second, he thought that it would cost relatively little to clear up the mess from the bubble after it had burst. This policy proved to be mistaken.

A second limit to macro-supervision is that it will fail to detect risks that will prove to be systemic. Some are inherently difficult to spot, much like finding a needle in the haystack – until the sunlight heats the needle to the point where it sets the haystack afire. Then of course it may be too late to take mitigating action. Such arguably was the risk to the financial system posed by sub-prime securities. Initially, the structuring and rating agency review process provided strong protection to investors. However, when the ratings agencies changed their procedures without too much fanfare or warning, risk rose. This only became transparent as the relaxed underwriting standards collided with rising interest rates to produce faster acceleration in arrears. By then it was too late to eliminate the risk that sub-prime ABS would pose to the financial system and ultimately to the real economy.

Macro-prudential supervision must also confront the possibility that reforms that strengthen the banking system may not improve the resiliency of the overall financial system. The first issue is whether strengthening the banking system will actually strengthen the overall financial and economic system, or whether strengthening the banking system will merely mean that when pressures arise, they are diverted to other areas. In other words, will strengthening the banking system be akin to reinforcing one portion of the levee whilst leaving another in disrepair?

This could result, if capital and liquidity requirements for banks were raised to the point where it became much more attractive for borrowers and lenders to interact directly with one another in the securities markets. This would tend to shift credit from the bank markets to the securities markets during the upswing of the business cycle, leaving the overall level of credit in the economy pretty much unaffected during the boom. But in the downturn, new issuance in the securities markets tends to contract very dramatically. Thanks to the higher capital and liquidity requirements, banks would be in stronger condition, able to absorb the losses on the assets that had remained in their portfolios, but they might be collectively too small to provide the credit that would be needed to offset the decline in new issuance in the securities markets. Care therefore needs to be taken in the design of capital and liquidity requirements for banks so that there is not an abrupt and potentially disruptive shift in financial activity from bank markets to securities markets.

Finally, risks to financial stability may arise from areas into which the macro-prudential bodies neglect to look. One such area might be monetary policy itself. This certainly has an impact on financial markets and may adversely affect financial stability. Indeed, some would contend that the asset-price bubble of 2003–2006/2007 was fuelled by the period of extraordinarily low interest rates from 2001 to 2004. Some would further contend that the sustained and sharp hike in interest rates from the end of 2004 to mid-2006 punctured the bubble and contributed to setting the stage for the crisis of 2007. Other areas might include the threat to financial stability that would arise if governments were unable to fulfil explicit or implicit guarantees that they had given, or if Eurozone Member States were unable to sustain the fiscal foundations for a single currency.

So we should embark on the road to macro-supervision with a clear idea of its limitations. Macro-supervision can identify possible risks and stimulate action to mitigate the risks that it does identify. Macro-supervision can do nothing about the risks that it does not look for and/or does not find, and these 'unknown unknowns' are ultimately the risks that may pose the greatest threat to financial and economic stability in the future.

14.4 Conclusion: the need for preventive policy

In summary, finance has much to learn from the general framework of forecasting, warning and preventive policy applied in other fields. Markets are effective in identifying and prioritising risks if and only if market participants perceive that they will be exposed to loss. Prior to the crisis, this was not necessarily the case, as the Great Moderation had lulled investors into the belief that recessions were a relic of the past, and resolution policy had created the impression that some financial firms were too big to fail. Central banks and governments also failed to identify the risk that the financial system could implode, perhaps as a result of the policy model that effectively assumed that the financial system was a straightforward pass-through mechanism for policy initiatives rather than an integral to the entire economy.

There are many measures under discussion to prevent the recurrence of a crisis, with a central focus on strengthening banks' capital and liquidity. But more will need to be done. Reform should not stop with banking. Reform must include instituting a gradual, but permanent, exit from 'too big to fail'. Finally, reform must include initiation of macro-prudential supervision.

But perhaps the key lesson from the application of the general crisis framework to finance is the need for preventive policy. This should supplement reform. Specifically, supervisors will have to force firms to adopt preventive policies, that is to prepare for severe stress. With the benefit of hindsight, it might be said that regulators and supervisors placed too much reliance on the assurances of central banks and governments that the business cycle had been tamed, too much reliance on the assumption that markets would adequately discipline firms that took undue risk, and too much reliance on the assumption that markets would remain stable. They need to drop that reliance, and to prepare themselves and the firms they supervise for the possibility that the environment will turn out to be much worse than commonly expected (see Chapter 16).

Regulators and supervisors have already shifted their stance during the crisis to much more proactive supervision of financial firms. For example, in 2009 the UK Financial Services Authority instituted a regime whereby banks have to demonstrate to the supervisor that they would be able to maintain their core Tier I capital ratio above 4% even under a severe stress. This led UK institutions to take management actions to bolster their capital and liquidity. Similarly, the United States instituted a similar stress test and this led various US banks to strengthen their capital (Huertas, 2010a: 89). The Committee of European Banking Supervisors also instituted stress testing for major European banks. These should not be one-off exercises in the midst of crisis, but part of the ongoing supervisory tool kit.

Notes

1. The author is Vice Chairman, Committee of European Banking Supervisors (CEBS) and Director, Banking Sector, Financial Services Authority (UK). The opinions expressed here are the author's own and do not necessarily represent the views of CEBS or the FSA.
2. The implicit guarantees provided to Freddie Mac and Fannie Mae, two US government-sponsored institutions, also diluted market discipline. Additionally, market discipline was also muted by the official tolerance of allowing money-market mutual funds to portray themselves as deposit equivalents (i.e. that they would not 'break the buck').
3. Perhaps the clearest proof for this is the forecasts of continued economic growth that central banks and governments made in the fall of 2007 – fully three months after the crisis had started. In the United States the November 2007 forecast by the Council of Economic Advisers called for real growth of 2.7 per cent in 2008 and 3 per cent in 2009, somewhat, but not significantly, below the forecasts made a year earlier in 2006. For the Eurozone, the ECB forecast in October 2007 that real growth would be 2.2 per cent in 2008 and 2.1 per cent in 2009. In the UK the Government predicted in October 2007 that real growth in 2008 would be 2–2.5 per cent and that growth in 2009 would be 2.5–3 per cent. The Bank of England made a similar forecast in its November 2007 Inflation Report. Its central forecast called for a slight fall in growth in 2008 to about 2 per cent, before a pick-up in growth to nearly 3 per cent in 2009 and 2010. A fall in output was considered so remote a possibility that it did not even appear on the fan chart that the Bank used to present its economic forecasts. That meant the Bank considered the possibility of a recession to be less than 5 per cent (Huertas, 2010a: 40).

15

Prospective Sense-Making: A Realistic Approach to 'Foresight for Prevention' in an Age of Complex Threats

Warren H. Fishbein

Prediction is hard – especially about the future

Variously attributed to Yogi Berra and Niels Bohr

15.1 Introduction[1]

Both governmental and academic experts increasingly recognise the necessity for systematic efforts to 'look ahead' in order to better address – and hopefully to head off – potential security crises in what is almost universally seen as an increasingly fast-changing, complex and danger-filled world. For instance, the 2008 report of the US Project on National Security Reform, probably the most authoritative recent review of security issues from a US perspective, argued that the 'current environment virtually puts a premium on foresight – the ability to anticipate unwelcome contingencies' (Project on National Security Reform, 2008: vii). Leading Canadian environmental-security expert Thomas Homer-Dixon has called for the development of 'prospective mind', and former national-security advisor to Vice President Al Gore, Leon Fuerth (2009), has advocated 'forward engagement': both are roughly comparable calls for systematic, sustained and highly proactive consideration of potential future challenges in a wide range of connected-issue domains (see also Homer-Dixon, 2006). And, in terms of concrete actions, numerous governments, multinational groupings and private sector organisations have in recent years established programs to more effectively anticipate challenges in security and other issue areas: among the most prominent are Singapore's Risk Assessment and Horizon Scanning program (RAHS), the UK's Horizon Scanning Unit, OECD's Futures Program, and the World Economic Forum's Global Risks Program (see, e.g., Habegger, 2008).

In any enhanced effort to probe the future, intelligence organisations, particularly their analytical wings, would seemingly have a very important role to play. For helping policy officials to 'anticipate unwelcome contingencies' has always been among their bedrock missions. These organisations have pursued this responsibility in two broad ways: strategic assessment and warning.

- *Strategic assessment*: the production of formal analyses of future trends and possible developments. These tend to be evidence and/or theory based, and usually feature probabilistic judgements highlighting the likeliest outcomes and their implications – although often with some attention to less probable developments. US National Intelligence Estimates are exemplars of this genre.
- *Warning*: the 'gold standard' of intelligence anticipation, warning involves the issuance of alerts about potential 'unwelcome contingencies' that are designed to be 'actionable' – to elicit policy responses. Warning may be strategic – alerts issued at a somewhat distant temporal remove from the expected event that aim to prompt preventive action or enhance readiness – or tactical where the aim is to be sufficiently specific about 'where, when, what, and how' to prompt the immediate mobilisation of available resources. Warning is embedded in most types of intelligence production but can (as in the United States) also involve a dedicated system in which 'early-warning indicators' are monitored for possible escalation of the danger posed by a pre-identified threat (see, e.g., Grabo, 2004).

Whatever the specific process employed, the expectation of the general public, many policy officials and, to a considerable extent, intelligence organisations themselves, is that intelligence should strive and be able to provide specific predictions – particularly of a tactical nature – of coming dangers that can help to head off 'strategic surprise.'

But intelligence organisations has been most heavily held to account for alleged failures to make correct 'calls' on what have later turned out to be harmful-to-disastrous developments. From the World War II era onwards, there have been repeated failures by intelligence organisations around the globe – including highly capable ones – to predict various types of events: surprise military and terrorist attacks such as Pearl Harbor, the outbreak of the Yom Kippur War, and 9/11; major internal upheavals such as the 1979 Iranian revolution, and game-changing political events, such as the 1998 Indian nuclear test (see, e.g., Kam, 2004; Chapter 3 in this book). To be sure, there have been known predictive successes as well (and perhaps many less-recognised ones also, because warning successes produce non-events that do not register with publics or with commissions of inquiry) and some failures have arguably turned out, on close academic inspection, to be more nuanced than widely believed, especially insofar as intelligence performance is concerned (i.e., as has been argued for Pearl Harbor and 9/11, sufficiently clear warning was given but not acted upon by policy officials).[2] Nevertheless, the judgement of most serious students of intelligence and national-security processes – taking into account not only this record but the comparably spotty prognostic achievements of experts in other sectors such as industry and finance – is that prediction of specific events is extremely difficult, meaning that strategic surprises are inevitable (see Chapter 2).

It is hard to quarrel with this judgement, when one considers the almost endless array of factors identified as impeding abilities to predict effectively or, for that matter, to translate predictions into effective preventive or preparatory actions. These include (among many other factors):

Uncertainty: Even in the case of the most straightforward threat (e.g., a cross border conventional military attack), events can usually unfold in a number of different plausible ways, making precise judgements problematic. Large volumes of ambiguous information (even just in the classified arena) make it difficult to separate the true signal of future developments from the 'noise.' And sophisticated deception efforts are very difficult to detect.

Perceptual distortions: Analysts – seasoned experts, in particular – as well as their policy consumers, are all subject to 'mindsets' that cause them to believe that the future will look very much like the past, thus blinding them to surprise developments. And they are subject as well to ingrained perceptual and judgemental biases, such as confirmation (looking most intently for evidence that supports one's case), linearity (expecting a proportional relationship between causes and effects) and mirror-imaging (thinking that others think like them), all of which may prevent them from seeking or understanding signs of dramatic change.

The warning-response gap: Policy officials are often loath to act upon warning because they put greater emphasis on avoiding current losses (resources put into prevention) than future gains; the 'cry-wolf' phenomenon – predictions and warnings that do not pan out – prompts scepticism; and overcrowded agendas deter consideration of all but today's crisis (see, e.g., Heuer, 1999; Fishbein and Treverton, 2004: 3–5; Woocher, 2008).

There are, of course, innumerable IT-based predictive methodologies that aim to overcome such obstacles, but the jury is out concerning their reliability and usefulness. Persuasive (though challenged) claims have been made, for instance, that decision modelling employing rational-choice theory has outperformed unaided intelligence-analyst judgements (Tetlock, 2009). And political-instability forecasting models are said to have achieved fairly high levels of reliability looking ahead several years (Nyheim, 2008: 20–35). At the same time, the spectacular failure of risk-assessment models in relation to the 2007 global financial crisis (due to the extreme undervaluing of risk of real-estate price declines, among other factors, see Chapters 12 and 14) demonstrates that even the most sophisticated forecasting methodologies can fail if underlying assumptions prove inaccurate or 'externalities' suddenly change (a growing problem, as will be argued below). In any case, even if progress is made in refining such methodologies, the willingness of decision-makers – who, in many governments, lack technical backgrounds – to trust the results of products emerging from 'black boxes' remains questionable.

Intelligence organisations can hardly evade the necessity to try to predict adverse developments but, in view of the identified obstacles, there has been considerable rethinking in recent years about other approaches to improved performance in addressing future uncertainty. One important strain of thought advocates placing greater emphasis on the strategic aspect of warning. For instance, the doyen of US community of experts on intelligence analysis, Jack Davis, has argued in favour of a dedicated system within intelligence focused on identifying and exploring the most significant longer-run threats facing the United States (Davis, 2003). The objective would be to provide a sound basis not only for preventive measures but also for more effective preparedness should, as Davis realistically believes will often be the case, preventive efforts prove ineffective. This system would involve a combination of sound strategic assessment, robust employment of alternative analysis (techniques to challenge assumptions and explore the implications of unexpected outcomes so as to help overcome mindsets and biases), and close interaction between analysts and policy makers to increase the chances that warning will have an impact. Significantly, because this approach is resource and labour intensive, threat triage would be absolutely required to strictly limit the number of issues so rigorously examined.

15.2 Surprise and sense-making

Davis's suggestions seem sensible, as does enhancing strategic intelligence work generally on potential adverse developments. However useful, can strategic intelligence assessment, even if supported by alternative analysis, significantly improve the capabilities of governments to prevent or better address emerging and future threats in the current security environment? One can make a strong argument that this approach has severe limitations by drawing upon the thinking of an emerging school of writers on the underlying theory of intelligence analysis – what might be called the 'complexity school' (see, e.g., Fishbein and Treverton, 2004; Kerbel, 2004; Andrus, 2005; Williams, 2005)[3]

The fundamental premise of this school is that the cumulative impact of changes in the global-security environment that have taken place since the end of the Cold War have created a new context for intelligence analysis – and for threat anticipation and warning, in particular. From the World War II era through the late 1980s – the formative years of the modern intelligence establishment – a handful of nation states were the driving force of 'international relations.' These states were themselves driven by hierarchical/bureaucratic decision-making structures, and they operated within a context shaped by established ideas and histories (e.g., democracy, Leninism, nationalism, etc.) as well as international norms and rules. As a result, the range of possible adverse outcomes was limited, not so much to be sure that prediction was generally feasible, but enough so that, through the marshalling of considerable evidence (both publicly-available and privileged) about the preferences of and constraints facing a small group of decision-makers and the capabilities at their disposal, one could make informed probabilistic forecasts about potential threats.

But due to the impact of such dramatic changes as globalisation, democratisation, the information revolution, and so on that have evolved over the past twenty years, we have entered into a very different environment of international – or, rather, global – relations. Among the most significant changes from a security point of view have been:

- The rise of networked transnational malefactors, such as terrorist groups, criminal organisations and proliferation rings, with substantial resources, the ability to 'embed' themselves surreptitiously within traditional social structures, and the potential (due to the informality and flexibility of their internal structures) to 'morph' – to change their identities and modes of operation – when under attack.
- The decline of state sovereignty and the rise of sub-national security actors and challenges, reflected in failing states, and ungoverned and partially-governed areas within semi-functioning states (e.g., no-go areas for law enforcement or military forces).
- Rapid advances in potentially 'dual-capable' technologies such as nanotechnology, synthetic biology and IT, and the diffusion of knowledge about the development and use of these and other potentially dangerous technologies throughout the world.
- The diffusion through the Internet not only of access to information and knowledge but the ability to create, easily and at little or no cost, content that can be widely shared.
- Vastly increased global flows of goods, people and services, facilitating the movement across borders of illicit goods and services, dangerous individuals and microbes, and promoting vastly increased interconnectivity/interdependence among countries and systems.
- As a result of all the above, the empowerment of small groups and individuals that have the capabilities to inflict harm or exert influence vastly disproportionate to their size and disposable resources (Costigan, 2007: 10–11; Shirky, 2008).

The combination of these changes has had three broad and interrelated effects on the security environment that affect abilities to anticipate change.

First, as opposed to what some term the 'complicated' security environment of the World War II/Cold War era – to repeat, an environment marked by a limited number of large actors operating within a context of known rules of behaviour – we have entered into a 'complex' environment, with that term connoting the behaviour of 'complex adaptive systems' (see Chapter 4). This is a world of a multiplicity of small actors who make decisions within a much more fluid set of rules. Change 'emerges' when an idiosyncratic confluence of decisions and conditions achieve 'ripeness,' and then a possibly small, unforeseeable event takes things to and beyond a 'tipping point.' Causes and effects are intertwined as a large number of adaptive actors respond to each other's moves and to cues from the environment. Actions can have very significant 'knock-on' effects as they propel themselves through connected systems. To be sure, complexity is nothing new (revolutions, economic cycles and military battles all being longstanding phenomena governed by complexity) and the world continues to feature complicated state-to-state relationships that demand intelligence attention. The point is simply that the former is of greatly increased significance within the global system due to the growth of networked actors, empowered groups and individuals, and global interconnectivity (Williams, 2005: 35–62; Kerbel 2009).

Second, the current environment is characterised by enhanced 'obscurity' – much of what takes place of importance, especially in the transnational and sub-national domain, is largely hidden, at least insofar as intelligence and other security officials are concerned. This is again due to the number and small size of significant actors, the global diffusion of capabilities and the growth of ungoverned spaces where possibilities for monitoring are limited. The IT revolution cuts both ways relating to this factor: on the one hand, it vastly increases capacity for information gathering and collation but on the other hand produces such a torrent of information that it contributes to the possibilities of 'hiding in plain sight.' Here again, we are talking about degrees of difference from the World War II–1989 era but, at least in that era, intelligence organisations knew pretty much where to look for information (adversary-state political/military/industrial complexes) and what they were needing to learn (Fishbein and Treverton, 2004: 8–9).

Finally, the current security environment is characterised by novelty – the continuous appearance of unprecedented capabilities and trends. This is most obviously the case in science and technology; indeed, many believe that we are but in the early stages of a revolution that, through the interactions of nano-, bio-, and info-technologies (among others), will fundamentally transform the nature of life and society over the next 10–20 years (Project Horizon, 2006: 9). But it is also in the more strictly social sphere that new trends and capabilities – for example, 'flash mobs' – seem to emerge much more rapidly and frequently than in the past, as the result of creative applications of existing technologies. And if extreme scenarios of climate change come to pass then the physical environment may also produce an unprecedented combination of events with regional and global-security ramifications (see Dumaine, 2009). The possible 'peaking' of oil production could, likewise, create an entirely new context for global relations.

Considering these three change factors together we can identify several important implications for the ability of intelligence (or any other type) of organisation to anticipate 'unwelcome contingencies.'

- We have entered an era of increased potential for 'Black Swans' – unforeseen (and unforeseeable) events with major consequences – that can result from idiosyncratic 'emergence' and game-changing innovations, all taking place under a veil of too much or too little information. Such birds may still only take flight occasionally – the world being sufficiently large and complex enough itself to absorb undisturbed the impact of many changes. But even an increased potential for unforeseen dramatic change means the aperture of the intelligence lens must be set much wider than in the past in order to have any chance of spotting them in a timely enough way to make a difference (Taleb, 2007).
- In addition to heightening uncertainty, these factors also combine to exacerbate the impact of other obstacles to effective anticipation and response. For instance, mindsets, linear thinking and mirror-imaging are among the perceptual/judgemental distortions that are all the more serious in a world in which non-linear change, unfamiliar actors and unprecedented events are more prevalent (see Chapter 11).
- Finally, these factors raise the fundamental question of the extent to which 'intelligence analysis' – the basic art form of intelligence organisations that underpins strategic assessment and warning – is really relevant to the emerging security environment. Strictly considered, 'to analyse' means to take an issue apart in terms of underlying causes and effects and then to use logic and evidence to understand and project relationships among the two (see Chapter 3). But if causes and effects are intertwined, if small factors can tip systems into major changes, if evidence is hidden in obscurity, and if novel situations tax our existing structures of logic, can analysis be effectively employed to understand and probabilistically forecast some of the most significant challenges that could emerge?
- In place of analysis, intelligence will increasingly rely upon 'sense-making': a less formal, more intuitive means for comprehending emerging reality. Sense-making is the process by which individuals, groups and organisations put ongoing events into context and progressively develop understandings through the application of expertise and common sense as well as through conversation. Sense-making is a fundamental (if unlabelled) process within intelligence agencies as in any other type of organisation: indeed, it probably better describes what analysts do in producing current intelligence on a fast-turnaround basis than does the term analysis, strictly considered. But the question arises as to how, in our highly uncertain

environment, one might seek to strengthen sense-making so that, as situations move to their tipping point, or as new challenges emerge as a result of innovation, this process might better identify and 'make sense' of the earliest signals of potential adverse change?[4]

15.3 Cognitive readiness through prospective sense-making

The changes in the global-security environment suggest that enhanced strategic assessment, and even the sophisticated strategic-warning program proposed by Davis, would not be sufficient to help policy makers cope with the broad array of potential threats. For they would only address a portion of the potential adverse developments that could take place, and would, in particular, be of little help in identifying developments that emerge as a result of a confluence of factors. Indeed, it is arguable that robust strategic-assessment programs focused on set of pre-selected issues, if not complemented by other approaches, could blind intelligence and policy communities to other serious adverse outcomes. They would do so either by providing false assurance that either the most probable or the most damaging developments that could take place were being addressed or that forecasts for specific issues had exhausted the range of possible outcomes.

The need for a new, or at least supplemental, approach to intelligence-based anticipation has been officially recognised in the United States in *Visions 2015*, an unclassified study of longer-term requirements for intelligence published in 2008 by the Office of the Director of National Intelligence. The study notes (paralleling the argument here) that 'our anticipated strategic environment models (to 2015) border closely on chaos theory: initial conditions are key, trends are non-linear, and challenges emerge suddenly due to unpredictable systems behaviour' (US Office of the Director of National Intelligence, 2008). 'To head off or better deal with strategic surprise in this environment' (Ibid.), adaptive intelligence also requires strategic capabilities for sensing and evaluating 'weak signals' and other indicators of emerging issues and security risks. This, in turn, requires, better *global awareness,* defined as 'the ability to develop, digest, and manipulate vast and disparate data streams about the world as it is today' (Ibid.) – something that appears to be very similar to sense-making as defined above. Another requirement is *strategic foresight,* which is defined somewhat vaguely as 'the ability to probe existing conditions and use the responses to consider alternative hypotheses and scenarios, and determine linkages and possibilities' (Ibid.). The term foresight is commonly used as a synonym for anticipation but, as argued by Josh Kerbel (2009), one of the leaders of the complexity school, 'strategic foresight' defines a specific approach to looking ahead that is focused on exploring a broad range of possibilities (see Chapter 4). This distinguishes this art from prediction (focused on the certain or near-certain), forecasting (probabilities), and arguably, even from the most popular form of scenario planning (the Royal Dutch Shell 'two by two' matrix), which looks at a broader but restricted range of plausible developments (but implicitly argues that the scenarios within the range are more probable than any others). Strategic foresight looks more broadly at possible developments, keeping in mind the criterion of plausibility as a practical consideration but stretching it more broadly than in other approaches to anticipation. Kerbel argues that such techniques as simulation and game-playing, agent-based modelling, and 'synthesis' – essentially structured sense-making to discover new patterns by connecting information – fall under the strategic-foresight rubric. The concept of 'horizon scanning,' defined as a 'systematic examination of potential threats, opportunities and likely developments including (but not limited to) those at the margin of current thinking and planning' is also synonymous with strategic foresight. Finally, what is termed 'analytic outreach' can be an essential element of strategic foresight if it involves interaction with a diverse range of outside experts in formats designed to stretch the thinking of all involved (Habegger, 2008: 7–12; Kerbel, 2009: 3–5).

Ideally, the results of strategic foresight would feed in directly to national-security planning efforts, creating the basis for longer-range efforts to prevent potential unwelcome contingencies. Fuerth (2009) has, indeed, set out a concept of 'anticipatory governance,' which would make strategic foresight a key feature of the policy process government wide. He argues that administrative changes such as strongly emphasising interagency coordination (thus helping to overcome the more parochial thinking of 'stove-piped' institutions) could promote the application of this concept. But Fuerth recognises that such changes will not have a decisive impact unless supported by a comparable evolution in the 'culture of governance.' What would be required is a culture displaying such qualities as 'open-mindedness, curiosity and constant questioning of assumptions, and willingness to examine alternative possibilities.' This is, of course, a tall order, which Fuerth recognises could only be realised 'over time' with revised bureaucratic incentive structures, among other changes (Fuerth, 2009: 7–10). Unless or until there were a dramatic transformation in this area, obtaining policy maker buy-in for extensive direct use of foresight results would pose a special challenge. If policy makers are often reluctant now to act upon the strong signals identified and conveyed in the warning process, how much more so would they be in the case of the 'weak signals' about a range of possible developments that emerge from foresight initiatives?

A somewhat less ambitious, but more realistic approach to operationalising strategic foresight, would be to employ it to raise governmental and societal 'resilience' – preparedness (as also advocated by Jack Davis, 2003) to respond quickly to a broad range of not totally foreseen developments, both to mitigate their effects and to manage their consequences. One important contributor to resilience that is especially relevant from an intelligence perspective is what has been termed 'cognitive readiness.' This concept has been employed primarily in discussions of 'network-centric' warfare, and is defined as the ability of combat personnel to deal effectively in real time with unexpected developments in the complex and highly uncertain environment of the battlefield – to which the complex nature of global relations increasingly bears a resemblance. The existing published literature on this subject is sparse and preliminary, with a focus on identifying factors that may enhance or inhibit cognitive readiness, including situational awareness (understanding what is taking place – or sense-making), memory (of training to adapt to this environment), decision-making and executive-function skills, and creativity (Fletcher, 2004). It stands to reason that having a rich mental library of potential twists and turns in the way ahead – and experience in thinking about how these could come about – should help intelligence analysts to be more ready to detect possible signals of change, both those identified through strategic foresight and those wholly unforeseen.[5] As complex situations ripen, intelligence analysts would then be better able to identify and alert policy makers to strengthening signals (ones still easily missed by those thinking in conventional terms) in ways that might be sufficiently persuasive to prompt the latter to pursue more effective policies aimed at mitigation and/or consequence management.

But it is no small challenge to sustain the mental readiness of large bureaucracies to address a potentially wide range of unwelcome contingencies. What is learned in creative exercises may easily be forgotten or neglected by intelligence analysts facing daily production pressures. And the fact that analysts change accounts and jobs over time will, of course, exacerbate the loss of institutional memory. This argues for institutionalising a link between the strategic foresight process and sense-making in order to enhance the possibility of noticing both weak and strengthening signals. This could be accomplished, for instance, by embedding foresight specialists in key nodes within intelligence organisations (e.g., crossing disciplinary and geographic lines) with the responsibility and resources to effect this linkage. These specialists would not only organise foresight exercises on a shifting array of issues but would also inject the results of such exercises (including from those done in the distant past for which these specialists would preserve institutional memory) into discussions – both face-to-face and, now increasingly, online – about ongoing security-related developments. This would help analysts to view these developments through different lenses and to see possibilities pregnant within them that might not be apparent through unaided perception. In addition, there could undoubtedly be automated systems to bring the wealth of insights from strategic foresight to bear on day-to-day intelligence production. Borrowing from Homer-Dixon's concept of 'prospective mind,' what is being proposed here might be called prospective sense-making – systematically considering the present in the context of a broad range of plausible – more accurately, not implausible – future outcomes.

15.4 An organisational context for prospective sense-making

In some respects, intelligence organisations are well positioned to undertake 'prospective sense-making' and to lead strategic-foresight efforts within governments. For one thing, they employ cadres of individuals with considerable substantive expertise about global relations and a mandate to think about future developments. As they are less encumbered with policy responsibilities than other governmental agencies, they are in a better position to view reality in policy-neutral terms, thus affording them better long-run vision and enhanced credibility for objectivity in intergovernmental debates. Their credibility is also strengthened by their access to privileged information, which provides a certain cachet, at the least, and may well be of use in evaluating the relevance of foresight for ongoing developments. Finally, and perhaps most importantly, they are, generally speaking, in regular communication with senior policy makers on national-security issues, giving them an unparalleled opportunity to influence ongoing thinking and to highlight possible dangers.

Set against these, there are some very important factors that inhibit the ability of intelligence organisations to take on such tasks effectively.

- Intelligence remains organised along traditional lines that evolved to address the more straightforward challenges of the Cold War era. Analysts work on narrowly-drawn geographic or functional accounts that certainly enhance subject matter expertise on defined issues but may inhibit adoption of the broader perspective essential to effective foresight. And there is still a decided preference for what one writer has called 'evidence-based scientism' – the application of evidence and theory to reach probabilistic conclusions about 'complicated' issues that makes it difficult to convince analysts and their mangers to find time for, or to pay serious attention to, highly speculative endeavours (Cooper, 2005: 29–39).
- There are intense demands for daily production to support policy makers and operational personnel (in the US case, war fighters in particular) as well as to meet bureaucratically-set targets (as in many knowledge-based organisations, the volume of production being an important criterion for judging employee and unit success). This means that it is difficult for analysts to find the time to go 'offline' to take part in foresight exercises, or to participate in what would be a time-consuming (and often fruitless) effort to integrate the results of foresight activity into day-to-day work.
- Finally and perhaps most importantly, intelligence organisations do not tend to be highly introspective: they do not regularly examine their work

> to consider how their judgements might be radically wrong. Analysis often evolves through a process of 'layering', in which in which past judgements provide the foundation for current assessment, inevitably constraining capacities to evaluate signals of surprise properly. Alternative analysis techniques and 'lessons learned' studies can combat these problematic tendencies but, despite steps in the right direction in recent years, these processes are probably still used too sporadically to have a real impact on deeply ingrained ways of thinking (see Cooper, 2005: 29–39; Treverton, 2009: 134–167).

In view of these very significant negative factors, it seems logical to conclude that major changes in the processes, incentive structures and the operational cultures of intelligence organisations would be needed before prospective sense-making could be implemented effectively.

Although this is not the place to discuss at length the complex issue of intelligence reform, it would be useful to discuss briefly the potential benefits of applying principles from one promising organisational model that has arisen in other sectors – 'the high reliability organisation' (HRO). The HRO is an organisation that, despite operating in a highly complex and uncertain environment, experiences exceptionally low rates of failure – largely conceived here in terms of major industrial accidents. HRO exemplars include nuclear power plants, aircraft carriers and the air-traffic control system. Such organisations succeed in their mission, whereas counterparts in similarly risky endeavours (e.g., hospitals) often do not, because they are intently focused on the possibility of operational failures, which, in their areas of activity, could potentially mean catastrophic loss of life and/or economic damage. Constructive fear of failure leads them to exhibit a quality that has been called 'mindfulness' – continuous, self-critical attention both to the environment and to their own operations, with an eye to identifying possible sources of things going wrong as early as possible. Such organisations avoid taking things for granted, rigorously examine – albeit in a non-punitive way – minor failures and 'near-misses' for operational lessons, and promote collaboration across the organisation in addressing new challenges in order to benefit from diverse perspectives and knowledge.

If one were to make the (not huge) mental leap of considering threat-anticipation failures as analogous to industrial accidents, then one could apply the HRO model to the intelligence process (see Fishbein and Treverton, 2004: 16–18; Weick and Sutcliffe 2007). For instance, a 'mindful' intelligence organisation would continually re-examine judgements and assumptions about current and future and developments and carefully consider why past or recent judgements had not panned out (see Cooper, 2005: 41–57; Treverton 2009: 165–167). Moreover a more mindful intelligence organisation would eschew 'mindless' practices such as 'layering' and production for their own sakes. It would also encourage analysts to take part in take part in strategic-foresight exercises, providing them with the time and incentives to engage in wide-ranging discussions with governmental counterparts and with outside experts on applying foresight results to ongoing sense-making.

To be sure, wholesale application of the HRO model to the intelligence sector would neither be feasible nor, more importantly, wholly desirable. Beyond commonplace bureaucratic resistance to fundamental change, intelligence organisations have strong, and in many respects, desirable cultures of analyst independence (reflecting the academic backgrounds of many of these professionals) that would be highly resistant to the full implementation of the regimented introspection and collaboration of an HRO. And the range of uncertainties dealt with by intelligence is so much broader than those related to industrial-type accidents, that an obsessive attention to the potential of failure could paralyse production of truly needed intelligence. That said, judicious application of some of the principles promoting 'mindfulness' in HROs could at least serve as a counterweight to standard operating procedures within intelligence organisations, perhaps providing sufficient space for the emergence of a prospective sense-making capability.

15.5 Implications for prevention

If the global-security environment is indeed becoming more complex, uncertain and, therefore, unpredictable, then the challenges of undertaking preventive action become so much more daunting. If it is very difficult, as the literature suggests, to convince government officials to undertake significant investments to head off adverse developments that can be said to be highly probable based upon strong evidence and logic, how much more so would it be in the case of a broader range of lower-probability outcomes? And in this new environment, there will be many developments that 'emerge' suddenly, without a long causal chain evident (except, as often appears to be the case, in retrospect), thus effectively precluding highly targeted 'early action.' All this does not, however, necessarily mean that governments are henceforward strictly confined to reaction-and-response management. First of all, even in a complex-threat environment, there will still be 'complicated threats' involving linear progressions for which conventional forecasting-based preventive measures will still be theoretically applicable, however difficult to implement in practice. Equally important, prospective sense-making may enable policy makers to think about broad-spectrum normative interventions to shape complex systems in ways that might head off or mitigate a range of potential future troubles. Drawing upon the language of behavioural economics, this might involve 'nudges' – modest changes in incentive structures – that might prove effective against pre-ripened troublesome patterns as well as possibly attractive to policy makers given their low cost (Thaler and Sunstein, 2008). Given limited understandings about how complex systems evolve and the ever-present potential for unintended consequences of any intervention, considerable thinking and real-world experimentation (some of which could well yield unpleasant results) would be required to develop this approach to prevention in a complex-threat environment.

But even if foresight only improves the 'cognitive readiness' of government officials to respond effectively to an adverse event just days or weeks before its onset, its importance should not be underestimated. Many past security disasters, such as Pearl Harbor, the Fall of France, and 9/11, could arguably have been significantly mitigated had there been serious consideration of alternative outcomes – some of which had actually been envisaged in previous foresight exercises – and of associated simple remedial measures during the period in which the associated threats became acute and widely recognised (see Fishbein and Treverton, 2004: 24–25). While prevention is certainly preferable to palliation, the latter is still infinitely better than being caught by complete surprise. And this, in itself, argues strongly in favour of considering ways to strengthen both the intellectual and organisational capacities of intelligence organisations to engage in prospective sense-making.

Notes

1. The views expressed in this chapter are personal and do not necessarily reflect those of the US Department of State or any other US government agency.
2. Cohen and Gooch, for instance, argued that the general warning of war issued in November 1941 should have been sufficient to prompt the Pearl Harbor commanders to adopt minimal preparatory measures (e.g., installation of torpedo nets and barrage balloons) that could have mitigated the impact of the attack (Cohen and Gooch, 1991: 50–51).
3. A broad review of this thinking and a discussion of its implications for strategic warning can be found in Mauer and Cavelty (2009).
4. The distinction between analysis and sense-making is described in Fishbein and Treverton (2004: 13–18) and Treverton (2009: 33–36).
5. Noted futurists such as Peter Schwartz (1991) and John Petersen (see, e.g., Petersen, 2008) have frequently argued that 'if you haven't thought about it first, you won't see it coming.' And as elegantly put by Pasteur (1854) in the context of the not very dissimilar arena of scientific discovery, 'chance favors only the prepared mind.'

16
Conclusion: New Perspectives for Theorising and Addressing Transnational Risks

Christoph O. Meyer and Chiara de Franco

Preventing serious harm at little cost through foresighted action is a tantalising prospect. It is also a highly elusive goal, as the contributions to this book show. Obstacles stretch all the way across the four challenges we identified in the introductory chapter and which form the analytical backbone of this book: forecasting, warning, learning and mobilising preventive action. The odds seem to be stacked against overcoming the warning-response gap, particularly when risks are transnational and require coordinated responses. Forensic inquiries into industrial accidents or plane crashes typically reveal multiple failures forming an idiosyncratic causal chain leading to disaster. The opposite appears to be true for warnings at a time when they would be most useful. Genuinely surprising warnings are transmitted through a long, fragile chain, where each link has to withstand extreme pressure and individuals need to make difficult balancing judgements under conditions of uncertainty. The chapters by Tom Huertas and Gillian Tett illustrate why this was the case with the near meltdown of the world financial system in 2008. However, there are important variations across different constellations of risks and actors in how the warning-response process unfolds, as illustrated by cases of more propitious conditions for preventive policies like air pollution (Chapter 5) and flooding (Chapter 9).

When we speak of a structural warning-response gap, we do not mean to suggest that more warning, higher receptivity or more preventive action are always the way out, as some of the literature implies (Bazerman and Watkins, 2008; Gerstein and Ellsberg, 2008; Perrow, 2007). In fact, the cases of Y2K, swine flu, genetically-modified foods, Brent Spar, the invasion of Iraq or the Icelandic volcanic-ash cloud show that warnings can be exaggerated in terms of scientific certainty, as well as in terms of the scope of potential consequences leading to over-reactive preventive action that imposes disproportionate costs and can create unintended risks. Societies can easily go from being ignorant, or at least naïve, about a given issue, to being overly fearful about certain risks after things have gone wrong (Kahneman et al., 1982; Lau and Redlawsk 2001; Sunstein 2005). When scientists become strategic actors in order to make an impact on politics, as occurred in the case of climate change in the run-up to the Kyoto summit in 1997, they risk damaging their credibility in the medium and long-term. Crying wolf repeatedly when no sheep are lost can not only lead to disproportionate and risky preventive action, but also to lower receptivity to warnings in the long-term.

This concluding chapter does not attempt to summarise all arguments advanced throughout this book, but to draw selectively on some contributions, in combination with other evidence, to discuss in more depth questions of performance relating to the interlinked processes of forecasting, communicating risks, learning and preventive action. As we have seen throughout this book, all four challenges require various kinds of balancing judgements. We will seek to theorise under what conditions we are likely to see better warning-response dynamics (see Chapter 1), but will also try to identify those conditions under which we can expect various pathologies to crop up more frequently. Finally, we will cross over from the analytical to the prescriptive by suggesting strategies to improve the prospects for prevention by dealing better with uncertainty, enhancing international collaboration, better scrutiny of international-risk management and, finally, combining prevention and resilience.

16.1 Theorising warning-response dynamics

Under what conditions are we most likely to see success of warning about transnational risks as outlined in the introductory chapter? The cases covered in this book, in combination with the wider literature on forecasting and prevention, provide a first ground for identifying some of the factors that can facilitate or hinder effective identification, communication, learning about, and management of, transnational risks. We have sought to illustrate in Table 16.1 which factors we think have the most explanatory power to shape strong or poor performance of the warning-response loop as elaborated in the introductory chapter. Of course none of the cases discussed in this book is able to illustrate the whole range of facilitating or constraining features, while each of them can highlight how some of the features can combine to create a unique set of problems. For instance, climate change is underpinned by arguably high scientific certainty about its fundamental dynamics, which is coupled with good credibility of warners among decision-makers and regular and frequent interaction between producers and consumers. Moreover, what is being warned about is truly catastrophic in the long-term with very limited upsides globally. However, effective action suffers from feasibility problems, given the need for public mobilisation to justify high upfront costs, the asymmetric distribution of

Table 16.1 Variables influencing warning-response performance

Performance key variables	Strong performance	Poor performance
Confidence in forecasts and source credibility	Long track-record of forecasting familiar risks Natural phenomena or man-made environmental risks Credibility of warning source established	New risks due to spillover or complexity, or concentration Man-made risks arising from new technologies Doubts over warner's credibility
Risk-opportunity ratio and cost-benefit distribution	Clear and symmetric impact of anticipated harm Warners do not benefit from either action/inaction Low-cost and low-risk preventive instruments available Warnings fit with users' pre-existing beliefs	Unclear and asymmetric distribution of harm across groups/countries Warners' self-interest in particular response High-cost and high-risk preventive instruments necessary Warnings contradict users' pre-existing beliefs
Timing and context	Late or crisis warning highlights immediate risk of harm Recent experience of failure increases sensitivity Organisations engaged in reviews of their own	Early warning is too early for decision-making horizon Failure is distant and complacency has set in Organisation preoccupied with managing ongoing crises or high-priority projects
Organisational culture and leadership	Organisational culture supporting learning and debateExperts regularly interact with potential users Scrutiny through external actors, NGOs and media	Organisational culture focused on belief/defence/blame Experts have little access to decision-makers No external scrutiny from NGOs and media

costs and benefits among countries in the short to medium term, and the vulnerability to agenda competition from more immediate threats.

16.1.1 Confidence and credibility

The worst-case scenario for forecasting and warning are low-probability/high-impact risks labelled by Nicolas Taleb as 'Black Swan' events (2007). In fact, as Warren Fishbein (Chapter 15) explains, the problem is not that these are 'low-probability' events, but that their likelihood cannot be reliably assessed because these risks are 'novel', 'obscure' and 'complex' as a result of new forms of global interconnectedness and the vagaries of the post-cold war environment. Similarly fraught with uncertainty are early warnings about 'old risks', such as inter-state or civil conflict where some of the parties involved have strong interest to disguise, deceive and surprise and where both intelligence producers and consumers are prone to be blind-sided by their own world-views and assumptions ('mirror imaging') about what is rational behaviour to foreign leaders (Chapter 3; Jervis, 2010).

The financial crisis, for instance, had both old and new features. As Tom Huertas points out in Chapter 14, economists did expect asset bubbles, but on the basis of their knowledge of old scenarios they also believed that any negative consequence could be managed and was ultimately preferable to pricking them through monetary policy. The new crisis, however, presented some novel features, like the unprecedented scale of leveraging, the existence of new institutions which were believed too big to fail, and the creation of financial products such as collateralised debt obligations (CDOs) which ended up making the whole system more vulnerable rather than more stable. Gillian Tett argued in Chapter 13 that the financial system is made up of 'non-communicating technical silos' which at least partially explains why the banks themselves failed to spot those risks and their possible consequences: not only were the top management of banks were ignorant of the risk, but also some of those who were developing risky products did not fully appreciate the scale of the risks they were building up for their very own institutions.

Compared to these dark scenarios, warning works better when knowledge claims about future risks are considered credible and reliable, as in the case of successful forecasting of 'familiar risks'. Meteorology is one of the prime examples used in the forecasting literature, because it is tested day after day and users acquire a good idea of how accurate it is. Indeed, if they can assess that today's weather forecast was reliable, users can decide to base some decisions on the forecasts for tomorrow or the day after tomorrow, despite some remaining uncertainty. But most users will also know that a forecast of next month's weather is not reliable enough to book a plane ticket to the sun. Moreover, few users will think that they are better at forecasting the weather than meteorologists with their training, computer models and unique access to data from sensors and satellite imagery. Similarly, Demeritt and Nobert (Chapter 9) show that flood warnings can trigger preventive action seven days before the anticipated event despite residual uncertainty. Similarly, in the case of air pollution discussed by Wagner (Chapter 5), the 20-year track-record of the RAINS/GAINS model also helps to explain why it is so widely used by policy makers.

Such forecasts work best for natural phenomena that are regularly occurring and can be studied on the basis of clocklike laws unearthed through empiricism and experimental methods, but there are cases when forecasts about man-made risks also reach a higher degree of credibility with users. This can be either because they are hybrid forecasts built on both hard and soft scientific methods, or because they relate to highly formalised and quantitative social science, as happens with demographics, population movements and even macro-economics. Warnings of pandemics combine, for instance, insights from the medical sciences with social-scientific theories about the movement of people that are expressed in quantitative terms. Warnings about famines combine insights from satellite imagery and meteorology, about future harvests with demographic data and mobility projects, making for quite reliable forecasts. Despite being focused on the behaviour of humans, its poor record in forecasting and strong disagreements within the discipline, economics is considered sufficiently scientific to deserve a Nobel Prize, attract decision-makers' attention and command high market premiums for those who have received training in this discipline. Other areas of social science with higher credibility are electoral polling and rational choice forecast à la Bruce Bueno de Mesquita (2009) about the outcome of political negotiations and internal power struggles.

16.1.2 Risk-opportunity ratios and their distribution

Even in those cases where risks associated with major discontinuities are identified early, and are based on relatively credible knowledge claims, a key obstacle to warnings being communicated well and taken seriously is the risk-opportunity ratio at a given moment in time and among relevant actors. Many man-made products or practices, for example, pose evident risks but deliver substantial benefits for those engaged in the risky activity, especially in the short term. These could be risks associated with highly profitable financial (CDOs) or pharmaceutical (Vioxx) products, as well as deep-sea oil drilling. The key obstacle here is that warnings can be highly dissonant with pre-existing beliefs or interests. Moreover, warnings may imply a kind of action in evident conflict with opportunity-seeking behaviours or beliefs that underpin existing policies.

The more asymmetrically distributed a given harm, the less likely is preventive action. This is particularly true when actors are operating in a highly competitive environment, where someone's gains are someone else's losses. In the market place, investors who bet against mainstream opinion, by shorting stocks vulnerable to subprime mortgages collapsing at the right time, reaped a huge profit. The probability of action rises as the number of significant socio-political cleavages diminishes and no neat separation exists between the groups that benefit from action and those that lose out. In these cases, however, the opportunity to benefit directly from acting on warning at the right time can be limited if effective preventive action requires coordinated efforts from everyone. Thus, if the harm is undesirable and catastrophic with hardly any upsides for anyone, as in the case of an asteroid hitting the Earth, then one could expect substantial support for transnational preventive action. In contrast, when gains and harms are asymmetrically distributed across time and space, coordinated preventive measures tend to stall or fall short. An individual state could, for example, take many costly measures to reduce CO_2 emissions, weakening the competitive position of its industry, but would not be able to reduce future harm significantly due to climate change if other states did not do the same. Climate change is indeed a problematic case, because harm is not uniformly distributed, at least not in the short term: some states such as small islands close to the waterline will be much more affected than others who might even benefit in the short to medium term due to more rainfall or a warmer climate.

In comparison to these more difficult cases, the establishment of 'late warning and response systems' is relatively easy, even in those cases where prevention is impossible and prediction difficult such as earthquakes, tsunamis or volcanic eruptions. However, this has also to do with the perception of the feasibility and cost of preventive action. If decision-makers are aware that proven and relatively low-cost/risk tools for prevention and mitigation are available, they are more inclined to listen to warnings than in cases, such as late warnings about impending genocide, where the preventive action would require costly decisions to sending their own citizens into harm's way.

In the case of transnational risks, the cost-benefit ratio can be expected to vary across national contexts (Renn 2008; Hulme 2009), as policy makers tend to have different perceptions not only of the harmfulness of a given risk but also of the cost of a given preventive measure. National specificities can also explain variations in the way a given warning is received, as it may or may not create 'dissonance'. Warnings, in fact, can confirm or challenge – implicitly or explicitly – existing ideas and world-views that underpin a policy. 'Bad news', for example, may run against so-called motivational biases, limiting warning consumers' receptivity. If a leadership's economic policies are based on the assumption of the market being rational and well-working, a warning that this assumption is wrong will have trouble being heard (e.g. New Labour and the financial crisis). A leader, whose defence policy rests on assumptions about the benign intentions of a particular state, will find it hard to believe that this very state is about to launch an attack against his country, almost regardless of the evidence presented (e.g. Stalin and the German invasion in 1941). A leadership whose policy of regime change is premised on the population being grateful and cooperative will not be very receptive to warnings that the country will be ungovernable due to sectarian tensions (the George W. Bush administration and the invasion of Iraq in 2003). It is, of course, not predetermined that inconvenient warnings will be ignored, but particularly in the arena of national security, where the stakes are high and interpreting intentions matters, decision-makers often consider themselves competent to judge a foreign leader's intentions and thus act as 'the last analyst' (Hughes, 1976).

16.1.3 Timing and context

The immediacy and timing of warnings in relation to previous or current crises matter as they affect the cost-benefit-calculation as well as cognitive receptivity. As a general rule, late or crisis warnings are more likely to be heeded than those which appear distant in time. In a world of limited material and cognitive resources, decision-makers tend to focus on the 'crocodile next to the canoe', rather than the waterfall many days downstream. It is true that late warnings also tend to have a higher degree of certainty, as there will be usually more indicators in support of them, but the timing can be expected to play a role, regardless of the certainty factor, as it suggests a short window of opportunity in which action can make a difference and can thus assert itself in the competition of issues to be on the top of decision-makers' agendas. The tendency of decision-makers to discount the future, that is to value gains and costs in the present higher than those some years down the line, can become a liability when coupled with misunderstandings of probabilistic forecasts among policy makers. In the case of hurricane Katrina, which led to the devastation of New Orleans in 2005, senior policy makers defended their decision not to invest billions of dollars into strengthening levees on the grounds that experts had judged the probability of a Katrina-type event as one per 100 years. This was erroneously interpreted by decision-makers in public as *one in a 100 years*, implying that plenty of time was left until a hurricane 'was due' (Gerstein and Ellsberg, 2008). Discounting the future can be also seen with climate change, which is expected to produce its worst effects decades down the line, whereas many of the preventive measures will be costly over the next few years.

Whether a given risk is short, medium or long-term cannot be defined absolutely, but only with reference to decision-makers 'normal' time horizon. For a stock-broker, for example, the coming year is an eternity away. In the run-up to the financial crisis, traders were incentivised to take high risks in the short term even if they suspected their bets would turn sour later, because they were paid bonuses annually but not held to account for losses at a later stage. Senior managers did not dispute potential risks associated with subprime mortgages, but did not care of when the markets would fall. As the Citigroup's chief executive, Charles Prince, said as late as summer 2007: 'As long as the music is playing, you've got to get up and dance. We're still dancing' (*Financial Times*, 9 July 2007). Cognitive dissonance theory tells us that timing is also important for how individuals process warnings. The history of warfare is full of examples of commanders who discounted warning information, not because a change of plan was not feasible, but simply because they had made up their mind after considerable effort. The same warning would have had a much higher chance of success if it had been received earlier in the decision-making process.

A variation on the importance of time in preventive policy is illustrated by David Demeritt's and Sebastien Nobert's (Chapter 9) use of Kingdon's analysis of converging policy streams to argue that new warning systems, such as EFAS, often emerge after crises or failures have put a problem on the public agenda. This can dampen or amplify risk perceptions. An important explanation for the unwillingness of the United States to intervene in Rwanda were 'lessons learned' from the 'failed' intervention in Somalia 1992/1993. After the Rwandan genocide, policy makers and the news media became much more attentive to warning signals about 'another Rwanda' with beneficial as well as problematic consequences. Contextual factors are thus essential to understanding why sometimes windows of opportunity are closed to risk communicators. Indeed, both neglecting risks and being over-sensitive to them are contingent social facts that swing like a pendulum over time and, in their course, impact on forecasting, warning, learning and responding to risks. Agenda competition, in particular, seems to be a critical key to understanding why sometimes governments and the public at large do not perceive a given issue as high on the agenda, or do not have time and resources to engage with warnings about that issue.

16.1.4 Organisational culture and leadership

In-house warnings are more likely to be ignored in organisational cultures which discourage dissent than those where reporting of errors and adversarial thinking are encouraged. As Gerstein and Schein explain in Chapter 10, many organisations do not treat whistle-blowers kindly, not even if they highlight risks to the organisation rather than to external others. Take for example the case of the head of a regulatory risk group at the British Bank HBOS in 2002–2005, who repeatedly warned about the Bank's increasingly risky bets. He was ostracised and eventually sacked by the hierarchy. When the financial crisis hit, HBOS was among the most exposed institutions and could only be rescued through a hasty and anti-competitive merger with Lloyds Bank (*Guardian*, 28 March 2010). The relationship between experts and managers within an organisation is often a highly asymmetric one, which increases the probability of under-warning as experts will worry about not being taken seriously as well as being penalised for early warnings which turn out to be false positives. Both warning and prevention take place in the shadow of anticipated blame and, much less frequently, praise.

A different culture is prevalent in high-reliability organisations (Weick and Sutcliffe, 2007) where a good dialogue and division of labour exist between various kinds of experts and managers, which enables decisions to be taken by individuals or networks of individuals on the basis of their relevant expertise rather than their formal position within the hierarchy. Close and frequent interactions are possible within an atmosphere of trust and mutual respect that allows analysts to tailor their warnings to the users both in terms of content and timing and to use informal and direct channels to raise an alarm. In these organisations, the leadership is also more likely to consider warnings as more credible and trustworthy as well as to defer to expertise. Such institutions may of course still miss risks that are outside their explicit competence as seen in the 'underlap' between the UK Financial Services Authority and the Bank of England about the systemic risks some institutions were representing, but they are good at spotting and preventing certain categories of mistakes, as Warren Fishbein argues (Chapter 15).

Some organisations start out with a good culture focused on expertise and warning, but are then gradually corrupted by conflicts of interests relating to their funding seeping into organisational practices. This is what seems to have happened with Credit Risk Rating Agencies, which for a while preserved their independence and the primacy of expertise until their gradually-changing business model dragged them ever deeper into co-designing and then rubber-stamping highly lucrative but also very risky financial products with Triple-A-ratings. Whether a given organisation will be allowed to slip in this way is not just a function of its culture and leadership, but also on whether the external environment incentivises it to stay independent and vigilant. This environment is often shaped by regulators whose task is monitoring that safety standards are adhered to and that competition is not incentivising companies to cut their 'non-productive' safety measures. The problem is of course that even those legally independent regulators formally charged with assessing and preventing certain kinds of risks are not operating in a vacuum, but are more or less dependent on political users for resources as well as on society and stakeholders for cooperation and support. Over time, regulatory bodies face the risk of being 'captured' by the industry they are regulating as a result of informal networks emerging through exchanges in personnel and a convergence of thinking.

Civil society is equally important to make organisations more open to warning. The presence of strong media scrutiny and consumer groups, for example, is an important incentive for regulatory authorities to avoid missing out on any abuse of market position and to take bold action against it. Similarly, safety procedures within nuclear-power plants would not be as strict as they are without the awareness of segments of public opinion organised through NGOs being opposed to nuclear power given its risks. Conversely, areas of risk that are not subject to this kind of media and NGO scrutiny will fare less well in being attentive to certain risks, as discussed above in the case of the financial crisis. However, it remains true that organisations also need a strong degree of autonomy to withstand external demands for action when its best judgement is that the risks are small and action would be disproportionate or risky. Similarly, there should be no financial incentive related to the number of risks spotted or acted upon as these can compromise the analytical process. There can be too much scrutiny, not only too little.

16.2 Improving warning and preventive action on transnational risks

The above discussion of factors favouring or hindering preventive policies has revealed that transnational risks pose particular challenges as (i) they are more difficult to forecast because globalisation and modernisation create novel, complex and uncertain risks; (ii) they raise particular communication problems arising from the mismatch between the assumptions, concerns and epistemic languages of national expert communities and those of international regimes for coordinating preventive action; (iii) they cause recognition and prioritisation problems because national users have varying sensitivities to particular types of risks as a result of cultural differences or anticipated differences in the geographic impact of harm, and finally, (iv) it is more difficult to organise or coordinate international preventive action that is timely, effective and proportionate given the immaturity of global governing arrangements and the concerns over the transfer of policy authority to international institutions.

Thus, which strategies might alleviate some of these problems? What could be done in practice to better anticipate and prepare for future harm that is transnational in origin and consequences? As we have argued earlier, the warning-response dynamics differ markedly across different types of transnational risks and given a range of different variables. It is thus difficult to formulate suggestions for improvement without discussing a particular cause of harm or, if we are talking about resilience rather than prevention, a specific area of vulnerability. In the next pages, we will therefore concentrate on potential future harm with the following characteristics: transnational in origin and consequences; with strongly negative consequences for the overwhelming majority of those affected, although some countries or groups within countries may well think they can benefit out of it; with a high degree of uncertainty about whether, when and in what specific form it will occur because of its novelty and of the state of knowledge in this area; generally thought as being not imminent despite uncertainty about its timing. To enhance the prospects for proportionate, early and better informed preventive action we want to elaborate on four recommendations: using models that take uncertainty into account; enhance international collaboration in risk assessment; better design and scrutiny of international-risk regulation; and balancing prevention and resilience.

16.2.1 Alternative models for dealing with uncertainty

Some contributors, such as Brummer et al., Vander Beken and Fishbein, have made the argument that reliable probabilistic forecasts about some phenomena are not possible because of their inherent characteristics such as the ability of crime organisations or terrorist groups to innovate or because of our current inability adequately to theorise complex interactions within and across environmental and social systems. One response has been to shift the focus to understanding vulnerabilities and increasing the resilience of organisations and systems; the other to use alternative methods of thinking about the future rather than those in the service of conventional risk-benefit calculations. However, forecasting techniques have to fit the purpose for which they are to be used. As Brummer et al. argue, security-foresight techniques involving scenario building do not seek to identify probable but only possible futures. Their primary goal is not to provide support for specific decisions about the allocation of scarce resources on the basis of relative risks and opportunities, but to help experts in their identification of potential new discontinuities and advance longer-term thinking among decision-makers about desirable futures and how they might be shaped. As Tom Vander Beken points out, scenarios are not random narratives in which everything is uncertain, but structured exercises that make assumptions about key drivers of change as well as about those factors that do not change. They acknowledge and identify, however, key uncertainties that over the medium term may imply different pathways to quite different worlds, some of which more desirable than others to decision-makers.

Fabian Wagner (Chapter 5) shows how the success of the non-probabilistic GAINS model is due to the fact that it gives stakeholders not only a glimpse into a possible future, but also into the ways this future may be influenced by different options for action and the respective costs and trade-offs. Scenarios generated in this and other ways could give an impetus to more in-depth research into novel threats that might eventually lead to probabilistic forecasting. However, scenarios' primary purpose lies, first, in giving 'strategic notice' (David Omand) to decision-makers normally focused on the short term and most probable events and in increasing their 'cognitive readiness' (Warren Fishbein). Certainty and specificity of these scenarios may not be enough for informed choices about preventive action, but may facilitate less costly contingency planning, further research, or modest investments in reducing key vulnerabilities. Vander Beken mentions the case of Royal Dutch/Shell, which had produced scenarios that allowed it to 'anticipate and prepare for the dramatic drop in oil prices in the 1980s'.

Brummer et al. highlight the importance of establishing clarity about the ultimate purpose of foresight techniques from the outset and manage the tension between the goal to discover specific new threats and question conventional wisdom and the need to create a consensus among various experts with different cultural and disciplinary backgrounds. Scenario building needs to provide sufficient space for adversarial and out-of-the-box thinking in order to spot genuinely new dynamics at the boundaries of different expert communities and to prevent maverick voices from being drowned out by hegemonic discourses. Fabian Wagner has highlighted in his contribution that models can be seen as languages that contain specific disciplinary and socio-political assumptions that not everyone will be able to share. Rather than seeking broad agreement on a single model, an alternative approach may be to facilitate a plurality of models with different assumptions that are likely to generate competing hypotheses. This would mitigate the problem of discipline-specific 'assumption drag' (William Ascher, 1978) that systematically distort outcomes and limit the impact of 'plausibility tests' tending to hinder the recognition of surprising dynamics. Wagner also argues that experts needs to resist the temptation and in some cases pressure to oversell their expertise and emphasises the benefits of being as open as possible about underlying assumptions and data vis-a-vis potential critics and of working closely with relevant stakeholders. Those alternative foresight techniques are thus much more than just tools for more accurate forecasting: they combine risk-identification and risk communication to create a programming language that both experts and decision-makers can use to jointly explore possible futures and how to shape them.

16.2.2 Enhancing international collaboration in forecasting risks

Transnational collaboration is essential to deal with the interrelated problems of divergent assessments about the probability as well as the gravity of certain risks across different national and cultural contexts. In some areas of forecasting, the problem is not that risks are essentially unknowable, but that the state of the art lacks credibility with users as there is no minimum international consensus about what is knowable and what is not, or because forecasts are insufficiently specific in order to be useful. Despite the recent and, in retrospect, misguided media headlines over 'climategate', the case of climate change is a success story of how scientists can self-organise to put an issue on the agenda of policy makers to the extent that an institution was created to develop and harness knowledge about the risks related to this phenomenon: the Intergovernmental Panel on Climate Change (IPCC). Created in 1988 by the United Nations Environment Programme (UNEP) and the World Meteorological Organization (WMO), the IPCC was the worthy recipient of the Nobel Peace Prize in 2007 for it had managed to largely maintain its scientific integrity in the face of high politicisation in its various environments but also to bring about policy-change.

This model could be replicated in a number of other areas of transboundary risks where there is a need for better, more fine-grained and more credible forecasting informed by interactions of various users. The basic principle is that such a forum or organisation needs to be open to all relevant 'experts' in a given area, regardless of country of origin and epistemic or ontological position. It needs continuity of funding and a minimum central staff to initiate and operate its activities. And it needs to promote regular interactions and dialogue with relevant decision-makers to reach a better understanding of what kind of knowledge users need, at what time in relation to the decision-making process and the lead time of key instruments, and a better understanding of how to interpret knowledge and accept its limitations. Such a model does not work for risks that are recognised only by a few and is badly suited for anticipating and preparing for some 'unknown unknowns'. One could envisage, for instance, that the UN initiates a similar forum for experts working on conflict prevention, given that its primary mission is the preservation and promotion of peace. There is no shortage of researchers and institutes in this area, but little consolidated and politically-independent advice on how to best forecast and deal with civil war. Instead of outsourcing this task to different national intelligence communities, the UN could initiate a high-profile and continuous focal point for knowledge generation with regard to forecasting armed conflict similar but not identical to the IPCC. In order to avoid silo-mentality and to recognise that security risks are affected by economic, technological and environmental phenomena, relevant expertise will be found beyond peace studies and national intelligence communities.

In those areas where risks emerge at the cross-section of different expert communities, and where substantial divergences are formulated about their gravity, an IPCC approach may not work because it presumes an agreement about the undesirability of a specific risks and a minimum degree of epistemic homogeneity for peer review to work. Here, somewhat looser forms of transnational collaboration may work better, particularly transnational networks such as the Swiss-sponsored Global Risk Forum (2010) with its focus on disaster prevention and resilience and its orientation to the UN, and secondly the US-sponsored Global Futures Forum (2010) with a strong involvement of national intelligence professionals and an emphasis on old and new security threats. The most useful contribution of such forums may not be in increasing knowledge about future risks, but in increasing sensitivity to cross-national differences in risk perceptions. While the developed industrial world has minimised most conventional risks to life and worries about funding increasing longevity, millions of people elsewhere have a much lower life-expectancy as they face the entirely predictable risks of dying early from multiple causes such as dirty water and malnutrition, inadequate medical treatment and lack of protection from exploitation and violence. They are also the ones who are disproportionately affected by some of the threats relating to the effects of new industrial processes, such as the repercussions of climate change or vulnerabilities arising from the breakdown of critical infrastructures. When industrialised nations worry about the risks arising from the depletion of natural resources and the loss of biodiversity, uncontrolled mass migration and security risks relating to piracy and terrorism, they need to understand that developing countries' cooperation in preventing new risk may well require substantial help in solving the old ones first.

16.2.3 Better design and scrutiny of international-risk regulation

There is currently a divergence in the governance of risk between those areas where international bodies already exist that are charged with monitoring and in some cases even preventing a given harm, as compared to others where risks are still predominantly managed at the national level despite having transnational causes and consequences. This creates 'regulatory underlap' due to the fact that no organisation exists with the responsibility, resources, legitimacy and instruments to assess and act against such risks. For instance, it is clear that the global repercussions of the US subprime mortgage crisis had escaped most national regulators and Central Banks, even though the major Central Banks have eventually avoided a meltdown of the global financial system by working together and in conjunction with key national policy makers. In order to avert such a scenario in the future, the Group of 20 major economies (G-20) has instituted a new Financial Stability Board (FSB) to 'identify problems in the financial system and oversee action to address them.' The IMF has floated a complementary mechanism based on a 'mutual assessment process' (MAP) whose aim is 'to reduce risks to the system by making the world's largest economies accountable to each other for ensuring the global consistency of their economic policies' (Strauss-Kahn, 2010). Even if this is not the place to discuss the merit of these plans in detail, it is worth highlighting that the financial system is one area where institutional arrangements for risk monitoring and prevention have proven inadequate and new institutions had to be created to deal with transnational systemic risks. Even where bodies exist that are in charge of monitoring certain trans-boundary risks, as in the case of fiscal policy under the EU's stability and growth pact, it is clear that they often lack the authority, the will or the appropriate instruments to warn and take action against risky behaviour such as pro-cyclical spending, as in the case of Ireland, or excessive debts, as in the case of Greece. The key lesson from the failure of the European Stability and Growth Pact to enforce fiscal discipline and prevent pro-cyclical policies in the Eurozone is that voting rules and preventive instruments are necessary that work in crisis situations rather than succumb to the kind of wishful thinking that usually lubricates intergovernmental agreements.

In other areas, such as air-traffic safety (Eurocontrol), public health (WHO), and nuclear security (IAEA), international bodies are already in charge of risk monitoring. However, variations of success are visible, depending in part on their organisational culture and on institutions' ability to learn and adjust their methodologies and instruments. They do suffer, in particular, from the absence of adequate scrutiny by the news media and NGOs, which is essential for preventing regulatory bodies being captured by industry and institutional complacency. This is not to dispute that media coverage can also lead to pathologies in risk regulations, as discussed in the chapter by de Franco and Meyer, but to underline that rather than relishing its absence, media coverage should be improved through better-balanced judgements about when and how to give publicity to risks. Journalists, in turn, need to become better in explaining to the public the limitations of knowledge in different areas, while press officials and experts should improve the way they describe and explain the underlying probabilities of worst-case scenarios and the trade-offs involved in different courses of action. Journalists also need to become better at judging knowledge claims as well as the track-record and objectivity of experts, as stressed by Philip Tetlock's findings that well-known experts in foreign affairs score on average less well in their forecast than their less publicised colleagues (2005: 68–69). Given the commercial pressures bearing down on quality journalism, a solution might be to create an independent not-for-profit organisation dedicated to developing and maintaining a directory of experts across a range of fields and national jurisdictions combined with their rating within their scientific community, as a one-stop-access to reliable knowledge.

16.2.4 Balancing and questioning prevention and resilience

One can currently distinguish two dominant official strategies for dealing with uncertain transnational threats – prevention and resilience. The first approach focuses on preventing harm by spotting warning signals and then tackling their causes. This approach has limitations when either the probability of the harm, or the risks created by preventive action itself, are uncertain. But uncertainty does not necessarily mean that it is impossible to decide whether and how much to invest in precautionary measures as Richard Posner has argued for catastrophic risks (2007). In a first step one could build scenarios as mentioned above to explore futures with a minimum level of plausibility and, in a second step, arrive at some rough cost-benefit assessment by using different techniques (Posner, 2007: 175–187) such as forecasts traded in information markets for insurances, implied probabilities of a risk by looking at what the government is currently spending on prevention, and the tolerable-windows approach, which tries to ascertain the right level of investment by comparing the functions for the marginal costs and benefits of precautionary measures.

This approach works best when the harm arises from a single phenomenon, however uncertain, as prevention could focus on tackling this particular cause. Prevention reaches its limits when harm could arise from multiple and even completely unknown sources, such as technological failure, terrorist attacks or natural disasters. Here, enhancing the resilience may be the most cost-effective and least intrusive strategy. Resilience in a more narrow sense can be defined as the ability of organisations and systems to stretch sufficiently, when under extraordinary stress, to avoid a disaster and bounce back quickly. Warren Fishbein argued in this book that organisations dealing with risks should learn from so-called high-reliability institutions such as nuclear-power plants and aircraft carriers. These organisations tend to succeed because they track small failures, resist oversimplification, are sensitive to operations, and defer to expertise (Weick and Sutcliffe, 2007). Similarly, Tom Huertas pointed out that asset bubbles are difficult to spot and even harder to prevent, which underlines the importance of solving the 'too big to fail' problem of big global banks through a range of means, and improving resolution schemes when they do fail through living wills. Charles Perrow has argued that vulnerabilities can be found in concentrations of corporate power, critical infrastructures, populations and energy (1999; 2007). He suggests enhancing the resilience of systems by 'shrinking the target', that is by de-coupling, de-concentrating and building in redundancies at the design stage (Perrow, 2007).

The problem with resilience is, however, that shrinking targets still entails some investments and downside risks, that need to be justified on the basis of at least reasonable accounts of some of the causes of harm. The case of counter-terrorism shows how potentially endless and ultimately self-defeating the quest for weak spots is, given human ingenuity to produce maximum harm with limited means. Secondly, resilience may be convenient rhetorical device for governments as it can lead to a 'normalisation' of risks and thus weakening public pressure on authorities to invest in spotting weak warning signals and to take politically difficult measures to prevent potentially catastrophic events from occurring. Consider the civil-protection campaigns launched in the late 1950s in the United States for children, which officially aimed to increase survival rates in the event of a nuclear strike ('duck and cover'), but de-facto helped to legitimise US nuclear strategy. The expanded use of resilience in national strategy documents may thus constitute a slippery slope towards learning to live with risks that are actually intolerable. Finally, resilience may hinder learning and innovation by being excessively sceptical about human ability to better recognise and deal with risks. History suggests that the boundaries of knowledge and technology are constantly shifting so that the uncertain and unpreventable risks of today may well be knowable and preventable tomorrow.

We can see that both approaches are valuable and can be usefully sequenced or even combined depending on the type of risk, what is to be protected and the state of knowledge, but this will work only if there is a proper dialogue between the relevant experts, decision-makers and the relevant publics about the inevitable trade-offs involved in both action and inaction. While cost-benefit calculations can help us to make these choices, they will not be able to resolve the political problems of handling uncertainty, differences in risk perception within and across countries, as well as questions of justice concerning the use of scarce resources and the redistributive effects of choices.

16.3 Conclusion

We have identified a combination of factors which influence the warnings-response process and highlighted the balancing judgements involved. Preventive action tends to be most difficult in issue areas where uncertainty is high, where conflicts of interests undermine experts' credibility and where the potential harm is highly asymmetric across political boundaries as well as over time. Conversely, preventive policy works best in those areas of harm arising from well-understood and regular phenomena, where social beliefs in expert credibility is high, and where the effects are uniform in space and perception as well as immediate in time. Identifying these factors should be seen as a first step towards designing more ambitious research projects capable of examining systematically the relative explanatory power of these factors in different national settings, for different types of risks and under different contextual conditions. It may also help practitioners to better understand the challenges facing them and better direct material and political resources to forecasting, planning and preventive action.

The contributions assembled in this book, as well as this concluding chapter, make a number of recommendations about how the warning-response gap can be closed. As we have argued in the introduction as well as throughout this book, we do not to suggest that this implies a simple or even complex technocratic solution. The emergence of trans-boundary risks raises profound questions about the role of knowledge in policy-making and democratic practice, the representativeness and legitimacy of international-risk regulation and questions of justice with regard to costs of action and inaction. Nor is it always defensible to argue for more warnings, higher receptivity and more vigorous preventive action at the earliest stage possible. On the contrary, in some situations, actor constellations, and areas of risk, there ought to be less and later warning, more sceptical users and news media and ultimately none of the disproportionate, self-interested and myopic action we have seen in some cases. These caveats should not detract from the key conclusion of this book: there is substantial need as well as scope for better warning and better prevention of transnational threats.

Bibliography

9/11 Commission (2004). *'9/11 Commission Report.'* United States of America Government Printing Office.

Adams, J. (1995). *Risk.* London: University College London Press.

Adger, W. N., N. W. Arnel and E. L. Tompkins (2004). 'Successful Adaptation to Climate Change across Scales.' *Global Environmental Change* 15: 77–86.

AFP (2002). 'Schroeder Invites Central Europe Premiers for Flood Summit'. 16 August, *Agence France Presse,* 13 April 2010.

Aguirre-Bastos, C. (2009). '1st Delphi Report.' FORESEC Deliverable D 4.3.

Aikman, D., P. Barrett, S. Kapadia, M. King, J. Proudman, T. Taylor, I. De Weymarn and T. Yates (2010) 'Uncertainty in macroeconomic policy making: art or science?' Royal Society Conference on 'Handling Uncertainty in Science', 8 August, http://www.bankofengland.co.uk/publications/news/2010/034.htm, accessed 10 September 2010

Albanese, J. (1987). 'Predicting the Incidence of Organized Crime: A Preliminary Model.' *Organized Crime in America: Concepts and Controversies.* T. Bynum. New York: Criminal Justice Press: 103–114.

Alford, F. C. (2001). *Whistleblowers: Broken Lives and Organizational Power.* Ithaca and London: Cornell University Press.

Allan, B. A. and C. Carter, Eds (2000). *Environmental Risks and the Media.* London: Routledge.

Allard, T., Riley, M. and Wilkinson, M. (2002). 'The Warning Tourists Never Heard', http://www.greenspun.com/bboard/q-and-a-fetch-msg.tcl?msg_id=00A5Vs, accessed March 2010.

Altalo, M. G. and L. A. Smith (2004) 'Using Ensemble Weather Forecasts to Manage Utilities Risk.' *Environmental Finance* 20 (October), 8–9.

Amara, R. (1981). 'The Futures Field: Searching for Definitions and Boundaries.' *The Futurist* 15: 25–29.

Ammon, R. (2001). *Global Television and the Shaping of World Politics: CNN, Telediplomacy, and Foreign Policy.* Jefferson, NC: McFarland.

Amnesty International (2004). 'Clouds of Injustice: Bhopal Disaster 20 Years On.' London: Amnesty International.

Andrus, C. (2005). 'The Wiki and the Blog: Toward a Complex Adaptive Intelligence Community.' *Studies in Intelligence* 49(3): 63–70.

Ansoff, I. H. (1976). 'Strategic Issue Management.' *Strategic Management Journal* 1(2): 131–48.

Antilla, L. (2005). 'Climate of Scepticism: Us Newspaper Coverage of the Science of Climate Change.' *Global Environmental Change* 15: 338–52.

Armstrong, P. J., Ed. (2001). *Principles of Forecasting: A Handbook for Researchers and Practitioners.* Berlin: Springer.

Arribas, A., K. B. Robertson, and K. R. Mylne (2005). 'Test of a Poor Man's Ensemble for Short-Range Probability Forecasting.' *Monthly Weather Review* 133: 1825–39.

ASA (2010) Advertising Standards Authority. *Adjudication on Department of Energy and Climate Change,* 2010/3.

Ascher, W. (1978). *Forecasting: an appraisal for policy-makers and planners.* Baltimore: Johns Hopkins University Press.

Ascher, W. (2009). *Bringing in the future: strategies for farsightedness and sustainability in developing countries.* Chicago: University of Chicago Press.

ATSDR – Agency for Toxic Substances and Disease Registry (2007). *Toxfaqs for Lead, August 2007.* 15 Aug. 2009 from http://www.atsdr.cdc.gov/tfacts13.html.

Atwater, T. (1985). 'Media Agenda-Setting with Environmental Issues.' *Journalism Quarterly* 62(2): 393–397.

Australian Standards and New Zealand Standards (2004). *'As/Nzs 4360 Risk Management Standard.'* AS and NZS.

Aven, T. (2003). *Foundations of Risk Analysis: A Knowledge and Decision-Oriented Perspective.* Chichester: John Wiley & Sons.

Bahador, B. (2007). *The CNN Effect in Action: How the News Media Pushed the West toward War in Kosovo.* New York: Palgrave Macmillan.

Bandler, J. and J. Hechinger (2001). 'Executive Challenges Xerox's Books, Was Fired.' *The Wall Street Journal.* 6 February 2001.

Barber, T. (2010). 'The Euro: Dinner on the edge of the abyss.' *Financial Times,* 10 October 2010.

Barré, R. (2001). 'Synthesis of Technology Foresight'. *Strategic Policy Intelligence: Current Trends, the State of Play and Perspectives.* A. Tübke, K. Ducatel, J. Gavigan and P. Moncada-Paterno-Castello: EUR 20137 EN December: 71–88.

Barredo, J. I. (2007). 'Major Flood Disasters in Europe: 1950–2005'. *Natural Hazards* 42: 125–48.

Baum, M. A. and P. B. K. Potter (2008). 'The Relationships between Mass Media, Public Opinion, and Foreign Policy: Toward a Theoretical Synthesis.' *Annual Review of Political Science* 11: 39–65.

Bazerman, M. H. and M. D. Watkins (2008). *Predictable Surprises: The Disasters You Should Have Seen Coming, and How to Prevent Them.* Boston, MA: Harvard Business School Publishing.

BBC News (2003) 'Wolfowitz Justifies 'Murky Intelligence.' 28 July from http://news.bbc.co.uk/1/hi/world/middle_east/3102409.stm.

BCBS – Basel Committee on Banking Supervision (2009a). 'Strengthening the Resilience of the Banking Sector.' *Consultative document.* Basel: BCBS.

BCBS – Basel Committee on Banking Supervision (2009b). 'International Framework for Liquidity Risk Measurement, Standards and Monitoring.' *Consultative Document.* Basel: BCBS.

BCBS (2010). Basel Committee on Banking Supervision, The Basel Committee's response to the financial crisis: report to the G20, October 2010, http://www.bis.org/publ/bcbs179.pdf, accessed 23 October 2010.

Beck, U. (1986). *Die Risikogesellschaft: Auf Dem Weg in Eine Andere Moderne.* Frankfurt am Main: Suhrkamp.

Beck, U. (1992). 'From Industrial Society to the Risk Society: Questions of Survival, Social Structure and Ecological Enlightenment.' *Theory, Culture and Society* 9: 97–123.

Beck, U. (1998). *World Risk Society.* Cambridge: Polity Press.

Bell, M. (1998) 'The Journalism of Attachment', In Kieran, M. (ed.) *Media Ethics,* New York: Routledge, pp. 15–22.

Bennett, L. (1988). *News: The Politics of Illusion.* New York and London: Longman.

Bennett, W. L. (1991). 'Toward a Theory of Press-State Relations.' *Journal of Communication* 40(2): 103–125.

Besançon, J., O. Borraz and C. Clergeau (2006). 'Is It Just About Trust? The Partial Reform of French Food Safety Regulation'. *What's the Beef? The Contested Governance of European Food Safety.* C. Ansell and D. Vogel. Cambridge, Mass.: MIT Press: 125–152.

Betts, R. K. (1978). 'Analysis, War and Decision: Why Intelligence Failures Are Inevitable.' *World Politics* 31(1): 61–89.

Betts, R. K. (2007). *Enemies of Intelligence: Knowledge and Power in American National Security*. New York: Columbia University Press.

Betts, R. K. (2009). 'Analysis, War, and Decision: Why Intelligence Failures Are Inevitable'. *Intelligence Theory: Key Questions and Debates*. P. Gill, S. Marrin and M. Phythian. London: Routledge.

Beven, K. (2002). 'Towards a Coherent Philosophy for Modelling the Environment.' *Proceedings of the Royal Society of London* 458: 2465–2484.

Bittner, E. (1970). *The Functions of the Police in Modern Society: A Review of Background Factors, Current Practices, and Possible Role Models*. Rockville: National Institute of Mental Health.

Black, J. (2005) 'Risk Based Regulation: Policy Innovation and Policy Transfer in Financial Services', *Public Law*, Autumn 2005: 512–522.

Black, C., T. Vander Beken, B. Frans and M. Paternotte (2001). 'Reporting on Organised Crime. A Shift from Description to Explanation.' *Belgian Annual Report on Organised Crime*. Antwerp-Apeldoorn: Maklu Publishers.

Blair, T. (2005) *Common Sense Culture Not Compensation Culture*. London: Institute of Public Policy Research. http://www.number-10.gov.uk/output/Page7562.asp.

Bogner K., Pappenberger F. (2011). 'Multiscale Error Analysis, Correction and Predictive Uncertainty Estimation of a Flood Forecasting System.' Accepted *Water Resources Research*.

Boin, A., P. t'Hart, E. Stern and B. Sundelius (2005) *The Politics of Crisis Management: Public Leadership under Pressure*. Cambridge: Cambridge University Press.

Bondi, H. (1985). 'Risk in Perspective'. *Risk*. S. Cooper. Oxford: Clarendon Press: 8–17.

Bora, A. (2004) 'Technologische Risiken.' From http://www.uni-bielefeld.de/iwt/personen/bora/publications.html.

Börjeson, L. M., M. Höjer, K. H. Dreborg, T. Ekvall and G. Finnveden. (2006). 'Scenario Types and Techniques: Towards a User's Guide.' *Futures* 38: 723–39.

Borraz, O. and C. Gilbert (2008). 'Quand L'etat Prend Des Risques'. *Politiques Publiques 1. La France Dans La Gouvernance Européenne*. O. Borraz and V. Guiraudon. Paris: Presses de Sciences Po: 337–357.

Bostrom, N. and M. M. Cirkovic, Eds (2008). *Global Catastrophic Risks*. Oxford: Oxford University Press.

Boykoff, M. and J. Boykoff (2004). 'Balance as Bias: Global Warming and the Us Prestige Press.' *Global Environmental Change* 14: 125–36.

Brand, S. and R. Price (2000). 'The Economic and Social Costs of Crime.' *Home Office Research Study*. London: Home Office.

Brante, J. (2009). 'Strategic Warning in an EU Context: Achieving Common Threat Assessments'. *European Security and Defence Forum*, Chatham House, http://www.chathamhouse.org.uk/files/16618_1109esdf_brante.pdf, accessed 10 June 2010.

Breakwell, G. M. (2007). *The Psychology of Risk*. Cambridge: Cambridge University Press.

Breakwell, G. M. and J. Barnett (2001). 'The Impact of Social Amplification of Risk on Risk Communication.' *Contract Research Report 332/2001*. Health and Safety Executive.

Brennan, G. (1991). 'Civil Disaster Management: An Economist's View.' *Canberra Bulletin of Public Administration* 64: 30–33.

Brickman, R., S. Jasanoff and T. Ilgen (1985). *Controlling Chemicals: The Politics of Regulation in Europe and the United States*. Ithaca and London: Cornell University Press.

British Standards (2008). 'Bs 31100:2008 Risk Management. Code of Practice'. B. Standars.

Brodeur, J.-P. (1998). 'Policing the Risk Society: Review.' *Canadian Journal of Criminology* 40: 455–465.

Brody, R. (1983). 'The Limits of Warning.' *The Washington Quarterly* 6(3): 40–48.

Broome, J. (1993). *Counting the Cost of Global Warming*. Cambridge: White Horse Press.

Brosius, H. and H. Kepplinger (1990). 'The Agenda-Setting Function of Television News: Static and Dynamic Views.' *Communication Research* 17(2): 183–211.

Brown, J. (1998). 'Open-Source Information and the Intelligence Based Decision Model, an Address.'*Optimizing Open Source Information Conference*. Canberra: 7–8 October.

Brown, J. D. (2004). 'Knowledge, uncertainty, and physical geography: towards the development of methodologies for questioning belief.' *Transactions of the Institute of British Geographers* 29: 367–381.

Brown, J. S. and P. Duguid (2002). *The Social Life of Information*. Cambridge, MA: Harvard Business School Press.

Bruen, M., P. Krahe, M. Zappa, J. Olsson, B. Vehvilainen, K. Kok, K. Daamen (2010). 'Visualising Flood Forecasting Uncertainty: Some Current European EPS Platforms – COST731 Working Group 3, *Atmospheric Science Letters* 2: 92–99.

Brummer, V., T. Könnölä and A. Salo (2008). 'Foresight within Era-Nets: Experiences from the Preparation of an International Research Program.' *Technological Forecasting and Social Change* 75(4): 483–495.

Brunelli, M. and B. Vettori (2005). 'European Music Sector'. *Organised Crime and Vulnerability of Economic Sectors: The European Transport and Music Sector*. Antwerp-Apeldoorn: Maklu Publishers, pp. 194–308.

Bryson, B. (2003). *A Short History of Nearly Everything*. New York: Broadway Books.

Bucquoye, A., K. Verpoest, M. Defruytier and T. Vander Beken (2005). 'European Road Transport of Goods'. *Organised Crime and Vulnerability of Economic Sectors: The European Transport and Music Sector*. Antwerp-Apeldoorn: Maklu Publishers, pp. 57–193.

Bueno de Mesquita, B. (2009). *The Predictioneer's Game: Using the Logic of Brazen Self-Interest to See and Shape the Future*. New York: Random House.

Buizza, R. (2008). 'The Value of Probabilistic Prediction.' *Atmospheric Science Letters* 9: 36–42.

Buizza, R., M. Miller, and T. N. Palmer (1999). 'Stochastic Representation of Model uncertainties in the ECMWF Ensemble Prediction System.' *Quarterly Journal of the Royal Meteorological Society* 125: 2887–2908.

Buizza, R., Houtekamer, P. L., Toth, Z., Pellerin, G., Wei, M. and Zhu, Y. (2005) 'A Comparison of the ECMWF, MSC and NCEP Global Ensemble Prediction Systems.' *Monthly Weather Review* 133: 1076–1097.

Burnley, C., H. Carlsen, A.-M. Duta, R. Magoni and P. Wikman-Svahn (2009). 'Report on Scenarios.' FORESEC Deliverable D5.2.

Bush, G. W. (2004). 'President George W. Bush to Reporters at Fort Hood, Texas.' *USA Today*. Cable News Network, 12 April.

Cabinet Office (2002). *Risk: Improving Government's Capability to Handle Risk and Uncertainty*. London: Cabinet Office.

Cabinet Office (2008). *The National Security Strategy of the UK. Security in an Interdependent World*. London: HMSO.

Cabinet Office (2009). *Security for the Next Generation*. London: HMSO.

Calovi, F. (2007). 'The Market of Counterfeit Luxury Leather Fashion Products: From Vulnerabilities to Opportunities for Crime.' PhD Thesis. Milan: Catholic University of Milan.

Calovi, F. and G. Pomposo (2007). 'The European Pharmaceutical Sector.' *The European Pharmaceutical Sector and Crime Vulnerabilities.* Antwerp-Apeldoorn: Maklu Publishers: 29–170.

Canfield, R. L. (2003). 'Intellectual Impairment in Children with Blood Lead Concentrations Below 10 µg Per Deciliter.' *New England Journal of Medicine* 348(16): 1517–1526.

Carvalho, A. (2005). 'Representing the Politics of the Greenhouse Effect: Discursive Strategies in the British Media.' *Critical Discourse Studies* 2(1): 1–29.

Carvalho, A. (2007). 'Ideological Cultures and Media Discourses on Scientific Knowledge: Reading News on Climate Change.' *Public Understanding of Science* 16: 223–243.

Castells, N. and J. Ravetz (2001). 'Science and Policy in International Environmental Agreements: Lessons from the European Experience on Transboundary Air Pollution.' *International Environmental Agreements: Politics, Law and Economics* 1: 405–425.

Chan, M. (2010). *External Review of WHO's Response to the H1N1 Influenza Pandemic.* Opening intervention at the International Health Regulations Review Committee, Geneva, Switzerland, 28 September 2010, http://www.who.int/dg/speeches/2010/ihr_review_20100928/en/index.html

Chomsky, N. and E. S. Herman (1988). *Manufacturing Consent: The Political Economy of the Mass Media.* New York: Pantheon Books.

Clarke, R. A. (2004). 'Against All Enemies inside America's War on Terror.' New York: Simon & Schuster Audio.

Clausewitz, C. V. (1873). *On War.* London: N. Trübner.

Cloke, H. L. and F. Pappenberger (2009). 'Ensemble Flood Forecasting: A Review.' *Journal of Hydrology* 375: 613–626.

Cloke, H. L., J. Thielen, F. Pappenberger, S. Nobert, G. Bálint, C. Edlund, A. Koistinen, C. de Saint-Aubin, E. Sprokkereef, C. Viel, P. Salamon and R. Buizza (2009). 'EPS Progress in the Implementation of Hydrological Ensemble Prediction Systems (HEPS) in Europe for Operational Flood Forecasting.' *ECMWF Newsletters* 121: 20–24.

CNN.com (2004) 'Bush: Memo Had No "Actionable Intelligence."' 25 April 2010 from http://www.cnn.com/2004/ALLPOLITICS/04/11/911.investigation/index.html, accessed March 2010.

Cohen, B. (1994). 'A View from the Academy'. *Taken by Storm: The Media, Public Opinion, and U.S. Foreign Policy in the Gulf War.* W. L. Bennett and D. Paletz. Chicago: Chicago University Press, pp. 8–11.

Cohen, B. C. (1963). *The Press and Foreign Policy.* Princeton, NJ: Princeton University Press.

Cohen, E. and J. Gooch (1991). *Military Misfortune: The Anatomy of Failure in War.* New York: Vintage.

Collier, S. (2008). 'Enacting Catastrophe: Preparedness, Insurance, Budgetary Rationalization.' *Economy and Society* 37: 224–250.

Cooper, J. (2005). *Curing Analytic Pathologies: Pathways to Improved Intelligence Analysis.* Washington, D.C.: Center for the Study of Intelligence.

Costigan, S. (2007). 'Emerging Threats in the 21st Century: Strategic Foresight and Warning.' *Seminar I: The Changing Threat Environment and Its Implications for Strategic Warning.* Zurich: Center for Security Studies, ETHZ.

Council of the EU (2001) 'Council Decision of 23 October 2001 Establishing a Community Mechanism to Facilitate Reinforced Co-operation in Civil Protection Assistance Interventions.' 2001/792/EC, *Official Journal of the European Union* L 297: 7–11.

Council of the EU (2007) 'Council Decision of 8 November 2008 Establishing a Community Civil Protection Mechanism (Recast).' 2007/779/EC, *Official Journal of the European Union* L 314/9: 9–19.

Culpepper, P. D., Hall, P. A., Palier, B. (eds) (2006) *Changing France. The Politics that Markets Make*, London: Palgrave Macmillan.

Czwarno, M. (2006). 'Misjudging Islamic Terrorism: The Academic Community's Failure to Predict 9/11.' *Studies in Conflict & Terrorism* 29: 657–678.

Davis, J. (2003). 'Strategic Warning: If Surprise Is Inevitable, What Role for Analysis'. *Sherman Kent Center Occasional Papers* 2(1), Available at https://www.cia.gov/library/kent-center-occasional-papers/vol2no1.htm, accessed May 2011.

de Goede, M. (2004). 'Repoliticising Financial Risk.' *Economy and Society* 33(2): 197–217.

de Goede, M. (2008). 'The Politics of Pre-Emption and the War on Terror in Europe.' *European Journal of International Relations* 14(1): 161–185.

de Franco, C. (2010). 'The Media and Post-Modern Conflict'. *International Studies Encyclopedia*. New York: Blackwell.

DEFRA – Department for Environment, Food and Rural Affairs (2005). '*Making Space for Water.*' London: DEFRA.

DEFRA – Department for Environment, Food and Rural Affairs (2009). 'Valuing Our Natural Environment, Final Report.' London: DEFRA.

Delpech, T. (2007). *Savage Century: Back to Barbarism*. Washington, DC: Carnegie Endowment for International Peace.

Demeritt, D. (2001) 'The Construction of Global Warming and the Politics of Science.' *Annals of the Association of American Geographers* 91: 307–37.

Demeritt, D., H. Cloke, F. Pappenberger, J. Thielen, J. Bartholmes, and M.-H. Ramos (2007). 'Ensemble Predictions and Perceptions of Risk, Uncertainty, and Error in Flood Forecasting'. *Environmental Hazards* 7: 115–127.

Demeritt, D., S. Nobert, H. Cloke and F. Pappenberger (2010). 'Challenges in Communicating and Using Ensembles in Operational Flood Forecasting.' *Meteorological Applications* 17: 209–222.

Demeritt, D. and J. Wainwright (2005) 'Models, Modelling, and Geography'. In N. Castree, A. Rogers, and D. Sherman (Eds) *Questioning Geography: Essays on a Contested Discipline*. Oxford and New York: Blackwell, pp. 206–25.

de Roo, A, D. Price, G. Schmuck (1999). 'Simulating floods in the Meuse and Oder Catchments Using the LISFLOOD Model', *Modellierung des Wasser- und Stofftransports in großen Einxzugsgebieten: Workshop am 19–20.11.98 in Rauischholzhausen bei Geißen*, N. Fohrer, Döll P (Eds), Kassel: Kassel University Press.

Dorn, N. and H. Vandebunt (2010) 'Bad Thoughts. Towards an Organised Harm Assessment and Prioritization System (Ochaps).' 6 April 2010 from http://www.wodc.nl/images/1703_volledige%20tekst_tcm44-257202.pdf, accessed April 2010.

Douglas, M. and A. Wildavsky (1982). *Risk and Culture: An Essay on the Selection of Technical and Environmental Dangers*. Berkeley, CA: University of California Press.

Douglas, M. and A. Wildavsky (1983). *Risk and Culture: An Essay on the Selection of Technological and Environmental Dangers*. Berkeley: University of California Press.

Dow Chemical (Union Carbide) '2001–2009.' Bhopal Information Center.

Downs, A. (1972). 'Up and Down with Ecology-the Issue Attention Cycle.' *The Public Interest* 28: 38–50.

Dumaine, C. (2009). 'Keynote Speech.' *International Security Forum in Geneva: Common Security, Uncommon Challenges: Resiliency in An Era of the Unthinkable*. Geneva: May 2009.

Dunn Cavelty, M. and V. Mauer (2009). 'Postmodern Intelligence: Strategic Warning in an Age of Reflexive Intelligence.' *Security Dialogue* 40(2): 123–144.

EC (2002) 'Commission Expresses Solidarity with Victims of Floods.' Press release IP/02/1220, 15 August, Brussels: European Commission.

EC (2003) .'Floods: European Research for Better Predictions and Management Solutions', Press release, IP/03/1381, 13 October, Brussels: European Commission.

EC (2009). 'European Union Solidarity Fund, Annual Report 2008 and Report on Experience Gained after Six Years of Applying the New Instrument. Report from the Commission.' Brussels: European Commission.

Edwards, P. N. (2010). *A Vast Machine: Computer Models, Climate Data, and the Politics of Global Warming*. Cambridge, MA: MIT Press.

EEA (2003). *Mapping the Impacts of Recent Natural Disasters and Technological Accidents in Europe*, European Issue Report 35. Copenhagen: European Environment Agency.

Eichenwald, K. (2005). *Conspiracy of Fools*. New York: Basic Books.

Ekengren, M., N. Matzén, M. Rhinard and M. Svantesson M (2006). 'Solidarity or Sovereignty? EU Cooperation in Civil Protection.' *European Integration* 28: 457–476.

Eliade, M. (1991). *The Myth of the Eternal Return: Cosmos and History*. Princeton, NJ: Princeton University Press.

Elkus, A. (2009). 'Complexity, Defense Policy, and Epistemological Failure.' *Small War Journal*, http://smallwarsjournal.com/blog/journal/docs-temp/286-elkus.pdf. Accessed May 2011.

Ellsberg, D. (2008) 'When the Leaders Are the Problem', http://www.ellsberg.net/archive/when-the-leaders-are-the-problem, accessed 11 August 2010.

Entman, R. (2000). 'Declarations of Independence: The Growth of Media Power after the Cold War' In B. Nacos, R. Shapiro and P. Isernia (Eds), *Decisionmaking in a Glass House: Mass Media, Public Opinion, and American and European Foreign Policy in the 21st Century*. Lanham, MD: Rowman and Littlefield, pp. 11–26.

Entman, R. M. (1993). 'Framing: Toward Clarification of a Fractured Paradigm.' *Journal of Communication* 43(4): 51–58.

Ericson, R. and K. Haggerty (1997). *Policing the Risk Society*. Oxford: Clarendon Press.

ESRIF – European Security Research and Innovation Forum (2009). 'ESRIF Final Report.' ESRIF.

European Community (2009) 'A European Security Research and Innovation Agenda – Commission's Initial Position on Esrif's Key Findings and Recommendations.' From *<http://eur-lex.europa.eu/LexUriServ/LexUriServ.do?uri=COM:2009:0691:FIN:EN:PDF>*.

European Security Research Advisory Board (2006). 'Meeting the Challenge: The European Security Research Agenda.' Luxembourg: European Communities.

European Union (2003). *A Secure Europe in a Better World: European Security Strategy*. Brussels: European Union.

European Union (2008). 'Report on the Implementation of the European Security Strategy – Providing Security in a Changing World.' Brussels: Council of the European Union.

Europol (2008) 'Octa. Eu Organised Crime Threat Assessment 2008.' 6 April 2010 from http://www.europol.europa.eu/publications/European_Organised_Crime_Threat_Assessment_(OCTA)/OCTA2008.pdf, accessed 10 May 2011.

Ewald, F. (1986). *L'etat Providence*. Paris: Grasset.

Fairclough, N. (1995). *Media Discourse*. London: Edward Arnold.

Finckenauer, J. (2005). 'Problems of Definition: What is Organized Crime?' *Trends in Organized Crime* 8(3): 63–83.

Fine, G. A. (2007). *Authors of the Storm: Meteorologists and the Culture of Prediction*. Chicago: University of Chicago Press.

Fishbein, W. and G. Treverton (2004). 'Making Sense of Transnational Threats.' *Sherman Kent Center Occasional Papers* 3(2), https://www.cia.gov/library/kent-center-occasional-papers/vol3no1.htm. Accessed May 2011.

Fleming, J. R. (2004). *Historical Perspectives on Climate Change*. Oxford: Oxford University Press.

Fletcher, J. D. (2004). *Cognitive Readiness: Preparing for the Unexpected*. Washington, D.C: Institute for Defense Analysis.

FORESEC (2009). 'Cooperation in the Context of Complexity: European Security in Light of Evolving Trends, Drivers, and Threats.' Unpublished Work.

FSB (2009). Financial Stability Board, 'FSB Principles for Sound Compensation Practices: Implementation Standards,' Available at http://www.financialstabilityboard.org/publications/r_090925c.pdf, accessed 23 October 2010.

Fuerth, L. (2009). 'Foresight and Anticipatory Governance.' *Institute for Alternative Futures Conference: Foresight for Smart Globalization*. Bellagio, Italy: March 16–20.

Fukuyama, F. (2007). 'The Challenges of Uncertainty: An Introduction'. *Blindside: How to Anticipate Forcing Events and Wild Cards in World Politics*. F. Fukuyama. Washington, DC: Brookings Institution Press, pp. 1–6.

Fumerton, R. (2006). *Epistemology*. London: John Wiley & Sons.

Galtung, J. and M. H. Ruge (1965). 'The Structure of Foreign News: The Presentation of the Congo, Cuba and Cyprus Crises in Four Norwegian Newspapers.' *Journal of International Peace Research* 2(1): 64–91.

Gans, H. J. (1979) *Deciding What's News: A Study Of CBS Evening News, NBC Nightly News, Newsweek, And Time*. New York: Pantheon Books.

Gaskell, G. (2005) 'The Social Science and the Humanities, European Commission, Key Technologies for Europe.' From ftp://ftp.cordis.europa.eu/pub/foresight/docs/kte_social_humanities.pdf, accessed April 2010.

Georghiou, L. (2001). 'Evolving Frameworks for European Collaboration in Research and Technology.' *Research Policy* 30(6): 891–903.

Georghiou, L. and M. P. Keenan (2005). 'Evaluation of National Foresight Activities, Assessing Rationale, Process and Impact.' *Technological Forecasting and Social Change* 73(7): 761–777.

Gerstein, M. (2010) 'Blood Simple: Columbia University's Ten-Year Cover-up of Patient Harm, Conflicts of Interest and Administrative Misconduct.' *Truthout*. 26 February 2010 from http://www.truthout.org/blood-simple56928, accessed April 2010.

Gerstein, M., M. Ellsberg and D. Ellsberg (2008). *Flirting with Disaster: Why Accidents Are Rarely Accidental*. New York: Union Square Press.

Giegerich, B. and R. Pantucci (2008). 'Synthesis Report.' FORESEC D 2.4.

Gilboa, E. (2003). 'Television News and U.S. Foreign Policy: Constraints of Real-Time Coverage.' *Harvard International Journal of Press/Politics* 8(4): 97–113.

Gilboa, E. (2009). 'Media and Conflict Resolution: A Framework for Analysis.' *Marquette Law Review* 93(1): 87–111.

Gill, P. (2006). 'Not Just Joining the Dots but Crossing the Borders and Bridging the Voids: Constructing Security Networks after 11 September 2001.' *Policing and Society* 16: 27–49.

Gillies, D. (2000). *Philosophical Theories of Probability*. London: Routledge.

Gitlin, T. (1980). *The Whole World Is Watching: Mass Media in the Making and Unmaking of the New Left*. Berkeley, CA: University of California Press.

Glazer, M. (1983). 'Ten Whistleblowers and How They Fared.' *The Hastings Center Report* 13(6): 33–41.

Global Futures Forum. (2010). Website, https://www.globalfuturesforum.org/, accessed 17 October 2010.

Global Risk Forum (2010). http://www.grforum.org/, accessed 17 October 2010.

Gneiting T. and A. E. Raftery (2005). 'Weather Forecasting with Ensemble Methods.' *Science* 310: 248–249.

Goffman, E. (1959). *The Presentation of Self in Everyday Life*. Garden City, NY: Doubleday.

Goldman, J. (2006). *Words of Intelligence: A Dictionary*. Lanham, MD: Scarecrow Press.

Gouweleeuw, B., P. Reggiani, A. de Roo (2004). *A European Flood Forecasting System EFFS*. Full Report. EUR 21208 EN. Ispra, Italy.

Gouweleeuw, B., J. Thielen, A. de Roo and R. Buizza (2005) Flood forecasting using medium range probabilistic weather prediction, *Hydrology and Earth System Science* 9: 365–380.

Gould, S. J. (1987). *Time's Arrow, Time's Cycle: Myth and Metaphor in the Discovery of Geological Time*. Cambridge, MA: Harvard University Press.

Gover, R. and M. S. Goodman, Eds (2009). *Spinning Intelligence: Why Intelligence Needs the Media, Why the Media Needs Intelligence*. New York: Columbia University Press.

Gowing, N. (1994). *Real-Time Coverage of Armed Coverage and Diplomatic Crises: Does It Pressure or Distort Foreign Policy Decisions? (Harvard Working Paper)*. Cambridge, MA: The Joan Shorenstein Barone Center on the Press, Politics, and Public Policy, Harvard University.

Grabo, C. (1987). 'Warning Intelligence.' *The Intelligence Profession Series* 4, McLean, VA: The Association of Former Intelligence Officers.

Grabo, C. M. (2004). *Anticipating Surprise: Analysis of Strategic Warning*. Lanham, MD: University Press of America.

Greenspan, A. (2005). 'Testimony on the Federal Reserve Board's Semiannual Monetary Policy Report to the Congress.' *Committee on Banking, Housing, and Urban Affairs*. US Senate.

Greimas, A. J. and J. Courtés (1982). *Semiotics and Language: An Analytical Dictionary*. Bloomington, IN: Indiana University Press.

Gudykunst, W. B., S. Ting-Toomey, B. J. Hall and K. L. Schmidt (1989). 'Language and Intergroup Communication'. In M. K. Asante and W. B. Gudykunst (Eds) *Handbook of International and Intercultural Communication*. London: Sage.

Habegger, B. (2008). *Horizon Scanning in Government, Concept, Country Experiences, and Models for Switzerland*. Zurich: Center for Security Studies, ETHZ.

Habegger, B. (2010). 'Strategic Foresight in Public Policy: Reviewing the Experiences of the UK, Singapore, and the Netherlands.' *Futures: The Journal of Policy, Planning and Futures Studies* 42(1): 49–58.

Hallin, D. (1986). *The Uncensored War: The Media in Vietnam*. New York: Oxford University Press.

Halloran, R. (1987). 'Soldiers and Scribblers: A Common Mission.' *Parameters* 17: 10–28.

Hamilton, B. (1997). 'Re: Ethyl – Product Details.' Personal Communication from http://yarchive.net/chem/tetraethyl_lead.html, accessed February 2010.

Hampton, P. (2005). *Reducing Administrative Burdens: Effective Inspection and Enforcement*. London: H. Treasury.

Harcup T. and O'Neill D. (2001) 'What is News? Galtung and Ruge Revisited', *Journalism Studies*, 2(2): 261–280.

Harff, B. (2003) 'No Lessons Learned from the Holocaust? Assessing Risks of Genocide and Political Mass Murder since 1955', *American Political Science Review* 97(1), 57–73.

Hastie, R. and R. M. Dawes (2001). *Rational Choice in an Uncertain World: The Psychology of Judgment and Decision Making*. Thousand Oaks, CA: Sage.

Havas, A. (2003). 'Evolving Foresight in a Small Transition Economy.' *Journal of Forecasting* 22(2–3): 179–201.

van der Heijden, K. (2005). *Scenarios: The Art of Strategic Conversation*. Chichester: John Wiley & Sons.

Heintz Bettina (2010) Numerische Differenz. Überlegungen zu einer Soziologie des (quantitativen) Vergleichs. *Zeitschrift für Soziologie* 39(3), 162–81.

Hekkert, M. P., R. A. A. Suurs, S. O. Negro, S. Kuhlmann and R. E. H. M. Smits (2007). 'Functions of Innovation Systems: A New Approach for Analysing Technological Change.' *Technological Forecasting and Social Change* 74: 413–432.

Henderson-Sellers, A. (1998). 'Climate Whispers: Media Communication About Climate Change.' *Climatic Change* 40: 421–456.

Heuer, R. (1999). *Psychology of Intelligence Analysis*. Washington, DC: Government Printing Office.

HLEGEU – High Level Expert Group for the European Commission (2002). 'Thinking, Debating and Shaping the Future: Foresight for Europe.' Brussels: HLEGEU.

Hoge, J. F. (1994). 'Media Pervasiveness.' *Foreign Affairs* 73(4): 136–44.

Holling, C. S. (1979). 'Myths of Ecological Stability'. In G. Smart (Ed.) *Studies in Crisis Management*. Montreal: Butterworth.

Holling, C. S. (1986). 'The Resilience of Terrestrial Ecosystems'. In W. Clark (Ed.) *Sustainable Development of the Biosphere*. Cambridge: Cambridge University Press.

Holmes, J. B., N. Henrich, S. Hancock and V. Lestou (2009). 'Communicating with the Public During Health Crises: Experts' Experiences and Opinions.' *Journal of Risk Research* 12(6): 793–807.

Home Office (2009). *Countering International Terrorism: The United Kingdom Strategy*. London: HMSO.

Homer-Dixon, T. (2006). *The Upside of Down: Catastrophe, Creativity, and the Renewal of Civilization*. New York: Island Press.

Hood, C., H. Rothstein and R. Baldwin (2001). *The Government of Risk. Understanding Risk Regulation Regimes*. Oxford: Oxford University Press.

Hood, C., James, O., Jones, G., Scott, C., Travers, T. (1999) Regulation Inside Government: waste-Watchers, Quality Police and Sleaze-Busters, Oxford: Oxford University Press.

Horizon, P. (2006). *Progress Report*. Washington, D.C.: US Government.

Huber, M. (1998). *Das Regulative Netzwerk. Risiko Und Regulative Politik Im Bundesdeutschen Kernenergikonflikt*. Frankfurt/Main: Lang.

Huber, M. (2010). 'Insuring Climate Change – Managing Political and Economic Uncertainties'. *Climate Research and Policy: The Calculability of Climate Change and the Challenge of Uncertainty*. G. G. and F. J. Heidelberg: Springer.

Huberman, B. and T. Hogg (1986). 'Complexity and Adaptation.' *Physica D* 22: 376–384.

Huertas, T. F. (2010a). *Crisis: Cause, Containment and Cure*. London: Palgrave Macmillan.

Huertas, T. F. (2010b). 'Improving Bank Capital Structures.' *Modigliani-Miller in Banking*. London: 18 January.

Huertas, T. F. (2010c). 'Living Wills: How Can the Concept Be Implemented? Conference Remarks.' *Cross-Border Issues in Resolving Systemically Important Financial Institutions*. Philadelphia, PA: 12 February.

Huertas, T. F. (2010d). 'Resolution and Contagion.' *CCBS/FMG Conference*. London: 26 February.

Huertas, T. F. (2010e), 'The Road to Better Resolution: From Bail-out to Bail-in', Speech at the 'The Euro and the Financial Crisis conference', The Bank of Slovakia, 6 September 2010 http://www.fsa.gov.uk/pubs/speeches/th_6sep10.pdf.

Hughes, T. L. (1976) *The Face of Facts in a World of Men: Foreign Policy and Intelligence-Making*. New York: Foreign Policy Association.

Hulme, M. (2009). *Why We Disagree About Climate Change: Understanding Controversy, Inaction and Opportunity*. Cambridge, UK, and New York: Cambridge University Press.

Hulnick, A. S. (2004). *Keeping Us Safe: Secret Intelligence and Homeland Security*. Westport, CT: Greenwood Publishing Group.

Humanitarian Futures Programme (2010). 'Works with NGOs on the Anticipation, Prevention and Mitigation of Future Humanitarian Crises.' http://www.humanitarianfutures.org/.

Hume, M. (1997). *Whose War Is It Anyway? The Dangers of the Journalism of Attachment*. London: Informinc.

Hutter, B. (2005) The Attractions of Risk-Based Regulation: Accounting for the Emergence of Risk Ideas in Regulation. Discussion Paper No. 33. CARR, LSE: London.

IFRC (2009) 'Moldova and Ukraine: Floods. Final Report on Emergency Appeal no. MDR67003'. 3 September. Geneva, International Federation of Red Cross and Red Crescent Societies. April 2010 from http://reliefweb.int/node/322974, accessed May 2011.

IIASA – International Institute for Applied Systems Analysis (2010) 'Cleaner Air for a Cleaner Future: Controlling Transboundary Air Pollution.' 13 May 2010 from http://www.iiasa.ac.at/Admin/INF/OPT/Summer98/feature.htm, accessed 10 May 2011.

IIASA – International Institute for Applied Systems Analysis (2009). 'Gains: Comparing Ghg Mitigation Efforts between Annex I Countries.' From http://gains.iiasa.ac.at/index.php/gains-annex-1, accessed 10 May 2011.

IIASA – International Institute for Applied Systems Analysis (no date). 'What Is IIASA?' From http://www.iiasa.ac.at/docs/IIASA_Info.html, accessed 10 May 2011.

ILGRA – Interdepartmental Liaison Group on Risk Assessment (1996). *Use of Risk Assessment within Government Departments*. London: Health and Safety Executive.

ILGRA – Interdepartmental Liaison Group on Risk Assessment (1998). *Risk Assessment and Risk Management: Improving Policy and Practice within Government Departments*. London: Health and Safety Executive.

ILGRA – Interdepartmental Liaison Group on Risk Assessment (2002). *Third Report Prepared by the Interdepartmental Liaison Group on Risk Assessment*. London: Health and Safety Executive.

Innes, M. (2006). 'Policing Uncertainty: Countering Terror through Community Intelligence and Democratic Policing.' *The ANNALS of the American Academy of Political and Social Science* 605: 222–241.

Innes, M., N. Fielding and N. Cope (2005). 'The Appliance of Science? The Theory and Practice of Crime Intelligence Analysis.' *British Journal of Criminology* 45: 39–57.

Institute of Public Policy Research (2009). 'Shared Responsibilities: A National Security Strategy for the UK.' London: IPPR.

IRM – Institute of Risk Management, AIRMIC – The Association of Insurance and Risk Managers and Alarm – The Public Risk Management Association (2002). *The Risk Management Standard*. London: IRM.

Irvine, J. and B. R. Martin (1984). *Foresight in Science: Picking the Winners*. London: Dover.

ISO – International Standard Organisation (2009). *Iso/Fdis 3100: Risk Management – Principles and Guidelines*. Geneva: ISO.
Jakobsen, P. V. (2000). 'Focus on the CNN Effect Misses the Point: The Real Media Impact on Conflict Management Is Invisible and Indirect.' *Journal of Peace Research* 37(2): 131–143.
Jervis, R. (2010). *Why Intelligence Fails: Lessons from the Iranian Revolution and the Iraq War*. Ithaca: Cornell University Press.
Johnson, L. (2009). 'Sketches for a Theory of Strategic Intelligence'. In P. Gill, S. Marrin and M. Phythian (Eds) *Intelligence Theory: Key Questions and Debate*. London: Routledge.
Joint Intelligence Committee (2002). *Iraq Dossier*. London: JIC.
Joly, P.-B. (2007). 'Scientific Expertise in Public Arenas: Lessons from the French Experience.' *Journal of Risk Research* 10(7): 905–924.
Jones, R. V. (1989). *Reflections on Intelligence*. London: Mandarin.
JRC-IPTS (2001). *Foresight for Regional Development Network. A Practical Guide to Regional Foresight*. Seville: FOREN.
Kahn, D. (2009). 'An Historical Theory of Intelligence'. In P. Gill, S. Marrin and M. Phythian (Eds) *Intelligence Theory: Key Questions and Debates*. London: Routledge.
Kahn, H. and A. J. Wiener (1967). *The Year 2000: A Framework for Speculation on the Next Thirty-Three Years*. New York: Macmillan.
Kahneman, D., P. Slovic and A. Tversky, Ed. (1982). *Judgment under Uncertainty: Heuristics and Biases*. Cambridge: Cambridge University Press.
Kam, E. (2004). *Surprise Attack, the Victim's Perspective*. Boston, MA: Harvard University Press.
Keenan, M. (2003). 'Identifying Emerging Generic Technologies at the National Level: The UK Experience.' *Journal of Forecasting* 22(2–3): 129–160.
Keenan, M. (2006). *Establishment of a Technology Foresight (TF) Regional Virtual Centre (RVC) for the Cee/Nis Countries*. Vienna: UNIDO.
Keman, W. N. (2000). *Phenylpropanolamine & Risk of Hemorrhagic Stroke*, Final Report of The Hemorrhagic Stroke Project. Washington, DC: FDA.
Kerbel, J. (2004). 'Thinking Straight, Cognitive Bias in the Us Debate About China.' *Studies in Intelligence* 48(3): 27–35.
Kerbel, J. (2009). 'Complicated to Complex: Transforming Intelligence for a Changing World.' *ISA Convention 2009*. New York: February 2009.
Kessler, O. and C. Daase (2008). 'From Insecurity to Uncertainty: Risk and the Paradox of Security.' *Alternatives: Global, Local Political* 33: 211–232.
Keynes, J. M. (1997). *The General Theory of Employment, Interest, and Money*. Amherst, NY: Prometheus Books.
Kingdon, J. W. (1995) *Agendas, Alternatives, and Public Policies*, 2nd ed. New York: Harper Collins.
Kinsella, J. (1989). *Covering the Plague: Aids and the American Media*. New Brunswick, NJ: New Jersey University Press.
Kirby, A. (2010). 'How the Media Reported Climate, and in Particular the Science of Climate Change.' *The Climate Change Media Partnership*, Conference paper available at http://reutersinstitute.politics.ox.ac.uk/fileadmin/documents/Conferences/Climate_Change/Alex_Kirby__How_the_Media_Reported_Climate.pdf.
Kitman, J. L. (2000). 'The Secret History of Lead.' *The Nation*. March 2: 15 August 2009 from http://www.thenation.com/doc/20000320/kitman/single.
Klerks, P. (2000). *Groot in De Hasj: Theorie En Praktijk Van De Georganiseerde Criminaliteit*. Alphen a/d Rijn: Samsom.

Klijn, F., M. van Buuren, and S. A. M. van Rooij (2004). 'Flood-Risk Management Strategies for an Uncertain Future: Living with Rhine River Floods in the Netherlands?' *Ambio* 33: 141–147.

Klima, N. (2009). 'Resilience Joins Research in Vulnerability of Economic Activity to Crime'. In M. Hildebrandt, A. Makinwa and A. Oemichen (Eds) *Controlling Security in a Culture of Fear.* The Hague: Boom Legal Publishers, pp. 247–266.

Könnölä, T., T. Ahlqvist, A. Eerola, S. Kivisaari and R. Koivisto (2009). 'Management of Foresight Portfolio: Analysis of Modular Foresight Projects at Contract Research Organization.' *Technological Analysis & Strategic Management* 21(3): 381–405.

Kopp, P. and F. Besson (2009). 'A Methodology to Measure the Impact of Organised Crime Activities at the Eu Level'. In Savona et al. (Eds) *Organised Crime in the EU: A Methodology for Risk Assessment.* Rotterdam: Erasmus University, pp. 204–231.

Kreibich, H. and A. Thieken (2009). 'Coping with Floods in the city of Dresden, Germany.' *Natural Hazards* 51: 423–36.

Kuhn, T. S. (1962). *The Structure of Scientific Revolutions.* Chicago: University of Chicago Press.

Kuhn, T. S. (1996). *The Structure of Scientific Revolutions.* Chicago, IL: University of Chicago Press.

Lang, G. and Lang, K. (1981) 'Watergate: An Exploration of the Agenda-Building Process'. *Mass Communication Review Yearbook* 2, 447–468.

Lau, R. R. and D. P. Redlawsk (2001). 'Advantages and Disadvantages of Cognitive Heuristics in Political Decision Making.' *American Journal of Political Science* 45(4): 951–971.

Leung, R. (2005). 'Uncertain Future for Us Spies.' *CBS News.* 15 April.

Levi, M. (2002). 'The Organization of Serious Crime'. In M. Maguire, R. Morgan and R. Reiner (Eds). *The Oxford Handbook of Criminology.* Oxford: Oxford University Press, pp. 878–913.

Levi, M. and M. Maguire (2004). 'Reducing and Preventing Organized Crime: An Evidence-Based Critique.' *Crime, Law & Social Change* 41: 397–469.

Levi, M. and N. Dorn (2008). 'Examining the Feasibility of the Methodology: A Pilot Study on International Fraud.' In Savona et al. *Organised Crime in the EU: A Methodology for Risk Assessment.* Rotterdam: Erasmus University, pp. 204–231.

Liberatore, A. (1999). *The Management of Uncertainty. Learning from Chernobyl.* Amsterdam: Gordon & Breach Publisher

Lippman, W. (1965). *Public Opinion.* New York: Harcourt Brace.

Livingston, S. (1997). 'Clarifying the CNN Effect: An Examination of Media Effects According to Type of Military Intervention.' *Joan Shorenstein Center on the Press, Politics and Public Policy* Research Paper R-18.

Lodge, M. (2001). 'Barking Mad? Risk Regulation and the Control of Dangerous Dogs in Germany.' *German Politics* 10(3): 65–82.

Löfstedt, R. E. (2003). 'Risk Communication: Pitfalls and Promises.' *European Review* 11(3): 417–435.

Longstaff, P. (2005). 'Security, Resilience, and Communication in Unpredictable Environments Such as Terrorism, Natural Disasters and Complex Technology.' Cambridge, MA: Program on Information Resources Policy, Harvard University and the Center for Information Policy Research.

Lorenzoni, I., Jones, M., Turnpenny, J., (2006) 'Climate Change, Human Genetics and Post-Normality in the UK'. *Futures* 39, 65–82.

Loudon, M. (2005) 'The FDA Exposed: An Interview with Dr. David Graham, the Vioxx Whistleblower.' 14 August 2009 from http://mrgreenbiz.wordpress.com/2009/06/20/the-fda-exposed-an-interview-with-dr-david-graham-the-vioxx-whistleblower, accessed March 2010.

Luhmann, N. (1991). *Soziologie De Risikos*. Berlin: De Gruyter.

Luhmann, N. (1998). 'Describing the Future.' In N. Luhmann (Ed.) *Observations on Modernity*. Stanford: Stanford University Press, 63–74

Lumbroso, D and B. von Christierson (2009) *Communication and Dissemination of Probabilistic Flood Warnings – Literature Review of International Material*. Science project SC070060/SR3 for Environment Agency/Defra Flood and Coastal Erosion Risk Management Research and Development Programme. Bristol: Environment Agency.

Magli, P. (2006) 'Efficacia Delle Immagini. Presentazione Del Convegno.' from http://www.documenti.ve.it.

Marrin, G. S. and M. Phythian (2009). *Intelligence Theory: Key Questions and Debates*. London: Routledge.

Martin, B. R. and J. Irvine (1989). *Research Foresight: Priority-Setting in Science*. London: Pinter Publishers.

Matveeva, A. (2006) 'Early Warning and Early Response: Conceptual and Empirical Dilemmas', Issue Paper, no. 1, Global Partnership for the Prevention of Armed Conflict (GPPAC), European Centre for Conflict Prevention, The Hague.

Mauer, V. and M. D. Cavelty (2009). *Postmodern Intelligence: Strategic Warning in an Age of Reflexive Intelligence*. Oslo: Sage Publications.

Mazzoleni, G. and W. Schulz (1999). '"Mediatization" Of Politics: A Challenge for Democracy?' *Political Communication* 16(3): 247–261.

McComas, K. and J. Shanahna (1999). 'Telling Stories About Global Climate Change: Measuring the Impact of Narratives on Issue Cycles '*Communication Research* 26(1): 30–57.

McLuhan, M. (1962). *The Gutenberg Galaxy: The Making of Typographic Man*. Toronto: University of Toronto Press.

McLuhan, M. (2001). *Understanding Media*. London: Routledge.

McNair, B. (1999). *An Introduction to Political Communication*. London: Routledge.

McQuail, D. (1983) *Mass Communication Theory*. London: Sage.

Meijerink, H. (2005) 'Understanding Policy Stability and Change: The Interplay of Advocacy Coalitions and Epistemic Communities, Windows of Opportunity, and Dutch coastal flooding policy, 1945–2003.' *Journal of European Public Policy* 12: 1060–1077

Mermin, J. (1999). *Debating War and Peace: Media Coverage of U.S. Interventionism in the Post-Vietnam Era*. Princeton, NJ: Princeton University Press.

Meyer, C. O. (2011). 'The Purpose and Pitfalls of Constructivist Forecasting: Insights from Strategic Culture Research for the European Union's Evolution as a Military Power.' *International Studies Quarterly* 55(3), DOI: 10.1111/j.1468-2478.2011.00648.x.

Meyer, C. O., F. Otto, J. Brante, and C. de Franco (2010) 'Re-casting the Warning-Response-Problem: Persuasion and Preventive Policy.' *International Studies Review*, 12(4): 556–578.

MIC (2008) 'EU Response to Floods in Romania, Ukraine, and Moldova.' Press release, IP/08/1243 Brussels: Monitoring and Information Centre, European Commission.

Michaels, D. (2005). 'Doubt Is Their Product.' *Scientific American* 292(6): 96–101.

Mitchell, J. K. (2003) 'European River Floods in a Changing World', *Risk Analysis* 23: 567–74.

Moeller, S. (1999). *Compassion Fatigue. How the Media Sell Disease, Famine, War and Death*. New York: Routledge.

Molloy College Philosophy Department. (12 April 2010). 'Sophia Project.' from http://www.molloy.edu/sophia/sophia_project.htm.

Molotsky, I. (1987). 'Critics Say F.D.A. Is Unsafe in Reagan Era.' *The New York Times*. 4 January: 44.

Moorcraft, P. L. and P. M. Taylor (2008). *Shooting the Messenger: The Political Impact of War Reporting*. Washington, D.C.: Potomac Books.

Morrison, J. (1992). 'Environmental Scanning'. *The Primer for New Institutional Researchers*. M. Whitely, J. Porter and R. Fenske. Tallahassee: The Association for Institutional Research, 86–99.

Mowlana, H. (1992). 'Roots of the War: The Long Road of Intervention'. In G. Gebner, H. I. Schiller and H. Mowlana (Eds) *Triumph of the Image*. Boulder, CO: Westview Press, pp. 30–50.

NATO (2003). *Handbook on Long Term Defence Planning*. NATO Research and Technology Organisation. RTO-TR-069.

NATO (2005). *Nato Future World Scenarios: Future Worlds*. Brussels: NATO.

Neal, M. (2000). 'Risk Aversion: The Rise of an Ideology'. *Safe Enough? Managing Risk and Regulation*. L. Jones. Vancouver: Fraser Institute, 13–30.

Neuman, J. (1996). *Light, Camera, War!* New York: St. Martin's Press.

NIST – National Institute of Standars and Technology (2001). *800–30 Risk Management Guide for Information Technology Systems*. Gaithersburg: NIST.

NISTEP (2005). 'Science and Technology Foresight Survey. Delphi Analysis.' Science and Technology Foresight Center, National Institute of Science and Technology Policy, Ministry of Education, Culture, Sports, Science and Technology (Japan). NISTEP report no. 97.

Nobert S., D. Demeritt, and H. Cloke (2010). 'Informing Operational Flood Management with Ensemble Predictions: Lessons from Sweden.' *Journal of Flood Risk Management* 3: 72–79.

Norris, F. (2003). '6 from Xerox to Pay S.E.C. $22 Million.' *The New York Times*. 6 Jun: C 1.

Nowotny, H. (2006). *Cultures of Technology and the Quest for Innovation*. New York, Oxford: Berghahn Books.

NRC – National Research Council (1983). *Risk Assessment in the Federal Government: Managing the Process*. Washington, D.C.: National Academy Press.

Nye, J. (1999). 'Ridefinire La Missione Della Nato Nell'era Dell'informazione.' *Rivista della NATO* 4: 12-15.

Nyheim, D. (2008). *Can Violence, War and State Collapse Be Prevented?* Paris: OECD.

OECD (Organisation for Economic Co-Operation and Development) (2010) *Risk and Regulatory Policy: Improving the Governance of Risk*. OECD: Paris.

Odoni, N. A., and Lane S.N. (2010). Knowledge-theoretic Models in Hydrology" *Progress in Physical Geography* 34: 151–171.

O'Malley, P. (2000). 'Uncertain Subjects: Risks, Liberalism and Contract.' *Economy and Society* 29(4): 460–484.

O'Neill, S. and S. Nicholson-Cole (2009). ''Fear Won't Do It': Promoting Positive Engagement with Climate Change through Visual and Iconic Representations.' *Science Communication* 30(3): 355–379.

Olausson, U. (2009). 'Global Warming-Global Responsibility? Media Frames of Collective Action and Scientific Certainty.' *Public Understanding of Science* 18: 421–436.

Omand, D. (2009). *National Security Strategy: Some Implications for the UK Intelligence Community*. London: IPPR.

Omand, D. (2010) *Securing the State*, London: Hurst and Co.

Oreskes, N., K. Shrader-Frechette and K. Belitz (1994). 'Verification, Validation, and Confirmation of Numerical Models in the Earth Sciences.' *Science* 263: 641–646.
Palmer, T. N. (2002). 'The Economic Value of Ensemble Forecasts as a Tool for Risk Assessment: From Days to Decades.' *Quarterly Journal of the Royal Meteorological Society* 128, 147–74.
Pappenberger, F., J. Thielen, J. Del Medico (2011). 'The Impact of Weather Forecast Improvements on Large Scale Hydrology: Analyzing a Decade of Forecasts of the European Flood Alert System' *Hydrological Processes* 25: 1091–113.
Pasteur, L. (1854). 'Lecture.' Lille: University of Lille.
PBS (2005). 'Interview with Thai Met's Smith Dharmasaroja.' *PBS News Hour With Jim Lehrer.* 21 November 2005 from http://www.pbs.org/newshour/bb/asia/july-dec05/tsunami_11-21.html, accessed March 2010.
Perloff, R. (2008). *The Dynamics of Persuasion: Communication and Attitudes in the 21st Century.* London: Taylor & Francis.
Perrow, C. (1999). *Normal Accidents: Living with High-Risk Technologies.* Princeton, NJ: Princeton University Press.
Perrow, C. (2007). *The Next Catastrophe: Reducing our Vulnerabilities to Natural, Industrial and Terrorist Disasters.* Princeton, NJ: Princeton University Press.
Peters, H. P. (1995). 'The Interaction of Journalists and Scientific Experts: Co-Operation and Conflict between Two Professional Cultures.' *Media, Culture and Society* 17: 31–48.
Petersen, J. L. (2008). *A Vision for 2012: Planning for Extraordinary Changes.* Golden, CO: Fulcrum.
Pidgeon, N. F., J. X. Kasperson, and P. Slovic, Eds (2003). *The Social Amplification of Risk.* Cambridge: Cambridge University Press.
Pielke, R. A. J. (1998). 'Rethinking the Role of Adaptation in Climate Policy.' *Global Environmental Change* 8(2): 159–170.
Plato (2007) *The Republic.* London: Penguin Books.
Popper, K. (2002) [1957]. *The Poverty of Historicism.* London: Routledge.
Porter, M. (1990). *Competitive Advantages of Nations.* New York: Free Press.
Porter, T. (1995). *Trust in Numbers: The Pursuit of Objectivity in Science and Public Life.* Princeton, NJ: Princeton University Press.
Posner, R. A. (2004). *Catastrophe: Risk and Response.* Oxford: Oxford University Press.
Power, M. (1997). *The Audit Society.* Oxford: Oxford University Press.
Power, M. (2007). *Organized Uncertainty: Designing a World of Risk Management.* Oxford: Oxford University Press.
Power, S. (2004). 'Reporting Atrocity: War, Neutrality, and the Danger of Taking Sides.' *Press/Politics* 9(3): 3–11.
Pozsar, Z., T. Adrian, A. B. Ashcraft, and H. Boesky (2010), 'Shadow Banking', Federal Reserve Bank of New York Staff Report No. 458, 1 July 2010.
Project on National Security Reform (2008). *'Forging a New Shield, Executive Summary.'* Arlington, VA: Center for the Study of the Presidency.
Propp, V. (1928). *Morphology of the Folktale.* Austin, TX: University of Texas Press.
Proske, D. (2008). *Catalogue of Risks: Natural, Technical, Social and Health Risks.* Berlin: Springer Verlag.
Ramos, M. H., J. Bartholmes and J. Thielen-del Pozo, J. (2007). 'Development of Decision Support Products Based on Ensemble Weather Forecasts in the European Flood Alert System.' *Atmospheric Science Letters* 8: 113–119.
Ransley, J. and L. Mazerolle (2009). 'Policing in a Era of Uncertainty.' *Police Practice and Research* 10: 1–17.
Rask, M. (2008). 'Foresight – Balancing Between Increasing Variety and Productive Convergence.' *Technological Forecasting and Social Change* 75(8): 1157–1175.

Rasmussen, B. and P. D. Andersen (2009). 'Review of Science and Technology Foresight Studies and Comparison with Gts2015.' from www.fi.dk.

Ravetz, J. (2003). 'Models as Metaphors'. In B. Kasemir, J. Jaeger, C. Jaeger and M. T. Gardner (Eds) *Public Participation in Sustainability Science*. Cambridge: Cambridge University Press.

RCMP – Royal Canadian Mounted Police (2000) 'The Long Matrix for Organised Crime. An Analytical Technique for Determining Relative Levels of Threat Posed by Organized Crime Groups.' 6 April 2010 from https://analysis.mitre.org/proceedings/Final_Papers_Files/135_Camera_Ready_Paper.pdf, accessed March 2010.

Renn, O. (2008). *Risk Governance: Coping with Uncertainty in a Complex World*. London: Earthscan.

Reuben, R. C. (2009). 'The Impact of News Coverage on Conflict: Toward Greater Understanding.' *Marquette Law Review* 93(1): 45–85.

Ringland, G. (1998). *Scenario Planning: Managing for the Future*. New York: John Wiley and Sons.

Rintakoski, K. and M. Partanen (2009). 'Concept of European Security: Implications for European Security Research.' FORESEC Deliverable D 4.6.

Rip, A. (1990) 'An Exercise in Foresight: The Research System in Transition ... to What.' *Kluwer Academic* from http://doc.utwente.nl/34815/1/K340____.PDF, accessed April 2010.

Rip, A. (2003). 'Constructing Expertise: In a Third Wave of Science Studies?' *Social Studies of Science* 33(3): 419–434.

RMS (2003). *Central Europe Flooding, August 2002*. London: Risk Management Solutions Ltd.

Robinson, P. (2002). *The CNN Effect: The Myth of News, Foreign Policy and Intervention*. New York: Routledge.

Rockart, J. F. (1986). 'A Primer on Critical Success Factors'. In J. F. Rockart and C. V. Bullen (Eds) *The Rise of Managerial Computing: The Best of the Center for Information Systems Research*. Homewood, IL: Dow Jones-Irwin, pp. 135–147.

Rose, M. (2000). 'The Media and International Security'. In S. Badsey (Ed.) *The Media and International Security*. London: Frank Cass, pp. 3–33.

Rose, N. and P. Miller (1992). 'Political Power Beyond the State: Problematics of Government.' *British Journal of Sociology* 43(2): 173–205.

Rothstein, H. and J. Downer (2008). 'Risk in Policy-Making: Managing the Risks of Risk Governance. Report for the Department for Environment, Food and Rural Affairs.' London: King's College London.

Rothstein, H. and Downer, J. (forthcoming 2012) 'Renewing Defra: Exploring the Emergence of Risk-Based Policymaking in UK Central Government'. *Public Administration*.

Rothstein, H., M. Huber and G. Gaskell (2006). 'A Theory of Risk Colonisation: The Spiralling Regulatory Logics of Societal and Institutional Risk.' *Economy and Society* 35 (1): 91–112.

Roulin, E. (2007). 'Skill and Relative Economic Value of Medium-Range Hydrological Ensemble Predictions.' *Hydrology and Earth System Science* 11: 725–737.

Rozenkrans, R. and E. Emde (1996). 'Organized Crime: Towards the Preventive Screening of Industries: A Conceptual Model.' *Security Journal* 7: 169–176.

Salamon, P. and L. Feyen (2009) 'Assessing Parameter, Precipitation, and Predictive Uncertainty in a Distributed Hydrological Model Using Sequential Data Assimilation with the Particle Filter,' *Journal of Hydrology* 376: 428–442

Salmenkaita, J.-P. and A. Salo (2002). 'Rationales for Government Intervention in the Commercialization of New Technologies.' *Technology Analysis and Strategic Management* 14(2): 183–200.

Salo, A. and K. Cuhls (2003). 'Technology Foresight: Past and Future.' *Journal of Forecasting* 22(2–3): 79–82.
Salo, A., Brummer, V. and Könnölä, T. (2009). 'Axes of Balance in Foresight - Reflections from Finnsight 2015.' *Technology Analysis and Strategic Management* 21(8): 287–1001.
Sammonds, P., W. McGuire and S. Edwards Eds (2010). *Volcanic Hazard from Iceland: Analysis and Implications of the Eyjafjallajökull Eruption*. London: UCL Institute for Risk and Disaster Reduction.
Sandman, P. (1994). 'Mass Media and Environmental Risk: Seven Principals.' *Risk: Health, Safety and Environment* 5: 251–260.
Savona, E. and B. Vettori (2009). 'Evaluating the Cost of Organized Crime from a Comparative Perspective.' *European Journal of Criminal Policy Research* 15: 379–393.
Scheffer, M., J. Bascompte, W. A. Brock, V. Brovkin, S. R. Carpenter, V. Dakos, H. Held, E. H. van Nes, M. Rietkerk and G. Sugihara (2009). 'Early-Warning Signals for Critical Transitions.' *Nature* 461: 53–59.
Schoemaker, P. J. H. and G. S. Day (2009). 'How to Make Sense of Weak Signals.' *Sloan Management Review* 50(3): 81–89.
Schulsky, A. and G. Schmitt (2002). *Silent Warfare: Understanding the World of Intelligence*. Washington, D.C.: Brassey's.
Schwartz, P. (1991). *The Art of the Long View: Planning for the Future in an Uncertain World*. New York: Doubleday.
Schwartz, P. and J. Ogilvy (2004) 'Plotting Your Scenarios. An Introduction to the Art and Process of Scenario Planning.' 6 April 2010 from http://www.gbn.com/articles/pdfs/gbn_Plotting%20Scenarios%20new.pdf, accessed 10 May 2011.
Schwarz, M. and Thompson, M. (1990) *Divided We Stand: Redefining Politics, Technology and Social Choice*, Philadelphia, PA: University of Pennsylvania Press.
Seib, P. (1997). *Headline Diplomacy: How News Coverage Affects Foreign Policy*. Westport, CT: Praeger.
Sen, A. K. (1984). *Resources, Values, and Development: Expanded Edition*. Oxford: Basil Blackwell.
Shanahan, J. and J. Good (2000). 'Heat and Hot Air: Influence of Local Temperature on Journalists' Coverage of Global Warming.' *Public Understanding of Science* 9: 285–295.
Shaw, D. and M. McCombs, Eds (1977). *The Emergence of American Political Issues: The Agenda-Setting Function of the Press*. St. Paul: West.
Scheffer, M.; Bascompte, J.; Brock, W. A.; Brovkin, V.; Carpenter, S. R.; Dakos, V.; Held, H.; Nes, E. H. Van; Rietkerk, M. and Sugihara, G. (2009) 'Early-warning signals for critical transitions,' *Nature* 461, 53–59.
Sheptycki, J. (1998). 'Policing the Risk Society: Book Review.' *British Journal of Criminology* 38: 521–525.
Shirky, C. (2008). *Here Comes Everybody, the Power of Organizing without Organizations*. New York: Penguin Press.
Sieber, A. (2005). 'Emerging Technologies in the Context of 'Security.' *Key Technologies for Europe*. European Commission.
Sismondo, S. (1999). 'Models, Simulations, and Their Objects.' *Science in Context* 12: 247–260.
van der Sluis, J. P. (2002). 'Integrated Assessment.' *Encyclopedia of Global Environmental Change*. London: Wiley.
Smith, D. (1980). 'Paragons, Pariahs and Pirates: A Spectrum-Based Theory of Enterprise.' *Crime and Delinquency* 26: 358–386.

Smits, R. and S. Kuhlman (2004). 'The Rise of Systemic Instruments in Innovation Policy.' *International Journal of Foresight and Innovation Policy* 1(1): 4–32.

Snook, S. A. (2000). *Friendly Fire: The Accidental Shootdown of U.S. Black Hawks over Northern Iraq*. Princeton, NJ: Princeton University Press.

Steiner, G. (1998). *After Babel*. Oxford: Oxford University Press.

Strauss-Kahn, D. (2010). 'The Managing Director of the International Monetary Fund Addresses the Bretton Woods Committee Annual Meeting.' *Bretton Woods Committee*. Washington D.C.

Strobel, W. P. (1997). *Late-Breaking Foreign Policy: The News Media's Influence on Peace Operations*. Washington, D.C.: United States Institute of Peace.

Sunstein, C. R. (2005). *Laws of Fear: Beyond the Precautionary Principle*. Cambridge: Cambridge University Press.

Surowiecki, J. (2004). *The Wisdom of Crowds: Why the Many Are Smarter than the Few and How Collective Wisdom Shapes Business, Economies, Societies, and Nations*. New York: Doubleday.

Sutherland, W. J. and H. J. Woodroof (2009). 'The Need for Environmental Horizon Scanning.' *Trends in Ecology and Evolution* 24(10): 523–527.

Taleb, N. N. (2007). *The Black Swan: The Impact of the Highly Improbable*. New York: Random House.

Tetlock, P. (2009). 'Reading Tarot on K Street.' *The National Interest Online*. 25 August 2009 from http://www.nationalinterest.org/Article.aspx?id=22040, accessed February 2010.

Tetlock, P. E. (2005). *Expert Political Judgement: How Good Is It? How Can We Know?* Princeton, NJ: Princeton University Press.

TFAMWG – Technological Futures Analysis Methods Working Group (2004). 'Technology Futures Analysis: Toward Integration of the Field and New Methods.' *Technological Forecasting & Social Change* 71(3): 287–303.

Thaler, R. and C. Sunstein (2008). *Nudge: Improving Decisions About Health, Wealth, and Happiness*. New Haven, CT: Yale University Press.

Thielen, J., J. Bartholmes, M.-H. Ramos, and A. de Roo (2009a). 'The European Flood Alert System – Part 1: Concept and Development.' *Hydrology and Earth System Science* 13: 125–140.

Thielen, J., P. Salamon, and F. Pappenberger (2009b). 'Minutes from 4th EFAS Meeting Held at ECMWF, Reading UK, from 27–28 January.' 4 April 2010.

Thielen, J., A. de Roo, G. Schmuck (2003) *First LISFLOOD Alert Workshop* (Ispra: Institute for Environment and Sustainability, JRC).

Thielen J, (2006) The benefit of probabilistic flood forecasting on European scale: Results of the European Flood Alert System for 2005/2006 EUR 22560 EN (Ispra: Institute for Environment and Sustainability, JRC).

Tol, R. S. J. (2005). 'Adaptation and Mitigation: Trade-Offs in Substance and Methods.' *Environmental Science and Policy* 8: 572–578.

Tonn, B., Hemrick, A. and Conrad, F. (2006) 'Cognitive Representations of the Future: Survey Results,' *Futures* 38: 810–29.

Topol, E. J. (2004) 'Failing the Public Health—Rofecoxib, Merck, and the FDA.' *New England Journal of Medicine* 351(17): 1707–1709.

Townsend, M. and P. Harris (2004). 'Now the Pentagon Tells Bush: Climate Change Will Destroy Us.' *The Observer*. 22 February. September 2009 from http://www.guardian.co.uk/environment/2004/feb/22/usnews.theobserver, accessed May 2010.

Travers, R. (1997). 'The Coming Intelligence Failure.' *Unclassified Studies In Intelligence* 1(1), Available at https://www.cia.gov/library/center-for-the-study-of-intelligence/

csi-publications/csi-studies/studies/97unclass/failure.html, accessed 16 May 2011.

Treverton, G. (2009). *Intelligence for an Age of Terror.* Cambridge: Cambridge University Press.

Trumbo, C. (1995). 'Longitudinal Modeling of Public Issues with the Agenda-Setting Process: The Case of Global Warming.' *Journalism and Communications Monographs* 152: 1–12.

Trumbo, C. (1996). 'Constructing Climate Change. Claims and Frames in U.S. News Coverage of an Environmental Issue.' *Public Understanding of Science* 5(3): 1–15.

Tsoukas, H. and J. Shepherd, Eds (2004). *Managing the Future: Foresight in the Knowledge Economy.* Malden, MA: Blackwell.

Tusikov, N. and R. Fahlman (2009). 'Risk and Threat Assessment: New Approaches'. In J. Rattcliffe (Ed.) *Strategic Thinking in Criminal Intelligence.* Cullompton: Willan Publishing.

US Congress (2004). Senate Committee on Finance, Hearing on 'FDA, Merck and Vioxx: Putting Patient Safety First?' Testimony of Gurkirpal Singh, M.D., November 18, 2004.

US Office of the Director of National Intelligence (2008). 'Visions 2015.' Washington, D.C.

US Securities and Exchange Commission (2002a). Securities and Exchange Commission v. Xerox Corporation, 11 April, http://www.sec.gov/litigation/complaints/complr17465.htm, accessed 16 August 2009.

US Securities and Exchange Commission (2002b). Litigation Release No. 17465, 11 April, http://www.sec.gov/litigation/litreleases/lr17465.htm, accessed 16 August 2009.

US Securities and Exchange Commission (2003). KPMG LLP, Joseph T. Boyle, Michael A. Conway, Anthony P. Dolanski, Ronald A. Safran and Thomas J. Yoho, 3 October, http://www.sec.gov/litigation/complaints/comp18389.htm, accessed 16 August 2009.

US Securities and Exchange Commission (2006). Litigation Release No. 19573, 22 February, http://www.sec.gov/litigation/litreleases/lr19573.htm, accessed 16 August 2009.

US Securities and Exchange Commission (2008). Litigation Release No. 20471, 29 February, http://www.sec.gov/litigation/litreleases/2008/lr20471.htm, accessed 16 August 2009.

US Senate Committee on Finance (2004). 'Testimony of David J. Graham.' 18 November from http://finance.senate.gov/hearings/testimony/2004test/111804dgtest.pdf, accessed March 2010.

Ungar, S. (1995). 'Social Scares and Global Warming: Beyond the Rio Convention.' *Society and Natural Resources* 8: 443–456.

Ungar, S. (2008). 'Global Bird Flu Communication: Hot Crisis and Media Reassurance.' *Science Communication* 29: 472–497.

Van Daele, S., T. Vander Beken and N. Dorn (2007). 'Waste Management and Crime: Regulatory, Business and Product Vulnerabilities.' *Environmental Policy and Law* 37: 34–38.

Van Duyne, P. (2006). 'Counting Clouds and Measuring Organised Crime.' In A. M. Petrus van Duyne, Maarten van Dijck, Klaus von Lampe James and Newell Nijmegen (Eds) *The Organisation of Crime for Profit: Conduct, Law and Measurement.* Nijmegen: Wolf Legal Publishers, pp. 1–16.

Van Duyne, P. and T. Vander Beken (2009). 'The Incantations of the EU Organised Crime Policy Making.' *Crime, Law and Social Change* 51: 261–281.

Vander Beken, T. (2004). 'Risky Business: A Risk – Based Methodology to Measure Organized Crime.' *Crime Law and Social Change* 41: 471–516.

Vander Beken, T. and S. Van Daele (2008). 'Legitimate Businesses and Crime Vulnerabilities.' *International Journal of Social Economics* 35: 739–750.

Vander Beken, T., L. Cuyvers, B. De Ruyver, M. Defruytier and J. Hansens (2004). *Kwetsbaarheid Voor Georganiseerde Criminaliteit: Een Gevalstudie Van De Diamantsector.* Gent: Academia Press.

Vander Beken, T., M. Defruytier, A. Bucquoye and K. Verpoest (2005). 'Road Map for Vulnerability Studies.' *Organised Crime and Vulnerability of Economic Sectors: The European Transport and Music Sector.* Antwerp-Apeldoorn: Maklu Publishers, pp. 7–56.

Vandivier, K. (1972). 'The Aircraft Brake Scandal.' *Harpers* (April): 45–52.

Various Authors (1999). 'Complex Systems – Special Issue.' *Science* 284 (Whole special issue).

Verfaillie, K. and T. Vander Beken (2008a). 'Interesting Times: European Criminal Markets in 2015.' *Futures* 40: 438–450.

Verfaillie, K. and T. Vander Beken (2008b). 'Proactive Policing and the Assessment of Organised Crime.' *Policing: An International Journal of Police Strategies & Management* 31: 534–552.

Vogel, D. (1986). *National Styles of Regulation: Environmental Policy in Great Britain and the United States.* Ithaca and London: Cornell University Press.

von Lampe, K. (2001). 'Not a Process of Enlightenment: The Conceptual History of Organized Crime in Germany and the United States of America.' *Forum on Crime and Society* 2: 99–116.

Wahlberg, A. A. F. and L. Sjöberg (2000). 'Risk Perception and the Media.' *Journal of Risk Research* 3(1): 31–50.

Wallensteen, P. (2002). 'Reassessing Recent Conflicts: Direct Vs. Structural Prevention'. In D. Malone and F. O. Hampson (Eds) *From Reaction to Conflict Prevention. Opportunities for the Un-System.* Boulder, CO: Lynne Rienner, pp. 213–229.

Waltz, E. (2003). *Knowledge Management.* Norwood, MA: Artech House.

WDEU (2003). *Best Practices on Flood Prevention, Protection, and Mitigation.* N.P.: Water Directors of the European Union. 4 April 2010 from http://www.floods.org/PDF/Intl_BestPractices_EU_2004.pdf, accessed May 2011.

Weart, S. R. (2003). *The Discovery of Global Warming.* Cambridge, MA: Harvard University Press.

Webster, B. (2010). 'Science Chief John Beddington Calls for Honesty on Climate Change.' *Times on line.* 27 January. April 2010 from http://www.timesonline.co.uk/tol/news/environment/article7003622.ece, accessed March 2010.

Weeks, J. (2004). *Unpopular Culture: The Ritual of Complaint in a British Bank.* Chicago: University of Chicago Press.

Weick, K. E. and K. M. Sutcliffe (2007) *Managing the Unexpected: Resilient Performance in an Age of Uncertainty.* San Francisco, CA: Jossey-Bass.

Weingart, P., A. Engels, and P. Pansegrau (2000). 'Risks of Communication: Discourses on Climate Change in Science, Politics, and the Mass Media.' *Public Understanding of Science* 9: 261–283.

Whiteside, K. H. (2006). *Precautionary Politics: Principle and Practice in Confronting Environmental Risk.* Cambridge, MA: MIT Press.

Wiering, M.A., and B. J. M. Arts (2006). 'Discursive Shifts in Dutch River Management: 'Deep' Institutional Change or Adaptation Strategy? *Hydrogiologia* 565: 327–338.
Wikipedia 'Bhopal Disaster.' 14 August 2009 from http://en.wikipedia.org/wiki/Bhopal_disaster#cite_ref-Kalelkar_10-0.
Wikipedia 'Scientific Model.' From http://en.wikipedia.org/wiki/Scientific_model.
Wikman-Svahn, P. (2009). 'State of the Art Scan – Meta-Analysis of Recent Security-Related Foresight Studies.' *Foresight and Scenarios*. ESRIF Working Group 5.
Williams, P. (2005). 'Intelligence Requirements for Transnational Threats: New Ways of Thinking, Alternative Methods of Analysis, and Innovative Organizational Structures'. *New Frontiers of Intelligence Analysis*. C. Dumaine and S. Germani. Washington, D.C.: Global Futures Partnership.
Williams, P. and R. Godson (2002). 'Anticipating Organized and Transnational Crime.' *Crime Law and Social Change* 37: 311–355.
Wilson, K. M. (2000). 'Drought, Debate, and Uncertainty: Measuring Reporters' Knowledge and Ignorance About Climate Change.' *Public Understanding of Science* 9(3): 1–13.
Wingardt, P. (1998). 'Science and the Media', *Research Policy* 27(8): 869–79.
Wohlstetter, R. (1962) *Pearl Harbor: Warning and Decision*. Stanford, CA: Stanford University Press.
Wolfe, S. M. (2006). 'Statement before the Institute of Medicine Committee Assessing the U.S. Drug Safety System.' Publication #1759.
Wolfsfeld, G. (1997) *The Media and Political Conflict*. Cambridge: Cambridge University Press.
Woocher, L. (2008). 'The Effects of Cognitive Biases on Early Warning.' *Bridging Multiple Divides: 49th Annual Convention of the International Studies Association*. San Francisco: 29 March 2008.
World Health Organization (2009a) 'Deaths.' 15 August 2009 from http://www.who.int/tobacco/statistics/tobacco_atlas/en/, accessed April 2010.
World Health Organization (2009b) 'Why Is Tobacco a Public Health Priority.' 15 August 2009 from http://www.who.int/tobacco/health_priority/en/index.html, accessed April 2010.
World Health Organization (2010). 'Floods in Moldova, Romania and Ukraine (2008). 'World Health Organization, Regional Office for Europe.' 4 April 2010 from http://www.euro.who.int/emergencies/20080730_1, accessed April 2010.
Worms, J.-P. (1966). 'Le Préfet Et Ses Notables.' *Sociologie du Travail* 66 (3): 249–275.
Zack, N. (2009). *Ethics for Disaster*. Lanham, MD: Rowan and Littlefield.
Zappa, M., S. Jaun, U. Germann, A. Walser and F. Fundel (2011) 'Superposition of Three Sources of Uncertainties in Operational Flood Forecasting Chains' *Atmospheric Research*, Thematic Issue on COST731. 100(2–3), 246–62.
Zedner, L. (2007). 'Pre-Crime and Post-Criminology?' *Theoretical Criminology* 11: 261–281.
Zinn, J. O. (2008). *Social Theories of Risk and Uncertainty: An Introduction*. Oxford: Blackwell.
Zizek, S. (2007). *How to Read Lacan*. New York: W. W. Norton & Co.
Zweig, S. (1964). *The World of Yesterday*. London: University of Nebraska Press.

Index

Accountability, 136, 144–6, 191–207
Accuracy, 8, 10, 75, 109, 143
Adversary, 23, 28–9, 36, 38, 46, 232
  see also Enemy
Advocacy, 109–10, 115, 123, 135
Agenda, 11, 13, 30, 47–8, 53–5, 63, 86, 108–10, 115, 135, 176, 197, 202, 220, 222, 243, 247–8, 252
Agenda Setting, 109–10
al Qaeda, 40, 124–5
ALARP, 24, 192
Alert, 8, 30, 92, 127–33, 139–40, 143–4, 147, 182, 236
Ambiguity, 36, 45, 121
Anticipation, 79–94, 228–38
Ash Cloud, 2–3, 241
Assessment, Strategic, 27, 228–34
  see also Risk, Assessment; Threat, assessment
Assumptions, 33–4, 41, 96, 118, 139, 184, 214–15, 226, 246, 251
Attitudes, 65, 151, 204
Awareness, Situational, 21–2, 27, 236

Banks, 9, 15, 209–26, 244, 255
BBC, 44, 107
  see also News, Media
Behaviour, 2, 22–3, 45, 50, 68, 71–2, 77, 83, 91, 100, 106, 109, 148–9, 155–6, 159–63, 194, 203, 232–4, 244–5, 254
Belief, 22, 36–7, 65, 71, 92–4, 123, 145, 207, 219, 225, 243
  see also World-views
Biases, 142, 144, 185
  Cognitive, 2, 9–13, 112, 123, 131, 146, 191, 208, 214–15, 236, 240, 246–7, 251
  Heuristic, 107, 138
  Motivational, 9, 12, 246
Blair, Tony, 187, 193
Bosnia, 110
British Joint Intelligence Committee, 23, 27–8, 118, 122–3
Budgeting, 25, 48, 72, 152
Bush, George W., 24, 44, 66, 246

Capabilities, 2, 6, 21–3, 36–8, 40–4, 63, 88, 105, 129, 164, 230–4
Career, 39, 159, 210
Catastrophe, 104, 111, 153
  see also Emergency; Hazard
Challenges, 3, 9–12, 49–50, 66, 71, 93, 114, 123, 131, 151, 157–9, 182, 211, 216, 230, 235–6, 246
CIA, 33, 42–3
Civil Protection, 127–8, 131–6
Civil War, 4, 99–114, 253
Climate change, 1, 4, 9–13, 20, 56–7, 66–74, 83–4, 99–129, 139, 189, 199, 232, 242, 246–7, 252–3
  see also IPCC
CNN Effect, 109–10, 113
Compassion Fatigue, 108, 112
Complexity, 2–9, 20, 26, 30, 43, 49–60, 67–81, 86, 100–4, 109–10, 115–18, 121, 153, 169–70, 175, 180–4, 190, 199, 206–21, 227, 230–43, 250, 257
Control Risk, 5, 10, 169, 178, 179, 184
Counter-terrorism, 14, 23, 24, 27, 43, 256
Credibility, 7, 10, 79, 106, 116, 124, 202, 237, 242–5, 252, 256–7
Crises
  Financial, 2, 8, 13–14, 187, 208, 218–20, 229, 244–9
  Humanitarian, 5, 61, 108, 109, 110, 125, 133
Cry-wolf syndrome, 229
Culture
  of blaming, 3, 38, 106, 146, 154–6, 194–5, 203–8, 243, 248
  High reliability, 238
Cyber-space, 20

Darfur, 124–5
Decision Support, 57–8, 62, 74

Decision-making, 4, 11, 21–4, 37, 45, 51, 57, 58–63, 82, 88, 93, 102, 116, 171, 176, 188–94, 198–204, 230, 236, 243, 247, 252
Developing Countries, 56, 105, 253
Disasters, 30, 39, 41, 95, 108–10, 129, 132–4, 148, 152, 156, 164, 208–10, 241, 253–5
Dissonance, 123, 246, 247

Education, 34, 115, 158, 187, 193, 198, 210, 216
EFAS, 127–47, 247
Emergency, 109, 127, 129–34, 221
  see also Catastrophe; Hazard
Enemy, 15, 25, 35–7, 94, 152
  see also Adversary
Epistemology, 19, 33–4, 38–9, 44–6, 101
Escalation, of Conflict, 99, 108, 112, 156, 163, 228
Ethics, 41
Ethnic cleansing, 112
EU, 5, 8–13, 26, 47–9, 53–63, 83, 89, 117–47, 188, 223, 254
Evidence, 3, 12, 20, 28, 45, 66, 104, 116, 151, 156, 160, 188, 196–7, 201–2, 207, 228–33, 237, 239, 242, 246
Expectations, 6– 9, 31, 57, 62–3, 114, 149, 169, 182, 195, 206, 219, 256
Expert, 1–4, 8, 79–80, 87, 114, 131, 138, 155, 165, 197–8, 202, 206, 227, 250–3, 257
  communities, 2–4, 250–3

Face-work, 148–9, 154
Fear, 3, 6, 31–2, 56, 106, 111–15, 149, 157, 238
Feasibility, 135–7, 242, 246
Federal Reserve, 208, 213, 218–19
Financial market, 11–13, 70, 217–18, 221, 225
Financial Service Authority, 213, 226
Flooding, 5, 10–11, 21, 127–47, 217, 241
Forecasting, 2–24, 29–34, 44–52, 62, 67–9, 96, 102, 127–46, 169, 175, 179–85, 217, 225–57
  Probabilistic, 8, 146, 251
FORESEC, 8, 47–64
Foresight techniques, 2, 47–63, 227, 234–40, 251, 252
Forewarning, 19, 21, 22, 26
  see also Warning
Fragmentation, 62–3, 200–15
Framework, Analytical, 6
Framing, 10–11, 23, 75, 100–15, 135, 172, 188, 191, 199, 202–7
France, 52, 132, 144, 147, 188–206, 240

GAINS, 8, 67, 74–84, 244, 251
Genocide, 2–5, 101, 106–13, 246, 248
Georgia, 124–5
Germany, 52, 81, 85, 107, 132–4, 145, 188–92, 199–206
Globalisation, 94, 105, 195, 231, 250

Harm, 2–17, 43, 88–90, 96, 101–2, 149–60, 187, 191–2, 202–4, 231, 241–6, 250–7
  see also Risk; Threat
Hazard, 131, 145, 191, 205
  see also Catastrophe; Emergency
Horizon-scanning, 2, 27
Human Rights, 24, 180
HUMINT, 43–5
Hurricane
  El Niño, 108
  Katrina, 247

Images, 28, 107–8, 151–6, 195, 199
Indicators, 69
Information, 2, 8–12, 21–2, 26–51, 57–63, 70–93, 100–6, 109, 115–28, 135–44, 151, 160, 165, 171–2, 181, 186–8, 193–205, 211–16, 229–37, 247, 255
  Gathering, 22, 115, 199–201, 205, 232
Innovation, 48, 51, 57, 60–3, 170, 208–10, 215–16, 234, 256
Inquiries, 27, 33, 194, 228, 241
Intelligence
  Actionable, 21, 42–5, 58, 92, 228
  Analyst, 9, 20, 26–31, 36, 39–44, 121, 236
  Community, 26, 35–46, 122, 186
  Cycle, 27, 33, 118
  Estimative, 35, 118, 122
  Failure, 2, 9, 29, 31–46
    compare Warning, failure of
  Physical, 35–6, 117
  Strategic, 37, 40, 44, 230
  Verbal, 35–6

IPCC, 71, 83, 199, 252–3
see also Climate change
Issues, 2, 31, 40, 50, 55, 69–72, 81, 86, 93–4, 103–18, 125–35, 144–6, 155, 162, 181, 197, 222–7, 233, 238, 241, 248, 252, 256

Journalists, 7, 80, 99, 102–15, 208, 215, 254–5
see also News, Media
Justice, 256–7
see also Law; Norms

Knowledge, 2–12, 19, 24, 29, 33–7, 43–52, 62–7, 73–9, 82, 89, 92, 95, 99, 100–7, 115, 124, 194, 202, 207, 210–11, 231, 237–8, 244–5, 250–7
Claim, 7, 12, 101, 104–5, 244–5, 255
Explicit, 45–6
Tacit, 45–6
Kosovo, 110
Kyoto Summit, 1, 83, 108, 242

Law, 20–3, 73, 85–8, 94, 149, 160–3, 170–2, 185, 197, 200–4, 231
see also Justice; Norms
Leadership, 27, 42, 152–4, 158–63, 176, 243, 246–9
Learning, 4–6, 11–12, 30, 93, 97, 129–30, 210, 241–8, 256
Loyalty, 151, 156–9

Media, 73, 79, 99, 100–17, 154, 162, 181–3, 188, 191, 194, 198, 204, 214, 243, 249, 252–4
Mediatisation, 101–5, 109, 115
Methodology, 20, 30, 47–9, 53, 59, 89, 91, 101, 170–1, 186
Methods
Ensamble, 129–30, 136–7
Qualitative, 101
Mitigation, 2, 7, 13, 67, 83, 106, 111, 172, 177–8, 186, 217, 236, 246
Mobilisation, 6, 45, 111, 114, 204, 228, 242
Models, 10, 23, 66–87, 92, 101, 111, 127, 137–44, 156–9, 220, 229, 234, 244, 250–1

Narratives, 69, 73, 80, 93, 103, 107, 112, 115, 251
National Security, 5, 14, 20–5, 39, 43, 44, 51, 57, 125, 195, 227, 231, 246
NATO, 51, 54–5, 61–2, 126
Networking, 22, 27, 44, 56, 59, 60–1, 181, 194, 248, 249, 253
News, 4, 6, 9, 11, 12, 44, 99, 100, 102, 103, 104, 105, 106, 107, 108, 109, 110, 111, 112, 113, 114, 115, 116, 156, 209, 215, 246, 248, 254, 257
Bad, 31, 150, 156
Management, 115
Media, 4, 6, 9, 11, 99, 100–5, 113–15, 248, 254, 257
Values, 100–6, 112
NGOs, 5–7, 64, 76–8, 102, 110, 117, 125, 156, 181, 190, 243, 249, 254
Norms, 14, 37, 106–7, 115, 159, 199, 231
see also Justice; Law
Novelty, 8, 137, 232, 250

Objectivity, 38, 106, 122, 184, 185, 237, 255
Obscurity, 8, 232–3
OECD, 188, 202, 227
Opportunities, 2, 6, 12–13, 24–7, 30, 43, 57–60, 65–6, 84, 88, 93–4, 111, 123–5, 134, 170, 178–83, 235–7, 243–8, 251
Organisations, 2, 10, 12, 57–8, 64, 92, 100–4, 123, 148–64, 180, 186, 189–91, 198, 202, 237–43, 248–9, 254
Culture, 27, 49, 65–6, 99–100, 125, 140, 144, 148–9, 154, 159, 160–4, 180–4, 187, 190, 194, 204, 235, 243, 248–9, 254
Secrets, 12, 28, 148–63
Structure, 6, 23, 45, 49, 73, 77, 79, 92, 118, 121–6, 158, 176, 184, 210–13
Organised Crime, 89
Overreaction, 2–3, 14, 115, 199

Pandemics, 2, 21, 109, 245
Pearl Harbor, 38–5, 228, 229, 240
Perception, 34, 39, 46, 51, 55, 72, 113, 150–1, 179, 218, 236, 246, 256–7
Persuasion, 115, 123

Policy
Defence, 43, 246
Exit, 221
Fiscal, 254
Foreign, 36, 43, 100
Macroeconomic, 218–19
Monetary, 208, 213, 220, 225, 244
Precautionary, 146
see also Principle, Precautionary
Preventive, 2, 14, 15, 109, 111–14, 145, 146, 225, 247, 257
see also Prevention
Resolution, 218–22, 225
Political Judgement, 119, 202, 229, 249
Pollution, 10, 66–7, 72–7, 80–4, 154–5, 200, 241–4
Power, Nuclear, 4, 12, 26, 200, 238, 249
Precaution, 201, 204
Precision, 22, 68, 122, 143, 145
Prediction, 19–23, 28, 31, 45, 52, 66–8, 81, 84, 92–3, 128, 136, 141–6, 227–34, 246
Preparedness, 13–15, 41, 57, 132, 142, 230, 235
Prevention, 1–7, 13–15, 86, 99–100, 148, 154, 158, 190–1, 201, 217, 227–9, 239–57
see also Policy, Preventive
Principle, Precautionary, 72, 198, 200, 201
see also Policy, Precautionary
Prioritisation, 48, 217–20, 250
Probability, 6, 8, 11, 13–14, 20, 26, 29, 52, 69–72, 81, 83, 88, 92, 99, 114, 122, 127–30, 138, 152, 173, 175, 177, 182–3, 187–91, 217–19, 222, 224, 239, 243, 245, 247–8, 252, 255
Projection, 67–9, 82, 183
Prophecy, 11, 65, 87
Self-fulfilling, 11, 87
Self-negating, 11
Public Opinion, 40, 52–3, 113, 123, 249

Receptivity, 12, 32, 241–2, 246–7, 257
Regime, 28, 173, 176, 188, 222, 226, 246
Regulation, 2–14, 24, 71–2, 91, 99–100, 148–52, 156–61, 170, 182, 187–226, 249–57
Report, 22, 40, 44, 52, 63, 87, 89, 102, 105, 107, 112, 116, 150–1, 161, 214, 226–7
Resilience, 13, 15, 30, 63, 93–6, 235, 242, 250–6
Resonance, 123–5
Resources, 14, 51, 62, 159, 183, 186, 191–2, 230
Response, 2–7, 13–15, 25, 29, 33, 37–44, 55, 72, 87, 90–9, 104–5, 110–13, 128–49, 163, 173, 191, 202, 223, 229, 233, 239–50, 256–7
see also Warning, Warning-response gap
Risk, 2–14, 21–6, 32, 47–58, 65–75, 82–105, 111–16, 121–6, 146–59, 169–212, 217–27, 234, 241–57
Assessment, 2, 8, 26, 50, 62, 67, 86, 121, 169, 171–88, 193–205, 227, 250
aversion, 130, 187, 190–3, 198
Calculus of, 24
Communication, 9–12, 100, 102, 114, 116, 252
Consultancy, 169, 185
Environmental, 4, 66–7, 71, 82–3, 87, 102, 106, 108–9, 243
Management, 5, 15, 20, 24–5, 30, 73, 128, 137, 140, 146, 151, 169–86, 194–9, 207, 209, 215, 222, 242
Recognition, 6, 217–20
Routines, Journalistic, 103
Rwanda, 106, 110, 248

Safety, 26, 137, 144, 149, 151–64, 187–207, 249, 254
Scenario, 8, 36, 51–69, 81, 93–6, 124, 134, 199, 235, 243, 251, 254
analysis, 69
building, 52–3, 251
workshop, 55, 59–60
Science, 1, 11, 28, 51, 66–7, 73–5, 79, 81, 95, 99–108, 115–16, 129, 216, 232, 245
Secrets, 12, 28, 148–9, 154–6, 157–9, 161–3
Self-image, 149, 151, 154, 156
Sense-making, 230–40
September 11, 2, 8, 9, 26, 29, 38, 40, 44, 50, 96, 131, 135, 228–9, 240

SIGINT, 45
Signals
  Noise, 12, 30, 35, 45, 120, 229
  Strong, 235
  Weak, 2, 12, 151, 158, 198, 204, 234, 235
Silo, 9, 22, 209–16, 221, 253
  Mentality, 9, 214, 221
Somalia, 110, 122, 248
Sovereignty, 51, 231
Specificity, 6, 8, 101, 129, 130, 137, 144, 251
Stakeholders, 10, 59–67, 74–83, 100, 170–80, 199–204, 249–52
Strategy, 20, 24–5, 30, 43, 48, 54, 61, 71–2, 93–4, 100, 111, 170, 177–9, 193, 210–14, 222, 255–6
Supervision, Macro-prudential, 222–5
Surprise, 2, 8, 26, 28, 37, 39, 42–5, 66, 118, 126, 195, 204, 228–30, 234, 238, 240, 244
Surveillance, 22, 27, 58

Technocracy, 3, 5, 87, 189, 257
Technology, 1–4, 19, 26–8, 35, 48–51, 54, 57–62, 76–7, 84, 99, 113, 125, 216, 231–2, 243, 256
Terrorism, 1–4, 20–5, 40, 44, 54, 56, 96, 173, 180, 195, 253
Threat, 2, 6, 13, 20, 23–9, 36–42, 49, 54, 56, 62, 85–9, 96, 100, 108, 113, 115, 126, 173–8, 182, 225, 228–30, 238–9
  assessment, 49, 54, 88–9
  domains, 20
Trade-offs, 60, 74–5, 82, 115, 130, 143, 151, 191, 194, 198–9, 251, 255–6
Training, 22, 34, 41, 78, 115–16, 132, 141, 145, 152, 158–9, 174, 210, 236, 244–5
Translation, 79–80, 111

UK, 2–5, 20–9, 52–3, 61, 118, 128, 146–7, 164, 171, 181, 187–213, 221–7, 248
UN, 86, 105, 122, 126, 133, 252–3
Uncertainty, 2–9, 15, 21, 24, 43, 45, 47–51, 70–1, 80–7, 94–6, 101, 115, 128, 137–8, 142–6, 182, 198, 229–33, 241–4, 250, 255–6
US, 1–5, 22–3, 27–9, 33, 38, 42–6, 107, 110, 122–3, 152–5, 160–5, 190, 209, 219–37, 253–6

Variables, 50, 148, 220
Vioxx, 153–6, 160–1, 245
Vulnerability, 24–5, 32, 42, 56, 76, 88–96, 175–80, 186, 243, 250

Warner, 12, 109, 119, 122–6, 243
Warning, 1–15, 24–46, 65, 82, 92, 99, 100–60, 196, 206, 217–19, 224–57
  early, 2, 9, 13, 15, 28, 110, 118–19, 128, 129–31, 142–5, 198, 243, 248
  failure of, 5, 31–4, 38–46
  late, 246–7
  mediatised, 100, 104–5, 109–16
  tactical, 118
  warning-response gap, 2, 229, 241, 257
Whistleblowers, 149, 157, 160–3
WHO, 3, 26, 129, 155, 254
WMD, 11, 29, 66, 124
World-views, 181, 186, 190, 244–6
WTO, 188, 202

Xerox, 153, 160–5

GPSR Compliance
The European Union's (EU) General Product Safety Regulation (GPSR) is a set of rules that requires consumer products to be safe and our obligations to ensure this.

If you have any concerns about our products, you can contact us on

ProductSafety@springernature.com

In case Publisher is established outside the EU, the EU authorized representative is:

Springer Nature Customer Service Center GmbH
Europaplatz 3
69115 Heidelberg, Germany

www.ingramcontent.com/pod-product-compliance
Ingram Content Group UK Ltd.
Pitfield, Milton Keynes, MK11 3LW, UK
UKHW020726070925
462611UK00024B/1293
* 9 7 8 1 3 4 9 3 3 4 2 2 3 *